Hands-On Networking Essentials with Projects

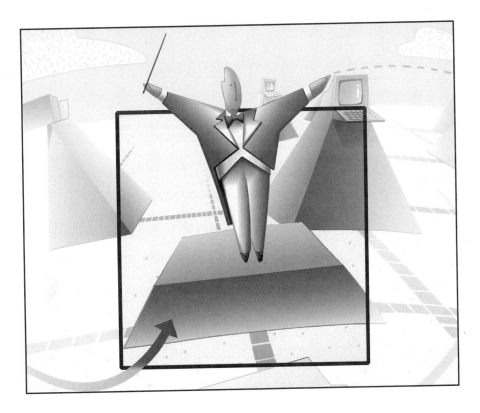

Michael J. Palmer, Ph.D.

COURSE
TECHNOLOGY

ONE MAIN STREET, CAMBRIDGE, MA 02142

an International Thomson Publishing company I T P®

Cambridge • Albany • Bonn • Boston • Cincinnati • London • Madrid • Melbourne • Mexico City
New York • Paris • San Francisco • Singapore • Tokyo • Toronto • Washington

Hands-On Networking Essentials with Projects is published by Course Technology.

Managing Editor:	Kristen Duerr
Product Manager:	Jennifer Normandin
Production Editor:	Nancy Benjamin
Development Editor:	Deb Kaufmann
Technical Editing:	Gate City Consulting, Inc.
Composition House:	GEX, Inc.
Text Designer:	GEX, Inc.
Cover Designer:	Doug Goodman
Marketing Manager:	Tracy Foley

© 1998 by Course Technology—I(T)P®

For more information contact:

Course Technology
One Main Street
Cambridge, MA 02142

International Thomson Editores
Seneca, 53
Colonia Polanco
11560 Mexico D.F. Mexico

ITP Europe
Berkshire House 168-173
High Holborn
London WCIV 7AA
England

ITP GmbH
Königswinterer Strasse 418
53227 Bonn
Germany

Nelson ITP, Australia
102 Dodds Street
South Melbourne, 3205
Victoria, Australia

ITP Asia
60 Albert Street, #15-01
Albert Complex
Singapore 189969

ITP Nelson Canada
1120 Birchmount Road
Scarborough, Ontario
Canada M1K 5G4

ITP Japan
Hirakawacho Kyowa Building, 3F
2-2-1 Hirakawacho
Chiyoda-ku, Tokyo 102
Japan

Trademarks

Course Technology and the Open Book logo are registered trademarks and CourseKits is a trademark of Course Technology. Custom Editions is a registered trademark of International Thomson Publishing.

I(T)P® The ITP logo is a registered trademark of International Thomson Publishing.

Some of the product names and company names used in this book have been used for identification purposes only and may be trademarks or registered trademarks of their respective manufacturers and sellers.

Disclaimer

Course Technology reserves the right to revise this publication and make changes from time to time in its content without notice.

ISBN 0-619-01628-0

Printed in the United States of America

3 4 5 6 7 8 9 BM 02 01 00

DEDICATION

To a quick-thinking young person, Jonathan Buffaloe,
who saved the life of someone in my family;
and to those who dedicate their lives to teaching others.

BRIEF TABLE OF CONTENTS

TABLE OF CONTENTS

CHAPTER ELEVEN

Managing the Network   353

CHAPTER TWELVE

Troubleshooting Network Problems   381

INTRODUCTION

Hands-On Networking Essentials with Projects is designed to enable you to learn the principles of computer networking using common network devices and Microsoft network operating systems to provide you with real-life experience. Each chapter features hands-on activities you can perform in the classroom or in a computer laboratory. The purpose of the book is twofold: (1) to give you theoretical knowledge and practical experience as a network administrator and (2) to prepare you for Exam 70-058, the Networking Essentials elective for certification as a Microsoft Certified Systems Engineer (MCSE).

If you are new to networking, this book starts from scratch to give you a solid background on which to launch a networking career. It teaches you networking theory, how to plan and design networks, and how to manage them. If you are preparing for Microsoft certification in networking essentials, the book provides the foundation you need to match all of the learning objectives for the certification. If you currently administer a network, the book has many up-to-the-minute design and management ideas to enhance any network environment.

Several types of projects and activities in each chapter make the material come alive, so you remember the lessons long after you have finished reading the book. In Hands-On exercises interspersed throughout the text, you design and diagram networks, set up networks, set up servers and workstations for networking, and monitor and troubleshoot networks. Each chapter concludes with practice Review Questions and Project assignments. The Review Questions are especially helpful for quick checks and act as a targeted study guide if you are preparing for the Microsoft certification exam. In the Project assignments, you act as an employee of Aspen Consulting, a company that specializes in setting up and maintaining networks for both large and small organizations. In these assignments you address realistic networking issues just as you will as a network administrator.

Every step of the way, this book is geared to thoroughly ground you in network administration by having you do the work of an administrator. Answers to the Review Questions and Aspen Consulting Project assignments can be obtained from your instructor. Your instructor also may assign one or more of the Optional Case Studies for Teams, which enable you to work with other members of your class to solve networking problems.

Many of the Hands-On exercises and Project assignments require access to computers running Windows NT Server, Windows NT Workstation, or Windows 95. Some also involve working with communications cable, hubs, test equipment, and other networking components. When you complete the Aspen Consulting Project assignments, you can submit them on separate pages, on the assignment pages at the end of each chapter, or by way of an electronic file. The Student Work Disk, available from your instructor, contains a Microsoft Word file for each end-of-chapter project and for the optional team case studies. You can record your answers in the space provided within the file and submit them to your instructor by disk, through the network, or through e-mail.

Features

To aid you in fully understanding Networking Essentials concepts, there are many features in this book designed to improve its pedagogical value.

- **Chapter Objectives.** Each chapter in this book begins with a detailed list of the concepts to be mastered within that chapter. This list provides you with a quick reference to the contents of that chapter, as well as a useful study aid.

- **Illustrations and Tables.** Numerous illustrations of networking components aid you in the visualization of common networking setups, theories, and architectures. In addition, many tables provide details and comparisons of both practical and theoretical information.

- **Hands-On Exercises.** Although it is important to understand the theory behind networking technology, nothing can improve upon real-world experience. To this end, along with theoretical explanations, each chapter provides numerous hands-on exercises aimed at providing students with real-world implementation experience.

- **Chapter Summaries.** Each chapter's text is followed by a summary of the concepts it has introduced. These summaries provide a helpful way to recap and revisit the ideas covered in each chapter.

- **Key Terms.** Throughout the text, key terms are bolded, with their definitions given in paragraphs marked by Definition icons. Definitions for all terms in the book are included in the Glossary at the back of the book. Having definitions displayed separately in the text encourages proper understanding of the chapter's key concepts and provides a useful reference.

- **Review Questions.** End-of-chapter assessment begins with a set of review questions that reinforce the ideas introduced in each chapter. These questions not only ensure that you have mastered the concepts, but are written to help prepare you for the Microsoft certification examination.

- **Aspen Consulting Project.** Located near the end of each chapter is a continuous running case. In this extensive case example, as an employee of a fictitious network consulting company you implement the skills and knowledge gained in the chapter through real-world networking scenarios.

- **Optional Case Studies for Teams.** Each chapter closes with a section that proposes certain networking situations, also in a case-based, scenario setting. You and a team of classmates are asked to evaluate the situation and decide upon the course of action to be taken to remedy the problems described. This valuable tool will help you to sharpen decision-making, teamwork, and troubleshooting skills—important aspects of network administration.

Text and Graphic Conventions

Wherever appropriate, additional information and exercises have been added to this book to help you better understand what is being discussed in the chapter. Icons throughout the text alert you to additional materials. The icons used in this textbook are described below.

 The Note icon is used to present additional helpful material related to the subject being described.

As an experienced network administrator, the author has practical experience with how networks work in real business situations. Tip icons highlight suggestions on ways to attack problems you may encounter in a real-world situation.

 The author has given cautions for concepts or steps that often cause difficulty. Each caution anticipates a potential mistake and provides methods for avoiding the same problem in the future.

 Each hands-on activity in this book is preceded by the Hands-On icon and a description of the exercise that follows.

 Project icons mark the running Aspen Consulting case projects. These are more involved, scenario-based assignments. In this extensive case example, you are asked to implement independently what you have learned.

 The Case icons mark the Optional Case Studies for Teams at the end of each chapter.

Supplements

All of the supplements available with this book are provided to the instructor on a single CD-ROM.

Electronic Instructor's Manual. The Instructor's Manual that accompanies this textbook includes:

- Additional instructional material to assist in class preparation, including suggestions for lecture topics, suggested lab activities, tips on setting up a lab for the hands-on activities, and alternative lab setup ideas in situations where lab resources are limited.

- Solutions to all end-of-chapter materials, including the Project assignments.

Student Work Disk. Files for creating a Student Work Disk are available from your instructor. Also available is an electronic glossary of networking terms.

Course Test Manager 1.1. Accompanying this book is a powerful assessment tool known as the Course Test Manager. Designed by Course Technology, this cutting-edge Windows-based testing software helps instructors design and administer tests and pre-tests. In addition to being able to generate tests that can be printed and administered, this full-featured program also has an online testing component that allows students to take tests at the computer and have their exams automatically graded.

PowerPoint presentations. This book comes with Microsoft PowerPoint slides for each chapter. These are included as a teaching aid for classroom presentation, to make available to students on the network for chapter review, or to be printed for classroom distribution. Instructors, please feel at liberty to add your own slides for additional topics you introduce to the class.

Simulations. Featured on the Instructor's Resource Kit CD-ROM are seven simulations, written in Visual Basic, which animate key concepts: sharing a folder as a network resource; setting up a network (shared) printer; setting up TCP/IP at the network client; creating accounts for network management; setting network account policies (password and account lockout management policies); installing the Network Monitor Agent; and using the NT Performance Monitor to monitor the network. These simulations work in conjunction with many of the Hands-On exercises in the book, and can be run in a 16-bit or 32-bit environment. The host workstation operating system and setup are unaffected by the viewing of this simulation software.

Transcender Certification Test Prep Software

Bound into the back of this book is a CD-ROM containing Transcender Corporation's Networking Essentials certification exam preparation software with one full exam that simulates Microsoft's Networking Essentials exam (Exam 70-058).

Acknowledgments

Computer networking is exciting work and writing about it is equally rewarding. An important side to working in this field is the opportunity to work with many dedicated people like those who have helped with this book. I want to thank Kristen Duerr, managing editor, for her interest in this project, for the resources to make it happen, and for her continued support. Deb Kaufmann has been a profound source of guidance as development editor. She has provided critical advice, added polish, tested exercises, and carefully tuned each chapter to make a significantly better book. I also want to thank Jennifer Normandin and Susan Roche for their contributions in the production of this book.

The technical reviewers and validators have played an important role, too. I owe thanks to reviewers B.J. Honeycutt of Clayton College and State University, Robert Bruce Sinclair of the University of Wyoming (one of the "100 most wired" schools), and Mike Wright of the State Technical Institute of Memphis. Their technical advice and comments have been extremely valuable. Validators Greg Bigelow, Li-Jiuan Jang, and Brian McCooey have contributed by thoroughly checking the book contents and hands-on activities. Margarita Donovan of Course Technology has coordinated distribution of each chapter for timely review.

Nancy Benjamin of Books By Design has supplied excellent copy editing and production efforts. I also want to thank Lisa Ayers, Sean Marr, Kim Rivers, Christine Spillett, and Tracy Wells of Course Technology for all of their contributions.

Finally, I want to acknowledge Ring Lake Ranch in Wyoming for providing facilities and inspiring views for the writing of several chapters in this book.

PREPARING FOR
MICROSOFT CERTIFICATION

Microsoft offers a program called the Microsoft Certified Professional (MCP) program. Becoming a Microsoft Certified Professional can open many doors for you. Whether you want to be a network engineer, product specialist, or software developer, obtaining the appropriate Microsoft Certified Professional credentials can provide a formal record of your skills to potential employers. Certification can be equally effective in helping you secure a raise or promotion.

The Microsoft Certified Professional program is made up of many courses in several different tracks. Combinations of individual courses can lead to certification in a specific track. Most tracks require a combination of required and elective courses. One of the most common tracks for beginners is the Microsoft Certified Product Specialist (MCPS). By obtaining this status, your credentials tell a potential employer that you are an expert in a specialized computing area such as Personal Computer Operating Systems on a specific product, like Microsoft Windows 95.

How Can Transcender's Test Prep Software Help?

To become a Microsoft Certified Professional, you must pass rigorous certification exams that provide a valid and reliable measure of technical proficiency and expertise. The CD-ROM contained in this book, Transcender Corporation's Limited Version certification exam preparation software, can be used in conjunction with the book to help you assess your progress in the event you choose to pursue Microsoft Professional Certification. The Transcender CD-ROM presents a series of questions that were expertly prepared to test your readiness for the official Microsoft Certification examination on Networking Essentials (Exam 70-058). These questions were taken from a larger series of practice tests produced by the Transcender Corporation—practice tests that simulate the interface and format of the actual certification exams. Transcender's complete product also offers explanations for all questions. The rationale for each correct answer is carefully explained, and specific page references are given for Microsoft Product Documentation and Microsoft Press reference books. These page references enable you to study from additional sources.

Practice test questions from Transcender Corporation are acknowledged as the best available. In fact, with their full product, Transcender offers a money-back guarantee if you do not pass the exam. If you have trouble passing the practice examination included on the enclosed CD-ROM, you should consider purchasing the full product with additional practice tests and personalized feedback. Details and pricing information are available at the back of this book. A sample of the full Transcender product is on the enclosed CD-ROM, including remedial explanations.

The Transcender product is a great tool to help you prepare to become certified. If you experience technical problems with this product, please e-mail Transcender at *course@transcender.com* or call (615) 726-8779.

Want to Know More about Microsoft Certification?

There are many additional benefits to achieving Microsoft Certified status. These benefits apply to you as well as to your potential employer. As a Microsoft Certified Professional (MCP), you will be recognized as an expert on Microsoft products, have access to ongoing technical information from Microsoft, and receive special invitations to Microsoft conferences and events. You can obtain a comprehensive, interactive tool that provides full details about the Microsoft Certified Professional program online at *www.microsoft.com/train_cert/cert/certif.htm*. For more information on texts at Course Technology that will help prepare you for certification exams, visit our site at *www.course.com*.

When you become a Certified Product Specialist, Microsoft sends you a Welcome Kit that contains:

- An 8½ x 11" Microsoft Certified Product Specialist wall certificate. Also, within a few weeks after you have passed any exam, Microsoft sends you a Microsoft Certified Professional Transcript that shows which exams you have passed.

- A Microsoft Certified Professional Program membership card.

- A Microsoft Certified Professional lapel pin.

- A license to use the Microsoft Certified Professional logo. You are licensed to use the logo in your advertisements, promotions, proposals, and other materials, including business cards, letterheads, advertising circulars, brochures, yellow page advertisements, mailings, banners, resumes, and invitations.

- A Microsoft Certified Professional logo sheet. Before using the camera-ready logo, you must agree to the terms of the licensing agreement.

- A Microsoft TechNet CD-ROM.

- A 50% discount toward a one-year membership in the Microsoft TechNet Technical Information Network, which provides valuable information via monthly CD-ROMs.

- Dedicated forums on CompuServe (GO MECFORUM) and The Microsoft Network, which enable Microsoft Certified Professionals to communicate directly with Microsoft and one another.

- A one-year subscription to Microsoft Certified Professional Magazine, a career and professional development magazine created especially for Microsoft Certified Professionals.

- A Certification Update subscription. Certification Update is a bimonthly newsletter from the Microsoft Certified Professional program that keeps you informed of changes and advances in the program and exams.

- Invitations to Microsoft conferences, technical training sessions, and special events.

- Eligibility to join the Network Professional Association, a worldwide association of computer professionals. Microsoft Certified Product Specialists are invited to join as associate members.

A Certified Systems Engineer receives all the benefits mentioned above as well as the following additional benefits:

- Microsoft Certified Systems Engineer logos and other materials to help you identify yourself as a Microsoft Certified Systems Engineer to colleagues or clients.

- Ten free incidents with the Microsoft Support Network and a 25% discount on purchases of additional 10-packs of Priority Development and Desktop Support incidents.

- A one-year subscription to the Microsoft TechNet Technical Information Network.

- A one-year subscription to the Microsoft Beta Evaluation program. This benefit provides you with up to 12 free monthly beta software CDs for many of Microsoft's newest software products. This enables you to become familiar with new versions of Microsoft products before they are generally available. This benefit also includes access to a private CompuServe forum where you can exchange information with other program members and find information from Microsoft on current beta issues and product information.

Certify Me!

So you are ready to become a Microsoft Certified Professional. The examinations are administered through Sylvan Prometric (formerly Drake Prometric) and are offered at more than 700 authorized testing centers around the world. Microsoft evaluates certification status based on current exam records. Your current exam record is the set of exams you have passed. To maintain Microsoft Certified Professional status, you must remain current on all the requirements for your certification.

Registering for an exam is easy. To register, contact Sylvan Prometric, 2601 West 88th Street, Bloomington, MN, 55431, at (800) 755-EXAM (3926). Dial (612) 896-7000 or (612) 820-5707 if you cannot place a call to an 800 number from your location. You must call to schedule the exam at least one day before the day you want to take the exam. Taking the exam automatically enrolls you in the Microsoft Certified Professional program; you do not need to submit an application to Microsoft Corporation.

When you call Sylvan Prometric, have the following information ready:

- Your name, organization (if any), mailing address, and phone number.

- A unique ID number (e.g., your Social Security number).

- The number of the exam you wish to take (#70-058 for the Networking Essentials exam).

- A payment method (e.g., credit card number). If you pay by check, payment is due before the examination can be scheduled. The fee to take each exam is currently $100.

READ THIS BEFORE YOU BEGIN

Setting up the lab or classroom.   To complete the assignments in the book, it is desirable to have access to a lab with several kinds of resources. Network resources can be expensive, and so the assignments in this book use commonly available resources in an attempt to reduce costs but still maximize what students learn. To complete the hands-on activities the students need access to a classroom or lab with different kinds of resources. Those resources are presented in the following three lists to help instructors decide how to prepare a lab corresponding to their budget.

Needed for Many Hands-On Exercises

- Two or more computers (but preferably many more in a lab) running Microsoft Windows 95 or Windows NT 4.0 (or higher) Workstation or a combination of both

- One or more computers running Microsoft Windows 4.0 (or higher) Server

- Microsoft Internet Explorer (or another Internet browser)

- Internet access

- Microsoft Paint

- Microsoft Network Monitor (included with Windows NT Server or Microsoft SMS)

Needed for Some Hands-On Exercises (Very Desirable)

- Sections of coaxial and UTP cable

- BNC and RJ-45 connectors

- Two or more 10BASE2 terminators

- A small section of fiber-optic cable for demonstration

- One or more wire strippers and wire cutters

- One or more crimping tools

- One or more 8-port 10BASE-T hubs or equivalent

- One or more cable scanners

Needed for a Few Hands-On Exercises

- Microsoft Windows NT Server Resource Kit with Net Watcher and other network tools

- MAU or CAU

- Tape drive for one of the lab computers and tapes

- Repeater

- Modular hub or ability to view one at a school or business

- FDDI network or ability to view one at a school or business

Using remote administration and dual boot options to stretch resources.   Consider setting up the Remote Administration Tools on one or more computers running Windows NT Server. Many of the hands-on activities involving Windows NT Server can be performed remotely on a computer running Windows 95 or NT with access to a server's Remote Administration Tools. This will help reduce the number of lab computers running Windows NT Server. Also, consider implementing some lab computers as dual boot systems so they can run Windows 95 or NT. This will help reduce the costs of computers, too.

Accepting assignments electronically.   The project files on the Student Work Disk are in Microsoft Word format. This enables the instructor to accept assignments electronically, if appropriate to the classroom setting. For example, students can submit their Work Disk directly or print specific project files to hand in. Or students may submit completed assignment files by copying it to a specified shared directory. Another option is to use Send from Microsoft Word and submit an assignment file by e-mail. Because these are Word files, instructors can use the Revisions tool to provide each student feedback through printed copy, or by electronic means such as e-mail. The project assignment files are labeled *proj1.doc* through *proj12.doc,* one for each chapter.

CHAPTER ONE

AN INTRODUCTION TO NETWORKS

Networking is a rapidly growing area in the computer industry. Nearly every law office, school, private business, corporation, university, and research organization has a network or plans to install one. Anywhere a group of people work with computers in the same office, on the same floor, or in the same building, a network is likely to be there, too. Networks also are used by people who work from home or on the road, where they can dial in to the office using a modem and telephone line.

Networks are everywhere for important reasons. They save organizations money by enabling employees to share equipment, such as printers. They enable people to share information faster and more effectively through sending mail and files electronically, instead of transporting them on foot. They open up ways for instantaneous communication with someone in another room, building, city, state, or country. The Internet is the most publicized network, with news agencies, car dealers, radio shows, and countless other entities encouraging users to visit their sites for information. Thousands of other less visible networks are available for private or public use, like the ones on college campuses, in community libraries, and at local newspapers.

AFTER READING THIS CHAPTER AND COMPLETING THE EXERCISES YOU WILL BE ABLE TO:

- EXPLAIN BASIC NETWORK TERMINOLOGY AND CONCEPTS
- DESCRIBE AND USE NETWORKING CAPABILITIES SUCH AS FILE SERVICES, PRINT SERVICES, AND E-MAIL SERVICES
- EXPLAIN PEER-TO-PEER NETWORKING AND SET UP PEER-TO-PEER CAPABILITIES THROUGH A WORKGROUP
- DESCRIBE THE ADVANTAGES OF NETWORK FILE SERVERS
- EXPLAIN CLIENT/SERVER NETWORKING
- EXPLAIN NETWORK SERVICES AND WHERE TO INSTALL THEM FROM A MICROSOFT NT SERVER
- COMPARE WIRED TO WIRELESS NETWORKING
- EXPLAIN THE DIFFERENCES BETWEEN LOCAL-AREA, METROPOLITAN-AREA, WIDE-AREA, AND ENTERPRISE NETWORKS

In this chapter, you start to learn more about networks and participate in hands-on exercises along the way. The chapter introduces you to basic networking concepts, some you may already know and some you may not. It also introduces you to networking applications such as file services, print services, and e-mail. Different network services are discussed, complemented by a hands-on activity to view network services on a Microsoft Windows NT server. The chapter also presents options for wireless networking.

BASIC NETWORK CONCEPTS

A **network** is a communication system that enables computer users to share computer equipment, application software, and data, voice, and video transmissions. Networks can link users who are in the same office or on different continents. Network information is transmitted by wire, through fiber-optic communications, or radio waves, such as microwaves (Figure 1-1).

 A computer **network** is a system of computers, network devices, printers, and software linked by communications cabling.

Figure 1-1

Network communication methods

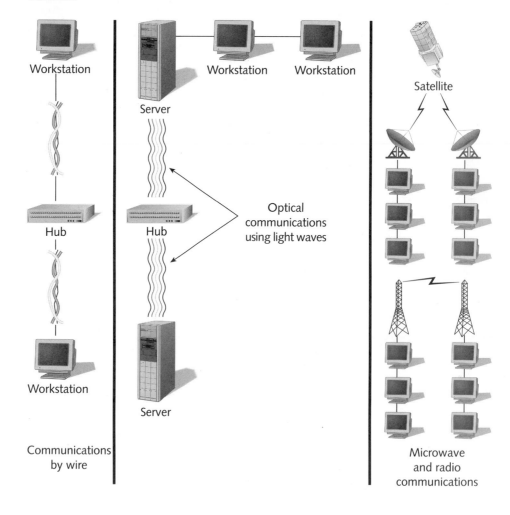

There are several reasons for having a network. First, by sharing software and equipment, network owners are able to save expenses on resources. One printer can be used for an entire office, saving the cost of attaching a printer to each computer. CD-ROM and disk storage can be shared to save on purchasing CD-ROM and disk drives for each computer on a network. Figure 1-2 illustrates 10 network computers sharing a single array of 14 CD-ROM drives.

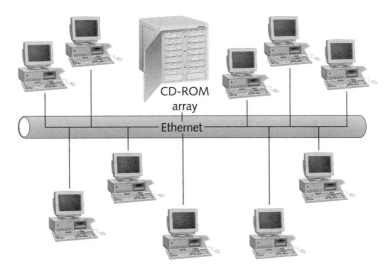

Figure 1-2

Computers connected to a CD-ROM array on a network

Second, networks make people more productive because they can share information without leaving their offices or homes. One university discovered that it took several trips between offices and the copy machine in the hiring of a single employee. Prospective employees filled out applications, which were passed to the human resources department. That department made a copy of each application and sent it to the head of the department that had the vacancy. The department head had more copies made for the department's hiring committee. Once a person was hired from the pool of applicants, more forms were completed for budget allocations, federal reporting, state reporting, hiring authorization, and payroll. Each of those forms was carried from office to office for the appropriate signatures.

That university found it could use its network to speed up the hiring process by scanning applications into electronic files. The files now are sent through the network to the appropriate department head, who forwards copies to the hiring committee. Once a decision is made, all the hiring forms are completed electronically, sent out for electronic signature, and then sent back to the human resources department.

Another reason for having a network is to open avenues to information. Libraries, research organizations, universities, corporations, and private individuals make all types of information available through networks connected to the **Internet**. For example, a college student who receives a diagnosis that he needs a knee operation decides to find out more by obtaining information from the Internet. He finds medical research sites that fully describe the procedures involved in the operation. He also finds private **World Wide Web (Web)** sites of people who have had the same operation, describing their experiences. An Internet discussion group provides even more information. All those resources help the student decide whether to have the surgery.

The **Internet** is a collection of thousands of smaller networks around the globe linked by a vast array of network equipment and communications methods.

The **World Wide Web (Web)** is a vast network of servers throughout the world that provide access to voice, text, video, and data files.

COMMUNICATIONS MEDIA AND NODES

A network comprises mainframes, minicomputers, microcomputers, printers, fax equipment, CD-ROM arrays, disk arrays, and other equipment. When directly connected to the network, each piece of equipment is a **node**. Nodes are physically linked into a network through **communications media** that consists of wire cabling, fiber-optic cable, or radio waves. The most common media are wire and fiber-optic cabling, which involve running communications cable between the nodes. The cable provides a physical medium for transmitting a signal. The signal contains data that is sent and received by the network nodes.

 A **node** is any device connected to a network, such as a microcomputer, a mainframe, a minicomputer, network equipment, or a printer.

 Communications media are the cabling or radio waves used to connect one network computer to another and to transport data between them.

Besides cabling, nodes can be linked by transmitting data on radio frequencies. Wireless commercial networks use **spread spectrum technology (SST)**, which takes advantage of high-frequency communications with the data-carrying signal transmitted from one location to another by low-power transmissions. Wireless networks are less common than cabled networks, but the technology is growing rapidly as higher data communication speeds are devised along with the associated network standards.

 Spread spectrum technology (SST) is used by wireless networks in place of cable for communications between network nodes. Network data is transmitted by means of reliable high-frequency radio signals.

WORKSTATIONS, HOSTS, AND SERVERS

Three of the most critical types of network nodes are workstations, hosts, and file servers. A **workstation** is a computer that is home to local applications such as Microsoft Office and that can run network applications, such as software that accesses data on a mainframe computer. The workstation has its own central processing unit (CPU) and operating system. When a workstation accesses software and data through the network on another computer, it is a **client** of that computer. The computer it accesses is a **host**.

 A **client** computer is one that accesses a mainframe, a minicomputer, or a microcomputer that allows access to multiple users. For example, a personal computer may access another computer for a file or a report or to use a software application. The client may use the accessed computer (host) to process data, or it may process accessed data using its own CPU.

A **host** has an operating system that allows multiple computers to access it at the same time. For example, several hundred clients may be logged in to one host simultaneously. Programs and information may be processed at the host, or they may be downloaded to the accessing computer (client) for processing.

 A **workstation** has its own CPU and may be used as a stand-alone computer for word processing, spreadsheet creation, or other software applications. It also may be used as a client to access another computer, such as a mainframe computer or a file server, as long as the necessary network hardware and software are installed.

The most typical client workstations on a network are personal computers, such as Pentium-based computers. Some workstations fulfill roles as both client and host. For example, on a Microsoft network, a Windows NT workstation may share a folder or an entire disk drive for others to access. In those roles, it acts as a workstation for a user who may be alternating work between a Microsoft Word document and updating payroll information on a mainframe. Serving as a host, the Windows NT workstation can be accessed by another workstation to download a spreadsheet to that workstation.

File servers are single computers that offer multi-user access. The server acts as a repository for software applications and data files that other network computers can use. A single server may allow access for as few as two users or as many as several thousand. A file server can host multiple users because it has a network operating system with that capability. For example, a server running the Microsoft Windows NT Server operating system can host up to 15,000 users at the same time (depending on the server hardware). One user may be accessing a spreadsheet, another may be installing software from the server, a third may be running a database application, while a fourth is running a data report. To host a small number of users, such as fewer than 100, the server may be a 80486 or Pentium computer. Hosting more than 100 users likely requires a Pentium-based server with several CPUs or an advanced workstation, such as a DEC Alpha or Sun Microsystems computer (both containing advanced or multiple CPUs).

 A **file server** is a network computer that makes software applications, data files, and network utilities available to other network computers.

Most networks have a combination of workstation clients and file servers. Some networks also have mainframes, minicomputers, and networked printers and faxes. Still others may have disk arrays and CD-ROM arrays available to users. Disk arrays are units that contain multiple hard disks that can be used for network access. Figure 1-3 illustrates a network containing these types of nodes.

Figure 1-3

A network with many types of nodes

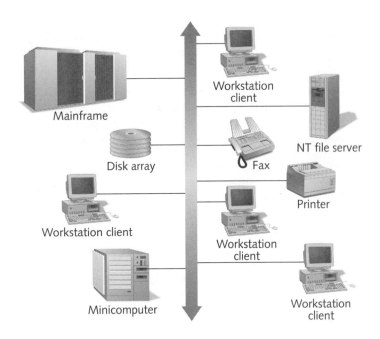

Network nodes are attached to the communications media through a **network interface card (NIC)**. The NIC is a board that is installed in the computer or network device, such as in an empty slot on the main board inside a workstation. One end of the card is accessible on the outside of the workstation and contains a receptacle or connector for attachment to the communication media. Figure 1-4 is an example of a NIC.

A **network interface card (NIC)** is an adapter card that enables a workstation, file server, printer, or other device to connect to a network and communicate with other network nodes.

In many new workstations, the NIC is built into the main board. When ordering such a workstation, make sure you specify one with a NIC that is compatible with the network setup and communications cable already in use.

Figure 1-4

A network interface card

PACKETS, FRAMES, AND CELLS

Data is sent from node to node in small units called **packets** or **frames**. Each node has communications software that codes the data into the units. Depending on the communications media, the data unit is converted to an electrical, radio, or light wave signal so it can be transmitted between nodes. For example, it takes many packets of data to print a single page of text on a network printer. The format of the packet is determined by the type of language, or **protocol**, used on the network. The protocol determines how the data is packaged, such as how to include information about which node sent the packet, which node is to receive the packet, the type of data to be transmitted, the size of the packet, the amount of data included, and a means of detecting damaged packets or transmission errors. Another important part of the packet is the timing information for multiple packet transfers, so packets are sent at known intervals. Figure 1-5 illustrates a generic packet format.

Figure 1-5

Generic
packet format

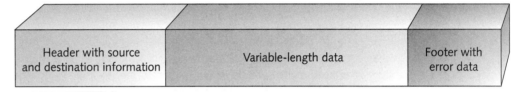

| Header with source and destination information | Variable-length data | Footer with error data |

 A **packet** is a unit of data formatted for transmission over a network. A packet normally is formatted with control information, a header that contains information about the packet's source and destination, the data to be transmitted, and a footer that contains error-checking information. Sometimes the terms *packet* and **frame** are used interchangeably. In this text, the term *packet* is used, except when discussing the packet format or contents, where the term *frame* is used (as is common practice among network administrators).

 A **protocol** is an established guideline that specifies how networked data is formatted into a packet, how the packet is transmitted, and how it is interpreted at the receiving end.

Data formatted in a packet can attain transmission speeds ranging from 1 to over 100 megabits per second (million bits per second, or Mbps), depending on the design of the network. Newer high-speed technologies have replaced packets with cells. A **cell** typically contains a fixed amount of data formatted to be transmitted at high speeds, such as from 155 Mbps to speeds over 1 Gbps (gigabits per second). It contains a header with information such as the following (Figure 1-6):

- Flow control information to coordinate transmission between the source node and the destination node

- Path and channel information to deliver the data along the fastest route

- Information to indicate whether the cell contains actual data or management information for the high-speed connection

- Error control information

Figure 1-6

Cell format

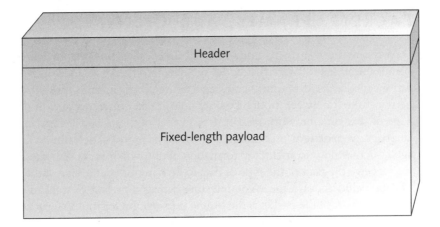

The cell's payload of fixed-length data is different from that of a packet. Depending on the protocol, packets contain a variable amount of data, such as multiples of 8 bits. For example, the amount of data in a packet used by the popular Ethernet transport method varies from several hundred to several thousand bits in length. The amount of data in a cell is always a certain length, such as 384 bits for the high-speed Asynchronous Transfer Mode (ATM) transport method. The fixed length enables more precise timing of data transmissions to attain high speeds and quality of service. (ATM is described in chapter 5.)

Definition

A **cell** is a unit of data formatted for high-speed transmission over a network. Typically a cell contains a fixed amount of data and performs less error checking than a packet to achieve faster transmission.

Packets and cells find their way from one node to another by means of addressing. Each network node must have a unique address. Addressing information also is used to identify different networks and the fastest path from one network to another. The dotted decimal notation addressing method is illustrated in Figure 1-7, which shows that each network node has a slightly different address. The first two numbers in the address identify the network and the last two numbers identify the node.

Figure 1-7

Network nodes with unique addresses

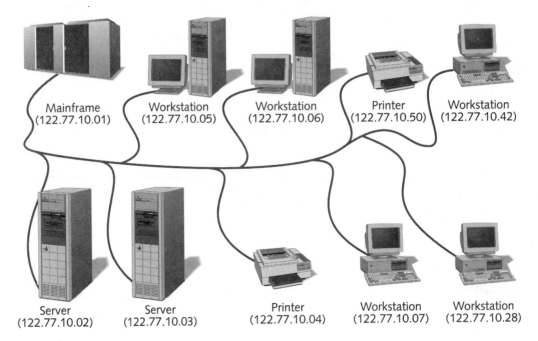

Mainframe (122.77.10.01) Workstation (122.77.10.05) Workstation (122.77.10.06) Printer (122.77.10.50) Workstation (122.77.10.42)

Server (122.77.10.02) Server (122.77.10.03) Printer (122.77.10.04) Workstation (122.77.10.07) Workstation (122.77.10.28)

NETWORK COMMUNICATIONS DEVICES

The transmission of packets and cells is assisted by the use of a range of devices that can be placed in strategic locations on the network. Some of the devices amplify the data-carrying signal so it can go farther, while others redirect a signal to another network. The following are examples of what some network devices can do:

- Connect different nodes into one or more networks
- Amplify packet signals to go farther
- Connect different networks into one or more networks
- Control the packet traffic to reduce network congestion
- Route packets and cells to particular destinations
- Establish alternative routes for packets when portions of the network are down
- Connect networks within a city or between continents
- Monitor for network problems

Many network devices are connected to the network, having a built-in NIC or similar interface. Other devices are connected using specialized techniques, depending on the function of the device. Some network devices are counted as a node, which is important in determining how many devices and computers can be supported on a single network, depending on the design. (Chapter 6 explains the different types of network devices.)

NETWORKING CAPABILITIES

Once a network has been installed, many new capabilities become available to increase a user group's productivity and range of information. Those capabilities include the following:

- File services
- Print services
- Software services
- E-mail services
- Internet and intranet services
- Commerce
- Network monitoring

FILE SERVICES

Before networks, a common way to share files was to carry files on disk from office to office (a method sometimes called the "SneakerNet"). At one university, a budget officer created disks of budget information, which were then distributed to the departments. Each department would review the disk files, make changes, and send its disk back to the budget officer to be incorporated in the calculations for the next budget. Creating a university-wide budget involved a lot of work—over a hundred disks were carried back and forth to distribute original data and to make corrections or additions.

The implementation of a network and the sharing of data files significantly changed the effort to create a new budget each year. With a network, the budget officer could put data files on a file server. Each department could access its own budget information, share it with others in the department, adjust the data, and return the file, all without anyone leaving the office or walking several blocks across campus.

Sharing files is a hallmark of networks. It enables files that need to be used by several people to be stored at one or more locations, such as on a file server. Those who have accounts or authorized access to the file server can obtain shared files quickly. By storing information in one place, controls can be set up to ensure that everyone obtains the same consistent data. It is easier to back up data, too, because of the central location.

Another file service option is for a single user to make certain files available to a limited set of users through the network. A professor can share the class syllabus with students by making a copy available from a file server or from the professor's hard drive. Class assignments can be distributed and handed back the same way.

Microsoft networks provide options to share files from a central server or from a user's hard drive by creating a shared folder. When a shared folder is available through the network, users with the right authorization can **map** that folder as though it is a drive on their computers.

A **mapped drive** is a disk volume or folder that is shared on the network by a file server or workstation. It gives designated network workstations access to the files and data in its shared volume or folder. The workstation, via software, determines a drive letter for the shared volume, which is the workstation's map to the data.

In this hands-on activity, you use Network Neighborhood to map a drive. You need access to a lab that has workstations with Microsoft Windows 95 or Windows NT Workstation 4.0. Before starting, ask your instructor for the name of the computer with the shared folder and the name of the folder. To start, you should be at the Windows desktop.

To map a network drive:

1. Double-click **Network Neighborhood** on the desktop of the workstation.

2. Double-click the workstation or server your instructor has set up with a shared folder.

3. Right-click the folder you want to map to your workstation so a shortcut menu is displayed.

4. Click **Map Network Drive** (see Figure 1-8).

Figure 1-8

Mapping
a drive

5. In the Map Network Drive dialog box, click the arrow in the **Drive**: drop-down box and select **M** (or another available drive if M is in use) as your mapped drive.

6. Click the **Reconnect at logon** box so the drive is automatically mapped the next time you log on.

7. Click **OK**.

8. Close the drive and then the Network Neighborhood dialog boxes by clicking the **Close** button ⊠ in the upper right corner.

9. Double-click **My Computer** on the desktop and look for drive M to verify that you mapped the drive.

10. Close My Computer.

 In this hands-on activity, you make a folder available for others to access through the network. File sharing should be enabled in Windows 95 and set to Share Level access control.

To create a shared folder:

1. Double-click **My Computer** on the desktop of the workstation.

2. Double-click drive **C**.

3. Right-click the folder you want to share, such as Apps or Utilities.

4. Click **Properties** on the shortcut menu.

5. Click the **Sharing** tab.

6. Click the **Shared As:** radio button.

7. Enter a name for the shared folder in the Share Name: text box.

8. If you are using Windows 95, click the **Full** radio button for full access to the folder (see Figure 1-9).

Figure 1-9

Sharing a
folder from
Windows 95

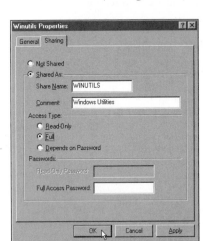

9. If you are using Windows NT Workstation, click the **Maximum Allowed** button so there is no limit to the number of people who can access your drive at the same time. Click the **Permissions** button to make sure the Everyone group has Full Control as the type of access. If it does not, highlight Everyone and change the Type of Access: box to Full Control. Your screen should look similar to Figure 1-10. Click **OK**.

Figure 1-10

Sharing a
folder from
Windows NT
Workstation

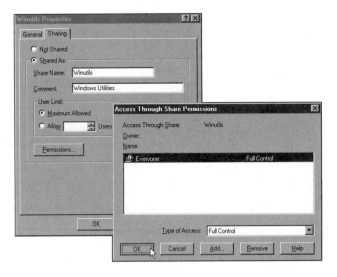

10. In Windows 95 or Windows NT Workstation, click **OK** on the Properties dialog box.

11. Back on the My Computer screen, a hand appears under the folder to indicate it is shared.

PRINT SERVICES

Network print services enable many kinds of printers to be shared on a network. For example, on a Microsoft network you can share a printer from a workstation running Windows 95 or Windows NT Workstation. The network administrator also can share one or more printers connected to the Windows NT server.

Many offices find that network print services save on making a substantial investment in printing equipment. For example, in an office with six people working in close proximity, all can share a single network printer instead of purchasing a printer for each employee, as shown in Figure 1-11. In another example, an architecture firm can save by sharing one expensive plotter for printing building drawings, instead of purchasing several lower-quality plotters, one for each architect. On a smaller scale, you may have a color inkjet printer and your office partner may have a laser printer. By setting up both as network printers, each of you can print from either printer.

Figure 1-11

Sharing a printer over a network

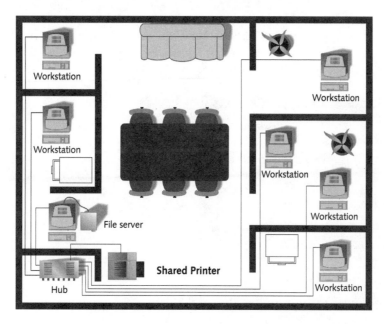

 In this hands-on activity, you use Windows 95 or Windows NT Workstation 4.0 to share a printer for others to use through the network. It requires you to work from a lab workstation that has its own printer already set up.

To share a printer over the network:

1. Double-click **My Computer** on the desktop.

2. Double-click the **Printers** folder.

3. Right-click the printer you want to share.

4. Click **Sharing** on the shortcut menu.

5. Click the **Sharing** tab.

6. Click the **Shared As:** radio button in Windows 95 or the **Shared** button in Windows NT.

7. If you are using Windows 95, use the Share Name: text box to enter a name for the shared printer and enter a comment to describe the printer, such as **LaserJet Printer**, as shown in Figure 1-12.

Figure 1-12

Sharing a
printer from
Windows 95

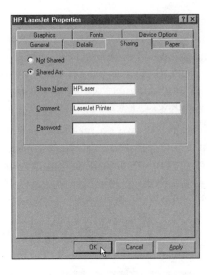

8. If you are using Windows NT Workstation, type a name for the shared printer
in the Share Name: box (for example, **LaserJet**) and double-click **Windows 95**
under Alternate Drivers: (see Figure 1-13).

Figure 1-13

Sharing a
printer from
Windows NT
Workstation

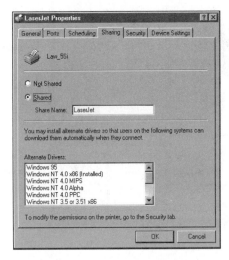

9. In Windows 95 or Windows NT Workstation, click **OK**.

10. Notice that a hand appears under that printer in the Printers folder to indicate
it is shared.

SOFTWARE SERVICES

Another advantage of a network is the ability to load or run software applications on workstations across the network. A site license can be purchased to have one shared copy of a
word processor or one shared copy of an entire suite of programs, such as Microsoft Office,
installed on a file server. For example, if the site license is for 400 users, then that many users
have the option to install the application from the file server to their workstations over the
network. Another option is to run a network version of the software, which means that only
a few utility files are permanently loaded at the workstation, while the main program files
are always loaded from the server each time the program is started. The advantage of that

method is that it saves workstation disk space. A disadvantage is that it may create an excessive load on the server and the network if several hundred users have network installations.

Using application services on a network can save the network administrator or client support people hours of work. When a software upgrade is released, the network administrator loads one copy on the server to be shared by all users. Doing that represents hours of savings compared to purchasing individual licenses and loading the software at each workstation of, say, 400 users. Also, by using the file server as the central application program source, it is easier to ensure that all users have the same software and version level. That saves many hours for client support people by reducing the need to support an extensive range of software and different software versions.

 When software applications are selected, their impact on the network should be determined before the purchase is made. Some software applications can slow network response for all users.

CLIENT/SERVER APPLICATIONS

A major push for networking services today is the drive to implement new client/server applications. **Client/server applications** involve computing that is performed on the client side (i.e., on individual workstations) as well as on the server side. This is a shift from host-based computing, in which all processing occurs on the host computer, such as a mainframe. It also is a shift from server-based computing, in which files are loaded from the server onto the workstation for processing at the workstation.

 A **client/server application** is one in which processing tasks are performed on the client or on one or more servers to achieve the best performance and to minimize network load.

An example of a client/server application is a payroll system designed to use both the server and the workstation. The payroll system's computations, such as calculation of payroll benefits and deductions, are performed at the workstation to relieve the CPU load on the server. Large, complex reports are processed by the server's database through a custom-built data view and then transmitted to the workstation for viewing.

There are efforts throughout industry to re-engineer how companies are organized. Many organizations and consultants are working with client/server applications to place more information in the hands of computer users and make it easier to use. That is possible only with extensive networking capabilities, which must be designed and implemented well before the client/server applications are released.

ELECTRONIC MAIL SERVICES

Electronic mail (e-mail) has become a critical application on networks. Many organizations rely on their e-mail services to communicate about projects, to discuss sales strategies, and to prepare for meetings. Students contact their college professors through e-mail for help on tests and assignments, and some instructors prefer to have assignments submitted by e-mail. Many software vendors provide assistance to their customers by e-mail. Even television viewers can contact their favorite news organizations through e-mail.

Electronic mail (e-mail) is the use of mail software on the client to compose a message and send it to mail or post office software on one or more servers that forward the message to the intended destination. E-mail is possible because of networks and can reach around the world through the Internet.

A major advantage of e-mail is that it is fast and convenient. Another advantage is that mail distribution lists can be built so that many people at different locations can receive the same message. Many networked organizations offer calendar and appointment software to complement e-mail. For example, Microsoft's Schedule+ and Outlook enable a user to view appointments on another person's calendar and send an invitation for a new appointment by Microsoft Mail, Microsoft Exchange, or Microsoft Outlook.

In this hands-on activity, you use Microsoft Exchange to send e-mail to yourself. Use a lab computer that has Microsoft Exchange or Outlook and Microsoft Word already installed. You also need to have a mail account on a school mail server.

To send e-mail using Microsoft Outlook:

1. Open Outlook by clicking the **Start** button on the Windows Taskbar, **Programs**, and **Microsoft Outlook** (or click the **Outlook** button on the Microsoft Office toolbar).

2. Click the **New Mail Message** button on the far left side of the Outlook toolbar. The Microsoft Word editor opens, as shown in Figure 1-14. Continue with step 3.

To send e-mail using Microsoft Exchange:

1. Open Exchange by clicking the **Inbox** icon on the desktop.

2. Click the **New Message** button on the left side of the toolbar. The Microsoft Word editor opens, as shown in Figure 1-14. Continue with step 3.

Figure 1-14

Sending an
e-mail message

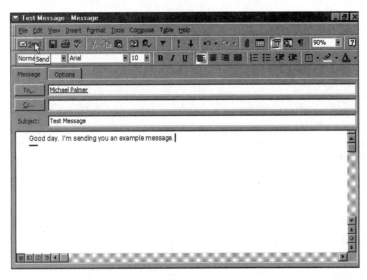

From the Microsoft Word editor:

3. Click the **To** button. The Select Names dialog box opens.

4. Click the **New** button on the Select Names dialog box.

5. Click the entry type, such as **Microsoft Mail** or **cc:Mail** and then click the **In this message only** radio button.

6. Enter your name and e-mail address (the dialog box will vary, depending on the mail system used). (For this exercise, you send e-mail to yourself.)

7. Click **OK**.

8. Press **[Tab]** twice.

9. Enter a message subject, such as **Test Message**, in the Subject: text box and press **[Tab]**.

10. Type an example message, such as **Good day. I'm sending you an example message.**

11. Click the **Send** button on the left side of the toolbar.

12. Wait a few minutes for the message to arrive. Click the **Inbox** folder on the left side of the screen in Outlook or Exchange, then double-click your message subject (e.g., **Test Message**) to read your message when it arrives.

INTERNET AND INTRANET SERVICES

The Internet is a prime example of networking capabilities. It is a vast collection of thousands of networks connected worldwide. Millions of computer users are attached to the networks in every part of the United States and in countries all over the world. The Internet brings together government, education, business, and research organizations. Internet participants share in discussion groups, work on leading-edge technological developments, conduct business, publish news stories, and obtain weather information. They access text, voice, and video files that are presented through a format called **Hypertext Markup Language (HTML).** An Internet user reads HTML files by using software called a **Web browser**, such as Microsoft Internet Explorer or Netscape Communicator.

Hypertext Markup Language (HTML) is a formatting process used to enable documents and graphics images to be read on the World Wide Web. HTML also provides for fast links to other documents, to graphics, and to Web sites.

A **Web browser** enables the user to search for information and to display text, graphics, sound, and video from the World Wide Web. Web browsers also can be used to search for information through private networks. Microsoft Internet Explorer and Netscape Communicator are two popular Web browsers.

An **intranet** is like the Internet in that it provides access to HTML-formatted documents from one or more servers. The difference is that an intranet uses tight controls to limit who has access. Many organizations make sales, performance, human resources, and accounting reports available to their managers through an intranet. Other organizations use an intranet to enable employees to update personal information, such as a new address or a change in health benefits. Colleges use intranets to enable students to look up their grades and degree progress.

An **intranet** is a private network within an organization. It uses the same Web-based software as the Internet, but access to it is highly restricted. Intranets are used, for example, to enable managers to run high-level reports, to let staff members update human resources information, and to provide authorized users access to other forms of private data.

Microsoft has a Web site with a wide range of information. Try this hands-on exercise to access their Web site from a lab workstation with Microsoft Internet Explorer.

To explore the Microsoft Web site using Internet Explorer:

1. Click the **Start** button, **Programs**, and **Internet Explorer**. Or double-click the **Internet Explorer** icon on the desktop.

2. You will see a Connect To dialog box if your school uses a dial-up service such as America Online, CompuServe, the Microsoft Network, or another Internet service provider (ISP). If you see the Connect To dialog box, click **OK**.

3. Enter **http://www.microsoft.com/** in the Address box on the Internet Explorer screen. Click **OK**.

4. In the left News for You column, click a topic to view, such as **Education** (see Figure 1-15).

5. Click the Close button ⊠ on the top right portion of the screen to exit.

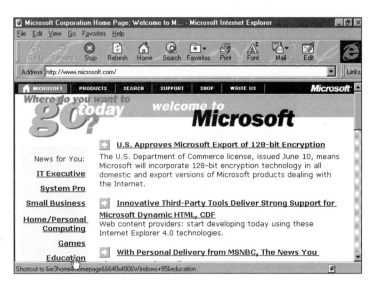

Figure 1-15

Accessing Microsoft's Web site

COMMERCE ON NETWORKS

The Internet has become a major source of commerce, where people can order just about anything electronically. With an account number or credit card, you can order almost any type of product, including flowers, a boat, books, art, computer equipment, shoes, or a mountain bike. Thousands of companies have established Web sites from which to advertise and sell products directly to Internet users. Many publications are now electronic only, available through subscription on the Internet.

Although the World Wide Web is receiving much publicity, many organizations have been conducting business on the Internet or through private networks for years. Universities, for example, handle large payroll transactions to multiple banks through electronic clearinghouses that specialize in electronic payroll transfers. Businesses have automated inventory purchases through networks so that stocks are resupplied automatically when they are low.

INTEGRATION ISSUES

There are many types of network operating systems and many manufacturers of network devices. As with any growing technological area, there are potential problems in making one vendor's product work with another vendor's product. The best advice is to research compatibility concerns before you buy a product. Mainstream operating systems are always a solid option because they typically work with other mainstream systems. For example, Microsoft Windows NT Server and Novell NetWare are popular network operating systems that have reliable integration paths, so both work well on the same network. Both also have options to interface with many other kinds of networks, such as the Internet, networks with IBM mainframes, and networks with UNIX computers.

Some network equipment manufacturers sell equipment that interfaces only with other equipment made by the same manufacturer. Such equipment is called proprietary network equipment because it is based on technology that is used by only one manufacturer. Using proprietary equipment severely limits your ability to integrate one network with another. Mainstream network equipment manufacturers, however, work with one another to follow networking standards. Those standards help remove the difficulties of integrating different kinds of equipment.

PEER-TO-PEER NETWORKING AND WORKGROUPS

A peer-to-peer network is one of the simplest ways to network. On a **peer-to-peer** network, each workstation communicates with other workstations strictly through its own operating system. Files, folders, printers, and the contents of entire disk drives can be made available on one computer for others to access. No file servers or host computers are needed to enable workstations to communicate and share resources. Figure 1-16 illustrates a simple peer-to-peer network.

 A **peer-to-peer** network is one in which any computer can communicate with other networked computers on an equal or peerlike basis without going through an intermediary, such as a server or a host.

Figure 1-16

A simple peer-to-peer network

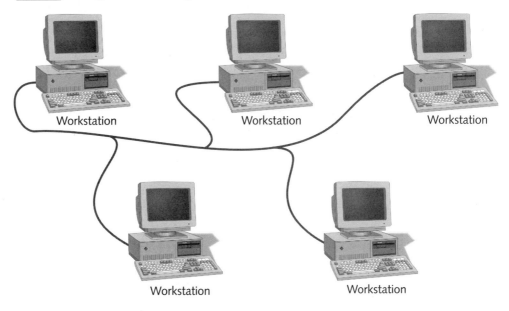

Workstation   Workstation   Workstation

Workstation   Workstation

Microsoft's workgroup concept is a good example of peer-to-peer networking. Any Windows 95 or Windows NT computer can set up resources to share with other Windows 95 or NT computers on the network. A **workgroup** is a grouping of computer users who share one or more resources in a decentralized way. For example, if Bob, Jane, Reuben, Jesse, and Gina all work in the accounting office where they share reports and files, any or all of them can set up a shared folder containing files that can be accessed over the network. In the process, access to the shared folder can be limited to members of the group only. Jane can run daily reports to share with the others, while Jesse can update vendor lists and investment accounts to share from his computer.

 In a Microsoft Windows environment, a **workgroup** consists of users who share drive and printer resources in an independent peer-to-peer relationship.

Strict peer-to-peer networking can be effective for very small networks, but there are problems when resource management is totally decentralized. For example, Gina may leave work sick, turning off her computer so no one can access it the rest of the day. Another problem is that a workstation operating system is not designed to handle a growing load of clients in the same way as a server operating system.

One situation in which peer-to-peer networking can be effective is in a small office, say, one with five tax accountants and one office assistant. Each accountant can share a drive on his or her computer containing client tax files. Every accountant can access the client files of any other accountant. The office assistant also can access files to prepare mailings to all clients.

As the tax firm grows to 10 or 20 accountants, however, peer-to-peer networking is much less effective, for several reasons. First, it offers only moderate network security. Access to information can be limited to a certain drive or directory, but not to individual files. Second, as the number of network users grows, so does the need to have a central place to store and manage information. With 10 or more accountants, it is much easier to manage files by locating them on a central file server for all to access. Security is increased because there are more options to control access through user accounts on the server and through sophisticated security to the level of specified directories or individual files. Network management also is easier because there is one place from which to manage users and critical files, including the backing up of important files. Third, and most important, peer-to-peer networks can experience slow response because the operating systems are not optimized for heavy multiple access to one computer. For example, if nine accountants all decide to access the tenth accountant's shared drive at the same time, all are likely to experience slow computer response from the load. If, instead, all 10 accountants access one server, the response is quick because the server operating system is designed to handle the load.

 Access to shared drives and printers is susceptible to slow response on a peer-to-peer network, such as one where all workstations are running Windows 3.11 or Windows 95 and there is no server. If the amount of file and printer sharing is high, even among a handful of users, consider installing a Windows NT server computer. The savings in time and productivity are well worth the extra expense.

In this hands-on exercise, you set up a workgroup in Windows 95. You need access to a computer file with sharing set up.

To set up a workgroup in Windows 95:

1. Double-click **My Computer** on the desktop.

2. Double-click the **C:** drive.

3. Right-click the shared folder you created in the hands-on activity in the File Services section of this chapter, such as **Apps** or **Utilities**.

4. Click **Properties** on the shortcut menu.

5. Click the **Sharing** tab (see Figure 1-9).

6. Enter a password in the Full Access Password box (you create the workgroup by letting only certain users know the password).

 For Windows NT, you created a workgroup of Everyone when you created a shared folder in the File Services section of this chapter. To designate a different group or only certain users, you would remove the Everyone group (see Figure 1-10) and click the Add button on the Access Through Share Permissions dialog box.

NETWORKING WITH SERVERS

The addition of a file server on a network creates a more robust environment in which to share resources. A file server is designed to handle several hundred or more users at once, resulting in faster response when delivering the shared resource and less network congestion as multiple workstations wait to access that resource.

A mainstream server operating system also has many options for multiple network applications. For instance, a Microsoft NT server also can function as a primary source of application software, as a remote access server for users who work at home, as a database server, a management server for all network workstations, a gateway to NetWare files, a print server, a Web server, and a server for specialized network services (e.g., assigning workstation addresses.) The server also comes with complete security options to restrict access to resources, folders, and files.

 Make sure enough memory, hard disk space, and other resources exist on a server to match all of the functions it provides to users on the network.

USING A SERVER TO MANAGE NETWORK RESOURCES

One way in which a Windows NT server helps manage a network is through domains. An NT **domain** is a collection of resources and users who have access to the resources. Resources are servers, printers, CD-ROM arrays, and other equipment. A single domain can have one or more servers as members. Users can be set up into groups to control who has access to what resources. The domain offers a way to manage resources, workstations, software, and the network from one central location. The network administrator can manage the network resources with minimum confusion and time expenditure.

Domains consist of network clients and the resources used by the clients. User workstations and user groups are the clients; file servers, print servers, and other network services are the resources.

CLIENT/SERVER NETWORKING

Client/server applications began appearing in the late 1980s as a means to provide more information to users than previously achieved from traditional mainframe or file server–based application systems. Mainframe solutions have not been successful in fully meeting the reporting and data query needs of users. File server systems have not been efficient in handling large databases of information. Client/server applications are designed to fill the gaps left by mainframe and file server approaches.

Client/server applications focus on bringing data to customers quickly. Users are able to build queries and reports to meet their information needs without writing complex computer code. These applications are made possible by a combination of technological tools that include the following:

- Relational databases
- Graphical user interfaces (GUIs)
- Rapid application development (RAD) tools
- Powerful reporting tools
- More powerful PC workstations
- Networks

Relational databases have made it possible to store large amounts of data on a server. They are designed for fast access to data for updating, query, or reporting. Modern relational databases can store voice and video information as well as data. They also provide open access paths (standard guidelines for reaching data) so a variety of reporting and development tools can access the data. Such connectivity has created an active market for companies that offer RAD tools and GUI reporting tools.

Ninety percent of client/server applications are developed in the Microsoft Windows GUI environment with RAD tools such as Microsoft Visual Basic. The GUI environment is easy for customers to use, and the RAD tools are easier for programmers to work with than older development methods. More powerful PC workstations have made it possible to use GUI and to access large amounts of data held in relational databases.

Networks provide the link to the applications and to the data. Many client/server systems are designed to be three-tiered, meaning there are three critical pieces (Figure 1-17). One piece is the PC client workstation, which contains the GUI presentation logic seen by the user. Another piece is the application server, which stores client/server applications and reports (business process logic) used by the client. The third piece is the database server, which provides data-related services, including security.

Figure 1-17

Three-tiered client/server system

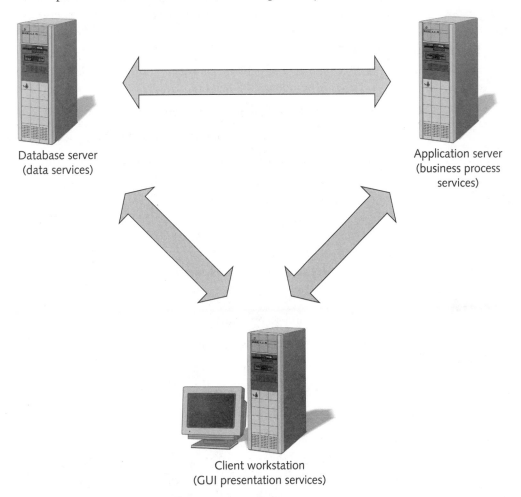

Database server
(data services)

Application server
(business process services)

Client workstation
(GUI presentation services)

The network demands for client/server applications continue to grow. GUI reporting tools make it possible for more clients to write their own database queries quickly. As more clients transport more ad hoc report data, network demands increase. That is particularly true when the data is video or voice information. The GUI format also is data intensive and puts demand on the network.

RAD tools reduce application development cycles, so developers can place more applications with more functionality on the network. Because the applications are developed in GUI format, they attract new customers who did not use computers in the past. That introduces more people to network computing, resulting in more network demand, such as for high-speed, high-capacity networks.

USING THE SERVER AS A NETWORK OPERATING SYSTEM

When you plan a network, it is critical to have a network operating system that offers a wide range of services. The more services, the more flexibility you have to match the network to the work requirements of your organization. There are many important services, such as connectivity services, network management services, services to browse resources and workstations, and Internet and intranet services. For example, Microsoft NT Server includes the following network services:

- A wide range of network protocols and communications services (in later versions of Windows NT Server)
- Network browsing services to identify who is connected to the network
- Network server and logon services to support user access
- Remote access services for dialing into the network from a modem
- Replication services to copy files from a folder on one computer to a folder on another computer
- Network file and printing services
- Backup services to save information on servers and workstations
- Gateway services to Novell NetWare file servers
- E-mail services
- Network and server management services
- Services for Macintosh computers
- Database connectivity services
- Internet and intranet services
- Fax services
- Software licensing services

 In this hands-on activity, you look at some of Microsoft Windows NT Server's network services. You can see which services are installed and how new services can be added. For this activity, you need access to a computer with Microsoft Windows NT Server.

To see which NT Server network services are installed:

1. Log on as an administrator (ask your instructor what account to use).
2. Click the **Start** button, **Settings**, and the **Control Panel** folder.
3. Double-click the **Network** icon on the Control Panel.
4. Click the **Services** tab. Use the scroll bar in the Network Services: list box to view which services are installed (Figure 1-18). (The services listed on your screen may vary from those shown in Figure 1-18.)

5. Click the **Add** button to view a full list of services that can be installed from the Control Panel Network icon. You can add any of the services by inserting the Windows NT Server CD-ROM and double-clicking the desired service. (From here, follow the instructions on the dialog boxes to complete the installation.)

Figure 1-18

Windows NT Server network services

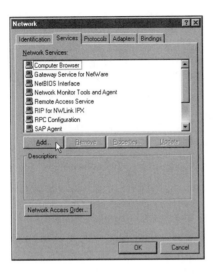

WIRED AND WIRELESS NETWORKING

The traditional way to build a network is through direct connections to network communications cable. Workstations, servers, hosts, and network equipment are physically connected to the cable through connectors, NICs, and other physical connection devices. In some cases, an organization needs to connect users in remote or hard-to-reach locations where it is difficult or expensive to run cable. An urban university may want to link networks in two adjoining buildings where there are no underground cabling tunnels. A small business that needs to link separate buildings may not have the budget to dig trenches and lay fiber-optic cable. Wireless networking equipment provides an answer to those types of situations.

Several vendors offer wireless networking equipment that links networks at two locations by using radio communications. For example, to connect two buildings, the network in one building would have wireless communication equipment connected to an antenna on top of the building. The network in the other building would have similar equipment connected to an antenna. Packets would be transmitted and received through the antenna at each location.

In another type of wireless communications, selected workstations can be equipped with a NIC that transmits and receives packets via an antenna on the NIC. A wireless device attached to the network communicates with the NIC through its own antenna.

On a wireless network, omnidirectional antennas are used for transmissions within a building; directional antennas are used for communications between local area networks (LANs) in separate buildings. Packets are transmitted as radio waves (packet radio) at ultra-high frequencies. The high-frequency ranges offer greater bandwidth transmissions at higher speeds than would be possible at lower frequencies. Because of the relatively high bandwidths, those frequencies are known as spread spectrum radio frequencies. Wireless bridges (discussed in chapter 6) operate on spread spectrum radio frequencies in the 902–928 MHz range. Radio transmissions in that frequency range are called line-of-sight transmissions because the waves travel only short distances. Wavelengths at lower frequencies, such as 20 MHz, are able to skip long distances in the atmosphere. They can travel several hundred or several thousand miles, but they do not have the high bandwidth characteristics needed for fast-packet radio transmissions.

Besides high bandwidth, the 902–928 MHz range offers several other advantages. One advantage is that transmissions at those frequencies are difficult to intercept. The military has long used such high frequencies to enhance security on its radio transmissions. Additionally, radio frequency interference (RFI) is much lower on spread spectrum frequencies than it is on conventional radio frequencies. Spread spectrum communications also are less susceptible to interference from weather conditions than some other frequencies. Another advantage is that the Federal Communications Commission (FCC) does not require licensing for radio transmissions in the 902–928 MHz range. (Countries other than the United States may require licensing; the laws should be checked before wireless network equipment is installed.)

Spread spectrum network communications do have some disadvantages. One is that although communications are faster than at lower frequencies, they are about half as fast or less than cabled communications. Another disadvantage is that because the frequencies are shared by the military and by licensed amateur radio operators, network communications may experience interference from those sources. Also, nonlicensed network applications cannot use high wattage levels to boost weak signals for longer distances or stronger reception. Table 1-1 summarizes the advantages and disadvantages of spread spectrum radio frequency.

Table 1-1

Advantages and disadvantages of spread-spectrum communication

Advantages	Disadvantages
Relatively high bandwidth	Transmission rates are slower than for cabled communications
Faster packet transmission compared to lower frequencies	Frequency range is shared with other competing sources, such as the military and amateur radio, that may cause interference
Security from interception	Transmission wattage levels are relatively low
Negligible RFI	
Less subject to problems from adverse weather than some other broadcast frequencies	
No FCC licensing requirement	

LANS, MANS, WANS, AND ENTERPRISE NETWORKS

Early networks connected users in close proximity, such as in the same office area or on the same floor of a building. They were truly **local area networks (LANs)** with a limited area of service. Once LANs became commonplace, the push was on to find ways to connect one LAN to another, for example, to connect a LAN in one building to a LAN in an adjacent building or in a building across town.

A **local area network (LAN)** is a series of interconnected computers, printers, and other computer equipment that share hardware and software resources. The service area usually is limited to a given floor, office area, or building.

Connecting multiple LANs within a city or metropolitan region creates a **metropolitan area network (MAN)**. A state university in one city is a MAN when it links several research centers and other facilities throughout the same city. A large business campus might have LANs used for administrative processing connected to LANs used for scientific research. Those are also examples of **enterprise networks**, because they link separate LANs with different computer resources into one large connected unit.

 A **metropolitan area network (MAN)** links multiple LANs within a large city or metropolitan region.

 An **enterprise network** reaches throughout a large area, such as a college campus, a city, or across several states, connecting many kinds of LANs and network resources.

The reach of networks has grown to extend across continents and oceans. **Wide area networks (WANs)** give college students at the University of Washington the ability to use supercomputers housed at the University of Illinois. A commercial vendor in Rochester, New York, can send software application updates to clients in Colorado and in London via network connections.

 A **wide area network (WAN)** is a far-reaching system of networks. WANs can extend across states and across continents.

Network technology is pervasive and has blurred the distinctions between LANs and WANs. It is difficult to define where a LAN ends and a WAN begins. The distinctions are growing more vague as television cable companies partner with telephone companies to bring networking into every home.

CHAPTER SUMMARY

To understand the basics of networks, you need to know a range of terms and concepts. Some of these concepts, such as the Internet, are easy to grasp, because they are in the public eye. Others, such as network protocols, become more meaningful as you progress through this book and try the hands-on activities. This chapter introduced terms such as network, workstation, client, server, and nodes.

It is equally important to have a strong understanding of the capabilities networks provide. File and print services are particularly important because they are two reasons why networks exist, as are services like running applications from the network and sending e-mail. Many people also rely on Internet access for information and to send e-mail long distances.

Network computers are able to communicate through peer-to-peer networking capabilities built into operating systems such as Microsoft Windows 3.1, 3.11, 95, and NT. Peer-to-peer networking enables computers to share information even when there is no server on the network. When there is a server, significantly more networking opportunities are created to share files and printers, manage the network, manage shared databases, and make software applications available.

As you look at implementing a server, make sure you take a close look at the services a server operating system offers. For example, a Microsoft Windows NT server offers services like full network communications, network browsing, e-mail, Internet and Web site management, network management, user management, and gateway services to Novell NetWare computers. The use of Microsoft domains through Windows NT Server offers many ways to reduce the effort needed to manage a network, such as managing access from one location instead of at each network workstation.

Wireless networks are an alternative to using communications cable. In some instances, wireless networking is cheaper and easier to install than cable. Because it uses ultra-high frequency ranges, this type of networking can be reliable and difficult for intruders to intercept.

Last, the differences between LANs, MANs, WANs, and enterprise networks are growing less distinct. Network connectivity is expanding to such an extent that networks soon will reach into every home or office where there is a computer.

In chapter 2, you explore networking standards and the organizations that set those standards. You also take a close look at one networking standard that has had a broad impact on networking, network design, software, and network communications.

REVIEW QUESTIONS

1. Which of the following might be good reasons to have a network?
   a. to share a printer
   b. to share a folder
   c. to save on equipment expenses
   d. all of the above
   e. both a and b

2. Which of the following is (are) true about wireless networking?
   a. It operates at ultra-high radio frequencies.
   b. It does not work well in snowy weather.
   c. It must be licensed by the FCC.
   d. all of the above
   e. both a and b

3. Workstations can communicate with one another on an equal basis through
   a. LAN-casting.
   b. peer-to-peer networking.
   c. mapping.
   d. link-casting.

4. Which of the following carry data on a network?
   a. cell
   b. packet
   c. sound wave
   d. all of the above
   e. both a and b

5. Which of the following is (are) best suited to carry data on a high-speed network in the gigabits-per-second range?

   a. cell

   b. packet

   c sound wave

   d. all of the above

   e. both a and b

6. A network extending through 15 buildings on a college campus is an example of a(n)

   a. local area network.

   b. wide area network.

   c. enterprise network.

   d. wireless network.

7. If you use Windows 95 to share a folder with two other people on a network, giving only those two people the password, you have formed a

   a. workgroup.

   b. domain.

   c. local area network.

   d. client/server application group.

8. On a Microsoft network, which of the following can offer a shared folder on the network?

   a. workstations only

   b. servers only

   c. only computers having Windows 95

   d. both workstations and servers

9. A workstation that is logged into a file server is that server's

   a. resource.

   b. client.

   c. node.

   d. share.

10. A _____ is like a language in that it determines the format and the rules of communication between computers on a network.

   a. linkup

   b. domain

   c. protocol

   d. node

ASPEN CONSULTING PROJECT: EXPLORING OPTIONS AVAILABLE FROM A NETWORK

You are employed as a network consultant for Aspen Consulting, located on the West Coast. Aspen Consulting specializes in helping large and small companies set up and maintain networks. Your assignment this week is to visit a small water consulting firm, called Ground Waters, that is struggling to take advantage of its network. Ground Waters has an office in the center of downtown with eight employees. Each employee has a Pentium computer with Windows 95. The firm already has paid another company to install a NIC in each PC and to cable the PCs together. The company they hired consisted of two people knowledgeable about networking but who decided to move to Boston to work for a multinational communications company. Your boss at Aspen Consulting, Mark Arnez, has asked you to visit Art Rossi at Ground Waters. Art, a geologist, has been assigned to help coordinate use of the firm's network.

 ## ASSIGNMENT 1-1

Art has several questions about some of the capabilities of the network. List and explain five network capabilities for him.

ASSIGNMENT 1-2

Show Art how to share a folder in Windows 95. As an example, use My Computer to access an existing folder, such as the Windows folder. As you go through each step, record it for Art in the following table.

Steps to Set Up a Shared Folder
Step 1:
Step 2:
Step 3:
Step 4:
Step 5:
Step 6:
Step 7:
Step 8:
Step 9:
Step 10:
Step 11:
Step 12:

ASSIGNMENT 1-3

Show Art how to give full access to the shared directory you created in Assignment 1-2. Describe how to do that in the following space.

Also, show Art how to place a password on the shared directory to limit access to only those who have the password. Describe how to do that in the following space.

ASSIGNMENT 1-4

Now that you have created a shared folder, explain folder mapping to Art:

Next, show him how another user might permanently map the folder to access it each time Windows 95 is started.

How to Map a Folder
Step 1:
Step 2:
Step 3:
Step 4:
Step 5:
Step 6:
Step 7:
Step 8:
Step 9:
Step 10:
Step 11:
Step 12:

ASSIGNMENT 1-5

Art is curious about how to use Microsoft Outlook to send e-mail. Describe the steps for Art in the table that follows.

Steps for Sending an E-Mail Message through Microsoft Outlook
Step 1:
Step 2:
Step 3:
Step 4:
Step 5:
Step 6:
Step 7:
Step 8:
Step 9:
Step 10:
Step 11:
Step 12:

ASSIGNMENT 1-6

Art is not aware that there is a way to share printers without having a file server. In a general way, explain how printers can be shared on a peer-to-peer vs. a file server network and discuss the advantages of each.

ASSIGNMENT 1-7

Ground Waters does not have direct access to the Internet from their network, but Art has a modem and can access an Internet service provider by calling a certain number. His computer is already set up to access the Internet through Internet Explorer, but Art has never tried out the software. Now he wants to access a white paper available from the government of Newfoundland and Labrador geological survey. The Internet site is located at *http://zeppo.geosurv.gov.nf.ca*. Use Internet Explorer to find the site. Describe the steps you took in the following table.

How to Use Internet Explorer to Find a Specific Internet Site
Step 1:
Step 2:
Step 3:
Step 4:
Step 5:
Step 6:
Step 7:
Step 8:
Step 9:
Step 10:
Step 11:
Step 12:

OPTIONAL CASE STUDIES FOR TEAMS

Sometimes Aspen Consulting encourages the use of teams for a project. Each case study that follows involves forming a team with your consulting associates to solve a particular client need.

 ## TEAM CASE 1

You are back in your office when Art calls you for some advice. Ground Waters is wondering if it would be a good idea to purchase a file server or if that would be a waste of money. You decide to assemble a small team of two or three consultants to discuss the pros and cons of the idea before reporting back to Art. Assemble your team and prepare a report for Art. What additional information might you need from Art to help Ground Waters make a more informed decision?

TEAM CASE 2

You have a new customer, information technology director Max Anderson at Golden Real Estate Company. Golden has offices in two buildings five blocks apart in a suburban area. Max wants to find out more about wireless computing and how it might be used to connect networks in the two offices. You form a small team to investigate and report back. Provide Max with the following information:

- Explain how wireless networking works.

- Explain the advantages and disadvantages of wireless networking.

- Search the Internet to find a company that makes wireless equipment for networks and provide a summary of the products available.

 ## TEAM CASE 3

Jennifer Sandos is the customer service manager for an accounting firm that employs 50 people. The firm has a network and four file servers and is interested in finding a financial package that uses network and client/server technology. You form another small team to investigate the following issues for them:

- Explain, in general terms, how client/server computing works.

- Explain the three-tier model of client/server computing.

- Why is a network critical to this kind of computing?

- Access the Microsoft Internet site at *http://www.microsoft.com* and find a relational database product that would work for client/server computing. Describe the product using Microsoft's information and explain its relationship to Microsoft NT Server.

NETWORKING STANDARDS AND MODELS

In chapter 1, you learned many networking terms, such as *packet*, *node*, *workstation*, and *network*. You explored networking capabilities and networking with file servers and compared different types of networks. From completing the hands-on exercises, you have a taste of what networks can do, such as sharing drives and printers or sending e-mail.

In this chapter, you look at networking standards to understand why they are vital and how they are applied in the real world. Standards are important to networks in the same way that traffic rules are important for traveling on the highway. Highway travel would be uncertain without speed limits, traffic signs, and stoplights. It would be even more uncertain if the rear lights on cars could be any color or if turn signals could be blinking lights, neon signs, or Morse code blared from roof-mounted speakers, depending on the preference of the car manufacturer.

Networks, like highways, need order to make certain everyone has the opportunity to communicate successfully. In this chapter, you get a glimpse of earlier times, when there were few computer and networking standards. You find out why standards are important and who sets the standards; most standards are developed by a consensus of business and government agencies through nongovernment organizations. You also discover information about one of the most important networking standards, the Open Systems Interconnect (OSI) model, which has a far-reaching impact on networking.

AFTER READING THIS CHAPTER AND COMPLETING THE EXERCISES YOU WILL BE ABLE TO:

- EXPLAIN WHY NETWORKING STANDARDS ARE NEEDED
- DESCRIBE THE TYPES OF NETWORKING STANDARDS
- DESCRIBE THE KEY NETWORKING STANDARDS ORGANIZATIONS
- EXPLAIN THE OPEN SYSTEMS INTERCONNECT (OSI) MODEL
- EXPLAIN COMMUNICATION BETWEEN STACKS
- DESCRIBE HOW THE OSI MODEL IS APPLIED

WHY NETWORKING STANDARDS ARE NEEDED

From the first mass-produced computers in the 1950s through the 1980s, the computer business was in some disarray as vendors tried to outmatch each other with new and secret technologies. Few standards guided the direction of how computers were constructed, how software ran on computers, and how computers communicated. If you purchased computer equipment, it often was necessary to stay with only one vendor to make sure all equipment and software were compatible. Even so, equipment or software designed by one division of a manufacturer still might not have been compatible with that of another division of the same manufacturer. For example, a printer designed for a mainframe might not have communicated with a minicomputer made by the same company.

Manufacturers believed they needed to maintain secrecy to be competitive and to guard new technologies. Their customers, however, suffered through the extra expense and wasted time of battling with incompatible equipment, coupled with rising equipment and software expenditures forced on them as old equipment support expired or was not compatible with new equipment.

A significant step away from secrecy was taken by IBM in the early 1980s, when that company developed its personal computer (PC). IBM took the unusual step of making the computer architecture public, so other companies could develop add-on equipment such as disk drives, floppy drives, display cards, monitors, printers, and modems. That risky step led many manufacturers to develop products to fit the IBM PC. It made the PC a great success, because there were so many ways to expand it while retaining the investment in the initial computer.

The next step was for computer manufacturers and government agencies to join in developing standards for computers. The initiative proved to be good for customers, who were desperate for more compatibility throughout the industry and, thus, good for computer sales.

When vendors began to develop networking equipment, there also was some chaos initially because of secrecy. There was no guarantee that network equipment made by one manufacturer would work with equipment made by another. The same was true for network operating systems on servers and for software developed for those operating systems. Again, the need arose for standards to protect customers and to advance networking technologies in a cooperative environment.

Compatibility issues remain, but manufacturers and governments have come a long way by using standards to bring consistency and reliability to the industry. For example, when you purchase a brand-name server operating system today, it is more compatible with a wider range of hardware and software than was the case a few years ago. When you purchase brand-name network equipment, it too is likely to be more compatible with another vendor's equipment than was true a few years back.

 Nonstandard, proprietary computer and network equipment still is on the market. Always check to make sure the equipment you purchase is a brand name and built to follow established or proposed standards (check the specifications). Nonstandard equipment may be cheaper up front, but more costly in terms of the time you spend to make it work.

TYPES OF STANDARDS

There are many types of standards for computer equipment, for example, for workstation and server hardware. Some of those standards affect the following:

- Bus design
- CPU design
- Serial port design
- Parallel port design
- Keyboard architecture
- Display architecture
- Modem communications
- Printer communications
- Network communications

Standards for networking provide common ground for transmitting data, manufacturing compatible network equipment, and designing operating systems for use on a network. Network standards define the maximum time a packet has to travel from one node to another before it is determined that the packet did not reach its destination. They define what to do when a packet is sent with only partial information, and they establish how to prevent confusion when too many packets are sent at once. More examples of areas influenced by networking standards are as follows:

- What communications media are used and specifications for those media
- How communications are established and maintained between nodes
- How to determine if a communications error has occurred
- What to do if an error occurs
- How fast and how far packets can travel on a network
- How a network can be designed for reliable communications
- What communications are used to manage a network
- What equipment can be attached to a network and how

KEY NETWORKING STANDARDS ORGANIZATIONS

The key organizations that help make standards for networking are the American National Standards Institute (ANSI), the Institute of Electrical and Electronics Engineers (IEEE), the Consultative Committee on International Telegraph and Telephone (CCITT), and the International Standards Organization (ISO).

AMERICAN NATIONAL STANDARDS INSTITUTE (ANSI)

One standards organization that has affected many areas of technology is the **American National Standards Institute (ANSI)**. Established in 1918, ANSI works with U.S. businesses, government agencies, and international groups to achieve agreement on standards for products ranging from bicycle helmets to communications cable. At this writing, ANSI has contributed to over 11,000 product standards. For the computer industry, ANSI has contributed to standards that affect screen display attributes, digital telecommunications, and fiber-optic cable transmissions. ANSI serves as the United States' representative to the International Standards Organization.

 The **American National Standards Institute (ANSI)** is an organization that works to set standards for all types of products, including computer network equipment.

 In this activity, you visit ANSI's Web site and discover first-hand why they think standards are important. You need access to a lab with computers that have Microsoft Internet Explorer or to a PC with Internet Explorer and Internet access. To begin the exercise, you should be at the Windows desktop.

To visit the ANSI Web site:

1. Click the **Start** button, **Programs**, and **Internet Explorer**. Or double-click the **Internet Explorer** icon on the desktop.

2. You will see a Connect To dialog box if the computer uses a dial-up service such as America Online, CompuServe, the Microsoft Network, or another Internet service provider (ISP). Click **OK** if the dialog box appears.

3. Enter **http://www.ansi.org/** in the Address line on the Internet Explorer screen. Click **OK**.

4. Click the topic **About ANSI**.

5. Click the button next to the topic *Standardization: A management tool for building success* (Figure 2-1).

6. Close Internet Explorer.

Figure 2-1

Accessing ANSI's Web site

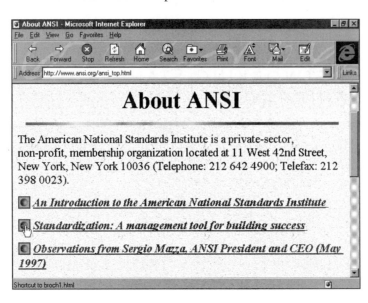

INSTITUTE OF ELECTRICAL AND ELECTRONICS ENGINEERS (IEEE)

An influential international organization that establishes communications standards is the **Institute of Electrical and Electronics Engineers (IEEE)**. The IEEE is a professional society of scientific, technical, and educational members active in over 140 countries. The Computer Society Local Network Committee of the IEEE has developed many networking standards in use today, especially its "802" standards for physical cabling and data transmission on local networks. Development of the 802 standards began in 1980 with the creation of the IEEE 802 committee and Project 802. The 802 specifications fall into several consecutive categories (802.1, 802.2, and so on). The most well-known are the 802.3 and 802.5 standards for networks, but all the standards are important to networking and are as follows:

- 802.1 An overview of the 802 standards

- 802.2 Standards for Logical Link Control (LLC) and other standards for basic network connectivity

- 802.3 Standards for Carrier Sense Multiple Access with Collision Detection (CSMA/CD)

- 802.4 Standards for token passing bus access

- 802.5 Standards for token ring access and for communications between LANs and MANs

- 802.6 Standards for LAN and MAN networks, including high-speed and connectionless networking

- 802.7 Standards for broadband cable technologies

- 802.8 Standards for fiber-optic cable technologies

- 802.9 Standards for integrated networking services, such as voice and data

- 802.10 Standards for interoperable LAN and MAN security

- 802.11 Standards for wireless connectivity

- 802.12 Standards for the demand priority access method

- 802.14 Standards for cable television broadband communications

The **Institute of Electrical and Electronics Engineers (IEEE)** is an organization of scientists, engineers, technicians, and educators that has influenced in particular standards for network cabling and data transmissions. For example, the IEEE 802.3 and 802.5 standards describe two commonly used access methods that determine how data is sent on a network.

In this hands-on activity, you go to the IEEE Web site to find out how you can obtain information about its 802.3 standards for networking. To start the exercise, you should be at the Windows desktop.

To find information about the IEEE 802.3 standards:

1. Click the **Start** button, **Programs**, and **Internet Explorer**. Or double-click the **Internet Explorer** icon on the desktop.

2. You will see a Connect To dialog box if the computer uses a dial-up service such as America Online, CompuServe, the Microsoft Network, or another ISP. Click **OK** if the dialog box appears.

3. Enter **http://standards.ieee.org/** on the Address line on the Internet Explorer screen. Press [Enter].

4. Click the **Products** selection on the screen, then search for information on 802.3 (Figure 2-2).

Although you may not have many questions about networking standards now, as a network administrator you probably will. Now you know how to find two sources for information, the ANSI and IEEE Web sites.

Figure 2-2

Accessing IEEE's Web site

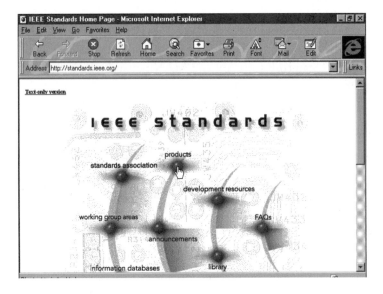

CONSULTATIVE COMMITTEE ON INTERNATIONAL TELEGRAPH AND TELEPHONE (CCITT)

A third international standards organization is the **Consultative Committee on International Telegraph and Telephone (CCITT)**. Based in Geneva, this branch of the International Telecommunications Union (ITU) sets standards for modems, e-mail, and digital telephone systems.

The CCITT addresses e-mail through its X.400 and X.500 standards. The X.400 standard contains guidelines for placing mail messages in an electronic envelope so that receiving units, or gateways, are able to receive and translate incoming mail. For example, Microsoft Mail's gateway can receive mail from cc:Mail's gateway successfully because both are X.400 compliant.

The **Consultative Committee on International Telegraph and Telephone (CCITT)** is an international standards body that develops telecommunications standards for modems, digital telephone systems, and e-mail. The CCITT X.400 standards are for international exchange of e-mail, and the X.500 standards are for creating a worldwide e-mail directory.

The X.400 standard also contains guidelines for mailing video, voice, and graphics files. That enables a Microsoft Excel spreadsheet or a Crystal Services database report to be sent from a Microsoft Mail gateway to any X.400 mail gateway.

The X.400 standards address the following areas:

- Mail service and user interface elements
- Guidelines for encoding and decoding mail objects
- Syntax for mail transfer
- Methods to ensure reliable mail transfer
- Guidelines for a message transfer layer
- Messaging protocol for telex

The CCITT has X.500 standards to complement X.400. The X.500 guidelines enable users of different mail packages to look up other mail users and address e-mail to them more effectively. The X.500 standards encourage the creation of universal directories, similar to a telephone company's white pages for private customers and yellow pages for commercial customers. For example, the X.400 and X.500 standards enable Lars Johnson in Stockholm to send an economics report with associated bar graphs and database reports to Michele Watson in Ontario. The X.500-compliant mail package at Lars's computer searches the naming service directory to find the network e-mail address. The e-mail address is encoded along with the text and graphics by the mail gateway at Lars's site, per the X.400 guidelines. It is then routed to the gateway that processes Michele's mail. The gateway strips off the X.400 encoding and forwards the mail to Michele's electronic post office box, so it is available to be read as soon as Michele turns on her computer.

Not all e-mail vendors have fully applied the X.400 and X.500 standards, but most are committed to that direction.

INTERNATIONAL STANDARDS ORGANIZATION (ISO)

The **International Standards Organization (ISO)** is a nongovernmental organization based in Geneva. Each nation has an option to belong to the ISO, with over 100 countries currently participating. The ISO was started in 1947 to promote international cooperation and standards in the following areas:

- Scientific
- Technological
- Economic
- Intellectual

The **International Standards Organization (ISO)** is an international body that establishes communications and networking standards. It is best known for its contributions to network protocol standards.

The ISO is particularly interested in the computer industry, which has a strong impact on global communications. It has been working to advance open systems in an effort to encourage worldwide competition and innovation among computer vendors.

OSI LAYERED COMMUNICATIONS

The ISO and ANSI have jointly developed a seven-layer network communications model known as **Open Systems Interconnect (OSI)**. The OSI model was developed in 1974 in an effort to standardize network communications. The goal was to encourage vendors to develop network equipment that would avoid proprietary design by following a standard way of communicating between nodes.

The OSI model is not a device or a set of software routines; it is a theoretical framework for understanding network communications. It does not perform any actual functions. The actual work is done by hardware and software devices. The OSI model simply defines the tasks that need to be done and which protocols are to be used for those tasks.

Developed by the ISO and ANSI, the **Open Systems Interconnect (OSI)** model provides a framework for network communications based on seven functional layers. It contains guidelines that can be applied to hardware and software network communications.

The OSI guidelines apply to the following issues:

- How network devices contact each other and how devices using different languages communicate

- How a network device knows when to transmit or not transmit data

- How the physical network devices are arranged and connected

- Methods to ensure that network transmissions are received correctly

- How network devices maintain a consistent rate of data flow

- How electronic data is represented on the network media

The OSI model consists of seven distinct layers stacked on one another: physical, data link, network, transport, session, presentation, and application (Figure 2-3). Each layer uses protocol communications to perform a particular function. The bottom layers perform functions related to physical communications, such as constructing packets and transmitting packet-containing signals. The middle layers coordinate network communications between nodes, for example, ensuring that a communication session continues without interruptions or errors. The top layers perform work that directly affects software applications and data presentation, including data formatting, encryption, and data and file transfer management. The set of layers is called a stack.

Although each layer performs a specific function, together they provide for integrated network services and communication and enable software communication between all layers of the model. As data is received by a node, portions of the data packet are extracted at one layer, beginning at the physical layer, and then sent to the next higher layer. When data is formatted to be sent, it starts at the top layer and gradually moves down the stack, with each successive layer adding specialized information, until the data is transmitted through the bottom physical layer. Layers in the stack communicate with one another on an equal basis.

 One way to remember the names of the seven OSI layers, from top to bottom, is the mnemonic "All People Seem To Need Data Processing."

Figure 2-3

The seven layers of the OSI model

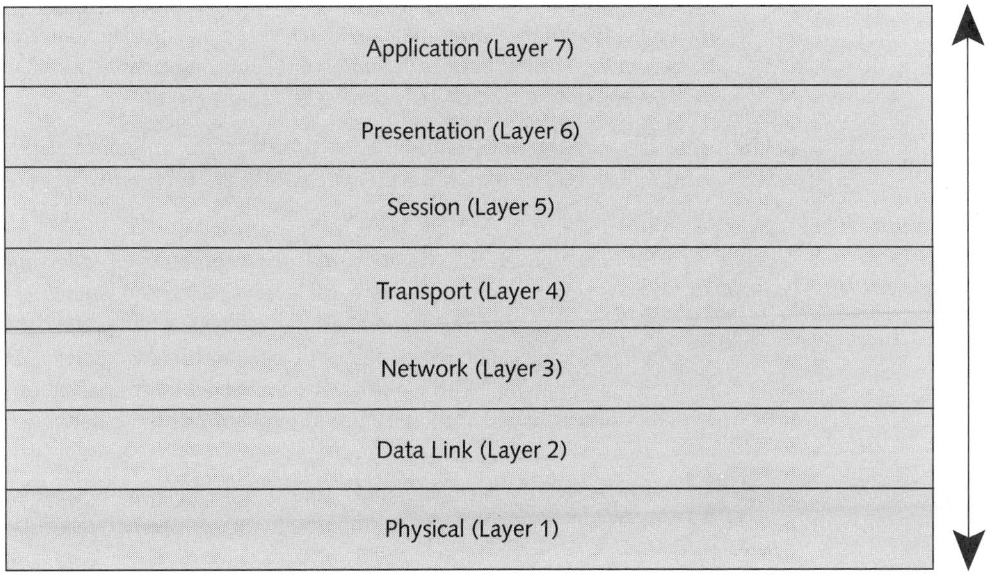

| Application (Layer 7) |
| Presentation (Layer 6) |
| Session (Layer 5) |
| Transport (Layer 4) |
| Network (Layer 3) |
| Data Link (Layer 2) |
| Physical (Layer 1) |

THE PHYSICAL LAYER

The lowest layer of the OSI model is the physical layer, which is the data transfer medium. Protocols used in the physical layer are responsible for generating and detecting voltage to transmit and receive signals that carry data. Data signals are transmitted as binary information consisting of 1s and 0s. For example, a 1 may be indicated by a 5-volt positive signal and a 0 might be 0 volts, all specially synchronized in distinct data streams that compose packets. The network cabling and equipment, including the physical layout of the network, also form the physical layer, as does the type of transmissions used, such as **analog** or **digital** transmissions.

 An **analog** transmission is one that can vary continuously, such as in a wave pattern with positive and negative voltage levels. An ordinary radio or telephone signal is an example of an analog transmission because it can have an infinite range for sound reproduction. Similarly, an analog TV or computer monitor can reproduce millions of colors in every range.

 A **digital** transmission has distinct levels to represent binary 1s and 0s, such as On and Off or +5 volts and 0 volts. For example, sound or pictures that are digitally transmitted use gradations, such as a music compact disc or a 256-color computer monitor. Neither has an infinite range of reproduction, like an equivalent analog device.

The physical layer handles the data transmission rate, monitors data error rates, and handles voltage levels for signal transmissions. It is affected by physical network problems, such as a missing cable terminator or electrical or magnetic interference. Interference is caused by nearby electrical motors, high-voltage lines, lighting, and other electrical devices.

 Electromagnetic interference (EMI) and **radio frequency interference (RFI)** are two sources of interference at the physical layer. EMI is caused by magnetic force fields that are generated by electrical devices such as motors. Sources of EMI are fans, elevator motors, electric drills, portable heaters, and air conditioning units. RFI is caused by electrical devices that emit radio waves at the same frequency used by network signal transmissions. RFI can be caused by cable TV components, radio and television stations, nearby amateur radio operators, ballast devices in fluorescent lights, inexpensively built computer or TV equipment, and citizens band (CB) radios.

The protocols developed by standards committees are built into the physical layer, as well as into other layers. They include the IEEE 802 protocols for network communications, cable specifications, and communications cable distance requirements.

 This hands-on exercise demonstrates the importance of following communications specifications at the physical level. As discussed in chapter 3, terminators must be connected at the ends of some types of networks, or the physical layer communication signal may not be transported correctly. This exercise requires a network with workstations connected by coaxial cable. Check with your instructor about the location of terminators on the network.

 Before starting this activity, make sure that the network is isolated from other users or that no one is doing important work on the network.

1. Turn on two or more computers that are connected to the network.

2. Access a shared drive or a file server on which you have an account, to make sure the network is working.

3. Remove one or both terminators.

4. Note problems you now may have when accessing the shared drive or file server.

5. Try logging on to other workstations and note if they have problems logging on or staying connected. (Problems may not show up at first, but soon you are likely to have problems accessing the network.)

THE DATA LINK LAYER

The construction of frames is performed by the data link layer. Each frame is formatted in a specified way so that data transmissions are synchronized from node to node. The data link layer enables the data to be encoded in an electrical signal by the transmitting node, decoded by the receiving node, and checked for errors. The data link layer also creates the formatting that allows frames to contain node addressing.

Once communication is established between two nodes, their data link layers are connected physically (through the physical layer) and logically (through protocols). The communication is first established by transmission of a small set of signals. As soon as the link has been made, the receiving data link layer decodes the signal into individual frames. The data link layer checks incoming signals for duplicate, incorrect, or partially received data. If an error is detected, the layer requests a retransmission of the data, frame by frame, from the sending node. Data link error detection is handled by use of a **cyclic redundancy check (CRC)**. As the data link layer transfers frames up to the next layer, the data link layer ensures that frames are sent in the same order as they are received.

Once a packet enters the stack, where its contents can be examined and where information can be added or extracted, it is typically called a frame.

A **cyclic redundancy check (CRC)** is an error detection method that calculates a value for the total size of the information fields (header, data, and footer) contained in a frame. The value is inserted at the end of the frame by the data link layer on the sending node and checked at the data link layer by the receiving node to determine if a transmission error has occurred.

On LANs that follow IEEE specifications, the data link layer incorporates the **logical link control (LLC)** and **media access control (MAC)** sublayers. The LLC sublayer ensures reliable communications by initiating a communications link between two nodes and then guarding against interruptions to the link. The MAC sublayer examines address information contained in each frame. For example, the MAC sublayer on a workstation examines each received frame for that workstation's address and sends the frame to the next higher layer if the address matches. The frame is discarded if the address is not a match. Another function of the MAC is to control how more than one device shares communication on the same network.

Logical link control (LLC) is a data link sublayer of the OSI model that initiates the communication link between nodes and ensures that the link is not unintentionally broken. The LLC is defined in the IEEE 802.2 standard.

Media access control (MAC) is a data link layer sublayer that examines addressing information contained in network frames and controls how devices share communications on the same network.

Two types of services are used for communications between the LLC sublayer and the network layer, which is the next layer up the stack. The Type 1 operation is a **connectionless service** that does not establish a logical connection between the sending and receiving nodes. Frames are not checked to ensure that they are received in the same sequence they were sent; there is no acknowledgment that a frame has been received; and there is no error recovery. The success of a data transmission is simply taken on faith.

Connectionless services, also known as Type 1 operation, occur between the LLC sublayer and the network layer and provide no checks to make sure data accurately reaches the receiving node.

The Type 2 operation is a **connection-oriented service** because a logical connection must be established between sending and receiving nodes before full communications begin. Frames contain a sequence number that is checked by the receiving node to ensure they are processed in the same order they are sent. Communications are established to make sure the sending node does not transmit data faster than the receiving node can handle it, and the receiving node provides an acknowledgment to the sending node on the success of data transmissions. Also, error recovery is made possible through the retransmission of data.

Type 1 operation is the most commonly used LLC class for protocols employed by Microsoft (NetBEUI), Novell (IPX/SPX), and the Internet (TCP/IP).

 Connection-oriented services, or Type 2 operation, occur between the LLC sublayer and the network layer and provide several ways to ensure data is successfully received by the destination node. Those ways include creating a logical communications connection, coordinating the speed of data transmission, providing notification that data is received, and providing a way to retransmit data.

THE NETWORK LAYER

The third layer up the stack is the network layer, which controls the passage of packets along the network. All networks consist of physical routes (cable paths) and logical routes (software paths). The network layer reads frame protocol address information and forwards each frame along the most expedient route, physical and logical, for efficient transmissions. This layer also permits frames to be sent from one network to another, through routers. **Routers** are physical devices that contain software to enable frames formatted on one network to reach a different network in a format that the second network understands. By controlling the passage of frames, the network layer acts like a switching station, routing frames along the most efficient of several different paths. The best path is determined by a constant gathering of information about the location of different networks and nodes, in a process called **discovery**.

 A **router** is an intelligent network device that can learn different network paths, forward data along certain paths for best network performance, and read data frames received in different formats. A router constantly gathers information about the network, such as about how many nodes are connected and where they are located. This information gathering is called **discovery**.

The network layer is able to route data on different paths by creating virtual (logical) circuits. **Virtual circuits** are logical communication paths set up to send and to receive data. The virtual circuits are known only to the network layer. Because the network layer manages data along several virtual circuits, the data frames can arrive in the wrong sequence. The network layer is responsible for tracking the situation and resequencing the frames before they are transported to the next layer.

A **virtual circuit** is a logical communication path established by the OSI network layer for sending and receiving data.

The network layer also addresses frames and resizes them to match the requirements of the receiving network. Another function of the network layer is to ensure that frames are not sent faster than the receiving layer can manage.

THE TRANSPORT LAYER

The transport layer ensures that data is sent reliably from the sending node to the destination node. For example, the transport layer ensures that frames are sent and received in the same order. Also, when a transmission is made, the receiving node may send an acknowledgment, sometimes called an "ack," that the data has been received. The transport layer establishes the level of packet error checking, with the highest level guaranteeing that frames are sent node to node, without error and in an acceptable amount of time.

The protocols used to communicate within the transport layer employ several reliability measures. Class 0 is the simplest protocol. It performs no error checking or flow control, relying on the network layer to perform those functions. The Class 1 protocol monitors for packet transmission errors. If an error is detected, the Class 1 protocol requests the sending node's transport layer to resend the packet. The Class 2 protocol monitors for transmission errors and provides **flow control** between the transport layer and the session layer. The Class 3 protocol provides the functions of Classes 1 and 2 and adds the option to recover lost packets in certain situations. Last, the Class 4 protocol performs the same functions as Class 3 but adds more extensive error monitoring and recovery.

 Flow control is used to make sure one device does not send information faster than can be received by another device.

THE SESSION LAYER

The session layer is responsible for the continuity of the communications link between two nodes. It establishes the link and ensures that the link is maintained for the duration of the communication session. The session layer also provides for orderly communication between nodes. For example, it establishes which node transmits first. It determines how long a node can transmit and how to recover from transmission errors.

The session layer also links each unique address to a given node, just as ZIP codes allow mail to be associated with appropriate postal regions. Once the communication session is finished, the session layer disconnects nodes.

One example of communications at this layer is when a workstation accesses a server on the Internet. The workstation and the server each has a unique dotted decimal address, such as 122.72.15.122 and 145.19.20.22, respectively. The session layer uses the address information to help establish contact between nodes. Once contact is made and the workstation is able to log on, a communication session is established via the session layer.

THE PRESENTATION LAYER

The presentation layer takes care of data formatting. Each type of network uses a particular formatting scheme, which is accomplished by the presentation layer. In one sense, the presentation layer is like a syntax checker. It ensures that numbers and text are sent so they can be read by the presentation layer at the receiving node. For example, data sent from an IBM mainframe computer may use **Extended Binary Coded Decimal Interchange Code (EBCDIC)** formatting and need to be translated into **American Standard Code for Information Interchange (ASCII)** format to be read by a workstation running Windows 95.

 Extended Binary Coded Decimal Interchange Code (EBCDIC), used mainly on IBM mainframe computers, consists of a specially coded 256-character set.

 American Standard Code for Information Interchange (ASCII) is a commonly used character set that consists of 96 uppercase and lowercase characters and numbers, plus 32 nonprinting characters.

The presentation layer also is responsible for data encryption. Encryption of data involves scrambling the data so it cannot be read by unauthorized users. Data encryption is used by many software systems for passwords but rarely for any other type of transmitted data.

Another function of the presentation layer is data compression. When data is formatted, there may be empty space that also gets formatted between portions of text and numbers. Data compression removes the space and compacts the data so it is much smaller to send. The data is then decompressed by the presentation layer at the receiving node.

THE APPLICATION LAYER

The application layer, the highest level of the OSI model, represents the computer user's most direct access to applications and network services on the computer. The application layer provides network services for application software, such as databases. Some of the services include file transfer, file management, remote access to files and printers, message handling for e-mail, and terminal emulation. This is the layer a computer programmer uses to access network services, such as linking an application into e-mail or database access over the network.

The Microsoft Windows **redirector** works through the application layer. The redirector is a service that makes one computer visible to another for access through the network. When you share a folder on a Microsoft network, other computers can find your computer and access that folder through the redirector.

 The Microsoft **redirector** is a service used via the application layer to recognize and access other computers with operating systems such as Windows 3.11, Windows 95, Windows NT, LAN Manager, and LAN Server.

Table 2-1 summarizes the functions of the seven OSI layers.

Table 2-1

Functions of the seven OSI layers

Layer	Functions
Physical (Layer 1)	• Provides the transfer medium (such as cable) • Translates data into a transmission signal appropriate to the transfer medium • Sends the signal along the transfer medium • Includes the physical layout of the network • Monitors for transmission errors • Determines the voltage levels used for data signal transmissions and to synchronize transmissions • Determines the signal type, such as digital or analog
Data Link (Layer 2)	• Constructs data packets using the appropriate format for the network • Creates CRC information • Checks for errors using CRC information • Responsible for data retransmission if there is an error • Initiates the communications link and makes sure it is not interrupted for node-to-node physical reliability • Examines packet addresses • Acknowledges receipt of a packet
Network (Layer 3)	• Determines the network path on which to route frames • Helps reduce network congestion • Establishes virtual circuits • Routes frames to other networks, resequencing packet transmissions when needed
Transport (Layer 4)	• Ensures reliability of packet transmissions from node to node • Ensures data packets are sent and received in the same order • Provides acknowledgment when a packet is received • Monitors for packet transmission errors and resends bad packets
Session (Layer 5)	• Initiates the communication link • Makes sure the communication link is maintained • Determines which node transmits at any point in time, such as which one transmits first • Disconnects when a communication session is over • Translates node addresses
Presentation (Layer 6)	• Translates data to a format the receiving node understands, such as from EBCDIC to ASCII • Performs data encryption • Performs data compression
Application (Layer 7)	• Enables sharing remote drives • Enables sharing remote printers • Handles e-mail messages • Provides file transfer services • Provides file management services • Provides terminal emulation services

COMMUNICATION BETWEEN STACKS

For two computers to be able to communicate on a network, they both must be operating under the same theoretical model, such as the OSI model. When a frame is constructed at the sending node, it starts at the top of the stack with the application layer. The frame information is sent next to the presentation layer and continues down the stack to the physical layer, where it is sent out to the network as a complete packet-carrying signal (Figure 2-4).

Figure 2-4

Building and receiving a frame from layer to layer

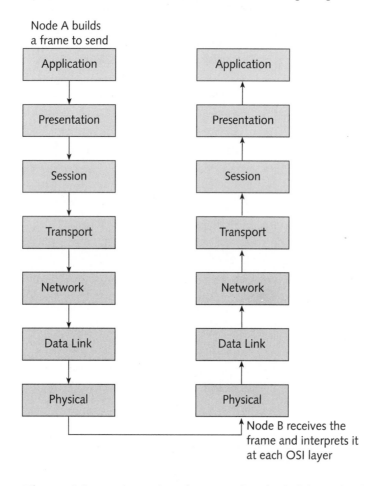

Node A builds a frame to send

Node B receives the frame and interprets it at each OSI layer

The receiving node receives frames at the physical layer (at the bottom of the stack) and then sends each frame to be checked by the data link layer, which determines if the frame is addressed to the workstation. The data link layer is similar to a postal worker who checks through all mail to see if any is addressed to your house. Letters with your address are left at the house to be passed along to the right person in the household. Other letters are sent on until their destination is found.

When the data link layer finds a frame addressed to that workstation, it sends the frame to the network layer, which strips out information intended for it and then sends the remaining information up the stack.

Each layer in the stack acts as a separate module performing one primary type of function and has its own format of communication instructions in the form of protocols. The protocols used to communicate between functions within the same layer are called **peer protocols**

(Figure 2-5). For example, when the data link layer on the sending node packages CRC information, it codes that information using a peer protocol that is understood by the data link layer on the receiving node.

Figure 2-5

Peer protocol communication between the same layers

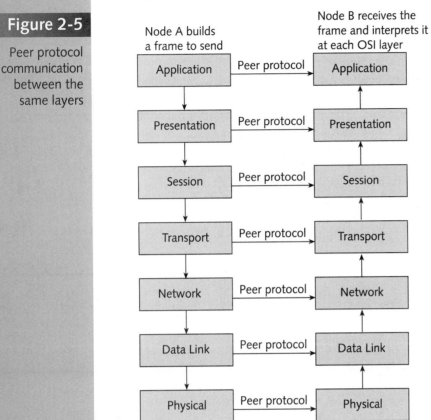

Figure 2-6

Using primitives to communicate between layers

Peer protocols enable an OSI layer on a sending node to communicate with the same layer on the receiving node.

Information from one layer is transferred to the next by means of commands called **primitives** (Figure 2-6). The information that is transferred is called a **protocol data unit (PDU)**. As the information progresses to the next layer, new control information is added to the PDU. When the PDU is ready to be passed to the next layer, instructions needed to transfer it to that layer are added.

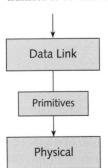

A **primitive** is a command used to transfer information from one layer in an OSI stack to another layer, such as from the physical layer to the data link layer.

A **protocol data unit (PDU)** is the information transferred between layers in the same OSI stack.

Once the PDU is received by the next layer, the control information and transfer instructions are stripped out. The resulting packet is called the **service data unit (SDU)** (Figure 2-7). As the SDU travels from one layer to the next, each layer adds its own control information. Thus, the frame grows as it travels through the layers.

A **service data unit** is the PDU minus control and transfer information used to transfer the data from the previous layer in the OSI stack.

Figure 2-7

Communications using service data units (SDUs) and protocol data units (PDUs)

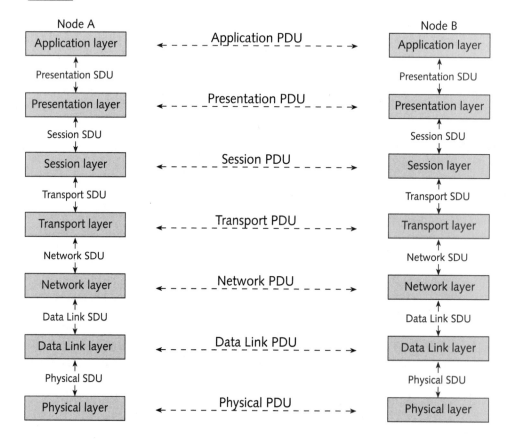

APPLYING THE OSI MODEL

Accessing a shared drive on another network computer is a good example of how layered communications work. The redirector at the application layer locates the shared drive. The presentation layer ensures that the data format is in ASCII format, which is the format used by both workstations. The session layer establishes the link between the two computers and ensures the link is not interrupted until you are finished accessing the shared drive's contents. The transport layer guards against packet errors, ensuring that the data is interpreted in the same order as it was sent. The network layer makes sure packets are sent along the fastest route, to minimize delays. The data link layer constructs packets and ensures that packets go to the right workstations. Finally, the physical layer makes the data transmissions possible by converting the information to electrical signals that are placed on the network communications cable.

The OSI model also is applied to network hardware and software communications. Network hardware and software that follow accepted standards should conform to specific layers of the OSI model in order to conform to standards. Later chapters discuss network hardware and software, but Table 2-2 presents a summary of what network hardware and software match specific OSI layers.

Table 2-2

Network hardware and software associated with the OSI model layers

OSI Layer	Corresponding Network Hardware or Software
Application	Application programming interfaces, gateways
Presentation	Data translation software, gateways
Session	Network equipment software drivers, computer name lookup software, gateways
Transport	Network equipment software drivers, gateways
Network	Gateways, routers
Data Link	NICs, intelligent hubs and bridges, gateways
Physical	Cabling, cable connectors, multiplexers, transmitters, receivers, transceivers, passive, and active hubs, repeaters, gateways

Note

A gateway is one of the most complex devices used to connect different network architectures, for example, a microcomputer to a mainframe or a mainframe to a telecommunications data network. For that reason, a gateway is a seven-layer device that provides protocol translation at any layer as needed.

Hands-On

In this hands-on activity, you have an opportunity to view what happens when a network connection is broken at the NIC. You need access to a lab computer connected to a network. To start the exercise, you should be at the Windows desktop.

To experience a connection broken at the NIC:

1. Use **Network Neighborhood** to access a shared drive.

2. Disconnect the cable to the workstation's NIC. Notice that an error message quickly appears; you have terminated at the physical and data link layers.

3. Reconnect the computer. Note whether the connection to the shared drive is re-established.

CHAPTER SUMMARY

Network standards are vital because they help ensure that manufacturers build equipment that can intercommunicate. Before standards, there were many problems of incompatibility. Equipment from one manufacturer might not work with the equipment of another. The same was true for network operating systems. Although incompatibility problems still exist, most manufacturers work to make hardware and software that follow accepted standards.

Several standards organizations have evolved, bringing nongovernmental solutions to help make networks reliable and compatible. They include ANSI (American National Standards Institute), IEEE (Institute of Electrical and Electronics Engineers), CCITT (Consultative Committee on International Telegraph and Telephone), and ISO (International Standards Organization).

One standards model that has a strong impact on networking is the OSI (Open Standards Interconnect) model. This seven-layer model, which is used throughout networking implementations, affects how signals are transmitted, how packets are constructed, the reliability of network communications, error detection, and the sharing of network resources. The OSI model affects how network equipment is designed and implemented and how it affects network software services.

In the next chapter, you learn about the physical layout of different types of networks, such as star designs and ring designs. You look at the different types of network cable media, including the popular use of telephone wiring for cabling networks. Also, you compare the costs of different kinds of networks.

REVIEW QUESTIONS

1. Which of the following would you find in networking standards?
   a. CPU design
   b. bus design
   c. what communications media to use
   d. all of the above
   e. both a and b

2. The network layer on one workstation communicates with the network layer an another through
   a. service data units.
   b. peer protocols.
   c. signal coding.
   d. a 4-bit data word.

3. Terminal emulation services would be performed at what OSI layer?
   a. network
   b. presentation
   c. application
   d. data link

4. _____ are commands used to transfer information from one OSI layer to the next.

5. The OSI model has how many layers?
   a. four
   b. seven
   c. eight
   d. ten
   e. fifteen

6. Which organization has contributed significantly to the X.400 and X.500 e-mail standards?
   a. IEEE
   b. CCITT
   c. ANSI
   d. ISO

7. Which sublayer in the data link layer has the ability to examine packet addresses?
   a. logical link control
   b. protocol data unit
   c. address link sublayer
   d. media access control

8. Which sublayer converts ASCII-formatted data to EBCDIC?
   a. data link
   b. physical
   c. presentation
   d. network

9. Which layer in the OSI model determines which node transmits first when communications are started?
   a. session
   b. network
   c. application
   d. transport

10. The _____ layer is the bottom layer in the OSI model.

ASPEN CONSULTING PROJECT: WORKING WITH STANDARDS AND THE OSI MODEL

Your boss, Mark Arnez, has you working this week with a newly hired network administrator for a mail order company called Collectibles. The company employs 45 people and is in the middle of installing a network. Their network administrator, Maria Korpitz, has been working in the company for a year as a PC support consultant. Your assignment is to provide Maria some training in networking standards and theory.

 ## ASSIGNMENT 2-1

Use the following space to record for Maria two reasons why network standards are important.

 ## ASSIGNMENT 2-2

Explain the ISO to Maria in the following space.

Next, find a computer with Internet access. Use a Web browser, such as Microsoft Internet Explorer, to access the ISO Web page at *http://www.iso.ch/*. Read the introduction to the ISO and research for Maria why the ISO believes standards are important. Why are international standards important? How are ISO standards developed? Go back to the ISO home page and read the selection about ISO worldwide members. Name four countries that are members. Use the following space to record your answers.

 ## ASSIGNMENT 2-3

Explain to Maria the functions of the physical layer of the OSI model.

Next, go into a lab or other area where there is a network. Point out three things in the network that operate at the physical layer and record them here.

ASSIGNMENT 2-4

Using Windows 95 or Windows NT, access e-mail on a network and send a message to another student or to your instructor. Use the following space to explain which OSI layers are involved in sending the message, including a brief description of the role of each.

ASSIGNMENT 2-5

Maria is interested in how a network packet travels from one type of network to another type of network in a different building. Before explaining the process, go to a lab and access a file server in another building across campus or use the Internet Explorer to download a file from an Internet site such as Microsoft's (*http://www.microsoft.com*). In the following space, explain for Maria how a packet finds its way from point to point so efficiently. What OSI layer plays an important role in making sure the packet finds the best way along the network. What network equipment plays a role?

ASSIGNMENT 2-6

Show Maria how a Microsoft NT Server locks out an account after a certain number of failed logon attempts. Use your own account or one provided by your instructor and try logging on several times using the wrong password. Explain why this type of security is important. Which OSI layers play a role in helping to encrypt passwords for security? What role do they play?

ASSIGNMENT 2-7

Maria has mentioned that Collectibles recently purchased two computers from a local store that builds them from scratch, using inexpensive components to reduce the purchase price. Both computers seem to work fine with Microsoft Word and Excel. The problem is that one computer will connect to the network but will not stay connected. The other computer will not connect at all. Both computers use a NIC made by a manufacturer you do not know. Maria tried a brand-name computer in both locations, and it worked without problems. Explain to Maria your opinion of using computers like the built-from-scratch ones on the network. What should Maria recommend to her company as a future direction for computer purchases?

ASSIGNMENT 2-8

Show Maria how dotted decimal addressing is used to access a Web site node. Open Internet Explorer, select the View menu, and make sure that Status bar and Toolbar are checked. Access Microsoft's Web site at *http://www.microsoft.com/*. As it is connecting, look at the bottom line of the Internet Explorer, just above the taskbar. Record the dotted decimal address that is displayed. Explain what OSI layer is responsible for making a network linkup using the dotted decimal addresses of two nodes. What other functions does that layer perform that might influence your connection?

OPTIONAL CASE STUDIES FOR TEAMS

TEAM CASE 1

Microsoft publishes a list of brand-name computer equipment and components that are compatible with Microsoft Windows NT Server. Form a small team and log on to Microsoft's Web site (*http://www.microsoft.com*) to find that list. Record five types of equipment or components on the list. Also, record the names of seven manufacturers listed. Explain why it is wise to use this type of information when purchasing computers and equipment for a network.

TEAM CASE 2

One of Aspen Consulting's customers owns a machine shop with five networked computers. Each time a machinist turns on machinery, the machine shop owner seems to have trouble with his network connection. Form a team and discuss in general terms what might be the problem. Explain how the OSI model could help in understanding the problem.

TEAM CASE 3

Mark Arnez has formed a small team to make a presentation about the OSI model to a networking class at the local community college. Use poster board, PowerPoint slides, or some other graphic means to reproduce the OSI model for your presentation. Show communications up and down the OSI stack and communications between layers in the stack.

CHAPTER THREE

TOPOLOGIES AND COMMUNICATIONS MEDIA

As you learned in chapter 2, standards have brought constancy and compatibility to networking. The OSI model in particular has influenced network communications, giving vendors a set of guidelines for hardware and software implementations. Through the hands-on exercises in chapter 2, you now know what happens behind the scenes when a NIC connection is broken or when the terminator is removed from a network. You also understand what happens when information travels from a Web site to your workstation through the stacks in the OSI model, to deliver text, sounds, and video.

In this chapter, you find out what is behind all the cabling that makes up a network. Just as there are principles and strategies for constructing a building or a bridge, there are principles and strategies for designing successful network layouts. Networking standards come alive as you run cable or put on a connector. Cable media must meet exacting standards for successful communications, such as length, composition, and signal-carrying qualities.

You start by looking at three general schemes for network design: bus, ring, and star. You also examine the different types of communication cable and how they are used. As you progress through this chapter, you get first-hand experience of how networks are designed and implemented. You also learn about the relative costs and merits of different types of networks, including wireless networking solutions. The hands-on exercises and chapter projects help you make decisions about the type of network topology and media that are most appropriate for different real-life situations.

AFTER READING THIS CHAPTER AND COMPLETING THE EXERCISES YOU WILL BE ABLE TO:

- EXPLAIN THE BUS, RING, AND STAR NETWORKING TOPOLOGIES AND DESCRIBE THE ADVANTAGES AND DISADVANTAGES OF EACH

- DRAW A BASIC NETWORK DIAGRAM

- DESCRIBE THE ADVANTAGES AND DISADVANTAGES OF VARIOUS TYPES OF NETWORK MEDIA: THICK AND THIN COAXIAL CABLE, SHIELDED AND UNSHIELDED TWISTED-PAIR CABLE, AND FIBER-OPTIC CABLE

- DISCUSS THE ADVANTAGES AND DISADVANTAGES OF WIRELESS NETWORK MEDIA

- COMPARE THE COSTS OF DIFFERENT NETWORK MEDIA AND UNDERSTAND IMPLEMENTATION CONSIDERATIONS

NETWORK TOPOLOGIES

Every network is created to address particular computing and organizational needs. Some networks house vital business functions, while others support scientific research. There are several ways to design a network to accommodate the needs of those who will be using it. Once a network is in place and fulfilling user needs, a significant investment has been made. That investment includes cabling, network equipment, file servers, workstations, hosts, software, and training. Network design and protecting the investment in a network are interrelated concerns. The network design affects the life of the investment in the network. Some designs are low in cost but expensive to maintain or upgrade. Other designs are more expensive in the beginning but are easy to maintain and offer simple upgrade paths.

The best starting point for understanding a network is through its topology. The **topology** is the physical layout of a network, combined with its logical characteristics. The physical layout is like an overhead picture or map of how the cabling is laid in an office or a building or through a campus. The total cabling often is called the **cable plant**. The logical side of a topology is the path taken by a packet as it moves around the network.

 Network **topology** has two components: the physical layout of the cable and the logical path followed by network packets sent on the cable.

 The **cable plant** is the total cabling of a network.

The network layout may be decentralized, with cable running between stations on the network, or the layout may be centralized, with each station physically connected to a central device that dispatches packets from workstation to workstation. Centralized layouts resemble a star, with rays reaching out to the individual network stations. Decentralized layouts resemble mountain climbers, each at a different location on the mountain but all joined by a long rope.

There are three main topologies: bus, ring, and star. Selecting the best topology for an installation requires the network administrator to consider several important questions, such as the following:

- What applications will be used on the network?
- What types of hosts and file servers are to be connected?
- Will the network be connected to other networks?
- Will the network have mission-critical applications?
- Is data transmission speed important?
- What network security is needed?
- What is the anticipated growth in the use of the network?

The applications intended to be used on a network influence the number and the frequency of packets to be transmitted, known as **network traffic**. If the network users primarily are accessing word processing software, the network traffic will be relatively low, and most of the work will be performed at workstations rather than on the network. Client/server applications generate a medium to high level of network traffic, depending on the client/server software design. Networks on which there is frequent exchange of database information, such as Microsoft Access or SQL Server files, have medium to high network traffic. Scientific and publications software generate high levels of traffic because they involve extremely large data files.

 Network traffic is the number, size, and frequency of packets transmitted on the network in a given amount of time.

The influence of hosts and servers on a network is closely linked to the type of software applications that are used. For example, a database server that constantly is accessed to generate reports of financial and sales figures is likely to cause more network traffic than a file server that is used occasionally to access business letters or templates for letters.

Whether other networks will be connected to the network also affects the topology used. The network topology for a small business that never will use more than four computers will be different from the topology required by an industrial campus. The small business is unlikely to connect to additional networks, except for perhaps an outside connection to the Internet. The industrial campus may consist of several interconnected networks, such as a network to control machines in the plant, a network for the business systems, and a network for the research scientists. Some topologies permit better network interconnectivity than other topologies.

The network administrator should ask whether the applications on the network are **mission critical**. A network used for a company's payroll is mission critical. This type of network topology needs to include system redundancy. For example, the network must include alternative routes for data transmission, so that failure of one part of the network does not prevent the payroll from running. This is called **fault-tolerance** technology.

 A **mission-critical** software application or hardware service is one that involves a vital business or support function, such as college registration, order-entry, or payroll.

 Fault tolerance is the availability of backup hardware or software so that computer functions can continue without interruption in the event of a problem, such as a power failure or a hard disk drive failure.

Some networks, such as those on which large files are transmitted, need high-speed data transmission capabilities. Network speed is important to the productivity of the users. High-speed capability is particularly needed when images, graphics, and other large files need to be transported over long distances.

Security is another issue that influences network design. Security is protection of data so that only authorized individuals have access to confidential information. Security involves network implementations that permit restrictions on who can access folders, files, printers, file servers, and application software. It also may include data encryption, which encodes packets and allows only authorized nodes to decode packets. On high-security networks, fiber-optic cable is used to minimize the risk of tapping into the cable and capturing packets.

Network topology directly influences a network's potential for growth. Once a network has been installed, more users commonly need to be added in the same office or from additional offices or floors. As a network administrator, you will find that a successful network implementation attracts more and more people who want to be networked.

In this hands-on activity you discover the importance of a reliable network topology in a real-life situation.

To complete this activity:

1. Contact a member of a business office at your school or a business in the community that is networked.

2. Ask that person what his or her day is like when a network problem halts work, such as a malfunctioning network device or damage to the network cable.

3. Contact the network administrator or information technology director and find out, in general, what topology is used.

BUS TOPOLOGY

The **bus topology** consists of running cable from one PC or file server to the next, similar to a city bus route. A city bus has a starting point and an ending point on its route, and along the way it stops at designated stations.

A **bus topology** is a network configured so that nodes are connected to a segment of cable in the logical shape of a line, with a terminator at each end.

In a bus topology, a terminator is connected to each end of a bus cable segment. Like a city bus, a data packet stops at each station on the line. Also like a city bus, a packet has a given amount of time to reach its destination, or it is considered late. A bus network segment must be within IEEE length specifications to ensure that packets arrive in the expected time. (Distance specifications are discussed in chapter 4.) Figure 3-1 shows a simple bus network.

Figure 3-1

Bus topology

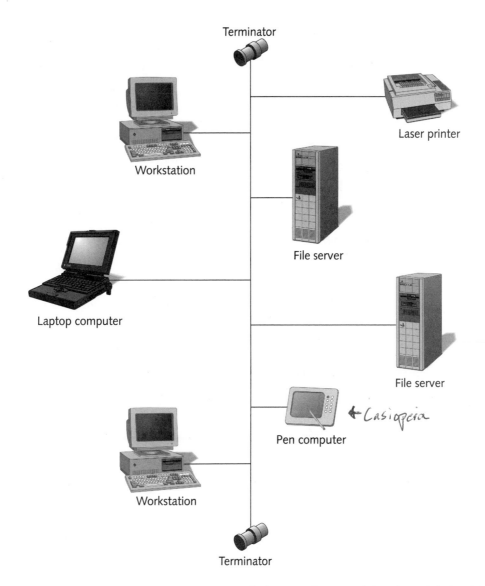

Terminator

Laser printer

Workstation

File server

Laptop computer

File server

← Casiopeia

Pen computer

Workstation

Terminator

The terminators are critical on bus networks because they signal the physical ends of the segment. A terminator is really an electrical resistance or block to the signal when it reaches the end of the network. Without a terminator, a segment violates IEEE specifications; signals are unreliable because the signal can be reflected back onto the same path it just covered.

The traditional bus design works well for small networks and is relatively inexpensive to implement. At the start, costs are minimized because a bus design requires less cable than other topologies. It also is easy to add another workstation to extend the bus for a short distance in a room or an office. The disadvantage is that management costs can be high. For example, it is difficult to isolate a single malfunctioning node or cable segment and associated connectors; one defective node or cable segment and connectors can take down an entire network. (Modern networking equipment, however, makes that less likely.) Another disadvantage is that the bus can become congested with network traffic, requiring the addition of bridges and other equipment to control the traffic flow. Table 3-1 summarizes the advantages and disadvantages of the bus topology.

Advantages	Disadvantages
Works well for small networks	Management costs often too high
Inexpensive to implement on a small scale	Difficult to isolate a malfunctioning node or cable segment and associated conectors
Requires less cable	Possible for defective node to take down the entire network
Easy to add another workstation	Subject to congestion from network traffic

RING TOPOLOGY

The **ring topology** is a continuous path for data with no logical beginning or ending point and thus no terminators. Workstations and file servers are attached to the cable at points around the ring (Figure 3–2). When data is transmitted onto the ring, it goes from node to node until the destination node is reached. Because the destination node may be reached before the data has gone full circle, the data often does not pass through all stations.

A **ring topology** is a network in the shape of a ring or circle, with nodes connected around the ring.

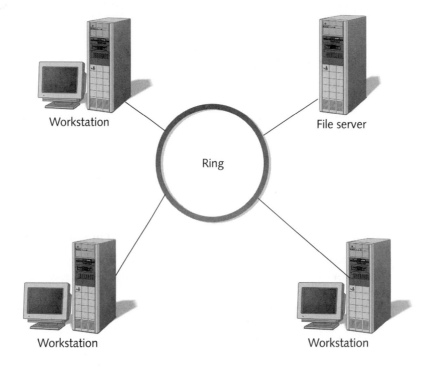

Workstation   File server

Ring

Workstation   Workstation

When it was first developed, the ring topology permitted data to go in one direction only, stopping at the node that originated the transmission. New high-speed ring technologies consist of two loops for redundant data transmission in opposite directions (Figure 3-3).

Figure 3-3

Dual ring topology

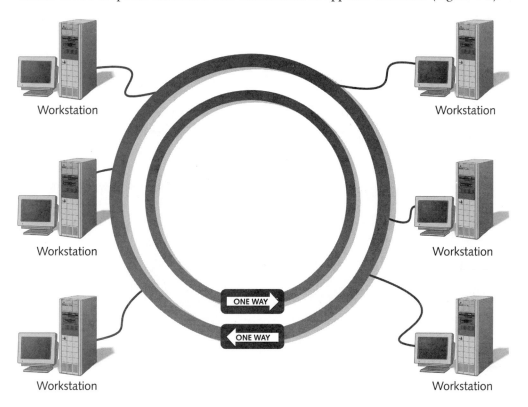

An advantage of the ring topology is that it is easier to manage than the bus. The network equipment used to build the ring makes it easier to locate a defective node or cable problem. This topology is well suited for transmitting signals over long distances on a LAN, and it handles high-volume network traffic better than the bus topology. Overall, the ring topology enables more reliable communications than the bus.

A disadvantage is that the ring topology requires more cable and network equipment at the start. Another disadvantage is that the ring is not used as widely as the bus topology, so there are fewer equipment options and fewer options for expansion to high-speed communications. Table 3-2 summarizes the advantages and disadvantages of the ring topology.

Table 3-2

Advantages and disadvantages of the ring topology

Advantages	Disadvantages
Easier to manage than a bus	Requires more network cable and equipment at the start than a bus
Easier to locate node and cable problems	Not as many equipment options as for a bus
Good over long distances	Not as widely used as the bus topology
Handles high-volume traffic well	
Very reliable	

STAR TOPOLOGY

The **star topology** is in the shape of a star. This is the oldest communications design method, with its roots in telephone switching systems. Although it is the oldest design method, advances in network technology have made the star topology a good option for modern networks. The physical layout of the star topology consists of multiple nodes attached to a central **hub** (Figure 3-4). Single communications cable segments radiate from the hub like the rays of a star.

 The **star topology** is a network configured with a central hub and individual cable segments connected to the hub, resembling the shape of a star.

 A **hub** is a central device used in the star topology that joins single cable segments or individual LANs into one network. Some hubs are called concentrators or access units.

Figure 3-4

Star topology

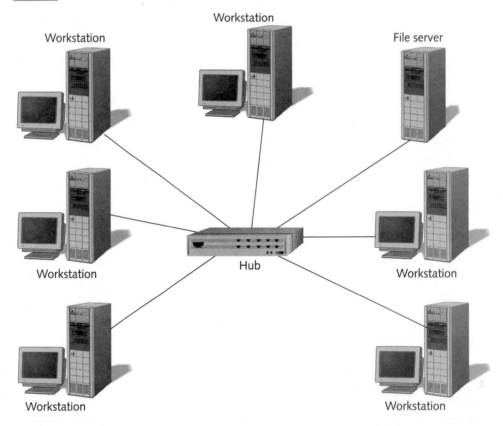

The start-up costs of the star topology are now lower than for a bus network and comparable to those of the ring network. That is because costs for network equipment are greatly reduced from what they were a few years ago.

Like the ring topology, the star is easier to manage than the traditional bus network, because malfunctioning nodes can be identified quickly. A damaged node or cable run is easily isolated from the network by the network equipment, and service to the other nodes is not affected. The star is easier to expand for connecting additional nodes or networks. It also offers the best avenues for expansion into high-speed networking. For those reasons, the star is the most popular topology, which means a wider variety of equipment is available for this topology.

A disadvantage is that the hub is a single point of failure; if it fails, all connected nodes are unable to communicate (unless there is redundancy built into the hub to include backup measures). Another disadvantage is that the star requires more cable to be run than do bus designs.

Table 3-3

Advantages and disadvantages of the star topology

Advantages	Disadvantages
Easier to manage than a bus	Susceptible to a single point of failure
Easier to locate node and cable problems	Requires more network cable at the start than a bus
Easier to expand than a bus or ring, especially for enterprise networking	
Well suited for expansion into high-speed networking	
More equipment options	

BUS-STAR LAYOUTS

Modern networks combine the logical communications of a bus with the physical layout of a star. In such a topology, each ray radiating from the center of the star is like a separate logical bus segment, but with only one or two computers attached. The segment still is terminated at both ends, but the advantage is there are no exposed terminators. On each segment, one end is terminated inside the hub and the other is terminated at the node's NIC.

Another advantage of the bus-star network topology is that multiple hubs can be connected to expand the network in many directions (Figure 3-5). The connection between hubs is a **backbone**, which often uses high-speed communications between hubs. Hubs are available with built-in intelligence to help detect problems and to isolate a malfunctioning segment or node, without affecting other network nodes. Also, there are expansion opportunities for the implementation of high-speed networking. Because this alternative is popular, a wide range of equipment is available for bus networks in the shape of a star. Table 3-4 summarizes the advantages and disadvantages of the bus-star topology.

A **backbone** is a high-capacity communications medium that joins networks and central network devices on the same floor in a building, on different floors, and across long distances.

Figure 3-5

Expanding a
bus-star
network

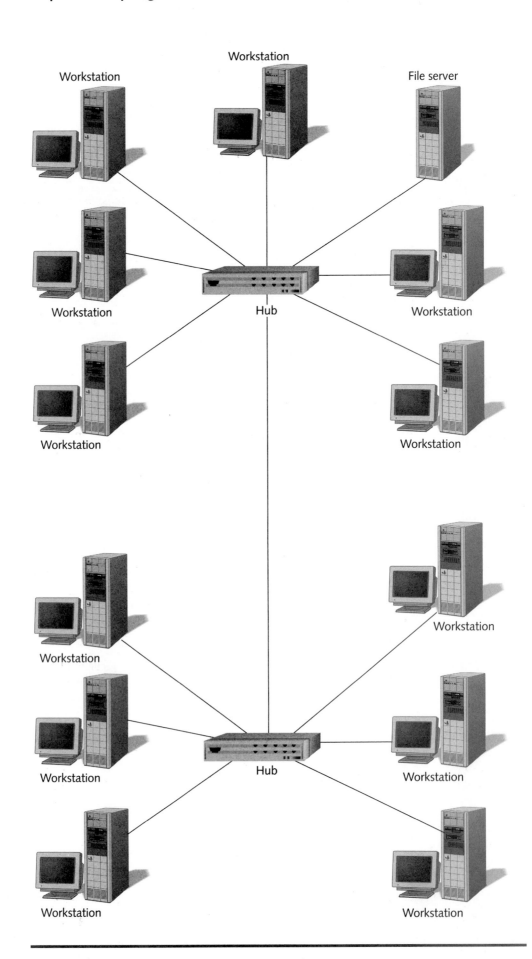

Table 3-4

Advantages and
disadvantages of
the bus-star
topology

Advantages	Disadvantages
Easier to manage than the traditional bus design	Susceptible to a single point of failure (the hub)
Easier to locate node and cable problems than the traditional bus design	Requires more network cable at the start than a bus
Many options for expansion	
Well suited for expansion into high-speed networking	
Many equipment options	
No exposed terminators	

In this hands-on activity, you use Microsoft Paint to draw a simple bus network that contains eight workstations. (You can substitute a different drawing package such as Visio or AutoCAD, in which case you will need help from your instructor.) It is good practice to learn to draw network representations as an aid to explaining and conceptualizing your network. Start at a lab computer with Windows 95 or NT Workstation and log on.

To draw a simple network diagram:

1. Click the **Start** button, **Programs**, **Accessories**, then **Paint**.

2. Click the **View** menu. If the Tool Box option has no check mark in front of it, click **Tool Box**. If the Tool Box option is already checked, press [Esc] to close the View menu. The Paint toolbar is displayed. If necessary, drag the toolbar to dock it to the left or the right of the drawing area.

3. Click the Line button ▧ on the toolbar. Place the crosshair cursor on the screen and, while holding down the Shift key to make a straight line, draw a vertical line from the top to the bottom of the screen.

4. Draw four separate short horizontal lines off the left side of the long vertical line (Figure 3-6). Do the same off of the right side at staggered intervals. These represent the connecting lines for your workstations.

5. Click the Rectangle button ▢ on the toolbar and drag to draw a small box anywhere on the screen (but not on the lines you just drew). This represents a workstation on the network.

6. Click the Text button **A** on the toolbar, click below the box you just drew, then type **Workstation** as the label for the box. Don't worry that the text does not fit on one line.

7. Use the horizontal and vertical sizing handles (the small boxes) around the text to size it so the word *Workstation* fits on one line. Place the cursor on the dotted border of the text box until it becomes a left-pointing arrow, then drag the text box inside the rectangle you drew in step 5.

8. Click the Select button ▢ on the toolbar and drag an outline around the workstation box and label you just made.

9. Move the workstation to connect to the end of one of the horizontal lines off of the main vertical line.

10. After the workstation box is in the desired place, right-click inside the outline still around the workstation and click **Copy** on the shortcut menu.

11. Right-click on an unused area of the screen and click **Paste** or press [Ctrl]+[V] to create another workstation box. While it is still outlined, move that workstation box to a vacant connecting line off the vertical line.

12. Repeat step 9 until each connecting horizontal line has a workstation attached, as shown in Figure 3-6.

13. If necessary, use the Eraser tool to clean up any ragged line ends.

14. Click the **File** menu option and click **Save** to save your work to use later. Name the file **simple bus network** and save it to a floppy disk in drive A or to the drive and directory your instructor specifies.

15. Print the drawing if a printer is available.

16. Close Microsoft Paint.

Figure 3-6

The beginning of a network diagram

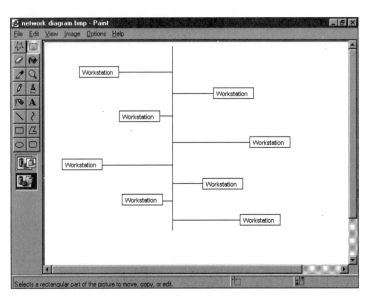

Many programs can be used to prepare network diagrams. Most run in Windows 95 and NT and use standard point-and-click techniques. Some examples of network diagramming programs are AutoCAD (Autodesk, Inc.), ClickNet (PinPoint Software), NetViz (NetViz Corporation), TurboCAD (IMSI), and Visio (Visio Corporation).

COMMUNICATIONS MEDIA

The communications media on a network are literally the tie that binds everything together. The media used in network communications include the following:

- Thick coaxial cable
- Thin coaxial cable
- Shielded twisted-pair cable
- Unshielded twisted-pair cable
- Fiber-optic cable
- Wireless technologies

In the next sections, you learn about each medium, including its advantages and disadvantages. The characteristics of the media types make them suitable for different types of networks. The most commonly used cabling is twisted-pair. Coaxial cable, though still common, is used mainly in older LANs. Fiber-optic cabling is used primarily to connect computers that demand high-speed access and to connect networks on different floors and in different buildings. Wireless technologies are used in situations where it is difficult or too expensive to use cable.

When choosing the best media for a network, you need to consider the characteristics of each medium, such as the following:

- Data transfer speed
- Use in specific network topologies
- Distance requirements
- Cable and cable component costs
- Additional network equipment that is required
- Ease of installation
- Immunity to interference from outside sources
- Upgrade options

COAXIAL CABLE

Coaxial cable comes in two varieties, thick and thin. Thick coaxial cable was used in early networks, particularly as a backbone to join different networks. It is used infrequently today because there are better alternatives, such as fiber-optic cable. Thin coaxial cable, which has a much smaller diameter than thick coaxial cable, is used on networks to connect desktop workstations.

Coaxial cable, also called coax, consists of a copper core surrounded by insulation. The insulation is surrounded by an another conducting material, such as braided wire, which is covered by an outer insulating material.

Thick Coaxial Cable

Thick coaxial cable (Figure 3-7) has a copper or copper-clad aluminum conductor as the core. The conductor has a relatively large diameter, compared with thin coaxial cable. The conductor is surrounded by insulation, and an aluminum sleeve is wrapped around the outside of the insulation. A polyvinyl chloride (PVC) or Teflon jacket covers the aluminum sleeve.

Figure 3-7

Thick coaxial cable

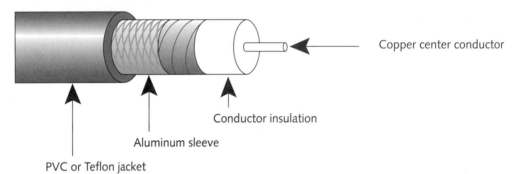

Copper center conductor

Conductor insulation

Aluminum sleeve

PVC or Teflon jacket

The cable jacket is marked every 2.5 meters to show where a network connecting device can be attached. If devices are attached more closely than that, network errors may result. Thick coaxial cable is also called RG-8 cable (RG means radio grade). The **impedance** of the cable is 50 ohms, and cable segments are terminated by a 50-ohm resistor.

 An electronics term, **impedance** is the total amount of opposition to the flow of current. In coaxial cable, a 50-ohm impedance influences how fast a packet can travel through the conductive material under optimal conditions.

Thick coaxial cable is difficult to bend, and a minimum bend radius must be followed because of the large diameter of the copper conductor. On the plus side, this cabling has better EMI and RFI (electrical interference) immunity than thin coaxial because of the larger-diameter conductor and aluminum shielding.

Thick coaxial cable works on bus networks that normally use transmission speeds of 10 Mbps. According to IEEE standards, the maximum cable length, or run, is 500 meters (m). The shorthand for those specifications is 10BASE5. The 10 indicates the cable transmission rate is 10 Mbps; BASE means that **baseband** transmission is used instead of **broadband**; and the 5 indicates 5 × 100 m for the longest cable run.

 A **baseband** transmission is one in which the entire channel capacity of the medium is used by one data signal. Thus, only one node transmits at a time.

 A **broadband** transmission employs several transmission channels on a single communications medium. That allows more than one node to transmit at a time. The capacity of a channel to transmit data is its bandwidth.

Thick coaxial cable can be used for baseband or broadband transmissions, but normally it is used for baseband transmission on data networks. Because of its diameter and the difficulty in manipulating and terminating it, thick coaxial is not as popular as other cabling. It also is expensive to purchase and install. On the plus side, thick coax is durable and reliable, with great resistance to signal interference.

Thin Coaxial Cable

Thin coaxial cable resembles television cable. Unlike television cable, however, the electrical characteristics of network cable must be precise and meet the specifications established by the IEEE. As for thick coaxial cable, those specifications require the cable to have 50 ohms of impedance. Thin coaxial cabling is labeled RG–58A/U (radio grade 58), which indicates that it is 50-ohm cable. Network administrators call the cable 10BASE2 (or thinnet or cheapernet), which means it has a maximum theoretical network speed of 10 Mbps uses baseband-type (BASE) data transmission, and can have wire runs up to 200 m. (These distinctions are becoming blurred because of the implementation of networking equipment that can amplify and retime signals for longer distances).

 Although 10BASE2 cable runs can be up to 200 m, a maximum of 185 m is preferred to allow for extra cabling needs required by network equipment. It is important to follow cable specifications carefully to ensure reliable data communications.

Thin coaxial cabling (usually referred to as coax) has a copper or copper-clad aluminum conductor at the core and an insulating foam material that surrounds the core. High-quality cable has an aluminum foil between the mesh and the foam around the core. A woven copper mesh and aluminum foil sleeve wraps around the insulating foam material and is covered with an outside PVC or Teflon jacket for insulation. It looks similar to the thick coaxial shown in Figure 3-7 but is much smaller in diameter. Coaxial cable comes in a variety of colors.

 In some locations, network cable is run through a plenum area, which is the space in a false ceiling where circulating air can reach other parts of the building. Because PVC produces a dangerous gas in a fire, it is safer to use plenum cable. Plenum cable is Teflon coated, so it does not emit a toxic gas when burned.

Coaxial cable is attached to a **BNC** connector, which is then connected to a T-connector. The middle of the T is connected to the NIC in the computer or network device. If that computer or device is at the last node on the cable, a terminator is connected to one end of the T-connector, as shown in Figure 3-8.

 A **BNC** connector is a connector with a bayonet-like shell, used for coax cable. (Various interpretations of what BNC stands for are bayonet naval connector, bayonet nut connection, and British Naval connector.) The female BNC connector has two small knobs that attach to circular slots in the male connector. Both connectors are twisted together for a connection.

Figure 3-8

A T-connector with a terminator at one end

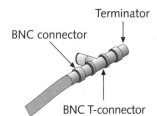

Thin coaxial cable is easier and cheaper to install than thick coaxial, but twisted-pair cable is much easier still to install and use, because it has better flexibility. That is one reason why coaxial is now used on a limited basis. An advantage of thin coaxial cable is that it is resistant to EMI and RFI.

In this hands-on activity, you have an opportunity to see thin coaxial cable and test its flexibility.

To examine thin coaxial cable:

1. In the classroom or in the lab, examine a small section of thin coaxial (RG-58A/U) cable.

2. Notice the RG-58A/U marking on the cable jacket.

3. Notice the inner copper conductor and outer mesh shield.

4. Try bending the cable.

5. Notice that the cable can be crimped or damaged if it is bent too much or caught under a chair leg.

 This hands-on activity gives you experience in attaching a BNC connector to coaxial cable, so the BNC connector later can be connected onto one end of a T-connector. The activity requires a crimping tool and a wire stripper designed for use with coaxial cable, a section of RG-58A/U cable, and a BNC connector.

To attach a BNC connector to coaxial cable:

1. Use a high-quality crimping tool for the type of connector you use.

2. Use a wire stripper intended for RG-58A/U coaxial cable.

3. Use a high-quality gold-plated BNC connector.

4. Follow the directions of the manufacturer of the stripper to strip the coaxial cable (including setting the stripper for the cable type).

5. After the cable is stripped, make sure all the strands in the center conductor are wrapped tightly, with no ends sticking out.

6. Slide the crimping sleeve onto the cable.

7. Insert the center conductor into the center contact of the connector; make sure all the braids are inside the center contact.

8. Use a crimping tool to crimp the center contact to the center conductor.

9. Carefully flare out the mesh braid away from its foam core.

10. Slide the BNC connector onto the foam core, making sure none of the braid is between the foam core and the sliding cylinder on the BNC connector and keeping the integrity of the aluminum foil as much as possible.

11. Slide the sleeve back up the cable flush with the bottom of the BNC connector.

12. Crimp the sleeve with a crimping tool.

TWISTED-PAIR CABLE

Resembling telephone wire, **twisted-pair** cable was approved for networking by the IEEE in 1990 and has become a popular communications medium. Twisted-pair is more flexible than coaxial cable for running through walls and around corners. Attached to the right network equipment, this cable can be adapted for high-speed communications of 100 Mbps or faster. For most applications, the maximum length to extend twisted-pair cable is 100 meters.

Twisted-pair is a flexible communications cable that contain pairs of insulated copper wires twisted together (for reduction of EMI and RFI) and covered with an outer insulating jacket.

Twisted-pair cabling is connected to network nodes with RJ-45 plug-in connectors, which resemble the RJ-11 connectors used on telephones. The connectors are less expensive than T-connectors and less susceptible to damage when moved. They also are easy to connect and allow more flexible cable configurations than coaxial cable.

The two kinds of twisted-pair cable are shielded and unshielded. Unshielded cable is preferred because of its lower cost and high reliability.

Shielded Twisted-Pair Cable

Shielded twisted-pair (STP) cable consists of pairs of insulated solid wire surrounded by a braided or corrugated shielding. Braided shielding is used for indoor wire, and corrugated shielding is used for outside or underground wiring. Shielding reduces interruptions of the communication signal caused by RFI and EMI. Twisting the wire pairs also helps reduce RFI and EMI, but not to the same extent as the shield. STP cabling is used where heavy electrical equipment or other strong sources of interference are nearby. The original types of STP, IBM type 1A and type 2A, transmit at the relatively low speed of 4 Mbps. Type 2A cable is used mainly indoors. Newer STP cabling is used in high-speed networks. Figure 3-9 shows examples of shielded and unshielded twisted-pair cable.

 Shielded twisted-pair (STP) cable contains pairs of insulated wires that are twisted together, surrounded by a shielding material for added EMI and RFI protection, all inside a protective jacket.

Figure 3-9

Twisted-pair cable

Shielded twisted-pair (STP)

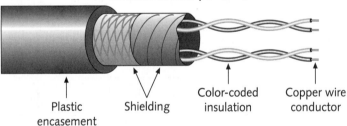

Plastic encasement   Shielding   Color-coded insulation   Copper wire conductor

Unshielded twisted-pair (UTP)

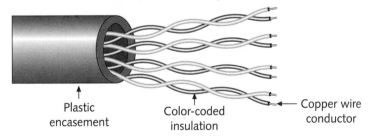

Plastic encasement   Color-coded insulation   Copper wire conductor

 Shielded cable and connectors along with the network equipment are more expensive than unshielded cable.

Unshielded Twisted-Pair Cable

Unshielded twisted-pair (UTP) cable is the most frequently used network cabling because of its low cost and relatively easy installation. UTP consists of wire pairs encased by an insulated covering. As with STP, each inside strand is twisted with another strand to help reduce interference to the data-carrying signal. An electrical device called a media filter is built into the network equipment, workstation, and file server connections to reduce EMI and RFI.

 Unshielded twisted-pair (UTP) has no shielding material between the pairs of insulated wires twisted together and the cable's outside jacket.

UTP is popularly called 10BASE-T cable, which means it has a maximum transmission rate of 10 Mbps (although actual cable specifications can be up to 16 Mbps for some data transmissions), uses baseband communications, and is twisted-pair. This version of UTP is also called category 3 cable. Category 4 UTP has a maximum transmission rate of 20 Mbps, and category 5 has a 100-Mbps transmission rate. Table 3-5 lists the most commonly used twisted-pair cable categories as specified by the **Electronic Telecommunications Association/Telecommunications Industry Association (EIA/TIA)**.

 In 1985, computer and telecommunications companies asked the **Electronic Industries Association (EIA)** to develop network cabling standards. The EIA develops standards for electrical interfaces, such as serial interfaces on computers. Formed in 1988, the **Telecommunications Industry Association (TIA)** was formed as a separate body within the EIA with the charge to develop telecommunications and cabling standards. The EIA/TIA-568 standard is for commercial building and telecommunications cabling. **Horizontal cabling** is used to connect to workstations and servers in the work area. **Backbone cabling** runs between network equipment rooms, floors, and buildings.

Table 3-5

Most commonly used twisted-pair cable categories

Twisted-Pair as Defined in the EIA/TIA-568 Specifications for Horizontal and Backbone Cable	Shielding	Maximum Transition Rate
IBM Type 1A	Shielded	4 Mbps
IBM Type 2A	Shielded	4 Mbps
Category 3	Unshielded	16 Mbps
Category 4	Unshielded	20 Mbps
Category 5	Unshielded	100 Mbps

 Category 5 twisted-pair cable is a good choice for new cable installations because it has high-speed networking capabilities at 100 Mbps.

In this hands-on activity, you have an opportunity to see UTP cable and test its flexibility.

To examine UTP cable:

1. In the classroom or in the lab, examine a small section of UTP cable.

2. Notice the twisted pairs of color-coded wires inside the outer insulation.

3. Try bending the cable.

4. Notice that the cable is easier to bend and less susceptible to damage than coaxial cable.

 This hands-on activity involves attaching 4-pair UTP cable to an RJ-45 connector. You need the cable, a crimper, a connector, and a wire stripper. These instructions and Figure 3-10 follow the EIA/TIA-568 standard.

To attach UTP cable to an RJ-45 connector:

1. Lay out the wires on a flat surface in the arrangement shown in Figure 3-10.

2. With a pair of wire cutters, trim all the wires to the same length.

3. Use a wire stripper intended for twisted-pair cable.

4. Follow the directions of the stripper manufacturer to strip the cable.

5. Insert the wires into the RJ-45 connector, making sure the connector is oriented the correct way, with the first pair of wires (blue and white/blue) to connectors 4 and 5 inside the RJ-45 connector, connecting the blue wire to connector 4 and the white/blue wire to connector 5 (Figure 3-10).

6. Make sure the second pair of wires go to connectors 1 and 2, connecting the white/orange wire to connector 1 and the orange wire to connector 2.

7. Make sure the third pair go to connectors 3 and 6, connecting the white/green wire to connector 3 and the green wire to connector 6.

8. Make sure the fourth pair go to connectors 7 and 8, connecting the white/brown wire to connector 7 and the brown wire to connector 8.

9. Make sure a portion of the cable jacket is inside the connector.

10. Insert the RJ-45 connector into the crimp tool and crimp the connector to the wires.

11. Test the installation by pulling the cable and connector in opposite directions to make sure your work does not come loose.

 After the cable is constructed, you can test it by using an inexpensive cable tester to test the cable pairs for accuracy end to end.

Figure 3-10

Connecting
twisted-pair
cable to an
RJ-45
connector

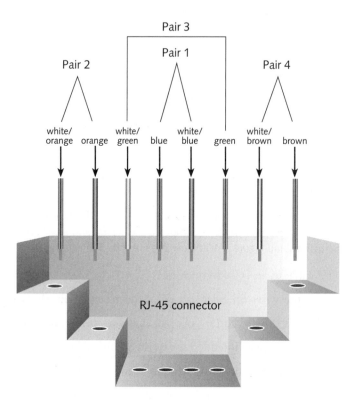

Twisted-pair cable

FIBER-OPTIC CABLE

Fiber-optic cable consists of a central glass cylinder encased in a glass tube, called cladding. The central core and the cladding are surrounded by a PVC sheath (Figure 3-11). The size of fiber-optic cable is measured in microns and has two components, the core diameter and the cladding diameter. For example, 50/125-micron (μ) fiber cable has a core diameter of 50μ and a cladding diameter of 125μ. (A micron is equal to 1 one-millionth of a meter.) The other two commonly used sizes are 62.5/125μ fiber cable and 100/140μ cable. All three types of cable have multimode transmission capability; which means that multiple light waves can be transmitted on the cable at once. The most commonly used fiber for multimode cable applications is 62.5/125.

Fiber-optic communications cable consists of one or more glass or plastic fiber cores inside a protective cladding material and covered by a PVC outer jacket. Signal transmission along the inside fibers is accomplished using infrared or, in some cases, visible light.

Figure 3-11

Fiber-optic cable

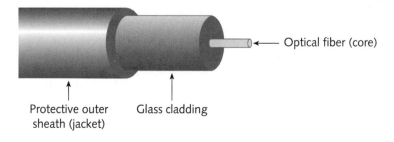

The cable core carries optical light pulses transmitted by laser or light-emitting diode (LED) devices. The glass cladding is designed to reflect light back into the core. Fiber-optic cable is well suited for high-speed network transmissions of 100 Mbps to over 1 Gbps. It is used in cable plant backbones, such as between floors in a building, between buildings, and beyond. The fiber backbone between floors in a building is sometimes called a **fat pipe**, because it has a wide bandwidth for baseband and broadband high-capacity communications. The most common use for fiber-optic cable in a campus environment is to interconnect different buildings to adhere to IEEE cabling specifications.

A **fat pipe** is fiber-optic cable used on a network backbone for high-speed communications.

One advantage of fiber-optic cable is that its high bandwidth and low **attenuation** enable it to sustain transmissions over long distances. Also, because the data travels by means of optical light pulses (on or off), there are no EMI or RFI problems associated with this type of cable. Another advantage is that, because cable installation requires a high level of expertise, it is difficult for someone to place unauthorized taps into the cable. A disadvantage of fiber-optic cable is that it is fragile and relatively expensive and requires specialized training to install.

Attenuation is the amount of signal that is lost as the signal travels through the communications medium from its source (transmitting node) to the receiving node. Attenuation in fiber-optic cable is measured as the drop in decibels.

The ability to transmit signals by light waves is related to the wavelength of the light. Some wavelengths travel through optical fiber more efficiently than others. Light wavelength is measured in nanometers (nm). Visible light, in the range of 400 –700 nm, does not travel through fiber-optic cable with enough efficiency for data transfer. Infrared light, in the range of 700 –1600 nm, travels with the necessary efficiency for data transmission.

Optical communications occur through three ideal wavelengths, or windows: 850 nm, 1300 nm, and 1550 nm. High-speed transmissions use the 1300-nm window. Power loss on fiber-optic cable is measured in decibels (dB). Loss of optical power is directly related to the length of the cable, along with the number of bends and the radii of those bends in the cable. There also is power loss as the wave passes through connectors and splices.

The wave must leave the transmitting device with a minimum level of power to be accurately translated at the receiving end. That minimum power level is called the **power budget**. For high-speed communications, the power budget must be 11 dB.

The **power budget** for optical-fiber cable communications is the difference between the transmitted power and the receiver sensitivity, measured in decibels. It is the minimum transmitter power and receiver sensitivity needed for a signal to be sent and received intact.

Fiber-optic cable comes in two modes: single-mode and multimode. Single-mode cable is used mainly for long-distance communications and has a central core diameter of 8–10µ and a 125µ cladding diameter. The central core diameter is much smaller than that of multimode cable. Only one light wave is transmitted on the cable at a given time. Laser light is the communication source for single-mode cable. The laser light source, coupled with a relatively large bandwidth, enables long-distance transmissions at high speeds.

The intensity of laser light makes looking into the cable hazardous, resulting in severe eye injury. Regardless of the light source, *never* look into a fiber-optic cable.

Multimode cable can support simultaneous transmission of multiple light waves for broad-band communications. The transmission distance is not as great as for single-mode cable, because the available bandwidth is smaller and the light source is weaker. The transmission source for multimode cable is an LED.

 In this hands-on activity, you have an opportunity to see fiber-optic cable and observe its fragile nature.

To inspect fiber-optic cable:

1. In the classroom or in the lab, examine a small section of fiber-optic cable.

2. Notice the glass conductive material inside the cladding. (The core is about the size of a human hair. Some of the cladding may need to be stripped away or an observation scope may be needed to see the glass core.)

3. Do not bend the cable but observe its fragility compared to coaxial and twisted-pair cables.

WIRELESS TECHNOLOGIES

Besides cable, several connectionless media are available for transmitting network packets: radio waves, infrared, and microwave. All these technologies transmit signals through the air or the atmosphere, a characteristic that makes them good alternatives in situations where it is difficult or impossible to use cable. It also is an important limitation in that these signals can experience problems due to interference from other signals using the same media and from sun spots, ionospheric changes, and other atmospheric disturbances.

Radio Technologies

Network signals are transmitted over radio waves in a fashion similar to your local radio station, but network applications use much higher frequencies. For example, an AM station in your area might transmit at a frequency of 1290, which is 1290 **kilohertz** (kHz), because the AM broadcast range is 535–1605 kHz. The FM range is 88–108 **megahertz** (MHz). In the United States, most computer network radio wave transmissions are at the much higher frequency range of 902–928 MHz.

 Hertz is the measurement of the frequency of the alternation of an electrical current or a radio wave. A **kilohertz** (kHz) is equal to 1000 hertz; a **megahertz** (MHz) to 1 million hertz; a **terahertz** (THz) to 1 trillion hertz.

In this type of transmission, a radio signal is transmitted in one or multiple directions, depending on the type of antenna used (Figure 3-12). The wave is very short in length with a low transmission strength (unless the transmission operator has a special license from the Federal Communications Commission, or FCC, for high-wattage transmission), which means it is better suited for short-range **line-of-sight** transmissions than for long-range transmissions. A low-power (1–10 watts) single-frequency signal has a data capacity in the range of 1–10 Mbps.

In a **line-of-sight** transmission, the signal goes from point to point, rather than bouncing off the atmosphere to skip across the country or across continents. A limitation of line-of-sight transmissions is that they are interrupted by large land masses, such as hills and mountains.

Figure 3-12

Radio wave communications between buildings

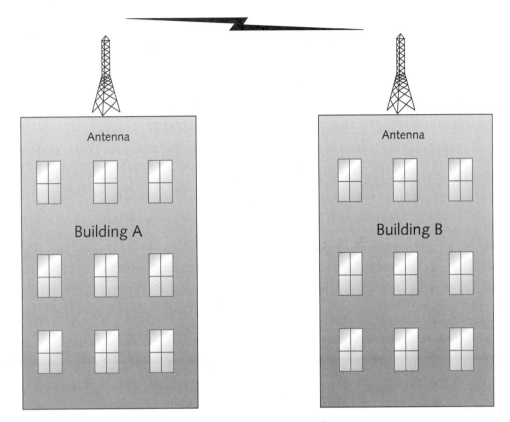

Most connectionless network equipment employs SST (spread spectrum technology) for packet transmissions. SST uses one or more adjoining frequencies to transmit the signal across greater bandwidth. Spread-spectrum frequency ranges are very high, in the 902–928 MHz range. Spread-spectrum transmissions typically send data at a rate of 2–6 Mbps.

Radio communications can save money where it is difficult or expensive to run cable. One example is an urban university that did not have a way to run underground cable between two adjacent buildings. At first they ran cable through two windows across an alley. One morning, the cable snapped when a tall garbage truck drove through the alley. The university found radio communications an inexpensive alternative for their situation. Radio wave installations also are useful in situations where portable computers are used and need to be moved around frequently. Compared to other wireless options, this one is relatively inexpensive and easy to install.

There are significant disadvantages to radio communications. One is that many network installations are implementing high-speed communications of 100 Mbps to handle heavy data traffic, including transmission of large files. Radio-based networks do not yet have the speeds to accommodate those needs. Another disadvantage is that the frequencies in use are unregulated. Amateur radio operators, the U.S. military, and cell phone companies also use these frequencies and may cause interference. Natural obstacles, such as hills, also diminish or interfere with the signal transmission.

Infrared Technologies

Network communications also can be performed through the use of infrared light. This technology probably is familiar to most people as the remote control devices used for televisions and stereos. Infrared can be broadcast in a single direction or in all directions, using an LED to transmit and a photodiode to receive. It transmits in light frequency ranges of 100 Ghz to 1000 THz.

Like radio waves, infrared can be an inexpensive solution in hard-to-cable areas or where the users are mobile. Another advantage is that the signal is difficult to intercept without the user's knowing it. There are, however, some significant disadvantages to this communication medium. One is that data transmission rates reach up to only 16 Mbps for directional communications and to less than 1 Mbps for omnidirectional communications. Another disadvantage is that infrared does not go through walls. (Take your stereo remote control into another room and try it from there.) Infrared also can experience interference from strong light sources.

Microwave Technologies

Microwave systems work in one of two ways. In a terrestrial microwave system, the signal is transmitted between two directional antennas shaped like dishes (Figure 3-13). The transmissions are in the frequency ranges of 4–6 GHz or 21–23 GHz and require the operator to obtain an FCC license.

Figure 3-13

Terrestrial microwave communications

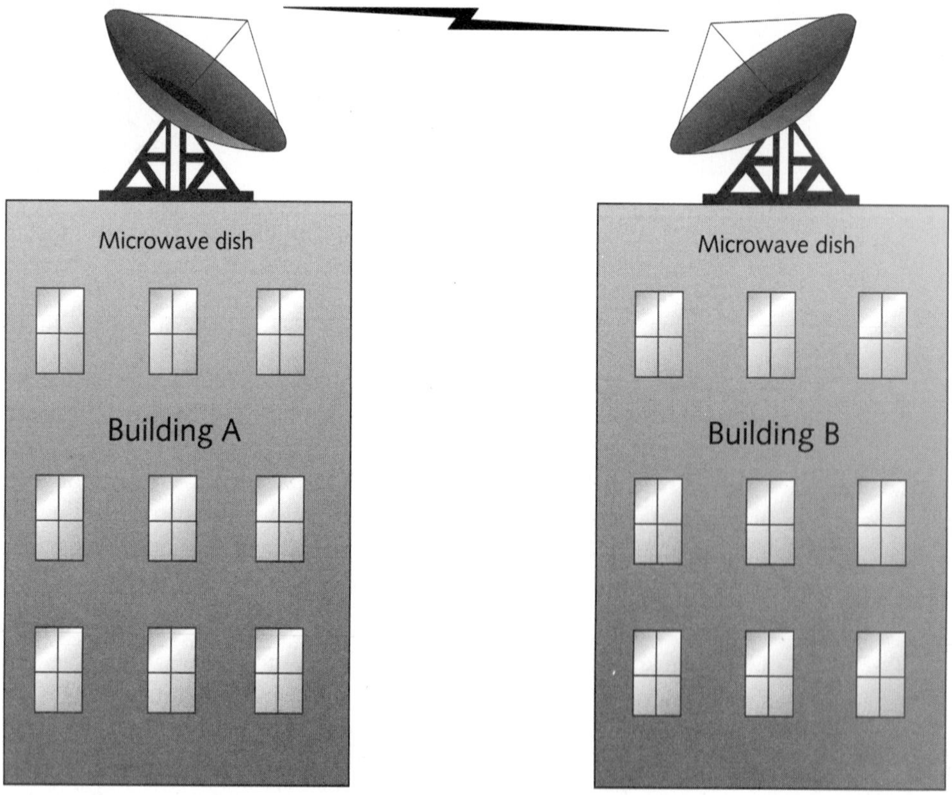

Microwave dish

Building A

Microwave dish

Building B

A satellite microwave system transmits the signal from the transmitting antenna to a satellite in space and then to the receiving antenna (Figure 3-14). To use this technology, you need to launch your own satellite or lease service from a company offering this technology, obviously very expensive options. Satellite microwave transmissions are in the 11–14 GHz range.

Figure 3-14

Satellite
microwave
communications

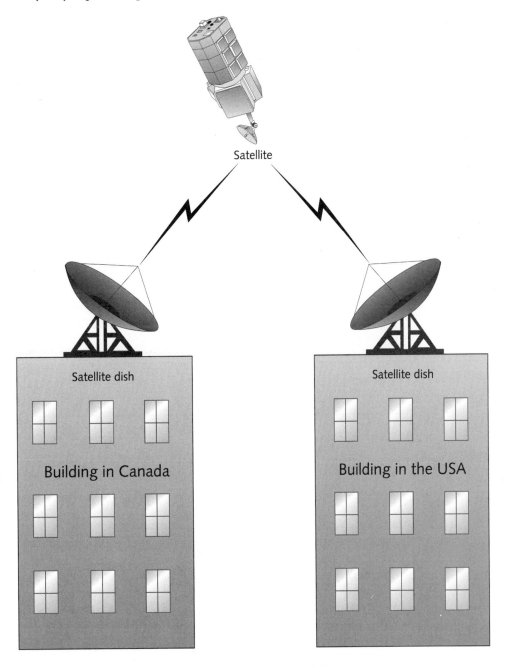

As with other connectionless media, microwave solutions are applied where cabling costs are too high or cabling is impossible. Terrestrial microwave may be a good solution for communications between two large buildings in a city. Satellite microwave is one solution for joining networks across a country or between two continents.

Both types of microwave media transmit at speeds of 1–10 Mbps, which is a limitation where higher network speeds are required. Microwave has some other limitations, too. It is expensive and difficult to install and maintain. Microwave transmissions also can be interrupted due to atmospheric conditions, bad weather, and EMI.

Table 3-6 compares the advantages and disadvantages of the three wireless technologies.

Table 3-6

Advantages and disadvantages of wireless communications

	Radio	Infrared	Microwave
Advantages	• An inexpensive alternative where communications cabling cannot be installed easily • An option for portable communications • Usually no licensing requirements	• An inexpensive alternative where communications cabling cannot be installed easily • Signal difficult to intercept secretly	• An alternative where communications cabling cannot be installed easily, such as over long distances
Disadvantages	• May not be feasible when high-speed communications are needed • Subject to interference from the military, amateur radio, cell phones, and other sources • Subject to interference from natural obstacles	• May not be feasible when high-speed communications are needed • Subject to interference from other light sources • Does not go through walls	• May not be feasible when high-speed communications are needed • Expensive to install and maintain • Subject to interference from bad weather, EMI, and atmospheric conditions

COMMUNICATIONS MEDIA COSTS AND CONSIDERATIONS

Two aspects must be considered in the calculation of network media costs: installation costs and maintenance costs. Let's look at several different scenarios to consider these types of costs. The first scenario is a small network with fewer than 30 nodes. A simple bus network with thin coaxial cable may be the least expensive to install. But the maintenance costs will be relatively high for replacing damaged BNC and T-connectors and cable and also in terms of personnel time expended to find network problems. Also, a coaxial-based network has fewer options for expansion to high-speed networking. Most manufacturers are moving away from BNC interfaces on their workstations, and the prices are going up for BNC interfaces on network equipment. The installation of a star network using twisted-pair cable may be a little more costly at first, because of the need to purchase more cable for the star topology. The twisted-pair cable and connectors, though, are less expensive to install than coaxial. Also, maintenance costs are lower because problems are easier to track and the cable is less expensive to replace than coaxial. If category 5 cable is used, it will be cheaper to convert to high-speed networking in the future because the twisted-pair cable is already in place.

In another scenario, let's say you need to plan a network to connect workstations on every floor of a five-story building. In this case, coaxial cable and the associated network equipment are likely to be an expensive alternative, although you could wire the building with a combination of coaxial and fiber-optic cable using the fiber cable between floors. A better alternative is to combine twisted-pair cable and fiber-optic cable. When the cost of running the cable through the walls is included, each floor can be wired at less cost using twisted pair. The hubs can be joined by fiber-optic cable on the backbone. The fiber-optic cable costs a little more to install, but it will significantly reduce later costs for expanding the network. Also, the fiber will increase the productivity of users, if backbone transmission speeds of 100 Mbps are used. The fiber-optic and twisted-pair combination is also a good choice for reducing troubleshooting costs, because network problems will be easier to locate and solve.

In the third scenario, you need to link networks in two downtown buildings eight blocks apart. An inexpensive option is to install spread-spectrum radio communications between the networks, placing the antennas on the roofs. That is less expensive and easier to install than microwave, and the impact of atmospheric or weather disturbances would be minimal. The equipment also is relatively inexpensive to maintain. It is likely to be less expensive than fiber-optic cable, because of the difficulty of installing the cable in this type of situation. Twisted-pair and coaxial cable are not a good choice, because of the distance and the installation expenses. The main limitation of spread-spectrum communications is the low transmission speeds.

 In this hands-on activity, you compare prices of UTP cable components to RG-58A/U.

To compare prices for different cable options:

1. Obtain a cable parts catalog from your instructor or search the Internet to find a cable vendor. (Some Internet addresses of cable parts providers are *www.shillsdata.com, www.m-i-c.com, www.anixter.com, www.ariesdirect.com,* and *www.sanbour.com.*)

2. Find the price of a BNC connector, a T-connector, 1 ft. of RG 58A/U cable, and a 50-ohm terminator. (Sample prices are $3.00 for the BNC connector, $6.00 for the T-connector, $.28/ft. for cable, and $7.00 for the terminator.)

3. Find the price of an RJ-45 connector and 1 ft. of category 5 4-pair PVC UTP cable. (Sample prices are $1.00 for the connector and $.25/ft. for the cable.)

CHAPTER SUMMARY

There are many ways to send a packet from one network node to another, as influenced by the network topology. Bus networks send the packet in a straight-line fashion from node to node, with terminators at both ends of the bus network. Ring networks have no distinct beginning or end point, sending packets to nodes around a ring. Star networks have a center connecting point, called a hub, with cable radiating from the hub in different directions.

Network designs are implemented through communications media. The media are thick and thin coaxial cable, shielded and unshielded twisted-pair cable, fiber-optic cable, radio waves, infrared waves, and microwaves. Each medium has advantages and disadvantages. For instance, thin coaxial cable is not as flexible as twisted-pair, and infrared waves will not go through walls, but radio waves will.

Selecting the right communication media depends on many factors, such as media capabilities, the cost of installation, and the cost of maintenance. One of the most popular media is twisted-pair cable, because it is versatile for many kinds of installations, is relatively inexpensive to install and maintain, and can be expanded as a network expands.

In the next chapter, you consider additional media factors as you examine the IEEE 802 standards and how to implement them. You are introduced to popular network protocols, including TCP/IP, which is widely used through the Internet. In the process, there will be hands-on opportunities to configure different protocols on a Microsoft network.

REVIEW QUESTIONS

1. Which type of cabling uses a T-connector?
   a. shielded twisted-pair
   b. unshielded twisted-pair
   c. coaxial
   d. fiber-optic

2. What is the amount of impedance for RG 58A/U cable?
   a. 20 ohms
   b. 50 ohms
   c. 75 ohms
   d. impedance is not important, but wattage is

3. 10BASE-T is what kind of cable?
   a. twisted-pair
   b. fiber-optic
   c. coaxial
   d. television

4. Category 5 twisted-pair cable has a transmission rate up to
   a. 1 Mbps.
   b. 10 Mbps.
   c. 50 Mbps.
   d. 100 Mbps.

5. Which type of cable is more flexible for bending around corners?
   a. fiber-optic
   b. twisted-pair
   c. coaxial
   d. all are equally flexible

6. Which communication medium is likely to be less costly to maintain?

   a. fiber-optic

   b. twisted-pair

   c. coaxial

   d. all of the above are inexpensive to maintain

   e. both a and b

7. Which of the following wireless communication media can connect networks on different continents?

   a. spread spectrum

   b. infrared

   c. satellite

   d. all of the above

   e. both a and c

8. An RJ-45 connector would be used with

   a. fiber-optic cable.

   b. a spread-spectrum antenna.

   c. coaxial cable.

   d. twisted-pair cable.

9. Which kind of fiber-optic cable normally is used for long-distance communications?

   a. single-mode

   b. multimode

   c. attenuated

   d. 4-wire

10. Which type of cable is capable of a transmission rate of over 1 Gbps?

   a. shielded twisted-pair

   b. unshielded twisted-pair

   c. coaxial

   d. fiber-optic

ASPEN CONSULTING PROJECT: THE PHYSICIANS GROUP

A group of physicians is building a new two-story building that is four blocks from the hospital. Their business manager, Gary Sharma, has contacted you about assisting them in selecting a basic network topology and what communications media to use. The plans for the building are not complete, but Gary wants to begin discussions on different options for networks that can be used. At this point, he can tell you that there will be over 30 workstations on each floor in different offices, labs, and work areas. Also, the group wants to link into the hospital's network.

ASSIGNMENT 3-1

On your first visit with Gary Sharma, he tells you he would like to know about some basic network designs. Use Microsoft Paint or another drawing package to draw examples of the basic network topologies for Gary. Then, use the space below to summarize those topologies.

ASSIGNMENT 3-2

Explain the advantages and disadvantages of the topologies you summarized for Gary in Assignment 3-1. Based on what you know at this point, which topology would you recommend for the physicians' building? Why would you recommend it?

ASSIGNMENT 3-3

Gary has read about using coaxial cable and twisted-pair cable to wire the building. Compare the advantages and disadvantages of each. Based on what you know at this point, what kind of cable would you recommend?

ASSIGNMENT 3-4

Gary is interested on comparing costs of thin coaxial and twisted-pair cabling. Find two cable sources on the Internet and prepare a table of example costs for him. You have decided to estimate costs by the foot, based on bulk purchases of cable (such as 500 or 1000 ft.) and connectors (70 to 80 connectors). Also, find out the cost of terminators. Use high-quality components, such as gold-plated connectors for the coaxial cable estimates. Before completing the table, use the following space to explain the kinds of connectors and terminators required by each communication medium.

	Thin Coaxial		Unshielded Twisted-Pair, Category 5 (Plenum)	
	Estimate 1	Estimate 2	Estimate 1	Estimate 2
Cable cost per foot				
Connectors				
Terminators				

ASSIGNMENT 3-5

What type of communications medium would you use to connect the floors of the building? What are the advantages and the disadvantages of that medium? Using Microsoft Paint or another drawing package, draw an example to show two floors in a generic building scheme having 35 computers on each floor. In your network diagram, show Gary in a rudimentary way how you would link the floors with the communications medium you are recommending.

ASSIGNMENT 3-6

As your discussions are beginning, Gary has found out that zoning laws and other obstacles make it unlikely you will be able to use any type of cable to connect to the hospital. Recommend a wireless option to Gary. Compare that option to other options and explain why you have chosen this particular one. Draw a simple network diagram to illustrate the option for Gary.

ASSIGNMENT 3-7

Before the planning goes much further, you want to know a few things about how the network will be used. Write down at least five questions you would ask Gary.

OPTIONAL CASE STUDIES FOR TEAMS

 ## TEAM CASE 1

Mark Arnez of Aspen Consulting has been contacted by a client who represents an international company with locations in your city, in Toronto, and in London. Each location has a plant for making parts for boilers used in large buildings. There also are sales and parts distribution offices at the plants. All buildings currently are networked using 10-Mbps communications to each workstation or server and 100-Mbps communications between floors. The client is exploring ways to link the business networks at all three locations. Form a team to determine the best way to connect the locations. Use the Internet to research some gross estimates of the costs.

 ## TEAM CASE 2

A new client, Sports Limited, has contacted Aspen Consulting because they are adding two new stories onto their existing building. The building they are expanding was originally a single-floor building with an eight-year-old network having a thick coaxial cable backbone and thin coaxial cable to the desktop units. They are wondering (1) if they should take this opportunity to convert their old network to some other type of communications media and (2) what they should use as communication media for the two new stories. Mark Arnez asks you to form a team and make some recommendations to this client.

 ## TEAM CASE 3

You and a couple of other consultants are interested in finding out more about local applications of fiber-optic cable. On your initiative, your small group has decided to visit the local telephone company and the local cable television company to find out how they use fiber-optic cable. Write a short report of what you found out to share with your co-workers at Aspen Consulting.

NETWORK TRANSPORT SYSTEMS AND PROTOCOLS

Several years ago, to install a network you needed false floors, troughs of cabling, and wide conduit to run thick coaxial cable. One highly networked plant owned by Hewlett-Packard was built with false floors wide enough to walk through on every story, each containing huge troughs of wire for network communications to all parts of the plant. Some state universities were able to put in networks quickly using thick coaxial cable because they already had machine rooms with 6 to 12 inches of false floors, originally designed to accommodate ventilation and cabling for mainframe computers. Soon thin coaxial cable was used to connect workstations and host computers into an ever expanding network. Today the urgency for high-capacity networks has prompted most organizations to replace older cable with combinations of twisted-pair cable to the desktops and fiber-optic cable as the backbone, providing speeds of 100 Mbps and higher. Network equipment advances and the need to build networks for future growth have combined to make the star topology commonplace in large and small networks.

AFTER READING THIS CHAPTER AND COMPLETING THE EXERCISES YOU WILL BE ABLE TO:

- EXPLAIN IEEE 802.3 (ETHERNET) NETWORK DATA TRANSPORT AND MEDIA SPECIFICATIONS
- EXPLAIN IEEE 802.5 (TOKEN RING) NETWORK DATA TRANSPORT AND MEDIA SPECIFICATIONS
- DESCRIBE MICROSOFT NETWORKING SERVICES AND PROTOCOL SUPPORT, INCLUDING NETBIOS, NETBEUI, NDIS, AND ODI
- EXPLAIN THE IPX/SPX AND NWLINK PROTOCOLS
- EXPLAIN THE TCP/IP PROTOCOL
- INSTALL A PROTOCOL IN MICROSOFT WINDOWS 95 OR NT
- SET UP A NIC AND NETWORK BINDINGS
- CONNECT TO AN IBM MAINFRAME USING DLC
- USE THE APPLETALK PROTOCOL TO CONNECT MACINTOSH COMPUTERS TO A MICROSOFT NT NETWORK
- SET PROTOCOL PRIORITIES
- RESOLVE A NIC RESOURCE CONFLICT
- SELECT THE RIGHT PROTOCOL FOR YOUR NETWORK

In this chapter, you build on your knowledge of network communications media and topology through the discussion of network transport methods and protocols. You discover the Ethernet and token ring transport methods, which are staples in the industry. You also take a closer look at networking protocols such as Microsoft's NetBEUI, Novell's IPX/SPX, and TCP/IP, which is used on the Internet. Essentially these "languages" enable different types of computers to communicate on common ground. Each discussion is followed by a hands-on activity in which you learn to use the protocol. You also look at protocols used with Apple computers and IBM mainframe computers.

ETHERNET AND THE IEEE 802.3 STANDARDS

Ethernet transport takes advantage of the bus and star topologies. This transport system uses a control method known as **Carrier Sense Multiple Access with Collision Detection (CSMA/CD)**. CSMA/CD is an **algorithm** that transmits and decodes formatted data frames. The algorithm detects node addresses and monitors for transmission errors.

The **Ethernet** transport system uses the CSMA/CD access method for data transmission on a network. Ethernet typically is implemented in a bus or star topology.

Carrier Sense Multiple Access with Collision Detection (CSMA/CD) is a network access control mechanism used in Ethernet networks. It regulates transmission by sensing the presence of packet collisions.

An **algorithm** is a block of computer code or logic designed to accomplish a certain task or to solve a problem, such as to control data communications or to calculate a payroll deduction.

There are several characteristics of Ethernet communications over a single cable run:

- No central control governs data transmission.
- The network can be accessed from many points, and all nodes have equal ability to transmit on the network.
- Data units are transmitted as encapsulated frames.
- Each transmitted frame contains addresses of the sending and receiving nodes.
- Frame addressing includes the ability to specify one node, multiple nodes, or all nodes on the network.
- The packets reach every network node.
- It is the responsibility of the receiving node to recognize and accept frames with its address as the destination.
- Data transmission is relatively fast (either 10 or 100 Mbps, although actual transmission speeds on a network vary, depending on the topology and traffic volume).
- Efficient error detection keeps transmission delays to a minimum.
- The communication specification discourages the implementing of special features that might lead to incompatible network variations.

When data is transmitted in Ethernet communications, it is encapsulated in frames (Figure 4-1). Each frame is composed of predefined parts. The first part is the preamble, which is 56 bits in length. The preamble synchronizes frame transmission and consists of an alternating pattern of 0s and 1s. The next field is the 8-bit start frame delimiter (SFD). The SFD bit pattern is 10101011. Following the SFD are two address fields, which contain the destination and source addresses. Under IEEE 802.3 guidelines, the address fields can be either 16 or 48 bits. Next, a 16-bit field specifies the frame length.

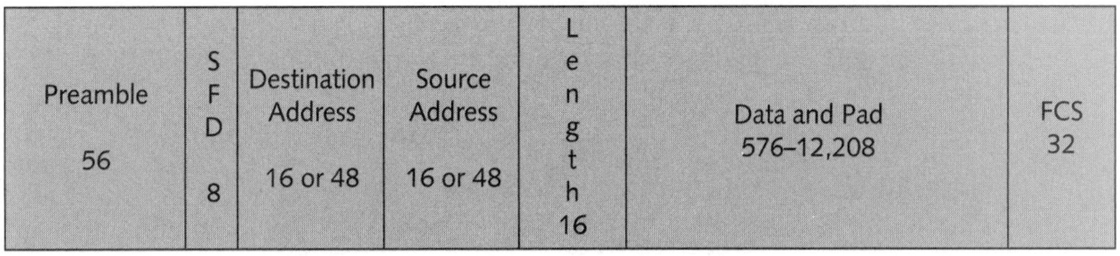

Figure 4-1

The 802.3 packet format

Preamble 56	S F D 8	Destination Address 16 or 48	Source Address 16 or 48	L e n g t h 16	Data and Pad 576–12,208	FCS 32

The data portion of the frame comes after the length field. The length of the encapsulated data is 576–12,208 bits and must be a multiple of 8. A pad field is included in case the data length is not a multiple of 8. The end portion of the frame is a frame check sequence (FCS) field, which is 32 bits long. The FCS field uses a cyclic redundancy check (CRC) value to enable error detection. The CRC value is calculated from the other fields in the frame at the time of encapsulation. It is recalculated when the destination node receives the packet. If the recalculation does not match the original calculated value, an error condition is generated and retransmission of the frame in error is requested.

ETHERNET II

Ethernet II is an Ethernet frame-formatting method used on the Internet and other modern networks. It is a slight variation from the IEEE 802.3 standard to make network transmissions more efficient. In Ethernet II, the preamble contains the start delimiter, is 64 bits in length, and includes the start of frame (SOF) delimiter. Destination and source addresses under Ethernet II are strictly limited to 48 bits (Figure 4-2).

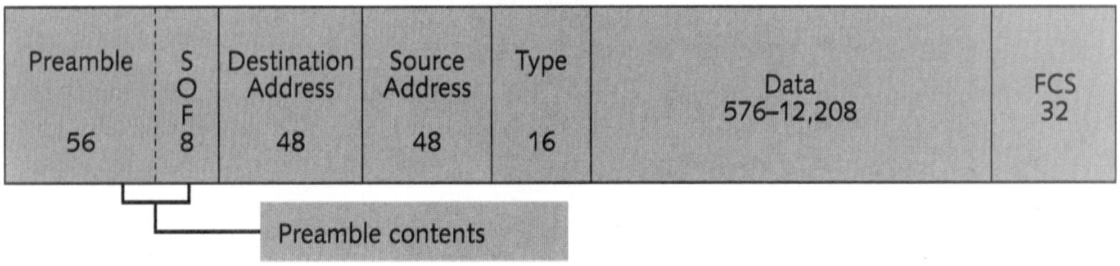

Figure 4-2

The Ethernet II packet format

Preamble 56	S O F 8	Destination Address 48	Source Address 48	Type 16	Data 576–12,208	FCS 32

Preamble contents

Ethernet II does not use a length field but a 16-bit type field instead. The type field is for upper-level network communications. The data field is encapsulated without a pad field and is between 576 and 12,208 bits in length. Minimum and maximum field sizes are used to improve packet collision detection and to ensure that a large packet does not occupy the network too long. The last field in the Ethernet II frame is the 32-bit long FCS field, which performs a CRC in the same way as the 802.3 standard.

 To avoid communication problems, Ethernet II and standard 802.3 frames should not be used on the same network.

SIGNAL TRANSMISSION

Using CSMA/CD, the Ethernet sending node encapsulates the frame to prepare it for transmission. All nodes that want to transmit a frame on the cable are in contention with one another. No single node has priority over another node. The nodes listen for any packet traffic on the cable. If a packet is detected, the nonsending nodes go into a "defer" mode. The Ethernet protocol permits only one node to transmit at a time. Signal transmission is accomplished by **carrier sense**. When no signal traffic is detected on the communication media for a given amount of time, any node is eligible to transmit. Figure 4–3 illustrates an 802.3 network in which one node is transmitting and the others are in defer mode.

Figure 4-3

One Ethernet node transmitting

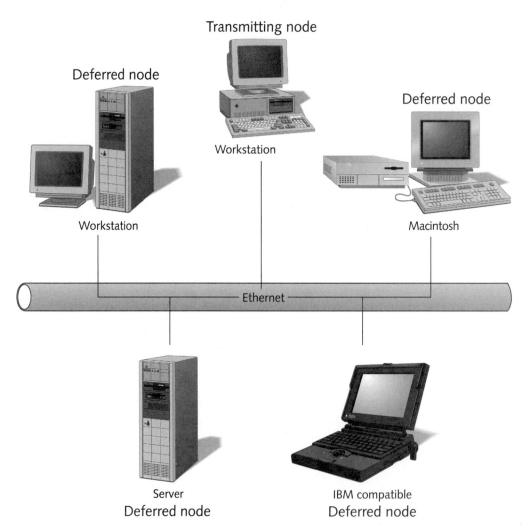

Carrier sense is the process of checking a communication medium, such as cable, for a specific voltage or signal level that indicates the presence of a data-carrying signal.

Occasionally, more than one node transmits at the same time. That is called a **collision**. The transmitting node detects a collision by measuring the signal strength. A collision has occurred if the signal is at least twice the normal strength.

A **collision** occurs when two or more packets are detected at the same time on an Ethernet network.

A transmitting node uses the collision detection algorithm to recover from packet collisions. The algorithm causes the stations that have transmitted to continue their transmission for 32 to 48 bytes. The continued transmission is a jam signal of all 1s that enables all listening nodes to determine that a collision has occurred. The software at each node generates a random number that is used as the interval to wait until retransmitting. That ensures that no two nodes attempt to transmit again at the same time.

NETWORK ADDRESSING

Ethernet addressing is accomplished through the OSI MAC (media access control) sublayer within the data link layer. The MAC sublayer uses an address associated with the NIC to direct encapsulated data to the data link layer of the receiving node. (See chapter 2 for a discussion of the OSI model and the MAC layer.)

Every network node has a unique physical MAC address that is burned into a programmable read only memory chip (PROM) in that node's NIC. Each vendor has a range of addresses it uses to burn into the PROM. Network equipment vendors are registered with the IEEE and receive a range of permitted addresses. MAC addresses are 48 bits long, with the first 24 bits used to identify the vendor. Some examples of vendor IDs follow:

- 02608C, assigned to 3Com Corporation

- 080020, assigned to Sun Microsystems

- 0000A2, assigned to Wellfleet Communications

The last 24 bits in the MAC address are assigned by the vendor. Some vendors use an assignment code to show that the network adapter is for particular types of equipment, for example, to distinguish a workstation from a router. To prevent confusion on the network, it is important that no two network cards have the same address. If that should happen and both NICs are active, network communications are unreliable. It is difficult for the network to determine if packets are being sent or received by a single, distinguishable node.

ETHERNET PHYSICAL LAYER MEDIA

Ethernet data encapsulation and decapsulation are performed at the physical and data link layers by the NIC in the network node. For example, all workstations are connected to the network through a NIC (Figure 4-4). The NIC is a transceiver (transmitter and receiver) and provides channel access to coaxial, twisted-pair, or fiber-optic cable. It also handles the logic that encapsulates the data with the preamble, start delimiter, addressing information, length or type field, data/pad field, and FCS. The NIC contains the algorithms for receiving, decapsulation, transmitting and deferring activity, collision detection, and collision response.

Figure 4-4

Connection
via a NIC

The software algorithms that perform those functions are compiled into programs and related files called network **drivers**. Every NIC requires specific network drivers suited for the network access method, data encapsulation format, cabling type, and physical MAC addressing. The network software drivers incorporate the standards for network layered communications set forth by the OSI model. The drivers enable the NIC to communicate at the physical and data link layers.

 A **driver** is software that enables a computer to communicate with devices like NICs, printers, monitors, and hard disk drives. Each driver has a specific purpose, such as to handle Ethernet network communications. The driver is installed on the computer.

Ethernet communications can use any of several different types of cable media:

- Thick coaxial

- Thin coaxial

- STP (shielded twisted-pair)

- UTP (unshielded twisted-pair)

- Fiber-optic

Tables 4-1 through 4-5 list the specifications for 10-Mbps communications using those media. (Chapter 5 discusses 100-Mbps communications.)

Table 4-1

10BASE5 thick coaxial Ethernet specifications

Specification	Value
Maximum length of one segment	500 m (approx. 1650 ft)
Maximum number of nodes	100 (including terminators)
Minimum distance between nodes	2.5 m (approx. 0.25 ft)
Maximum number of segments	5
Maximum number of segments containing nodes	3
Maximum number of repeaters	4
Maximum total length via repeaters	2500 m (approx. 1.5 miles)
Impedance	50 ohms

Table 4-2

10BASE2 thin coaxial Ethernet specifications

Specification	Value
Maximum length of one segment	185 m (approx. 610.5 ft)
Maximum number of nodes, including terminators and network equipment	30
Minimum distance between nodes	0.5 m (approx. 1.65 ft)
Maximum number of segments	5
Maximum number of segments containing nodes	3
Maximum number of repeaters	4
Maximum total length via repeaters	925 m (approx. 3052.5 ft)
Impedance	50 ohms

Table 4-3

10BASE-T unshielded twisted-pair Ethernet specifications

Specification	Value
Maximum length of one segment	100 m (approx. 330 ft)
Maximum number of nodes per segment	2
Minimum distance between nodes	3 m (approx. 9.9 ft)
Maximum number of segments	1024
Maximum number of segments with nodes	1024
Maximum number of daisy-chained hubs	4
Impedance	100 ohms

Table 4-4

10BASE-T shielded twisted-pair Ethernet specifications

Specification	Value
Maximum length of one segment	100 m (approx. 330 ft)
Maximum number of nodes per segment	2
Minimum distance between nodes	3 m (approx. 9.9 ft)
Maximum number of segments	1024
Maximum number of segments with nodes	1024
Maximum number of daisy-chained hubs	4
Impedance	150 ohms

Table 4-5

10BASE-FL fiber-optic Ethernet specifications (for multimode cable)

Specification	Value
Maximum length of one segment	2000 m (approx. 1.2 miles)
Maximum number of nodes per segment	2
Maximum attenuation	3.75 dB/km for transmissions with a wavelength of 850 nm; 1.5 dB/km for transmissions at 1300 nm
Maximum number of segments	1024
Maximum number of segments with nodes	1024
Maximum number of daisy-chained hubs	4
Cable type	62.5/125 μ

TOKEN RING AND THE IEEE 802.5 STANDARDS

The **token ring** access method was developed by IBM in the 1970s and remains a primary LAN technology. Today the token ring transport method is defined by IEEE's 802.5 standard. The token ring transport method uses a physical star topology but with the logic of a ring topology. Although each node is connected to a central hub, the packet travels from node to node as though there is no starting or ending point. Nodes are joined by use of a **multistation access unit (MAU)** (Figure 4-5). The MAU is a specialized hub that ensures the packet is transmitted around the ring of nodes. Because the packets travel as though in a ring, there are no terminators at the workstations or in the MAU.

The **token ring** network transport method uses a ring topology to pass a token from node to node. The token is used to coordinate transmission of data, because only the node possessing the token can send data.

A **multistation access unit (MAU)** is a central hub that links token ring nodes into a topology that physically resembles a star but in which packets are transferred in a logical ring pattern. Because of the ring logic, a MAU contains no terminators.

The multistation access unit also is referred to by the acronym MSAU. Another name is SMAU, for smart multistation access unit.

Figure 4-5

A token ring network connected through a MAU

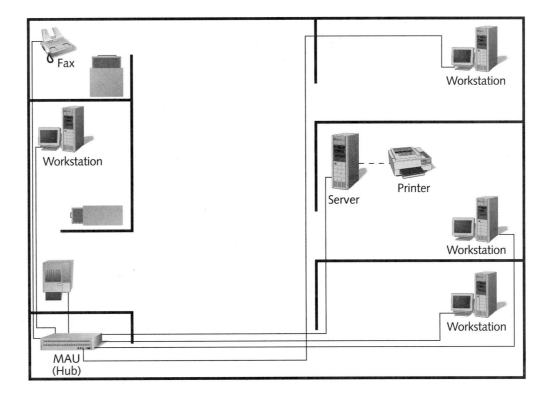

A specialized token is continuously transmitted on the ring to coordinate when a node can send a packet. The token is 24 bits in length, with three 8-bit fields. The fields are the starting delimiter (SD), access control (AC), and the ending delimiter (ED).

The SD is a signal pattern unlike any other on the network, which prevents it from being interpreted as anything else. It is seen as a nondata signal. The unique combination of 8 bits is recognized only as an SOF identifier.

The 8-bit AC field indicates whether an encapsulated data frame is attached to the token. That is, it indicates whether the token is busy carrying data or is free to be used by a node. The ED also is a uniquely encoded nondata signal. The 8 bits compose a signal that is not confused with the SD and that cannot be interpreted as data. The ED portion of the token shows whether more contiguous frames are to be transmitted by a node (a last-frame identifier). It also carries information about any error conditions detected by other stations.

In most implementations, only one token is available on the ring, although the IEEE specifications permit two tokens for networks operating at 16 Mbps or faster. When a node wants to transmit, it must capture the token. No other node can capture the token and transmit until the active node is finished. The station that captures the token builds a frame with the SD and the AC field at the beginning of the frame. The ED is placed at the end of the frame. The resulting packet is sent around the ring until it is read by the target node. It continues around the ring until the original transmitting station picks it up and checks the token to determine if it was received. The transmitting station then encapsulates the next frame of data with the token or builds a token without data to return to the ring so a different station will grab it.

Figure 4-6 shows a token ring frame with the token fields attached to the data fields. The first 16 bits are the SD and the AC fields. Following those fields is the frame control field, which identifies the frame as a data frame or as a frame used for network management, such as reporting network errors. The next two fields are either 16 bits or 48 bits in length and are used for addressing. The first address field contains the destination node address, and the second holds the source node address. Following the addressing fields is the routing information field (RIF), which is 144 bits or less in length. The RIF contains source-routing information that can be used at the network layer of the OSI model.

Figure 4-6

The 802.5 frame format

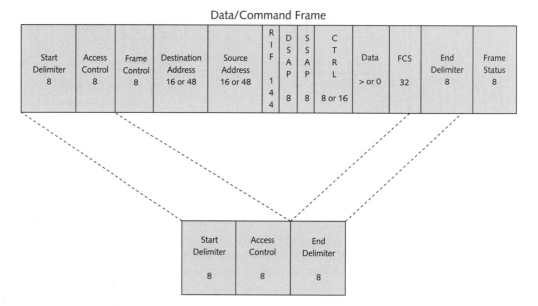

Data/Command Frame

The next three fields enable the data link layer to manage frames and communicate with higher layers of the OSI model. These fields are the destination service access point (DSAP), source service access point (SSAP), and control fields. The DSAP and SSAP are each 8 bits long. Service access points enable the network layer to determine which network process should accept a frame. The DSAP specifies the access point to use to deliver data to the target node. The SSAP is the network layer access point that sent the data. The control field indicates the function of the frame, such as whether it holds data or error reporting information.

The control field is either 8 bits or 16 bits long. After the control field is the data field, which contains data to be sent to a node or error-reporting information to be used for network management. The data field has no determined size. The 32-bit FCS field is used to check the accuracy of the full frame. Similar to an Ethernet frame, it uses a CRC algorithm to ensure that the information is sent and received as intended. The CRC value in the frame received must match the value that was sent.

The ED comes after the FCS field and contains information to show the receiving node that the end of the frame has been reached. It also indicates whether another packet is to be sent from the same node or whether this is the last packet from that node. Finally, it may contain information showing that another station has found an error in the frame and that the frame will be retransmitted. If the frame has an error, the sending node strips (removes) it from the network.

One more field is contained in a token ring frame after the ED. That field is the 8-bit frame status field. Two of those bits are of particular importance to the transmitting node. The address-recognized bit shows that the target node recognized its address as formatted in the frame. The other bit is the frame-copied bit, which shows whether the target node successfully copied the frame as sent.

ERROR DETERMINATION THROUGH BEACONING

Each token ring network designates one node as the active monitor, usually the first station to be recognized when the network is brought up. The active monitor is responsible for packet timing on the network and for issuing new token frames if problems occur. Every few seconds, the active monitor broadcasts a MAC sublayer frame to show it is functioning properly. The other workstation nodes are standby monitors. Periodically, the standby monitors broadcast frames, called "standby monitor present" frames, to show that each is working normally and is available to become the active monitor in case the current active monitor station malfunctions.

If no broadcasts are detected from the active monitor or one of the standby monitors, the ring goes into a beaconing condition. **Beaconing** starts when a node sends a beacon frame to indicate that it has detected a problem. The ring tries to self-correct the problem, such as assigning a new standby monitor if the original has gone out of action. When beaconing occurs, no data tokens are transmitted until the problem is resolved.

 Beaconing is the error condition on a token ring network that indicates one or more nodes is not functioning.

TOKEN RING COMMUNICATIONS MEDIA

Token ring communications use shielded and unshielded twisted-pair and fiber-optic cabling. Seven IBM cable types are used with token ring communications, as shown in Table 4-6.

Table 4-6

Token ring cable specifications

IBM Cable Type	Description
Types 1 and 1A	STP cabling using two pairs of 22-gauge AWG wire surrounded by a mesh shield and used in conduits, inside walls, and in wire troughs
Types 2 and 2A	The same as Type 1 cable, but includes four additional pairs of 22- to 26-gauge AWG conductors outside the shield for telephone use
Type 3	Unshielded four-pair wire, 22- to 24-gauge AWG; not quite as suitable for use as types 1 and 2 due to susceptibility to EMI and RFI
Type 5	62.5/125 or 100/140 μ fiber-optic cable primarily used as a ring backbone
Types 6 and 6A	Shielded 26-gauge AWG wire pairs used as a patch cable and for token ring network adapter cables
Type 8	Shielded 26-gauge AWG twisted-pair wire with a plastic protective ramp; designed for use on the floor when cable cannot be run in walls
Type 9	Shielded single-pair 26-gauge AWG wire with a plenum jacket

At the physical and data link layers, the NIC functions in one of three modes: repeat, transmit, or copy. In the repeat mode, the node has no data to be transmitted. The node's NIC simply reads the token and passes it to the next node. In the transmit mode, the node wants to transmit data. The node's NIC reads the token each time it circulates around the ring, until the token is not busy or reserved by another node. The NIC captures the token and formats a frame with the token and accompanying data. Other nodes on the ring are unable to transmit because the token is not available.

When a node transmits a frame, it is transmitted to all the other nodes for examination. The bits after the SD are read by each node to determine if the frame is intended for that node. If not, the node retransmits the uncopied frame for the next node to read. If the frame is intended for that node, then that node's NIC enters the copy mode. The receiving node copies the frame and returns it to the ring with the information that the frame was successfully addressed and read.

The node that originated the frame receives it last and strips it from the network. Only the sending node is able to strip the frame from the ring. If the sending node has more data to transmit, it places another formatted frame on the ring. When it has finished sending data, the node constructs a 24–bit token to place on the ring for another node to capture.

Originally, token ring networks transmitted at a rate of 4 Mbps. Today the transmission rate is 16 Mbps, and IBM is releasing even faster token ring technology. Nodes equipped to work at 4 Mbps cannot be mixed with those equipped to work at 16 Mbps and vice versa. Table 4-7 lists the IEEE 802.5 specifications for connecting a token ring network.

 At this writing, IBM is working to release NICs and networking equipment for 100-Mbps and 128-Mbps token ring communications. Other networking companies, such as Cisco Systems and 3Com Corporation, also are working to release new high-speed token ring network equipment. The "fast token ring" technologies thus far are designed to operate more like traditional token ring than like the FDDI technology described in chapter 5.

Table 4-7

Token ring design specifications

Specification	Value
Number of nodes per MAU	8
Maximum segment length for type 1 cable when using only 1 MAU	300 m (approx. 990 ft)
Maximum segment length for types 1, 2, 3, and 9 cable	100 m (approx. 330 ft)
Maximum number of MAUs per entire ring	12
Maximum number of nodes per ring for cable types 1, 2, and 9	260
Maximum number of nodes per ring for type 3 cable	72

Token ring networks are extremely reliable and for that reason are used in some mission-critical situations. One advantage of token ring networks over Ethernet networks is that **broadcast storms** and workstation interference are rare. Broadcast storms sometimes occur on Ethernet networks when a large number of nodes attempt to transmit at once or when nodes persist in transmitting repeatedly. Network interference also occurs on Ethernet networks when a damaged NIC continues to broadcast transmissions regardless of whether the network is busy. Those problems are rare on token ring networks, because only one node is able to transmit at a time.

 A **broadcast storm** occurs on an Ethernet network when one or more nodes broadcast continuously, interrupting or delaying successful network transmissions.

MICROSOFT NETWORKING SERVICES

Microsoft operating systems use several networking tools to provide network services over Ethernet and token ring networks: NetBIOS/NetBEUI, NDIS, NWLink, ODI, TCP/IP, DLC, and AppleTalk. The services provided by these tools are summarized in Table 4-8 and described in detail in the following sections.

Table 4-8

Microsoft tools
for Ethernet
and token ring
communications

Service	Function
NetBIOS (Network Basic Input/Output System)	A link to programs that use the NetBIOS interface
NetBEUI (NetBIOS Extended User Interface)	Software drivers for a data transport protocol used on small Microsoft-based networks
NDIS (Network Driver Interface Specification)	Specifications for and software drivers to enable Microsoft-based network protocols to communicate with a NIC
ODI (Open Datalink Interface)	Novell-developed software drivers for communications with Novell NetWare networks
NWLink (NetWare Link)	Microsoft-developed drivers for communications with Novell NetWare networks
TCP/IP (Transmission Control Protocol/Internet Protocol)	Software drivers for TCP/IP communications with mainframes, UNIX computers, and Internet servers
DLC (Microsoft Data Link Protocol)	Software drivers for communications with IBM mainframe and minicomputers
AppleTalk	Software drivers for communications with Apple Macintosh computers

NETBIOS AND NETBEUI

NetBIOS Extended User Interface (NetBEUI) is a communications protocol that is native to Microsoft network communications. First developed by IBM in 1985, it is an enhancement of **Network Basic Input/Output System (NetBIOS)**. NetBIOS, which is not a protocol, is a method for interfacing software with network services. It also provides a naming convention.

 NetBIOS Extended User Interface (NetBEUI) is a protocol that incorporates NetBIOS for communications across a network.

 Network Basic Input/Output System (NetBIOS) is a combination software interface and network-naming convention. It is available in Microsoft operating systems through the file NetBIOS.dll.

NetBIOS

When a software application is written for compatibility with the NetBIOS interface, it calls the NetBIOS.dll file, which links the software to a transport driver. The transport driver communicates with NetBEUI for network transmissions. Microsoft Windows 3.1, 3.11, and 95 are most compatible with older programs requiring the NetBIOS interface. Microsoft NT uses a NetBIOS emulator (a program that simulates NetBIOS) for communications between NetBIOS and NetBEUI. Figure 4-7 illustrates the communication flow from NetBIOS applications to NetBEUI to transport data over a network.

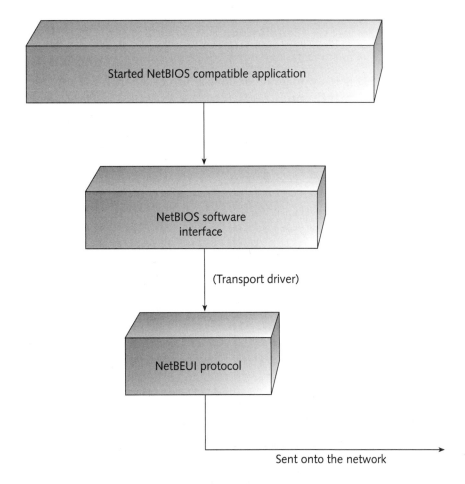

Figure 4-7

NetBIOS/
NetBEUI
communications

NetBIOS names are used to name objects on a network, such as a workstation, a server, or a printer. For example, your workstation might use your last name for identification to other network users, the network printer you access might be named HPLaser, and the server you access might be named Netserver. The NetBIOS Name Query services translate those names, which make it easy for humans to identify particular network resources, into addresses for network communications.

There are two important elements to remember about NetBIOS names. First, each name must be unique. No network object can have the same name as another object; otherwise, there would be great confusion about how to communicate with objects having the same name. Second, names can be no more than 16 characters. The first 15 characters are a user-assigned name; the last character identifies the type of network resource, such as a server or a printer, which the operating system handles using a hexadecimal number.

In this hands-on activity, you use Microsoft Windows 95 to name your computer. You should be at a networked workstation with the Windows 95 desktop displayed.

To give your computer a network name with Windows 95:

1. Click the **Start** button, **Settings**, and **Control Panel**.

2. Double-click the **Network** icon on the Control Panel.

3. Click the **Identification** tab (Figure 4-8).

4. Enter a name for your workstation in the Computer name: text box.

5. Enter a workgroup or domain name (although you may not have one yet), such as **MyGroup**.

6. Enter a description of your computer, such as **Desktop workstation**.

7. Click **OK** at the bottom of the Network dialog box.

Figure 4-8

Entering a
workstation
name

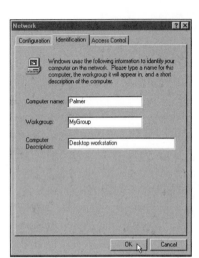

 Name workstations, servers, and printers so others can quickly recognize them. For example, it is easier for someone to realize that a workstation having your last name is associated with you than if you name it BigHoncho or Oyster.

NetBEUI

NetBEUI was developed when computer networking primarily meant local area networking for a relatively small number (e.g., 2 to 200) of computers. It was not developed to take into account enterprise networks where frames are directed from one network to another through routing and routers. For that reason, NetBEUI is well suited for small LANs using Microsoft or IBM operating systems such as the following:

- Microsoft Windows 3.1 or 3.11

- Microsoft Windows 95

- Microsoft LAN Manager

- Microsoft LAN Manager for UNIX

- Microsoft Windows NT

- IBM PCLAN

- IBM LAN Server

NetBEUI on a computer running Windows NT is also called *NBF*, for NetBEUI Frame.

The NetBEUI protocol conforms to the OSI model at several layers. It uses the physical and data link layers for network interface communications. Within the data link layer, it uses the LLC (logical link control) and MAC (media access control) sublayers for work such as flow control of frames, encoding frames, and addressing. It also performs functions that correspond to the transport and session layers, such as ensuring the reliability of transmissions, acknowledging transmissions, and establishing and ending sessions.

NetBEUI is a good choice on small Microsoft networks for several reasons. First, it is simple to install and is compatible with Microsoft workstation and server operating systems. Second, it can handle nearly limitless communication sessions on one network, because the 254-session limitation of earlier versions has been removed. Microsoft specifications, for example, show that a Windows NT server can support 1,000 sessions on one NIC. Third, NetBEUI has low memory requirements and can be transported quickly over small networks. Fourth, it has solid error detection and recovery.

The inability to route NetBEUI is a major disadvantage for medium and large networks, including enterprise networks. That means a NetBEUI frame cannot be forwarded by a router from one network to another, because there is not enough information in the NetBEUI frame to identify specific networks. Another disadvantage is that fewer network analysis tools are available for it than for other protocols. NetBEUI also is not widely supported by computers running non-Microsoft operating systems.

Consider two different networking scenarios. In the first, you are responsible for setting up a network for a credit union that has 52 workstations, 4 network printers, and 1 Microsoft NT server. The network is a star bus topology that contains no routers. This is a good situation in which to use NetBEUI as the sole protocol. In a second scenario, you are setting up communications on a busy college network with 520 nodes, including an IBM mainframe, 10 Microsoft NT servers, and Internet access. This network also is a star bus topology, but it has four routers linking different LANs across campus. NetBEUI is not a good choice in this situation; another protocol, such as TCP/IP (discussed later in this chapter), would be a better choice.

The following hands-on activities show you how to install the NetBEUI protocol in Windows 95 and set up a NIC to work with it.

 In this hands-on activity, you install the NetBEUI protocol. You need a computer with Windows 95 and with a NIC already installed. This activity uses the Intel EtherExpress Pro 100 NIC as an example. Before starting, obtain the NIC driver software disk from your instructor or lab monitor. Start at the Windows desktop.

To set up the NetBEUI protocol for Windows 95:

1. Click the **Start** button, **Settings**, and **Control Panel**.

2. Double-click the **Network** icon.

3. Click the **Configuration** tab, then the **Add** button.

4. Double-click the **Protocol** selection in the Select Network Component Type dialog box (Figure 4-9).

5. Click **Microsoft** in the Manufacturers: text box and double-click **NetBEUI** in the Network Protocols: text box in the Select Network Protocol dialog box (Figure 4-10).

6. If a dialog box is displayed asking for a Windows 95 disk or CD-ROM, insert the disk or CD-ROM, provide the path to the disk, if asked, and click **OK** or **Continue** (depending on the dialog box that is displayed).

Figure 4-9

Setting up a protocol

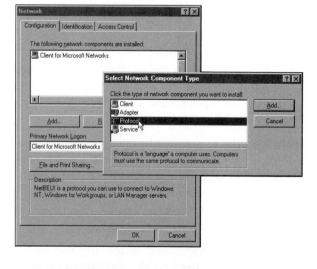

Figure 4-10

Selecting NetBEUI as the protocol

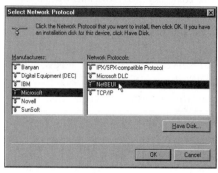

After setting up NetBEUI in Windows 95, you can configure the NIC for your computer. The Network dialog box should be displayed from the last hands-on activity.

To configure a NIC in Windows 95:

1. Click the **Configuration** tab on the Network dialog box.

2. Click the **Add** button.

3. Double-click **Adapter** in the Select Network Component Type dialog box (see Figure 4-9).

4. Select the vendor of your NIC adapter in the Manufacturers: text box and double-click the type of NIC in the Network Adapters: text box. (In Figure 4-11, the vendor is Intel, and the adapter is the Intel EtherExpress PRO/100 (PCI)).

Figure 4-11

Selecting a NIC

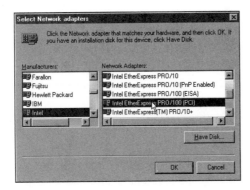

5. Insert the NIC driver disk and enter the path to the disk, such as **A:**, in the Copy manufacturers files from: text box. Click **OK**.

6. Back on the Configuration tab, highlight the NIC, which now appears on the tab, and click the **Properties** button.

7. Click the **Driver Type** tab and click the radio button for **Enhanced mode (32 and 16 bit) NDIS driver** (Figure 4-12). (NDIS is discussed shortly.)

8. Click the **Bindings** tab and check the box for **NetBEUI** (Figure 4-13).

9. Click **OK** on the Properties dialog box and **OK** on the Network dialog box.

Figure 4-12

Entering the driver type

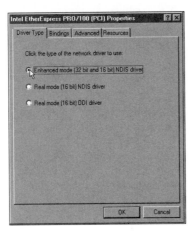

Figure 4-13

Setting
network
bindings

  Establishing **network bindings** is a process that identifies a computer's NIC or a dial-up connection with one or more network protocols to achieve optimum communications with network services. For Microsoft operating systems, you should always bind each protocol used to each network card that is installed.

NDIS

The **Network Driver Interface Specification (NDIS)** is a software driver specification that enables Microsoft network protocols to communicate with a NIC. Binding a protocol to a NIC is accomplished through the NDIS driver. NDIS can bind one or more protocols to a single NIC, allowing the protocols to send information at the same time. For example, you may have one process sending information using the NetBEUI protocol while another process is sending information using the IPX/SPX protocol to communicate with a Novell NetWare server. NDIS operates at the data link LLC sublayer, as shown in Figure 4–14.

Figure 4-14

NDIS
communications

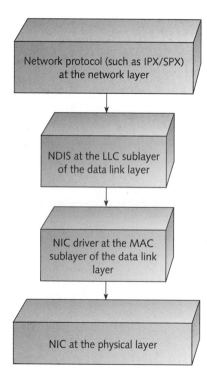

Network Device Interface Specification (NDIS) is a set of standards developed by Microsoft for network drivers that enables communication between a NIC and a protocol, and that enables the use of multiple protocols on the same network. On a computer running Microsoft Windows 95 or NT, NDIS is the file *Ndis.sys*.

ODI

Another driver that can be used to transport multiple protocols is the **Open Datalink Interface (ODI)** driver. This driver is used on Novell NetWare networks to support communications with NetWare file servers, mainframe computers and minicomputers, and the Internet, similar to NDIS. ODI communications can be used on a Microsoft network, but that is not advised. The Microsoft implementation of the ODI driver is as an older 16-bit application, compared to NDIS, which can support both the 16-bit and the more advanced 32-bit drivers.

 The **Open Datalink Interface (ODI)** driver is used by Novell NetWare networks to transport multiple protocols on multiple networks.

 In this hands-on activity, you see where NDIS and ODI drivers are set up. You need a computer with Windows 95 and a NIC that is already installed and set up.

To view where to set up the NDIS and ODI drivers:

1. Click the **Start** button, **Settings**, and **Control Panel**.

2. Double-click the **Network** icon on the Control Panel.

3. Click the **Configuration** tab.

4. Highlight the NIC in the text box labeled, *The following network components are installed:*. Click the **Properties** button.

5. Click the **Driver Type** tab. Notice the three options that are available: Enhanced mode (32 bit and 16 bit) NDIS driver, Real mode (16 bit) NDIS driver, and Real mode (16 bit) ODI driver (see Figure 4-12).

6. Click **Cancel** when you have finished viewing the options.

 Enhanced mode is when the computer processor is set to indirectly access computer memory, enabling it to run several programs at once. **Real mode** is when a computer processor is set to run programs so the programs have direct access to memory locations at 1024K or below and only one program can be run at a time. Real mode may be needed for older MS-DOS and 16-bit Windows programs.

IPX AND NWLINK

Novell adapted one of the early LAN protocols, the **Xerox Network System (XNS)** protocol, for use with its NetWare file server operating system. XNS was introduced by the Xerox Corporation as a means to communicate over Ethernet. In the early 1980s, several vendors implemented their own versions of XNS. Novell's adaptation is called the **Internet Packet Exchange (IPX)** protocol for use with NetWare.

Xerox Network System (XNS) is a protocol developed by Xerox in the early networking days for Ethernet communications.

Internet Packet Exchange (IPX) is a protocol developed by Novell for use with its NetWare file server operating system.

One advantage that IPX has over NetBEUI is that it has routing capabilities, so data is transported over multiple networks in an enterprise. Also, along with IPX, Novell implemented a companion protocol called **Sequence Packet Exchange (SPX)**. SPX enables the exchange of application-specific data with greater reliability than IPX. One use of SPX is for exchange of database data on the network. Novell's remote console utility and print services also take advantage of SPX. That utility enables a workstation to display the same information that appears on a NetWare file server monitor. With the remote console software, a workstation user can execute file server console commands without having to be at the file server keyboard.

Sequence Packet Exchange (SPX) is a Novell protocol used for network transport when there is a particular need for data reliability. IPX is a somewhat faster protocol, but it uses connectionless services, which means there is less checking to make sure that a packet has reached its destination. SPX uses connection-oriented services, making data transport more reliable. In most cases, IPX and SPX are referenced together as IPX/SPX.

IPX/SPX can be deployed on a Microsoft network in one of two ways. One way is to install the ODI driver instead of NDIS at workstations and servers. That method offers limited 16-bit real mode support, so the better way is to use NetWare Link (NWLink). **NWLink** is a network protocol used on Microsoft networks to emulate IPX/SPX. To use NWLink, you first must install the NDIS driver.

NWLink is a network protocol that simulates the IPX/SPX protocol for Microsoft Windows 95 and NT communications with Novell NetWare file servers and compatible devices.

The best way to install NWLink is as part of Client Service for NetWare, which installs the following three elements:

- Client Service for NetWare
- NWLink IPX/SPX Compatible Transport
- NWLink NetBIOS

NWLink offers several advantages, such as routing over enterprise networks. It is easy to install and provides more effective communications with NetWare file servers than the ODI driver. Its disadvantages are that it is not transported as fast as NetBEUI. Also, IPX/SPX and the NWLink emulation really are designed as proprietary protocols used mainly on NetWare networks. Another disadvantage is that IPX/SPX is a "chatty" protocol—each packet transmitted must be acknowledged by the receiving node.

The most common situations for using Microsoft's NWLink to emulate IPX/SPX are (a) to enable a workstation running Microsoft Windows 95 or NT Workstation to communicate with one or more NetWare servers and (b) to set up a Microsoft Windows NT server as a gateway to one or more NetWare servers. For example, assume you are configuring workstations running Windows 95 for a network with five Novell NetWare servers and no other host computers. In that situation, you would configure all workstations to use NWLink. However, consider another situation in which there is one NetWare server and four Windows NT servers on a network and some print services are to be handled through the Windows NT servers. One solution would be to configure all Windows-based workstations for NWLink and NetBEUI. Depending on the access needs to the NetWare server, a better solution would be to configure one of the Windows NT servers for NWLink and set it up to act as a gateway to NetWare by installing Microsoft's Gateway Service for NetWare. Now the workstations would need to use only NetBEUI, because they would access the NetWare server through the Windows NT server gateway. In that instance, the gateway functions to make the NetWare directories appear as a shared folder on the Windows NT server.

In this hands-on activity, you have an opportunity to install NetWare Client Service on a computer running Windows 95 (part 1) or Windows NT 4.0 (part 2). The computer you select should have the NDIS 16-bit/32-bit driver installed.

Part 1: To install NetWare Client Service for Windows 95:

1. Click the **Start** button, **Settings**, and **Control Panel**.

2. Double-click the **Network** icon.

3. Click the **Configuration** tab and then the **Add** button.

4. Double-click the **Client** selection in the Select Network Component Type dialog box (see Figure 4-9).

5. Highlight **Microsoft** in the Manufacturers: text box and double-click **Client for NetWare Networks** in the Network Clients: text box in the Select Network Client dialog box (Figure 4-15).

Figure 4-15

Setting up a client for NetWare Networks

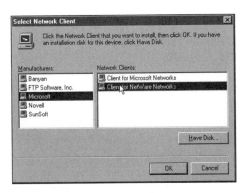

6. If a dialog box is displayed asking for a Windows 95 disk or CD-ROM, insert the disk or CD-ROM, provide the path to the disk, if asked, and click **OK** or **Continue** (depending on the dialog box that is displayed).

7. Click the **Configuration** tab, highlight your NIC, and click **Properties**.

8. Click the **Bindings** tab and check **IPX/SPX-compatible Protocol** for that NIC. Click **OK**.

9. Click **OK** to finish.

Part 2: To install Client Service for NetWare in Windows NT 4.0:

1. Click **Start**, **Settings**, and **Control Panel**.

2. Double-click the **Network** icon.

3. Click the **Services** tab in the Network dialog box and click **Add**.

4. In the Select Network Service dialog box, double-click **Client Service for NetWare** (Figure 4-16).

Figure 4-16

Installing Client Service for NetWare in Windows NT 4.0

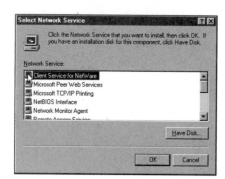

5. Insert the Windows NT CD-ROM. In the Windows NT Setup dialog box, enter the CD-ROM drive letter (such as **E:**) and the **\I386** path (which contains files for Intel-based computers). Click **Continue** to begin loading the NetWare client drivers.

6. Click the **Bindings** tab to automatically bind the protocol.

7. Click **OK** when you have finished.

8. A message appears to say you need to reboot the computer for the protocol to take effect. Click **Yes** to reboot.

TCP/IP

Many network users need to connect to a host computer, such as a mainframe running IBM's Multiple Virtual Storage (MVS) operating system or a minicomputer with UNIX. Another common need is to connect to a host computer that provides access to the Internet or to a Web server. The protocol for those jobs is **Transmission Control Protocol/Internet Protocol (TCP/IP)**. TCP/IP is used around the world for reliable network communications. TCP/IP is many protocols wrapped into one, all working together to establish the most error-free communications possible. The IP portion of the protocol provides network addressing to ensure that data packets quickly reach the correct destination. It uses the dotted decimal notation system of addressing, which consists of four numbers separated by a period, such as 129.77.15.182. The first two numbers identify the network, and the last two are the host number.

Transmission Control Protocol/Internet Protocol (TCP/IP) is a protocol particularly well suited for medium and large networks. The TCP portion was originally developed to ensure reliable connections on government, military, and educational networks. It performs extensive error checking to ensure that data is delivered successfully. The IP portion consists of rules for packaging data and for ensuring that it reaches the correct destination address.

For example, if you needed to access an IBM mainframe connected to your network, you would configure your workstation to use TCP/IP. As a start, the workstation would need a unique IP address, either specified at the workstation or obtained from a server that assigns temporary addresses for a communication session. Depending on the mainframe and application software in use, you might also need special software to emulate an IBM **terminal**, such as an IBM 3270 terminal emulator. The emulation software runs on the workstation so it responds in a way similar to a terminal.

A **terminal** is a device consisting of a monitor and a keyboard to communicate with a host computer that runs the programs. The terminal does not have a processor to use for running programs locally.

Before setting up TCP/IP, you need to make some decisions about how to set up IP addressing on the network. The options are to use what Microsoft calls **static addressing** or **dynamic addressing**. Static addressing involves assigning a dotted decimal address that is each workstation's permanent, unique IP address. This method is used on many networks, large and small, where the network administrator wants direct control over the assigned addresses. Direct control may be necessary when network management software is used to track all network nodes and the software depends on each node having a permanent, known IP address. Permanent addresses give consistency to monitoring network statistics and to keeping historical network performance information. The disadvantage is that IP address administration can be a laborious task on a large network. Most network administrators have an IP database to keep track of currently assigned addresses and unused addresses to assign as new people are connected to the network.

Static addressing is an IP (Internet Protocol) addressing method that requires the network administrator to assign and set up manually a unique network address on each workstation connected to a network.

Dynamic addressing is a method in which an IP (Internet Protocol) address is assigned to a workstation without the need for the network administrator to hard-code it in the workstation's network setup.

Dynamic addressing automatically assigns an IP address to a computer each time it is logged on. An IP address is leased to a particular computer for a defined period of time. This addressing method uses the **Dynamic Host Configuration Protocol (DHCP)**, which is a convention supported by Microsoft for dynamic addressing. The protocol enables a server with DHCP services to detect the presence of a new workstation and to assign an IP address to that workstation. On your network, that would require you to load DHCP services onto a Microsoft NT server and configure it to be a DHCP server. It still would act as a file server but with the added ability to assign IP addresses to workstations automatically. A Windows NT DHCP server leases IP addresses for a specified period of time, which might be one week, one month, one year, or permanently. When the lease is up, the IP address is returned to a pool of available IP addresses maintained by the server. On NT servers that provide Internet communications, when an NT DHCP server is configured, **Windows Internet Naming Service (WINS)** also is installed so that the NT server is both a DHCP and a WINS server. A WINS server is able to translate a workstation name to an IP address for Internet communications, such as translating the workstation name Palmer to its IP address, 129.77.15.182.

Dynamic Host Configuration Protocol (DHCP) provides a way for a server automatically to assign an IP address to a workstation on its network.

The Windows Internet Naming Service (WINS) enables the server to convert workstation names to IP addresses for Internet communications.

When using the DHCP services on a Microsoft network, make sure you use the scope option to set a known range of IP addresses that will be used. That is important to make sure the network is permitted to connect to the Internet using a predetermined set of IP addresses.

In this hands-on activity, you install TCP/IP on a computer running Windows NT 4.0 Workstation or Server.

To install the TCP/IP protocol on a Windows NT computer:

1. Start Windows NT and log on as Administrator or via an account with Administrator access privileges.

2. Click the **Start** button, then **Settings**, then **Control Panel**.

3. Double-click the **Network** icon on the Control Panel.

4. Click the **Protocols** tab on the Network dialog box, then click **Add**.

5. Highlight the **TCP/IP Protocol** option and click **OK**. The TCP/IP Setup dialog box opens, asking if you want to use DHCP.

6. Determine if there is a Windows NT DHCP server on the network. If there is one, you could click Yes to have the server provide IP addressing information for your workstation communications. The TCP/IP configuration would be performed automatically. If there is not a DHCP server, you would need to designate manually an IP address and a **subnet mask** for the adapter card on your workstation. In this example, assume there is not a DHCP server and click **No** (Figure 4-17).

A **subnet mask** is a method to show which part of the IP address uniquely identifies the network and which part uniquely identifies the workstation. For example, on a simple network, the subnet mask might be 255.255.0.0; the first two sets of digits (255 and 255) identify the network, and the third and fourth sets of digits (the 0s) identify the workstation.

Figure 4-17

Indicating if there is a DHCP server

7. Insert the Windows NT Workstation CD-ROM, as requested, enter the path to the CD-ROM drive and **\I386**, and click **Continue**. The \I386 directory contains the drivers needed for Intel-based computers (the I represents Intel, and 386 represents the 80386 and higher-level computers, including Pentiums). The installation program returns to the Protocols tab after the files are loaded.

8. Click the **Bindings** tab to configure automatically the NIC for TCP/IP.

9. Click the **Protocols** tab, highlight **TCP/IP Protocol**, and click the **Properties** button, as shown in Figure 4-18.

Figure 4-18

Accessing the TCP/IP protocol properties

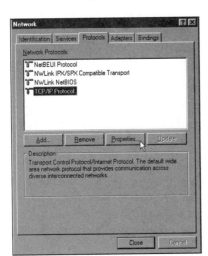

10. Enter the IP address and the address of the network subnet mask in the Specify an IP address section (Figure 4-19).

Figure 4-19

Entering the IP address and subnet mask

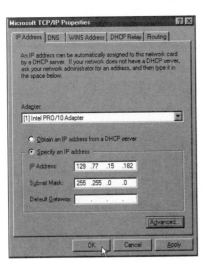

11. If there is a WINS server, click the **WINS Address** tab and enter the addresses of the primary and secondary WINS servers. The primary server is the main server, and the secondary is a backup. If those servers are in use, obtain the addresses from your instructor. Click **OK**.

12. Click **Yes** to reboot your computer to activate the new protocol.

TCP/IP ADVANTAGES AND DISADVANTAGES

TCP/IP has several advantages. It is well suited for medium to large networks and enterprise networks, and the protocol is designed for routing and has a high degree of reliability. It is used worldwide for directly connecting to the Internet and by Web servers. Also, it is compatible with standard tools for analyzing network performance. The parallel ability to use DHCP and WINS through a Microsoft NT server is another strong reason for using TCP/IP.

A disadvantage is that it is more difficult to set up and maintain than NetBEUI or IPX/SPX. Also, TCP/IP is somewhat slower than IPX/SPX and NetBEUI on networks with light to medium traffic volumes. However, it may be faster on heavy-volume networks, where there is a high frequency of routing frames.

One situation in which you would use TCP/IP would be on a large enterprise network, such as on a college or business campus that extensively uses routers and connectivity to mainframe or UNIX computers. You also would use it in smaller network situations, where 100–200 Windows-based workstations access intranet or Internet services through an NT server offering Web services from Microsoft's Internet Information Server.

PROTOCOLS ASSOCIATED WITH TCP/IP

Complementing the main protocols are four application services provided through TCP/IP:

- Telnet
- File Transfer Protocol (FTP)
- Simple Mail Transfer Protocol (SMTP)
- Domain Name Service (DNS)

Telnet is an application protocol within TCP/IP that provides support for terminal emulation, such as for an IBM 3270 terminal or a DEC VT220 terminal. Telnet enables a user to connect to a host computer so that the host responds as though it were connected to a terminal. For example, Telnet with a 3270 emulator can connect to an IBM ES9000 mainframe like a terminal. The ES9000 requires a login ID and a password, just as though it were directly connected to a terminal. Telnet runs in the TCP/IP equivalent to the OSI session layer.

Telnet is a TCP/IP application protocol that provides terminal-emulation services.

Another TCP/IP application protocol, the **file transfer protocol (FTP)**, is an algorithm that enables the transfer of data from one remote device to another, using TCP and Telnet protocols. Through FTP, a user in England can use the Internet to log on to a host computer in California and download one or more data files from the host. (The user first must have an authorized user ID and password on the host.)

The **file transfer protocol (FTP)** is an application protocol within TCP/IP used to transfer data files from one computer system to another, such as from a workstation running a Microsoft operating system to a computer with the UNIX or IBM MVS operating system.

FTP is designed to transfer entire files only in bulk. It does not provide the capability to transfer a portion of a file or records within a file. The FTP transmission is composed of a single stream of data concluded by an end-of-file delimiter. FTP can transfer binary files and ASCII text files.

A popular alternative to FTP is the **network file system (NFS)** software offered by Sun Microsystems. NFS sends data in record streams instead of in bulk file streams. NFS is used by UNIX computers for transferring files, sharing disk storage, and enabling a UNIX workstation to act as a file server.

The **Simple Mail Transfer Protocol (SMTP)** is designed for the exchange of electronic mail between networked systems. UNIX, MVS, and other computer operating systems can exchange messages if they have TCP/IP accompanied by SMTP.

 The **network file system (NFS)** is a UNIX-based network file transfer protocol that ships files as streams of records.

 Simple Mail Transfer Protocol (SMTP) is an e-mail protocol used by systems having TCP/IP network communications

SMTP is an alternative to FTP for sending a file from one computer system to another. SMTP does not require use of a logon ID and a password for the remote system. All that is needed is an e-mail address for the receiving end. SMTP is limited to sending ASCII text files, so files in other formats must be converted to text before they are placed in an SMTP message.

Messages sent through SMTP have two parts: an address header and the message text. The address header can be very long, because it contains the address of every SMTP node through which it has traveled and a date stamp for every transfer point. If the receiving node is unavailable, SMTP can bounce the mail back to the sender.

SMTP is not an X.400 protocol (see chapter 2), but it does establish rules for how the sending and receiving computers need to format and exchange mail. One method employed by SMTP is to create a queue in a file directory. The queue serves as a "post office" for local users on the machine where it resides. If the queue contains messages for another computer system, it notifies the SMTP application on that system and forwards the message.

Another application protocol is **domain name service (DNS)**, which is used to translate domain computer names, such as *microsoft.com*, to an IP address. The DNS software runs on one computer that acts as a network server for the address translations. The process of translating names to addresses is called **resolution**, a process you have used already to access the Internet.

 A **domain name service (DNS)** is a TCP/IP application protocol that translates domain computer names to IP addresses or IP address to domain names. **Resolution** is another term used for the word *translation* in the DNS process.

CONNECTING TO IBM MAINFRAMES WITH DLC

Another way to connect to an IBM mainframe is to use the **Data Link Control Protocol (DLC)**. Microsoft Windows NT 4.0 Workstation and Server and Windows 95 offer a DLC driver that can be installed. DLC is needed to connect to IBM computers when TCP/IP is not available. It does that by providing connectivity to IBM's communication system, called Systems Network Architecture (SNA). Another use for DLC is to communicate with printers directly connected to the network, such as a Hewlett-Packard laser printer equipped with print services and network connectivity.

 The **Data Link Control Protocol (DLC)** is a protocol designed for communications with an IBM mainframe or minicomputer.

The main advantage to using DLC is that it is an alternative to TCP/IP. A disadvantage is that the protocol is not routable. Also, DLC is not truly designed for peer-to-peer communications between workstations but only for connectivity to a computer such as an IBM ES9000 mainframe or an AS/400 minicomputer.

 In this hands-on activity, you install the DLC driver on a Windows 95 workstation.

To install the DLC driver in Windows 95:

1. Click the **Start** button, **Settings**, and **Control Panel**.

2. Double-click the **Network** icon.

3. Click the **Configuration** tab, then the **Add** button.

4. Double-click the **Protocol** selection in the Select Network Component Type dialog box (see Figure 4-9).

5. Highlight **Microsoft** in the Manufacturers: text box and double-click **Microsoft DLC** in the Network Protocols: text box in the Select Network Protocol dialog box (see Figure 4-10).

6. If a dialog box is displayed asking for a Windows 95 disk or CD-ROM, insert the disk or CD-ROM, provide the path, if asked, and click **OK** or **Continue** (depending on the dialog box that is displayed).

7. Click the **Configuration** tab, highlight the workstation's NIC listed under the heading The following network components are installed. Click the **Properties** button for the NIC.

8. Click the **Bindings** tab and check the box for **Microsoft DLC**.

9. Click **OK** and click **OK** again.

CONNECTING TO MACINTOSH COMPUTERS WITH APPLETALK

Macintosh computer networks use a peer-to-peer network protocol called **AppleTalk**. AppleTalk is supported only in very limited ways on non-Macintosh networks. On a Microsoft network, Macintosh computers are linked in by setting up the Windows NT Server Services for Macintosh. The NT server becomes a file server for Macintosh computers as well as for computers running Microsoft operating systems. The NT server also is able to communicate with the Macintosh computers through the AppleTalk protocol and to operate as a print server.

AppleTalk is a peer-to-peer protocol used on networks for communications between Macintosh computers.

A separate disk volume can be created on the Windows NT server for Macintosh files, resembling a shared volume. Access permissions can be set up and logon authentication can be performed to ensure that only authorized users have access.

SETTING PROTOCOL PRIORITY

When you set up a workstation to use multiple protocols, you may experience slow response from the protocol you use most. For example, you might be set up to use NetBEUI to access a Microsoft NT server, IPX/SPX to access a NetWare server, and TCP/IP for Internet access. You access the NT server most, but response is slower than when you access the NetWare server or the Internet (which you access almost as much as the NT server). The solution is to give NetBEUI the first priority in communications, TCP/IP the next priority, and IPX/SPX the third priority.

In this hands-on activity, you set the access priority when multiple protocols are used on a Windows NT 4.0 Workstation computer. You need to make sure two or more protocols are set up already on the computer (such as NetBEUI and IPX/SPX).

To set protocol priorities in Windows NT:

1. Log on as Administrator or via an account with Administrator access privileges.

2. Click the **Start** button, **Settings**, and **Control Panel**.

3. Double-click the **Network** icon.

4. Click the **Services** tab.

5. Click the **Network Access Order** button on the tab.

6. Highlight **Microsoft Windows Network** and click the **Move Up** button until it has the top priority.

7. Click **OK** to finish.

8. Click **OK** again to exit the Network dialog box.

RESOLVING A NIC RESOURCE CONFLICT

When you set up the NIC, check for **resource** conflicts to make sure communications work properly. A workstation's resources include the interrupt request (IRQ) lines, which notify the CPU that an input/output device needs service, and other components such as the input/output address and reserved memory area. A limited number of IRQ lines (say, 1 to 15) are in a computer. The video display, each disk drive, each serial and parallel port, and the sound card use a dedicated IRQ to communicate with the processor. Each also needs reserved memory addresses for input/output operations.

There are two meanings for **resource** in a Microsoft network. The meaning used in the context here refers to the physical components on a workstation. Those components are the IRQs, I/O addresses, and memory that can be allocated to a computer component, such as a disk drive or a communications port. When applied to a network, a resource is a file server, a shared printer, or a shared folder that can be accessed by users.

Often a resource conflict is more subtle than two devices using the same IRQ. A common example is the I/O address range of one device overlapping slightly into that of another device, such as a serial port using the range 02F8-0300 and a NIC using 0300-030F. In that case, both devices are using location 0300, and the easiest solution is to change the range for the serial port.

In this hands-on activity, you see how to detect and solve a resource conflict in Windows 95.

To resolve a resource conflict in Windows 95 using the Network icon:

1. Click the **Start** button, **Settings**, and **Control Panel**.

2. Double-click the **Network** icon.

3. On the **Configuration** tab, highlight the NIC and click the **Properties** button. The Properties dialog box for the NIC opens.

4. Click the **Resources** tab (Figure 4-20).

Figure 4-20

Checking for a resource conflict

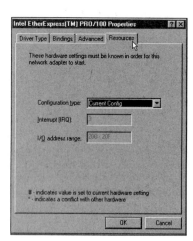

5. A conflict is indicated by an asterisk (*) next to one of the settings. If a conflict exists, the text box Interrupt (IRQ): or I/O address range: not only shows * but also becomes active with up and down arrows to select other resource options to solve the conflict. The absence of an asterisk means no conflict is detected.

6. If you detect a conflict, select another resource option.

7. Click **OK** and click **OK** again.

Another way to solve a resource conflict in Windows 95 is to open the Control Panel and use the System icon. This hands-on exercise shows you how.

To resolve a resource conflict in Windows 95 using the System icon:

1. Double-click the **System** icon on the Control Panel.

2. Click the **Device Manager** tab.

3. Double-click the **Network adapters** icon and click the **Resources** tab. Assume you find an I/O address range conflict with serial port 2 (COM2), and you want to change the resource used by COM2.

4. Double-click the **Ports (COM & LPT)** icon (Figure 4-21).

Figure 4-21

Fixing a conflict with a serial port

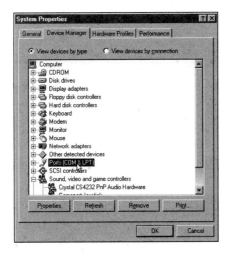

5. Double-click **Communications Port (COM2)**.

6. Click the **Resources** tab.

7. Click to remove the check from **Use automatic settings**.

8. Click the list arrow on the Settings based on: scroll box.

9. Select another Configuration setting in which there is no conflict.

10. Click **OK**.

11. Double-click the **Network adapters** icon and click the **Resources** tab to make sure there is no conflict.

12. Click **OK**.

13. Click **OK** to leave the Network dialog box.

SELECTING THE RIGHT PROTOCOL

The protocols you employ on a network depend on several factors:

- Do frames need to be routed?
- Is the network small (under 100 connections), medium (100 to 500 connections), or large (over 500 connections)?
- Are there Microsoft NT servers?
- Are there mainframe host computers?
- Are there NetWare servers?
- Is there direct access to the Internet or to Web-based intranet applications?
- Are there mission-critical applications?

If there is a need to route frames, such as on an enterprise network, your best choice is likely to be TCP/IP because it is designed for routing and is used on many types of networks. For a small nonrouted network with only Microsoft NT servers, NetBEUI is a good choice because it is native to Microsoft networking and provides fast, reliable communications. A NetWare-only network would use IPX/SPX, while a network with a combination of NetWare and NT servers needs to employ NetBEUI and IPX/SPX. NWLink is a good choice for NetWare client communications from workstations running a Microsoft operating system.

Connectivity to Internet or Web-based services requires that TCP/IP be implemented, so that FTP services can be used to transfer files. TCP/IP also is the first choice for connectivity to mainframe and UNIX computers. The Telnet terminal emulation available through TCP/IP may be needed to connect to the mainframe. If TCP/IP cannot be used, DLC is another option for IBM mainframe and minicomputer communications.

TCP/IP is the protocol of preference for medium- to large-size networks. It can be routed, is reliable for mission-critical applications, and has solid error checking. Network monitoring and analysis are important on such networks, and TCP/IP has associated protocols to accomplish those activities, too.

In many cases, it is necessary to use a combination of protocols for different types of network applications. Modern networks often combine the major protocols, TCP/IP, NetBEUI, and IPX/SPX.

CHAPTER SUMMARY

Protocols are the lifeblood of communications on a network. This chapter began by examining the IEEE 802.3 and 802.5 protocol standards. Both standards are employed widely on networks variously using star, ring, and bus topologies. You also looked at the communication media used with those standards. Because there are many network equipment and high-speed communication options for 802.3, that standard is used on more networks than 802.5. IEEE 802.3 and Ethernet networks are the preferred choices because they dominate the installation base and there is far more vendor development. IEEE 802.5 support and development are much less widespread, the user base is shrinking, and support likely will dwindle in the future.

Microsoft network services include many options for protocol communications. The NDIS driver is fundamental to taking advantage of the Microsoft options. The Microsoft protocol options include NetBEUI, NWLink (for IPX/SPX), TCP/IP, DLC, AppleTalk, among others. All those options provide flexibility for small single-segment networks to large enterprise networks. You had hands-on opportunities to practice installing the protocols in Windows 95 and Windows NT 4.0. You also practiced setting up a NIC, binding protocols to it, and checking for resource conflicts.

In the next chapter, you continue your investigation of protocols by examining high-speed communications. Those communication techniques, such as X.25, Fast Ethernet, and ATM, are becoming more critical each day as users place higher demands on networks.

REVIEW QUESTIONS

1. NetBIOS names
   a. can be up to 16 characters.
   b. must match the name of the domain.
   c. must be unique.
   d. none of the above
   e. both a and c

2. A token ring NIC can operate in which modes at the physical and data link layers?
   a. copy
   b. repeat
   c. transmit
   d. all of the above
   e. both b and c

3. IEEE 802.3 communications use what transport method?
   a. CSMA/CD
   b. token passing
   c. token sharing
   d. flow matching

4. Which of the following protocols cannot be routed?
   a. NetBEUI
   b. TCP/IP
   c. IPX/SPX
   d. none of the above

5. If TCP/IP cannot be used for communications with an IBM mainframe, what other protocol might you use?
   a. NetBEUI
   b. IPX/SPX
   c. DLC
   d. FTP

6. Which protocol is native for communications with Novell NetWare?

    a. NetBEUI

    b. IPX/SPX

    c. TCP/IP

    d. DLC

7. What is the maximum length of a 10BASE-T segment?

    a. 55 m

    b. 80 m

    c. 92 m

    d. 100 m

8. 10BASE2 uses what kind of communications cable?

    a. thin coaxial

    b. thick coaxial

    c. fiber-optic

    d. shielded twisted-pair

    e. unshielded twisted-pair

9. Microsoft's NWLink emulates which protocol?

    a. DLC

    b. TCP/IP

    c. NetBEUI

    d. IPX/SPX

10. What protocol would you most likely use on a Microsoft Windows NT Server network having 42 nodes all using Windows 95 or Windows NT 4.0 Workstation?

    a. DLC

    b. TCP/IP

    c. NetBEUI

    d. IPX/SPX

ASPEN CONSULTING PROJECT: THE PHYSICIANS GROUP, CONTINUED

You still are working with Gary Sharma of the Physicians Group to help him network their new building. Gary has decided to install a Microsoft NT server on his network. Besides connecting to the NT server, the group also will have access to the hospital's computers, an aging IBM AS/400 minicomputer and two Novell NetWare file servers (Figure 4-22). In these assignments, you work with Gary to explore protocol and connectivity options for his situation.

Figure 4-22

Physicians Group project

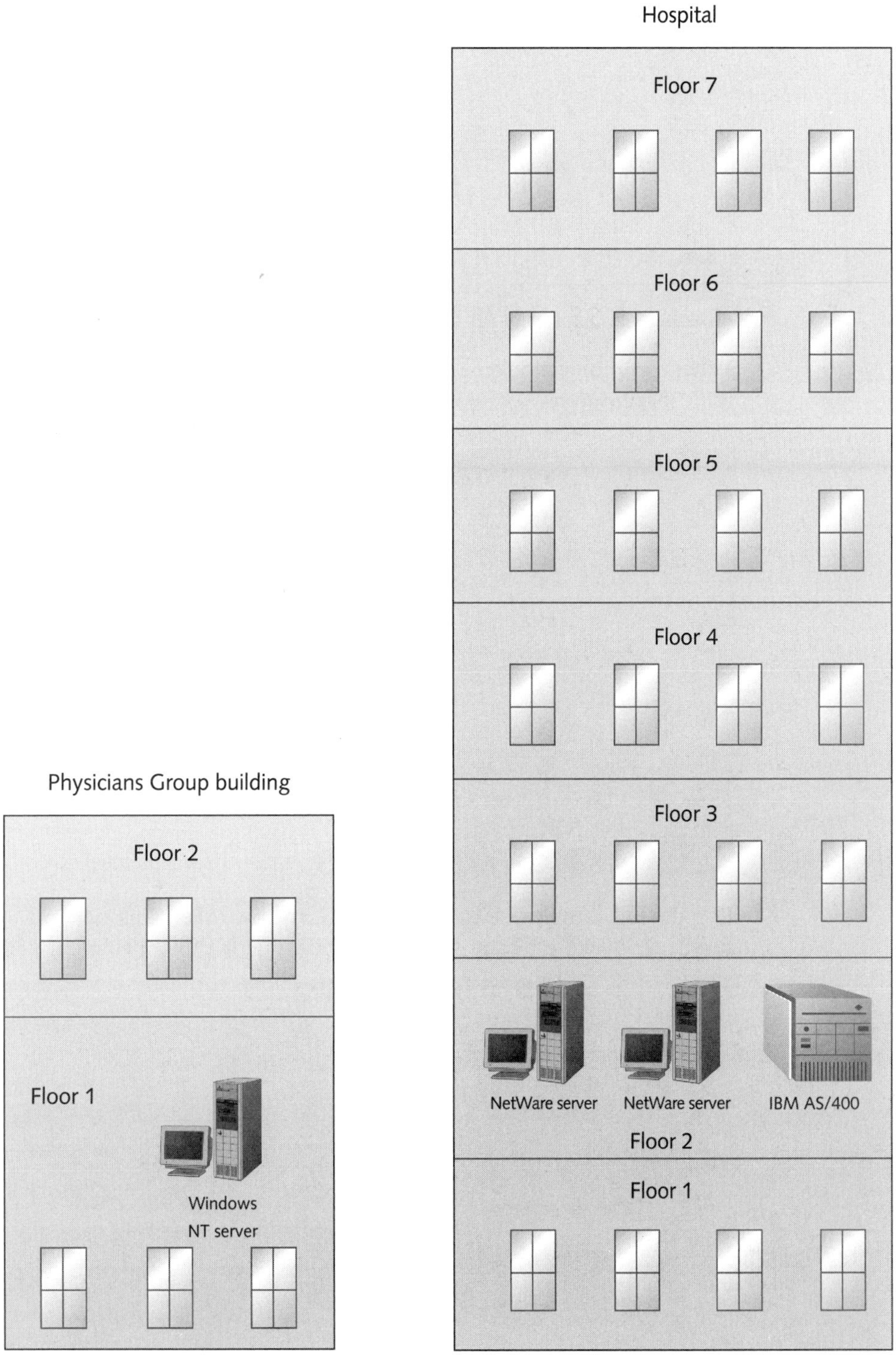

Hospital

Floor 7

Floor 6

Floor 5

Floor 4

Floor 3

NetWare server   NetWare server   IBM AS/400

Floor 2

Floor 1

Physicians Group building

Floor 2

Floor 1

Windows NT server

ASSIGNMENT 4-1

Gary has heard about Ethernet technology, but he is uncertain how it works. Use the space that follows to provide him an explanation of Ethernet. Would you recommend Ethernet for his installation? Why or why not?

 ASSIGNMENT 4-2

What communications media can be used with Ethernet? List three types of media and their specifications.

 ASSIGNMENT 4-3

Use the following space to explain to Gary how token ring networking works. After you finish, use Microsoft Paint to draw an example of a token ring network.

ASSIGNMENT 4-4

Gary has never set up a protocol in Microsoft Windows 95 or Microsoft NT 4.0 Workstation. You decide to show him how to set up NetBEUI. Open the Control Panel and go through the process, writing down the steps in the following table. Use either Windows 95 or NT Workstation to set up NetBEUI, noting in the table which one you used.

Steps to Set Up NetBEUI
Step 1:
Step 2:
Step 3:
Step 4:
Step 5:
Step 6:
Step 7:
Step 8:
Step 9:
Step 10:
Step 11:
Step 12:

ASSIGNMENT 4-5

Show Gary how to set up a NIC in Microsoft Windows 95 or Windows NT 4.0 Workstation. Go through the process and write down the steps in the following table. User either Windows 95 or NT Workstation to set up the NIC, noting in the table which one you used.

Steps to Set Up a NIC
Step 1:
Step 2:
Step 3:
Step 4:
Step 5:
Step 6:
Step 7:
Step 8:
Step 9:
Step 10:
Step 11:
Step 12:

ASSIGNMENT 4-6

While setting up the NIC, you discover there is an IRQ conflict with the parallel port. Go through the steps to resolve the conflict, taking notes for Gary's reference (note if you resolved it in Windows 95 or Windows NT Workstation).

Steps to Resolve an IRQ Conflict
Step 1:
Step 2:
Step 3:
Step 4:
Step 5:
Step 6:
Step 7:
Step 8:
Step 9:
Step 10:
Step 11:
Step 12:

ASSIGNMENT 4-7

You and Gary have been discussing what protocols will be needed for his network. Complete the following table showing the protocols you recommend, why you recommend them, and their overall advantages. If possible, after you finish, ask a network administrator at your school or elsewhere to evaluate your recommendation.

Protocol	Why You Would Use It	Advantages

ASSIGNMENT 4-8

Gary is curious about what happens when an Ethernet segment is too long. In a lab, recreate this type of situation using UTP cable or thin coaxial cable with too much cable in the segment. Answer the following questions:

What type of cable did you use and how long was the segment?

What happened to workstations on the network when you made the segment too long?

OPTIONAL CASE STUDIES FOR TEAMS

 ## TEAM CASE 1

Mark Arnez of Aspen Consulting has a client with an aging IBM mainframe that is worth only $12,000 on the used-equipment market. They have always directly connected to the mainframe using terminals. Now they have a budget to install a network and purchase additional PCs. The client's question is whether to try to connect the PCs to the mainframe or to convert to using file servers. Form a group and list some of the elements involved in the decision, such as ease of network communications, user productivity, and other advantages and disadvantages. What would you recommend?

 ## TEAM CASE 2

Government representatives in Latvia have contacted your consulting firm for help in making a decision. They want to network government offices in the 10 largest cities of the country in order to provide services to those communities. The offices have 50 to 250 workstations each and need to connect to one another to provide critical services. Their question for you is whether to use Ethernet or token ring communications. Form a group to discuss the advantages and the disadvantages of each. Make a recommendation based on your discussion.

 ## TEAM CASE 3

You are working with a small business college that has five labs, each containing 20 to 30 computers and a token ring network. None of the labs is connected to any of the other labs. The college has contacted you for a recommendation on whether to connect the labs keeping token ring communications or to convert to an Ethernet network. Cost is no object because they have a large grant from an anonymous sponsor. Note that the college does want to be able to have high-speed communications capabilities to one lab that is used to teach computer video and graphics techniques. Form a group and make a recommendation.

HIGH-SPEED NETWORK TRANSPORT

A few years ago the instructional computing coordinator at a community college wanted to connect two new offices that had been set up for four instructors. The existing network in that part of the campus was a 10BASE2 thin coaxial Ethernet network. The coordinator removed the terminator from the last workstation on the network and connected some coaxial cable purchased at a local electronics store. He ran the cable through a false ceiling and connected the four workstations (two in each office), placing the terminator on the last workstation. When he finished, all the nodes on the network started to experience problems. Some workstations hung and had to be rebooted, others would not connect at all, and some would work for a short time but then show a disconnection message. After a few days of struggling with these problems, the coordinator contacted a network administrator on campus to help find a solution. The network administrator first counted the number of nodes on the cable segment and found that there were now 32 nodes (including the network devices), two nodes over the 30-node limit. Next she attached a cable scanner to the network to determine if it violated any other IEEE 802.3 specifications (see chapter 4). A **cable scanner** is a device that measures and tests a cable segment. The network administrator found that the end-to-end distance was now 244 meters, well over the 185-meter limit. She also found that the new portion of the cable had an impedance of 54 ohms, instead of 50 ohms.

AFTER READING THIS CHAPTER AND COMPLETING THE EXERCISES YOU WILL BE ABLE TO:

- UNDERSTAND FAST ETHERNET
- DISCUSS FDDI COMMUNICATIONS
- DESCRIBE THE X.25 PACKET-SWITCHING PROTOCOL
- EXPLAIN ISDN COMMUNICATIONS FOR DATA NETWORKS
- UNDERSTAND FRAME RELAY CONCEPTS
- DESCRIBE ATM COMMUNICATIONS
- EXPLAIN SMDS
- DESCRIBE SONET COMMUNICATIONS

A **cable scanner** measures the length of a network cable segment and tests for electrical opens (breaks) and shorts.

In another example, a NetWare server administrator created a new account for an employee. The employee had previously accessed the company's NT server from her workstation running Windows 95 but now needed to use the NetWare server, too. That employee tried to connect to the NetWare server but was never able to view it in Network Neighborhood. She called the administrator, who checked the new account to make sure it was set up properly. When he visited the employee's office, the administrator checked the cable and its connection into the computer. Finally, he realized that her workstation was set up to use NetBEUI for the NT server, but NWLink was not set up for the SPX/IPX protocol communications required by the NetWare server.

Both examples show why a network administrator must have a sound knowledge of the IEEE specifications and of network protocols covered in chapter 4. It also is vital to know about technologies and protocols that enable your network to grow to meet new needs. A basic rule of networking is that you can never have too much bandwidth, in other words, your success as a network administrator leads to demands from users to do more and do it faster. This chapter addresses building more capacity by transporting data on LANs and WANs through high-speed networking options. You'll learn about packet switching, Fast Ethernet, FDDI, X.25, ISDN, frame relay, ATM, SMDS, and SONET, all technologies used for high-capacity WANs and enterprise networks.

WAN AND ENTERPRISE NETWORK COMMUNICATIONS

Many networks start small, such as a network used in a small business or in a single building on a college campus. As the organization grows, so does the network. For example, consider the water consulting company started by a hydrologist in Wyoming. After two years in business, he had eight employees and decided to install a network and a Microsoft NT file server. Before long he had fully networked offices in Wyoming, Colorado, Utah, and California, each with over 30 employees. Because the work involved complex graphical drawings, the hydrologist soon purchased a graphics design company located in the same city as his original office. Two needs quickly emerged: (1) to connect the graphics company with the main office in the same city to form an enterprise network, and (2) to connect the offices in the four states to form an enterprise and wide area network. Figure 5-1 shows a diagram of the four-state network.

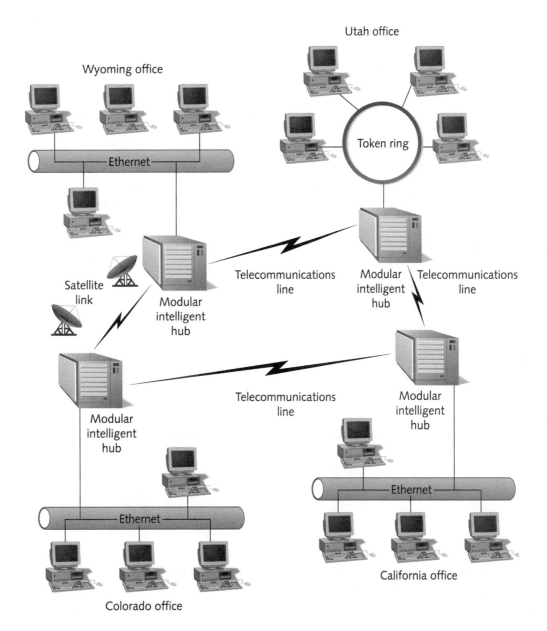

Figure 5-1

A WAN linking offices in four states

Such a network requires special planning. Because the company makes extensive use of large graphics files, the networks must have high-speed, high-capacity ability at each location. The same is true for communications between locations. Several technologies provide alternatives for enterprise and WAN requirements:

- Fast Ethernet
- FDDI
- X.25
- ISDN
- Frame relay
- Cell relay
- ATM
- SMDS
- SONET

This chapter considers each alternative.

In this hands-on activity you practice making a network diagram of a WAN that comprises networks in three cities: Los Angeles, Chicago, and New York.

To diagram a WAN:

1. Open Microsoft Paint from Windows 95 or Windows NT 4.0 Workstation (or use another network drawing application, such as VISIO).

2. Click the **Edit** menu and **Paste From**. Open the network cloud clip art (**cloud.bmp**) provided by your instructor and paste it into the drawing area.

3. Drag the cloud to the upper right corner of the drawing area.

4. Press **[Ctrl]+[C]** to copy the cloud, then press **[Ctrl]+[V]** to paste a duplicate image in the drawing area.

5. Drag the new cloud near the lower center of the drawing area.

6. Press **[Ctrl]+[V]** again to paste another cloud in the drawing area and drag that cloud so it is in the upper left corner.

7. Click the **Line** button 🔲 on the toolbar.

8. Use the crosshair cursor to draw a lightning bolt (to represent the communications link) between the upper-right cloud and the cloud in the lower center of the drawing area. Repeat the process to link the lower-center cloud to the one in the upper left and to connect the upper-left cloud to the upper right one (Figure 5-2).

9. Label the networks **Los Angeles**, **Chicago**, and **New York**.

10. Save your drawing as **WAN diagram** on a floppy disk or to the directory your instructor specifies.

Figure 5-2

Drawing a diagram of a WAN

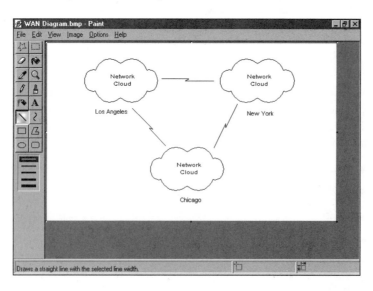

FAST ETHERNET

The need for high-speed solutions has created rapid development of Ethernet products capable of packet transfer rates of 100 Mbps. Manufacturers are offering hubs that can quickly convert a standard 10 Mbps 10BASE-T twisted-pair network to 100 Mbps (if 100 Mbps cable is used), and many Ethernet NICs are available with combined 10/100 Mbps capacities. Prompted by this broad interest, the IEEE has standardized high-speed Ethernet, called **Fast Ethernet**.

Fast Ethernet is Ethernet communications at speeds up to 100 Mbps and is defined under the IEEE 802.3u standard. Besides the 100 Mbps speed, Fast Ethernet has full duplex capability, which means it can send and receive packets at the same time.

At 100 Mbps, a multiple-volume encyclopedia set can be transmitted over a network segment in well under a minute.

Because vendors were divided in the beginning about how to implement Fast Ethernet, two techniques evolved. Hewlett-Packard led the way in developing 100BASE-VG, also called 100VG-AnyLAN, while a group of vendors that includes Bay Networks, Sun Microsystems, and 3Com developed 100BASE-X. Equipment exists for both approaches, but only 100BASE-X is accepted by the IEEE as the Fast Ethernet standard. 100BASE-VG/100VG-AnyLAN is endorsed by the IEEE for fast network communications but not as true Ethernet using CSMA/CD transport. Both techniques employ twisted-pair or fiber-optic cable using a star topology.

Although both 100BASE-VG/100VG-AnyLAN and 100BASE-X are explained here, you should plan to implement 100 Mbps communications using 100BASE-X on your Ethernet network because it is accepted by the IEEE as truly Ethernet-based. There are more network equipment options for 100BASE-X and more assured compatibility with other network options.

THE IEEE 802.12 STANDARD

Adopted by the IEEE as the 802.12 standard, the **100BASE-VG/100VG-AnyLAN** approach abandons the CSMA/CD transmission technique for one called **demand priority**. Demand priority ensures that the transmitted signal travels in only one direction. It is used in star networks, in which workstations are linked by a central hub. In that scheme, each node sends the hub a request to transmit. Requests are granted one by one. Incoming packets are examined for their destination address and sent directly to the recipient node on the star. Because of the physical star configuration, none of the other nodes sees the packet, since it never travels past other nodes. Each packet is moved from the transmitting node through the hub directly to the recipient node (Figure 5-3).

100BASE-VG, also called **100VG-AnyLAN**, is 100 Mbps communications that users demand priority to transmit packets.

Figure 5-3

100BASE-VG/
100VG-AnyLAN
communications

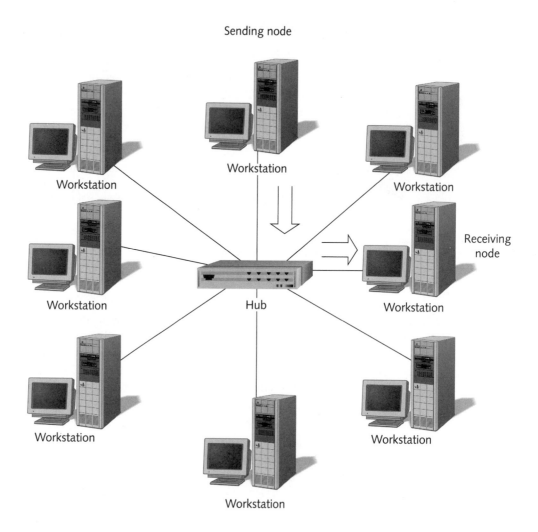

 Demand priority is a data communications technique that transmits a packet directly from the sending node, through a hub, and to the receiving node, without making it available to other network nodes.

Demand priority enables packets to travel up to 100 Mbps by eliminating the possibility of collisions. Besides fast transmission, demand priority has two other important benefits. One is security. Because only the receiving node sees the transmitted packet, data cannot be viewed and decoded at any other node. No other transmission mode can guarantee that type of network security. The other benefit of demand priority is its ability to handle multimedia and time-sensitive transmissions. The highest priority can be given to such transmissions, so that voice and video are transmitted in appropriate time sequences to prevent interruptions.

THE IEEE 802.3U STANDARD

The IEEE 802.3u standard for Fast Ethernet is called **100BASE-X** and uses the CSMA/CD media access method for transmission of signals. Unlike 100BASE-VG/100VG-AnyLAN, the signal is propagated in more than one direction on the network. Signal transmission is on unshielded twisted-pair (UTP) or fiber-optic cable. To work, the 100BASE-X algorithm requires that the total length of the network be limited to 250 meters and that the signal cannot go through more than two repeaters (repeaters are discussed in chapter 6).

100BASE-X is the 100 Mbps Fast Ethernet standard that uses the CSMA/CD access method for communications, as specified in the IEEE 802.3u standard.

As shown in Table 5-1, there are three ways to implement 100BASE-X, depending on the communication medium: 100BASE-TX, 100BASE-T4, and 100BASE-FX. 100BASE-X communications are accomplished by using a switching hub. A switching hub creates many logical communication channels on the communications cable (switching techniques are described later in this chapter and in chapter 6). For example, one way to convert a 10BASE-T network to 100BASE-TX is the following procedure:

1. Replace the 10 Mbps Ethernet NICs with 10/100 or 100 Mbps Ethernet NICs.

2. Make sure all nodes have category 5 UTP cable.

3. Replace the 10BASE-T hub with a 100BASE-TX switching hub.

Figure 5-4 illustrates a 100BASE-TX LAN.

Figure 5-4

A 100BASE-TX LAN

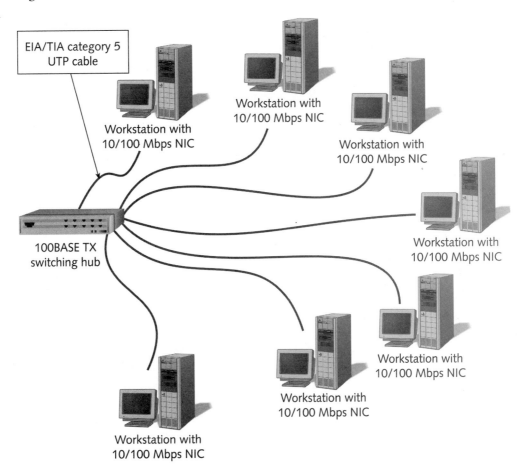

EIA/TIA category 5 UTP cable

Workstation with 10/100 Mbps NIC

Workstation with 10/100 Mbps NIC

Workstation with 10/100 Mbps NIC

Workstation with 10/100 Mbps NIC

100BASE TX switching hub

Workstation with 10/100 Mbps NIC

Workstation with 10/100 Mbps NIC

Workstation with 10/100 Mbps NIC

Workstation with 10/100 Mbps NIC

Table 5-1

100BASE-X
communications
options

100BASE-X Implementation	Description
100BASE-TX	Uses EIA/TIA type 1 or 1A 150-ohm STP (two pairs) or category 5 100-ohm UTP (two pairs) for 100 Mbps communications
100BASE-T4	Uses EIA/TIA 100-ohm category 3, 4, or 5 100-ohm UTP (4 pairs) for 100 Mbps communications
100BASE-FX	Uses duplex (two-way) single- or multimode fiber-optic cable for 100 Mbps communications

Although it is possible to use cable other than category 5 for Fast Ethernet communications, category 5 cable provides the best assurance of reliable high-speed communications.

In this hands-on activity you research the costs of Fast Ethernet switches.

To complete this activity:

1. Search the Internet to find a switch vendor, such as 3Com, Bay Networks, Cabletron, or Hewlett-Packard.

2. Find the price of some Fast Ethernet hubs with about eight connections. Note whether the hubs are 100BASE-VG/100VG-AnyLAN or 100BASE-X technology.

3. Find the price of a Fast Ethernet card for a modular hub (a hub that can be expanded for different communication needs) or for a switch with more than eight connections.

4. Create a document that lists your findings from steps 2 and 3.

FDDI

The **Fiber Distributed Data Interface (FDDI)** standard was developed in the mid-1980s to provide higher-speed data communications than those offered by Ethernet (10 Mbps at the time) or token ring (4 or 16 Mbps). The FDDI standard is defined by the ANSI X3T9.5 standards committee, providing an access method to enable high-capacity data throughput on busy networks. At a data throughput rate of 100 Mbps, FDDI is an improvement over 10 Mbps Ethernet and token ring, but it is used less and less since the development of Fast Ethernet. FDDI uses fiber-optic cable as the communications medium.

Fiber Distributed Data Interface (FDDI) is a fiber-optic data transport method capable of a 100 Mbps transfer rate using a ring topology.

FDDI supports up to 500 nodes on a single fiber-optic cable segment. The ultimate performance capability is a transmission speed of 450,000 packets per second, or 30 times the capacity of 10 Mbps Ethernet communications, which has a 15,000 packets-per-second maximum. Data traffic consisting of voice, video, and **real-time applications** all are supported by FDDI.

 A **real-time application** is one that involves immediate processing results, such as entering a new employee into a human resources database through an application that immediately updates the database as you are working.

THE TIMED TOKEN METHOD

FDDI is similar to the token ring access method because it uses token passing for network communications. It differs from standard token ring in that it uses a timed token access method. An FDDI token travels along the network ring from node to node. If a node does not need to transmit data, it picks up the token and sends it to the next node. If the node possessing the token does need to transmit, it can send as many frames as desired for a fixed amount of time, called the target token rotation time (TTRT). Because FDDI uses a timed token method, it is possible for several frames from several nodes to be on the network at a given time, providing high-capacity communications.

Once a node transmits a frame, the frame goes to the next node on the network ring. Each node determines if the frame is intended for it, and each node checks the frame for errors. If the node is the intended target, it marks the frame as having been read. If any node detects an error, it marks a status bit in the frame to indicate an error condition. When the frame arrives back at the originating node, it is read to determine whether the target node received it. The frame also is checked for errors. If an error is detected, the frame is retransmitted. If no errors are found, the frame is removed from the ring by the originating node. Figure 5-5 shows the FDDI timed token access method.

Figure 5-5

Timed-token access method

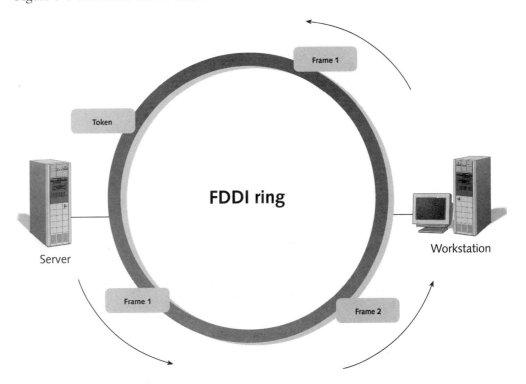

Two types of packets can be sent by FDDI: synchronous and asynchronous. **Synchronous communications** are used for time-sensitive transmissions that require continuous transmission, such as voice, video, and real-time traffic. **Asynchronous communications** are used for normal data traffic that does not have to be sent in continuous bursts. On a given network, the TTRT equals the total time needed for a node's synchronous transmissions plus the time it takes for the largest frame to travel around the ring.

Synchronous communications are continuous bursts of data controlled by a clock signal that starts each burst (like a starter at a cross-country foot race who fires a starting pistol at certain intervals to start different heats of runners on the same course). **Asynchronous communications** occur in discrete units in which a start bit at the front signals the start of a unit and a stop bit at the back signals the end of the unit (similar to a starter at a race who fires a pistol to start a race and again at the end).

FDDI PACKET FORMAT

FDDI's frame format is similar but not identical to that used by standard token ring (Figure 5-6). The beginning field in the packet is the preamble. Its purpose is to synchronize each station's transmission of the packet. The synchronization is important because, unlike token ring, FDDI permits more than one token on the network at a given moment. The preamble holds 64 bits that have no purpose other than as clocking signals. The start delimiter is part of the FDDI token and is 8 bits long. As with standard token ring, it signifies the start of the token. The next field is called the frame control. This 8-bit field shows the type of frame being transmitted, synchronous or asynchronous. It also shows if the address lengths are 16 bits or 48 bits, and it specifies if the frame carries data or network control information. As specified in the frame control, an FDDI address can be 16 or 48 bits. The first address field contains the destination address. The next address field has the source address.

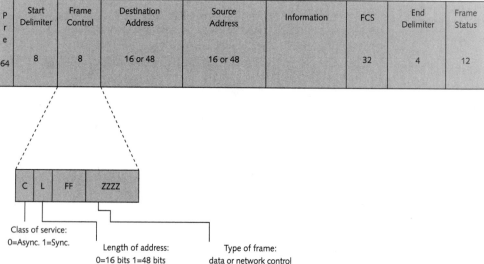

Figure 5-6

FDDI frame format

Following the address fields is the information field, which contains data for the receiving station or information about the network status. No specific size is associated with the information field.

Similar to Ethernet and token ring, FDDI has a frame check sequence (FCS) that uses a CRC value. The CRC value, calculated by the destination node, must be the same as the corresponding value sent by the source node. If not, an error condition is generated. The CRC value is calculated from information in the frame control field, the address fields, and the information field. The FCS field is 32 bits in length. The end delimiter shows that the end of the frame has been reached. Like the start delimiter, it is part of the FDDI token. The end delimiter is 4 bits long.

Last in the FDDI packet frame is the frame status field. It enables further error checking by showing whether the destination address was recognized and copied by the target node. The frame status field also may contain information on whether an error has occurred, for example, if a packet is received malformed and needs to be retransmitted. The frame status field is 12 bits long.

An FDDI token consists of the preamble, start delimiter, frame control, and end delimiter.

FDDI ERROR DETECTION

FDDI nodes monitor the network for two types of error conditions: long periods of no activity and long periods in which the token is not present. In the first instance, the token is presumed to be lost; in the second instance, a node is assumed to be transmitting continuously. If either error condition is present, the node that detects the error sends a stream of specialized frames called claim frames. The claim frames contain a proposed TTRT value. The first node stops transmitting, and the next node on the ring compares its proposed TTRT value with the value sent by the previous node. After the comparison, the second node sends the lower of the TTRT values in its claim frames to the next node. By the time the last node is reached, the smallest TTRT value has been selected. At that point the ring is initialized by transmitting the token and the new TTRT value to each node until the last node is reached.

FDDI COMMUNICATIONS MEDIA

FDDI employs single-mode or multimode fiber-optic cable. A mode is like a bundle of light entering the fiber at a particular angle. Single-mode cable allows one bundle of light to enter the fiber, whereas multimode cable allows many bundles of light to enter at a given time. Single-mode fiber is used for network backbones in which data must travel over long distances. Multimode fiber is used for desktop workgroup applications that involve shorter transmission distances.

FDDI networks have data transmission redundancy, making them highly reliable. Redundancy is accomplished by using two network rings. One ring is defined as the primary cable run for information transmission. The secondary ring provides a backup route for transmitted information, should the primary ring be broken. Data on the secondary ring travels in the opposite direction from data on the primary ring (Figure 5-7). If there is a failure in the FDDI primary ring, the logic of the cable architecture provides wrapping. That means the signal is directed onto the cable route so it doubles back to become a single ring. Fault-tolerant wrapping is shown in Figure 5-8.

Figure 5-7

FDDI dual ring

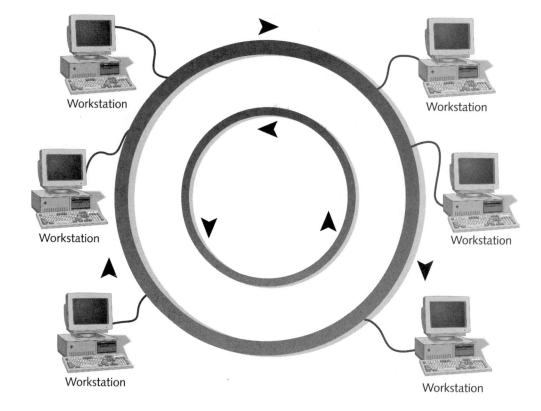

Figure 5-8

FDDI wrapping
in an error
condition

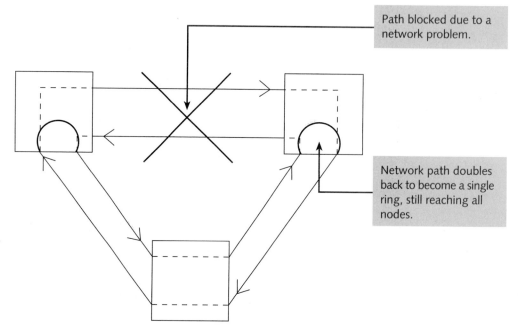

Path blocked due to a
network problem.

Network path doubles
back to become a single
ring, still reaching all
nodes.

Two classes of nodes connect to FDDI. **Class A nodes** are attached to both network
rings and consist of network equipment, such as hubs. Class A nodes have the ability to
reconfigure the ring to enable wrapping in the event of a network failure. **Class B nodes**
connect to the FDDI network through Class A devices and attach to the primary ring
only. Class B nodes are servers or workstations.

A **Class A node**, or dual-attached node, on an FDDI ring is a network device, such as a hub, that is connected to both rings in the FDDI architecture.

 A **Class B node**, or single-attached node, in FDDI is a workstation, server, or host computer that connects to the primary ring only and through that connects to a Class A node (hub).

 In this hands-on exercise you gain experience with FDDI. It requires that FDDI equipment be available.

To investigate FDDI transmission:

1. If your school or lab has an FDDI installation, schedule a time to see it.

2. Examine an FDDI network interface to a hub.

3. Find out what communications media are used to Class A and Class B nodes.

4. If the installation is used in a live setting, find out how it is used, for example, for academic or administrative computing.

5. Create a document and record your findings from steps 3 and 4.

X.25

The **X.25** protocol is a packet-switching protocol developed by the CCITT to ensure reliable data communications, even over networks with low-quality transmission equipment. The X.25 protocol is used internationally for public data networks. With a transmission rate up to 64 Kbps, it is suitable for connecting older networks with low transmission rates. X.25 is not commonly used in the United States, because it is too slow to provide services for most WANs. At 64 Kbps, X.25 is not as fast as newer technologies, but it offers some advantages until the technology in less-developed countries catches up. Its strength is that it is a well-established, dependable technology. For example, X.25 continues to be a reliable way to connect older mainframes, minicomputers, and early LANs with communications slower than 10 Mbps.

 X.25 is a packet-switching protocol for connecting remote networks at speeds up to 64 Kbps.

SWITCHING TECHNIQUES

Switching is a technique for sending an information-carrying signal from one point on a network to another but along different paths, much as trains are switched over multiple tracks. There are three ways to perform switching: circuit switching, message switching, and packet switching. **Circuit switching** involves creating a dedicated physical circuit between the sending node and the receiving node. Circuit switching acts as a straight channel on which to send data back and forth without interruption, similar to making a telephone call between two parties. The transmission channel remains in service until the two nodes disconnect.

Circuit switching is a network communication technique that uses a dedicated channel to transmit information between two nodes.

Message switching uses a store-and-forward communication method to transmit data from the sending node to the receiving node. The data is sent from one node to another one that stores it temporarily until a route is open on the next leg of the journey so the data can be forwarded. Several nodes along the route store and forward the data until it reaches the destination node. One example is sending an e-mail message on an enterprise network with five servers acting as "post offices." The message goes from one post office to the next until it reaches the intended recipient.

Message switching sends data from point to point, with each intermediate node storing the data, waiting for a free transmission channel, and forwarding the data to the next point until the destination is reached.

Packet switching is a combination of circuit and message switching. It establishes a dedicated circuit between the two transmitting nodes, but the circuit is a logical connection, not a physical one. Several different physical routes may be used during the session, but each node is aware only that there is a dedicated channel. The advantages of packet switching are that the best route can be established for the type and the amount of data sent, creating an opportunity to make the transmissions high speed. It is similar to looking through a periscope: the view appears to be in a straight line, but the image actually travels from point to point along a nonlinear path.

Packet switching is a data transmission technique that establishes a logical channel between two transmitting nodes but uses several different paths of transmission to continually find the best routes to the destination.

X.25 TRANSMISSION MODES

An X.25 network can transmit data packets using one of three modes: switched virtual circuits, permanent virtual circuits, or datagrams. A **switched virtual circuit** is a two-way channel established from station to station through an X.25 switch. The circuit is a logical connection that is established only for the duration of the data transmission. Once the transmission is completed, the channel can be made available to other nodes. **Permanent virtual circuits** are logical communication channels that remain connected at all times. The connection remains in place even when data transmission stops. Both switched and permanent virtual circuits are examples of packet switching.

Datagrams are packaged data sent without the establishment of a communication channel and are a form of message switching. The packets are addressed to a given destination and may arrive at different times, depending on which path is selected. Datagrams are not used on international networks but were included in the CCITT specifications for the Internet. The X.25 Internet datagram encapsulates the IP (Internet Protocol) layer within the X.25 packet, so the X.25 device is not aware of the IP component. The IP network address is simply mapped to the X.25 destination address.

A **switched virtual circuit** is a communication channel that is established for only as long as the communication session lasts.

In a **permanent virtual circuit** the communication channel stays connected at all times, even after the communication session is over.

An X.25 **datagram** does not use a particular communication channel. Data arrives at the destination node at different times, because each datagram may follow a different route to the destination.

X.25 PACKET SWITCHING

The X.25 standard defines communications between two types of entities: data terminal equipment and data communications equipment. **Data terminal equipment (DTE)** can be a terminal, a PC, or a host computer. **Data communications equipment (DCE)** is network equipment that functions as a packet-switching node. In the most common configuration, the DTE is attached to a **packet assembler/disassembler (PAD)**. The PAD translates data from the DTE into X.25 format. It also translates the received X.25 formatted data into a format understood by the DTE. Software at the PAD formats the data and provides extensive error checking. PADs also can send out data from several DTEs at the same time, which they do through packet switching.

Data terminal equipment (DTE) consists of terminals, workstations, servers, and host computers that operate on a packet-switching network.

Data communications equipment (DCE) consists of network devices that perform packet switching.

A **packet assembler/disassembler (PAD)** is a device that converts data from a format used by a DCE to one that can be placed on an X.25 communications network, and it translates data received in an X.25 communications format to a format that can be read by a DCE.

This form of packet switching involves transmitting messages using a store-and-forward technique. The data messages are broken into packets by the DTE and sent to the PAD. The PAD can send data from multiple DTEs over one cable medium to a packet-switched node (DCE). The DCE is a switch that is physically connected to several other DCEs. On an X.25 network, the DCE is a physical switch that can send data over several logical channels created by the X.25 protocol design. The switch receives the transmitted packets and stores them in a buffer until the intended transmission channel becomes available. Then the packets are forwarded to their destination, where the DTE reassembles the packets in their original order.

Because X.25 supports multiple channels, several DTEs can transmit at the same time. The switch sequentially switches from channel to channel, transmitting the data from each DTE. Figure 5-9 illustrates an X.25 network.

Figure 5-9

X.25 network

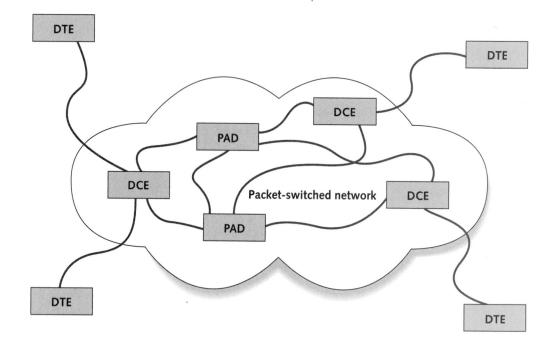

X.25 COMMUNICATION LAYERS

The CCITT specifications have defined three layers in X.25 for communications between DTEs and DCEs (Figure 5-10). The physical layer, or layer 1, is described by CCITT's X.21 standard. This layer is associated with physical connections, data–bit representation, and timing and control signals. The physical interface is similar to the EIA-232C/D standard for a serial communications port on a PC.

X.25's layer 2 is equivalent to the OSI data link layer. This layer provides the basic point-to-point connection between the DTE and the network. It is responsible for data transfer, error checking, and flow control. Layer 3 is like the OSI network layer and handles packet formatting and packet switching. It can switch up to 4,095 simultaneous logical connections over one link–level physical connection.

Figure 5-10

Relationship of X.25 communication layers and the OSI mode

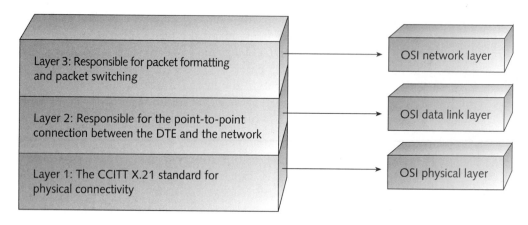

ISDN

Integrated Services Digital Network (ISDN) was introduced in the 1970s by the CCITT to provide voice, data, graphics, and video digital services. The first CCITT set of standards was made official in 1984 and later refined in 1988. The "I" series of standards from 1988 includes the following:

- I.100. This portion of the standards is an introduction to ISDN, and a glossary of terms.

- I.200. The services provided to users include:
  - Complete guaranteed end-to-end compatibility
  - Standardized terminals and procedures
  - Listing of ISDN subscribers in an international directory
  - Standard testing and maintenance procedures
  - Charging and account rules

- I.300. This series focuses on network issues such as numbering and addressing.

- I.400. This portion deals with network interface topics such as equipment configurations, transmission rates, and protocol specifications.

- I.500. This defines the interface between ISDN and dissimilar networks.

- I.600. Subscriber installation, access services, and general architecture are defined here.

Integrated Services Digital Network (ISDN) is a standard for delivering data services over telephone lines, with a current practical limit of 64 Kbps and a theoretical limit of 622 Mbps.

The benefits of ISDN are summarized in Table 5-2. Implementation of ISDN has been expensive for long-distance carriers. Because ISDN is entirely digital, old analog and electromechanical switches have to be replaced. The major U.S. long-distance carriers, such as AT&T, MCI, and Sprint, are implementing ISDN as they replace aging equipment.

Table 5-2

Advantages of ISDN

Provides voice, data, and video services over one network
Has a layered protocol structure compatible with OSI
Offers communications channels in multiples of 64 Kbps, 384 Kbps, and 1,536 Kbps
Has switched and nonswitched connection services
Has broadband ISDN capabilities of 155–622 Mbps

I.200 Services for Networking

The I.200 portion of the CCITT specifications for ISDN offers various networking capabilities, divided into bearer services, teleservices, and supplementary services. The bearer services include circuit-mode and packet-mode options. The circuit-mode options are shown in Table 5-3. Packet-mode bearer services include virtual call and permanent virtual call circuits that are modeled after X.25 switched and permanent virtual circuits. The second column in Table 5-3 lists the names of the ISDN communications channels used to deliver the services.

Table 5-3

ISDN circuit modes

Information Rate	Channel	Applications
64 Kbps	B	8-KHz general purpose communications
64 Kbps	B	8-KHz digitized speech
64 Kbps	B	3.1-KHz audio
64 Kbps	B	8-KHz alternate transfer of speech
8 or 16 Kbps	C	8-KHz signaling
384 Kbps	D	8-KHz video and PBX link ■ Fast fax ■ Computer imaging ■ High-speed data ■ LAN internetworking
1,536 Kbps	H11	Same services as 384 Kbps
155 Mbps	H4X	High-speed data, voice, and video

The teleservices provide for 3.1-KHz speech communications. They also include telex for interactive text communications, fax, and videotex, which provides for retrieval of digital mailbox information, including text and graphics. Supplementary services are available primarily for voice communications, including caller ID and conference calling.

Digital Communications Techniques

Two interfaces are supported in ISDN: basic rate interface and primary rate interface. The **basic rate interface (BRI)** has an aggregate data rate of 144 Kbps. Because many conventional LANs have data rates of 1–16 Mbps, ISDN BRI is not suitable for some network applications such as file transfer and graphics.

The ISDN **basic rate interface (BRI)** consists of three channels. Two are 64-Kbps channels for data, voice, and graphics transmissions. The third is a 16-Kbps channel used for communications signaling.

The **primary rate interface (PRI)** supports faster data rates, particularly on channel H11, which offers switched bandwidth in increments of 1,536 Kbps. As high-speed networks are developing, so are advances in **broadband ISDN (B-ISDN)** with data rates of 155–622 Mbps.

The ISDN **primary rate interface (PRI)** consists of switched communications in multiples of 1,536 Kbps.

 Broadband ISDN (B-ISDN) is being developed to provide an initial ISDN data transfer rate of 155 Mbps. The theoretical limit is 622 Mbps.

ISDN is compatible with many existing digital networks and telecommunications technologies, such as ATM, X.25, and T1. As shown in Table 5-3, ISDN is divided into 64-Kbps channels, which include channels B, C, D, H11, H12 (used in Europe), and H4X (broadband). Digital signals are placed on the network in two ways. One method is time-compression **multiplexing**, which sends 16- to 24-bit blocks of data in alternating digital bursts. A quiet period between bursts allows the line to settle before the next burst. Consequently, the first burst goes in one direction, followed by a pause. The pause is followed by a burst in the opposite direction. Each burst is 288 Kbps. Because of the direction switching, the total data rate is 144 Kbps. The data bursts are managed by central timing control.

 Multiplexing is a form of circuit switching in which several physical channels are connected to a switch called a multiplexer. Multiple computers also are connected to the switch, transmitting along the channels whose access is controlled by the switch. (Multiplexers are described in chapter 6.)

The second method is echo cancellation. This method transmits data in two directions at the same time. A device called a hybrid connects the transmitter and the receiver to the subscription line. The two-way simultaneous transmissions often cause reflection (echo) of the transmitted signal. Echo of signals on the line may be three times greater than the power of the true signals, thus obscuring the data. ISDN uses an echo canceler to overcome the reflected signals. The echo canceler determines the amplitude of the echoed signals and subtracts the amplitude from the incoming signals. Since the amount of echo can vary, the echo canceler employs a feedback circuit that enables it to continuously measure the amplitude of the signal reflection.

T-CARRIER

A **T-carrier** is a dedicated telephone line that can be used for data communications to connect two different locations. For example, some universities use T-carrier lines to connect to one another for Internet communications. Some states use T-carrier lines to connect branch offices and colleges into the government headquarters in the state capitol. T-carrier lines offer dependable service over long distances.

 A **T-carrier** is a dedicated telephone line for data communications.

T-carriers use switching techniques (time division multiple access, which is discussed in chapter 6) to offer high-speed data transmission options. The smallest carrier service, T1, offers 1.544 Mbps data communications that can be switched to create multiple data channels for high-speed communication (Table 5-4). For example, switching T1 to the next level of service, called T2, creates four channels. T3 has 28 channels, and T4 has 168 channels. Because T-carrier service is expensive, telephone companies offer fractional services that use a portion of the T1 service, utilizing subchannels with 64-Kbps speeds. That is possible because each T1 service consists of twenty-four 64-Kbps subchannels, called data signal at level 0 (DS-0) channels.

Table 5-4

T-carrier services and data rates

T-Carrier	Data Transmission Rate	T1 Switched Channels	Data Signal Level
Fractional T1	64 Kbps	1 of 24 T1 subchannels	DS-0
T1	1.544 Mbps	1	DS-1
T2	6.312 Mbps	4	DS-2
T3	44.736 Mbps	28	DS-3
T4	274.176 Mbps	168	DS-4

ISDN AND OSI LAYERED COMMUNICATIONS

ISDN incorporates the physical, data link, network, and transport layers of the OSI model (Figure 5-11). It uses the data link layer to ensure maximum detection of communication errors for highly reliable communications.

Figure 5-11

Relationship of ISDN layered communications to the OSI model

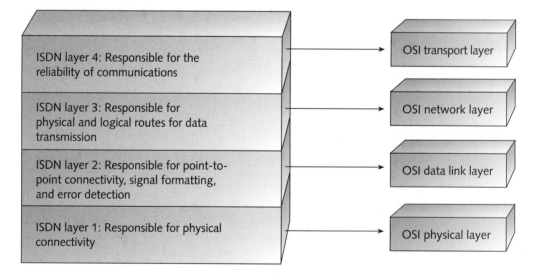

In this hands-on exercise you determine the costs of ISDN and T-carrier communications.

To complete the exercise:

1. Call your local telephone company or contact a telephone company through the Internet.

2. Find out what areas in your region have ISDN services.

3. Ask about the rates for ISDN services, including residential and commercial rates.

4. Find out what equipment and software are needed to connect to the ISDN services.

5. Ask about rates for fractional T1 and T1 services.

6. Create a document that summarizes your findings.

FRAME RELAY

CCITT standards for **frame relay** were introduced in 1988 to meet the demands of high-volume, high-bandwidth WANs. Additional standards were approved in 1990, 1992, and 1993 to meet the evolving demand for frame relay. Nearly 60% of Fortune 1000 companies use frame relay or plan to do so.

The concept behind this technology is similar to X.25, in that frame relay uses packet switching along with virtual circuit techniques. Unlike X.25 and ISDN, frame relay is designed to interface with modern networks that do their own error checking. It achieves high-speed data transmission by recognizing that newer network technologies have error checking on intermediate nodes, so it does not incorporate extensive error checking. For example, frame relay is used with TCP/IP- or IPX-based networks, where those protocols handle the end-to-end error checking.

Frame relay is a communications protocol that relies on packet switching and virtual circuit technology to transmit data packets. It does not incorporate extensive error checking, assuming that intermediate nodes will perform that task.

Frame relay does look for bad frame check sequences. If it detects errors that were not discovered by intermediate nodes, it discards the bad packets. It also discards packets if it detects heavy network congestion, a disadvantage that should be considered.

SWITCHING AND VIRTUAL CIRCUITS

Frame relay uses multiple virtual circuits over a single cable medium. Each virtual circuit provides a data path between two communicating nodes. As is true for X.25 communications, the virtual circuits are a logical rather than a physical connection. Two types of virtual circuits exist in frame relay: permanent and switched.

A permanent virtual circuit is a continuously available path between two nodes. The path is given a circuit ID that is part of every transmitted packet. Once the circuit is defined, it remains open, so communication can occur at any time. Permanent virtual circuits apply only the physical and data link layers of the OSI model. Signal transmission is handled at the physical layer, and virtual circuits are part of the data link layer. A single cable medium can support multiple virtual circuits to different network destinations.

A switched virtual circuit transmission is based on the need to establish a transmission session. A call-control signal is sent between the nodes to establish communication. Once the communication is finished, the call control signal issues a command for each node to disconnect. A switched virtual circuit connection is designed to allow the network or the T-carrier provider to determine the data throughput rate. It can be adjusted based on the needs of the application and the current network traffic conditions. Multiple switched virtual circuits can be supported on a single cable from point to point. Switched virtual circuit standards were issued in early 1994 for frame relay. Switched virtual circuits represent a newer technology in frame relay than permanent virtual circuits.

Switched virtual circuits use the physical, data link, and network portions of the OSI model. The physical and data link layers perform the same functions as in permanent virtual circuits. The network layer is used for call-control signaling protocols.

Frame relay technology is used with fiber-optic or compatible twisted-pair cable, including T1 and T3 fiber-optic media. Currently, it can deliver packets at speeds up to 1.544 Mbps (T1 speeds). The anticipated maximum data transfer rate for evolving broadband applications includes speeds up to 44.7 Mbps.

CELL RELAY

Cell relay is a developing technology that takes frame relay a step further. Because frame relay breaks data into packets designed for switched store-and-forward transmission, it is not suitable for voice and video applications. Cell relay creates large fixed-length data entities called **cells**. When transmitted, a cell may be empty or full of data. The cell relay technology enables information to be sent without the packet-switching delays of frame relay.

 Cell relay is a communications protocol that uses large fixed-length cells to transmit voice, video, and data.

 A **cell** is a large fixed-length data-carrying unit primarily consisting of a header with transmission control information and a large payload section that contains data.

ATM

The existence of multiple communication standards, such as Ethernet, token ring, and FDDI, has pointed out the need for an international standard. **Asynchronous Transfer Mode (ATM)**, developed by CCITT, is such a standard and has gained wide acceptance for network interoperability. The acceptance of ATM is related to several factors:

- It handles data, voice, and video transmissions.

- Because there is flexibility in geographic distance, it can be used for LAN and WAN communications.

- It can accommodate high-speed communications.

- It can provide high-speed communications between Ethernet, token ring, Fast Ethernet, FDDI, and other kinds of networks.

 Asynchronous Transfer Mode (ATM) is a transport method that uses multiple channels and switching to send voice, video, and data transmissions on the same network. ATM data transfer stresses efficient, quality of service (QOS), high-capacity data transport.

Many networks must use separate media for voice, video, and data, because the transmission characteristics are different for each. Voice and video transmissions tend to be continuous streams of signals along the cable, and video signals can occupy large bandwidths. Data signals need less bandwidth but are transmitted in bursts. Because ATM can handle voice, video, and data on a single network medium, it represents a large potential savings in network resources. ATM can be used for both LAN and WAN communications, which eliminates the need for separate short- and long-distance networks.

Connectivity between local, metropolitan, and worldwide networks would be greatly simplified if all users implemented a single networking system such as ATM. ATM is gaining attention in the networking industry because it can handle transmission speeds that range from 155 Mbps to 622 Mbps, with a theoretical limit of 1.2 Gbps. That offers very high capacity networking as more organizations begin to tax their networks with object-oriented, multimedia, and client/server applications.

An ATM-formatted packet is called a cell. The cell has a fixed-length format and contains two primary sections. The first section, the header, is 40 bits long. The second section, the payload, consists of 384 bits, as shown in Figure 5-12.

Figure 5-12

ATM cell

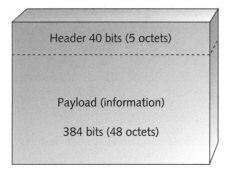

Header 40 bits (5 octets)

Payload (information)

384 bits (48 octets)

The header contains information to manage the cell transmission, such as flow control, which network path to follow, addressing information, and error-control information. The payload portion of the ATM cell is always the same length and contains voice, video, or data transmissions.

ATM is a layered communications system (Figure 5-13). The physical layer consists of the electrical transport interface, which conducts the cell as a signal. ATM cells can be transported over coaxial, twisted-pair, and fiber-optic cable systems. The next layer up is the ATM layer, which constructs the cell header and adds it to the payload data. The third layer is the adaption layer, which takes voice, video, and data and constructs the cell payload.

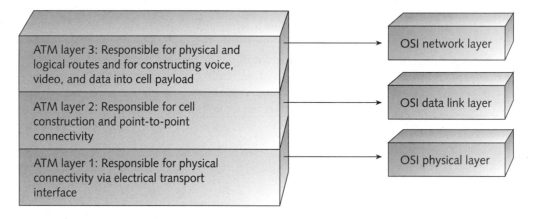

ATM layer 3: Responsible for physical and logical routes and for constructing voice, video, and data into cell payload → OSI network layer

ATM layer 2: Responsible for cell construction and point-to-point connectivity → OSI data link layer

ATM layer 1: Responsible for physical connectivity via electrical transport interface → OSI physical layer

ATM connectivity is accomplished through a network ATM switch, which dictates the path a cell can take from source to destination (Figure 5-14). When a node is prepared to transmit data, it "negotiates" with the switch for an open path to the destination node. In the negotiation, the sending node indicates the type of data to be sent, the transmission speed needed, and other information about the requested transmission. The information determines the type of transmission channel to be made available to the node. For example, continuous stream data, such as voice, may require a higher-speed channel than nonvoice data sent in bursts. Voice data also needs a channel with more bandwidth than nonvoice data.

Figure 5-14

ATM switching

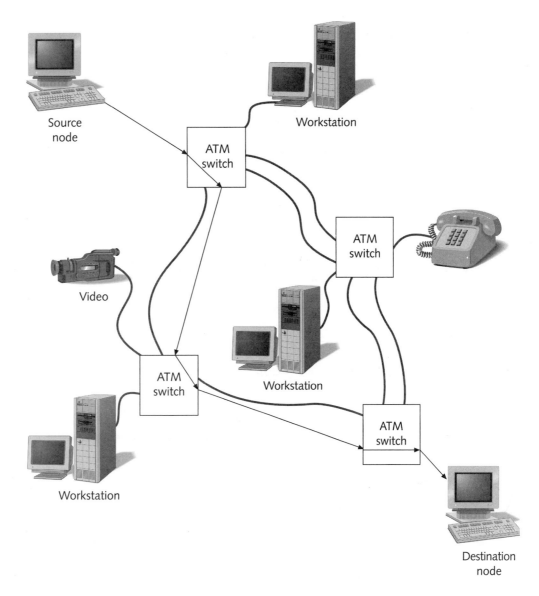

The ATM switching technology permits the network to handle many types of data transfer needs. Compared to other technologies, ATM switching has the following advantages:

- ATM switching enables data to be transmitted at access speeds appropriate to the type of data sent.

- ATM permits use of higher bandwidths.

- Each ATM connection (communication session) has its own dedicated bandwidth.

- Connection processes are more clearly defined with ATM, because they are handled by the switch from point to point.

SMDS

Developed by Bell Communications, **switched megabit data service (SMDS)** was first demonstrated in 1990 as a telecommunications-based system to link FDDI networks into a MAN (metropolitan area network). SMDS is a cell-based data transmission technology capable of speeds up to 155 Mbps over T-carrier lines. SMDS incorporates the physical, data link, and network layers of the OSI model (Figure 5-15). At the physical layer it uses the IEEE 802.6 standard for MAN communications; at the data link layer it employs LLC sublayer communications. The network layer consists of the communications paths used to transmit data.

Figure 5-15

Relationship of SMDS layered communications to the OSI model

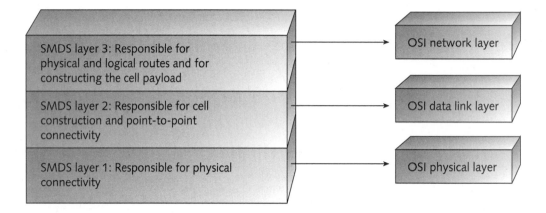

Switched megabit data service (SMDS), also called switched multimegabit data service, was developed by regional telephone companies to provide cell-based, high-speed communications between MANs.

SMDS was developed to provide high-speed data connectivity similar to that of SONET (discussed next) for applications like the following:

- Providing a high-speed link for regional networks

- Transmitting large image files, such as medical X-rays

- Transmitting architectural drawings and other CAD graphics

- Providing fast access to library holdings and electronic catalogs

SMDS was first incorporated by regional telephone companies, such as Bell Atlantic and Pacific Bell. Many of those companies have turned their attention to SONET, which provides greater high-speed options.

SONET

SONET (for **synchronous optical network**) is a fiber-optic technology that can transmit data at more than 1 Gbps. SONET has grown rapidly in popularity as more telephone companies have added this capability to their services. The Alliance for Telecommunications Industry Solutions (ATIS) developed the standard, which is endorsed by ANSI and boasts data transmission rates of 2.488 Gbps, with the promise of 13.271 Gbps in the future.

SONET (for **synchronous optical network**) fiber-optic technology allows for high-speed (more than 1 Gbps) data transmission. Networks based on SONET can deliver voice, data, and video.

One advantage of SONET is that it is nonproprietary, so point-to-point network equipment can be purchased from a variety of vendors. SONET can connect to interfaces for ATM, ISDN, routers, and other equipment to provide very high-speed communications. Another advantage of SONET is that high-speed communications are possible over long distances, such as between cities and states. Some applications of SONET are as follows:

- Providing very high-speed data connectivity between distant networks (for example, between college campuses and research centers sponsored by private businesses)

- Video conferencing between distant sites

- Long-distance teaching

- High-quality sound and video reproduction

- High-speed transmission of complex graphics, such as topographic maps and images created through satellite photography

COMMUNICATIONS MEDIA AND CHARACTERISTICS

SONET high-speed communications use single-mode fiber-optic cable and T-carrier communications (starting at T3). SONET operates at a base level of 51.84 Mbps, which is called Synchronous Transport Signal Level 1 (STS-1). From there, the signal can be incrementally switched to higher speeds as needed for a particular type of service. The currently available range of speeds is shown in Table 5-5. Future SONET transmission speeds are anticipated to reach STS-256 at 13.271 Gbps.

Table 5-5

SONET transmission rates

STS Level	Transmission Rate
STS-1	51.84 Mbps
STS-3	155.52 Mbps
STS-9	466.56 Mbps
STS-12	622.08 Mbps
STS-18	933.12 Mbps
STS-24	1.244 Gbps
STS-36	1.866 Gbps
STS-48	2.488 Gbps

SONET NETWORK TOPOLOGY AND FAILURE RECOVERY

SONET travels in a ring topology capable of providing three options for failure recovery: unidirectional path switching, automatic protection switching, and bidirectional line switching. In unidirectional path switching there is only one fiber-optic ring. The data signal is transmitted in both directions around the ring. The receiving node determines which signal to accept. If there is a break in one path, the signal on the alternative path still reaches the destination node. The data sent along the alternative path warns the receiving node that only one path is open.

Automatic protection switching is another form of recovery for a network failure. If a failure is detected at some point on the SONET network, the data is directed to an alternative switching node and is redirected to the assigned destination.

The third method of recovery, bidirectional line switching, provides the highest level of redundancy, up to 99%. It uses a dual ring topology, so there are always two paths to a node (Figure 5-16). The data is sent to both rings, but in opposite directions. If there is a break along one path, the data on the second path still gets through.

Figure 5-16

SONET bidirectional line switching

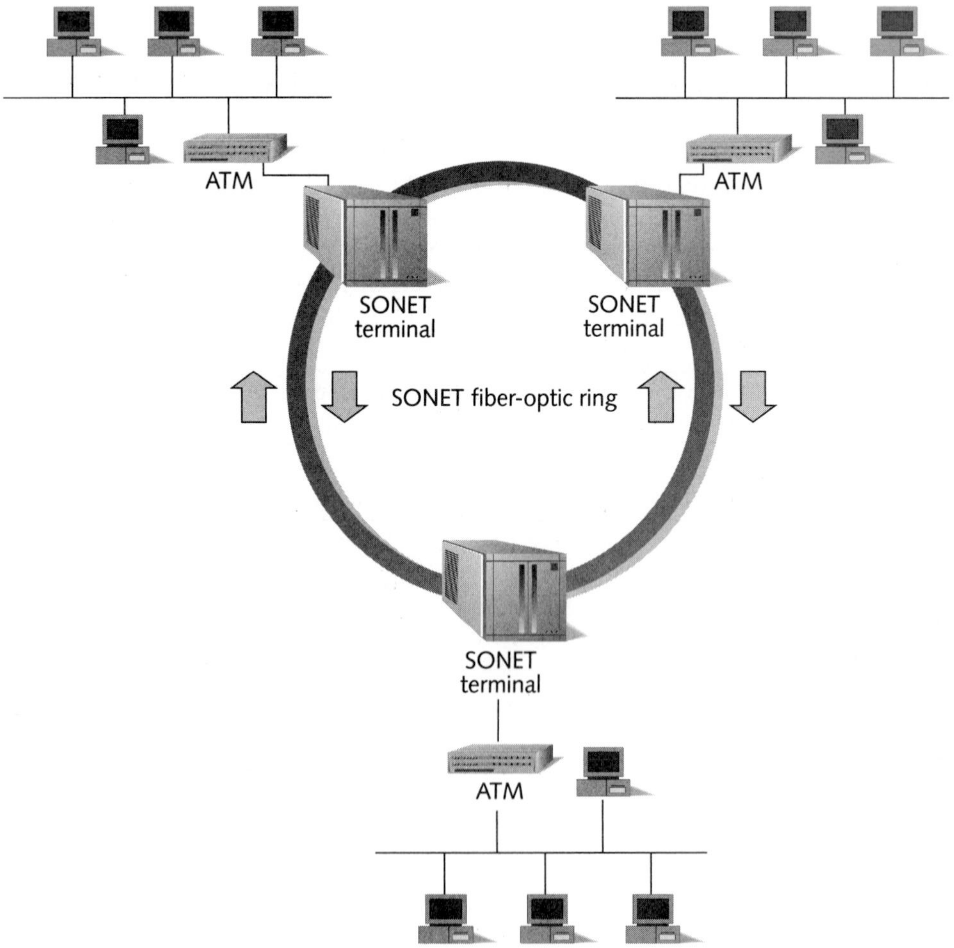

SONET LAYERS AND THE OSI MODEL

Four protocol layers are used in SONET (Figure 5-17). The bottom layer is the photonic layer, which is similar to the physical layer of the OSI model. It handles transportation and conversion of the transported signals. The transmitted electrical signals are changed into optical signals to be placed on the fiber-optic cable, and the received optical signals are changed back to electrical signals.

Figure 5-17

Relationship of SONET layered communications to the OSI model

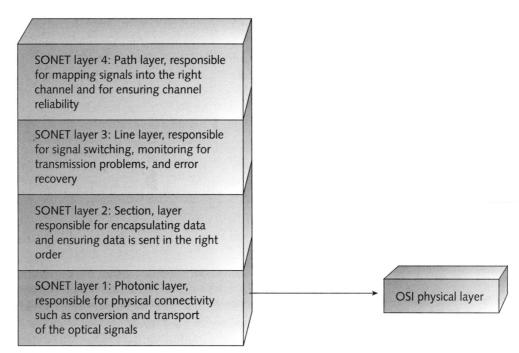

The second layer, the section layer, encapsulates data, ensures that data is sent in the correct order, ensures the timing of each frame, and checks for transmission errors. Next is the line layer, which monitors for problems and handles recovery switching if a problem is detected. The line layer is also responsible for switching the signal and for ensuring that the entire frame reaches its destination.

The top, or path, layer provides signal mapping into the communication channels. For example, it might map an ATM signal into one channel and an ISDN signal into another. It also ensures the reliability of a channel from source to destination.

 In this hands-on activity you access Pacific Bell's Web page to find out more about its SONET services.

To complete this activity:

1. Access Pacific Bell's Web page on the Internet at **http://www.pacbell.com/**.

2. Search for information about SONET services offered by Pacific Bell.

3. Find out which error recovery method is used by Pacific Bell's implementation of SONET.

4. Find out their objective in terms of keeping service available. (Is it 89% of the time? 99%?)

5. Create a document that lists your findings for steps 2–4.

CHAPTER SUMMARY

High-speed communications have generated great interest as network administrators work to provide more capacity on their networks and to provide connectivity to more places. The costs of Fast Ethernet and ATM have gone down dramatically, making those technologies very attractive. For example, a NIC with a combination 10/100 Mbps capability now costs the same as a 10 Mbps NIC cost a few years ago. In some situations, a 10 Mbps network can be converted to 100 Mbps with the implementation of a Fast Ethernet hub and 100 Mbps NICs (given 100 Mbps capable cable).

ATM technologies have exploded with options for high-speed networking. Many network administrators are implementing ATM for enterprise and WAN communications. Besides high-speed networking capabilities, ATM is highly compatible with SONET. Expect large corporations, universities, research centers, and other organizations to implement ATM and SONET networks for high-speed communications that will span continents. If you are expanding a network for enterprise communications or are installing a new large network, consider ATM as part of your network design.

FDDI, which was an early contender for high-speed communications, is generating less interest now. Fast Ethernet is a lower-cost and more flexible alternative than FDDI, and ATM provides faster communications, at 155 Mbps and more. ISDN has come into its own as telephone companies spend time and money to upgrade telephone lines and equipment. Not only does ISDN bring caller ID into the home, it brings Internet connectivity into many businesses. The home will be the next frontier for direct data communications. X.25 still has a place in global areas where network communications have not yet matured to speeds higher than 10 Mbps. For those situations, it is a proven and dependable technology.

In chapter 6 you anchor more of what you have learned so far to actual networking devices. You explore the devices you have heard about, such as MAUs, hubs, and routers. Other networking devices are introduced, including bridges, repeaters, and multiplexers. Network diagrams, illustrations, and hands-on activities in that chapter help you understand how they work.

REVIEW QUESTIONS

1. The speed of a T1 line is

    a. 1.544 Mbps.

    b. 2 Mbps.

    c. 44.736 Mbps.

    d. 274.176 Mbps.

2. SONET uses which topology?

    a. star

    b. bus

    c. ring

    d. peer

3. 100BASE-X is

    a. frame relay communications.

    b. Fast Ethernet.

    c. FDDI.

    d. SONET.

4. Continuous bursts of data controlled by clock signals describe _____ communications.

    a. asynchronous

    b. synchronous

    c. bus

    d. router

5. ISDN handles which of the following?

    a. voice

    b. video

    c. data

    d. all of the above

    e. both b and c

6. ATM handles which of the following?

    a. voice

    b. video

    c. data

    d. all of the above

    e. only b and c

7. Which of the following provides data communications at 155 Mbps?

    a. X.25

    b. ATM

    c. FDDI

    d. Fast Ethernet

8. If you needed to interface WAN communications with an older, slow LAN (transmission rate under 10 Mbps), the best solution would be

   a. X.25.

   b. ATM.

   c. FDDI.

   d. frame relay.

9. Packet switching

   a. is used in high-speed communications.

   b. employs store-and-forward transmissions.

   c. creates a continuous logical channel for communications.

   d. all of the above

   e. only a and c

10. Which of the following WAN technologies leaves most of the error checking to the LANs it connects into the WAN?

    a. X.25

    b. FDDI

    c. frame relay

    d. Fast Ethernet

ASPEN CONSULTING PROJECT: A MEDLEY OF ASSIGNMENTS

In these assignments, your boss, Mark Arnez, has several clients who need your assistance. Your clients include a graphics design company, a medical research organization, and an auto parts company. All three clients need assistance with high-speed communications implementations.

 ## ASSIGNMENT 5-1

Design Graphics has a 10BASE-T network wired with category 5 cable. Half of the users have NICs that are combination 10/100 Mbps cards. The company would like to upgrade to high-speed networking and needs your advice. What do you recommend? Why?

ASSIGNMENT 5-2

Winston Research Labs has large medical research centers in Boston, Atlanta, Houston, and Phoenix. Each center is an enterprise network with hundreds of users, and each already has ATM technology set up for high-speed communications at each site. None of the four research centers is connected to the others, but all want to use high-speed communications to build a WAN to join the four sites. What do you recommend? Why? Use Microsoft Paint or another drawing package to illustrate how you would connect the four research centers.

ASSIGNMENT 5-3

One of your colleagues at Aspen Consulting does not understand token-passing communications. Use the following space to compare the token-passing method of FDDI to that of standard token ring. Illustrate the differences using Microsoft Paint or another drawing package.

ASSIGNMENT 5-4

Easton Car Parts is debating whether to use X.25 or ISDN for communications between two Wisconsin plants with 10BASE-T networks, which are 100 miles apart. In an initial telephone conversation, you have discovered they are working on a plan to use photographs of their products in the shared inventory system. What other questions would you ask them about their needs? Based on what you know now, what would you recommend? Would you recommend they look at any other alternatives?

ASSIGNMENT 5-5

The people at Easton Car Parts are not certain how switching technologies work. Briefly explain circuit switching, message switching, and packet switching. Next, use Microsoft Paint or another drawing package to illustrate how they work.

ASSIGNMENT 5-6

A plant manager at one of Easton's plants is not sure how two plants might be connected via ISDN. Briefly explain one way to connect them and create a basic network diagram to illustrate how that would be done.

ASSIGNMENT 5-7

You are making a presentation about high-speed networking to five Easton Car Parts executives. One topic you will be covering is communications media. Use the following table to list five high-speed networking technologies and the media used in each.

High-Speed Technology	Media Options

OPTIONAL CASE STUDIES FOR TEAMS

 ## TEAM CASE 1

Mark Arnez has been contacted by your state university to perform a study on connecting all the state's community colleges with the university for high-speed communications. Form a group to develop a list of questions for networking people at the community colleges and the state university. Try out your list of questions at one of the community colleges or at a state university in your state.

 ## TEAM CASE 2

Mark is not certain if your local telephone company has SONET services. He wants you to form a small group to contact the telephone company and find out what services it offers (prepare a list of questions first). If SONET is not offered, use the Internet or another means to find a SONET provider. What form of fault tolerance does that provider offer? Draw a network diagram to illustrate the type of fault tolerance available.

 ## TEAM CASE 3

After Mark asks you to research SONET services, he is interested in having your group compare the merits of different high-speed technologies. What technologies would you recommend to a company planning to build two new factories 500 miles apart and needing high-speed data, voice, video, and teleconferencing capabilities between the factories?

CHAPTER SIX

DEVICES FOR NETWORK AND INTERNETWORK CONNECTIVITY

The high-speed networking options you learned about in chapter 5 have enabled networks to handle growing demands for expanded services. For example, one college campus of 15,000 students discovered heightened demand for access to their 10 Windows NT file servers, all originally connected to the network using a 10BASE-T star network. The demand initially was met by placing all the file servers on a 100 Mbps FDDI ring that campus workstations accessed through a hub. The high-speed FDDI network significantly cut down on access time to the file servers and sped up communications between servers. Later, even faster access was provided by installing ATM for 155 Mbps communications between buildings on campus.

In another example, a furniture manufacturing business uses the Internet daily to upload data to another company that handles the accounting and prepares the invoices. At first, the furniture manufacturer used a telephone line to provide the link to the Internet. Today, the company sends information faster and more reliably over an ISDN line installed by the regional telephone company.

Regular and high-speed networking is made possible by networking devices. In this chapter, you learn about token ring and Ethernet networking devices. Some devices, such as repeaters, offer inexpensive means to expand the scope of a network. Other devices, like intelligent modular hubs, combine several functions in one place. An intelligent modular hub helps the network administrator manage nodes while providing connectivity to workstations and servers. You begin by learning about basic networking equipment, including MAUs, multiplexers, and repeaters. Next, you learn about more complex devices such as bridges, routers, hubs, gateways, and ATM switches. The exercises throughout the chapter give you hands-on experience with those devices and in diagramming networks that use them.

AFTER READING THIS CHAPTER AND COMPLETING THE EXERCISES YOU WILL BE ABLE TO:

- EXPLAIN THE FUNCTION OF COMMONLY USED NETWORK DEVICES SUCH AS MAUs, MULTIPLEXERS, REPEATERS, BRIDGES, ROUTERS, BROUTERS, HUBS, AND GATEWAYS

- DETERMINE WHEN AND HOW TO USE THOSE DEVICES

- DESCRIBE WHAT OSI LAYER OR LAYERS CORRESPOND TO THE FUNCTION OF EACH DEVICE

- EXPLAIN THE FUNCTION OF ATM SWITCHING

- DESCRIBE HOW VLANs ARE AN IMPORTANT TOOL FOR MANAGING LARGE NETWORKS

MULTISTATION ACCESS UNITS (MAUS)

As you learned in chapter 4, a **multistation access unit (MAU)** acts as a central hub on a token ring network. Used exclusively on token ring networks, MAUs can perform the following tasks:

- Connect workstations in a logical ring through a physical star topology
- Move the token and packets around the ring
- Amplify data signals
- Connect in a daisy-chained manner to expand a token ring network
- Provide orderly movement of data

All token ring network devices connect to the network through a MAU, typically using Type 1, 2 (both shielded), or 3 (unshielded) twisted-pair cable. The MAU passes packets from one node to the next using a physical star topology but transporting packets as though they are going around a ring. Operating as a central hub, a MAU functions at the OSI physical and data link layers.

 A **multistation access unit (MAU)** is a central hub that links token ring nodes into a topology that physically resembles a star but in which packets are transferred in a logical ring pattern.

 MAU technology has evolved into new devices, such as the controlled access unit (CAU), which contains options to connect several units (stackable) to count as one MAU on a token ring network. CAUs also come with options to gather information used in network performance management.

The most basic MAU connects up to eight single-wire segments (Figure 6-1). Newer MAUs have 16 ports to connect nodes. A MAU can be a passive or an active hub. A **passive hub** does nothing more than pass the signal from workstation to workstation. Some of the signal strength is absorbed each time it goes through the MAU, reducing the maximum transmission capability of the network. For example, a network using passive hubs and Type 3 cable (UTP) has an actual limit of 72 nodes. An **active hub** regenerates, retimes, and amplifies the signal each time it passes through to the next node. That ensures delivery of a stronger signal to outlying nodes and more than doubles the number of nodes supported. A network composed of Type 3 cable can expand up to 150 nodes by using active MAUs, and a network using Type 1 or Type 2 cable can have up to 260 nodes. (The maximum number of nodes for Type 3 cable is less than for Types 1 and 2 because Type 3 cable has significantly more signal distortion, called jitter.)

 A **passive hub** connects nodes in a star topology, performing no signal enhancement as the packet moves from one node to the next through the hub. Each time the signal moves through the hub, it is weakened slightly because the hub absorbs some of the signal, reducing the total number of nodes that can be attached to a token ring network.

 An **active hub** connects nodes in a star topology, regenerating, retiming, and amplifying the data signal each time it passes through the hub. Using active hubs more than doubles the total number of nodes that can be connected to a token ring network.

Figure 6-1

MAU with
eight
connections

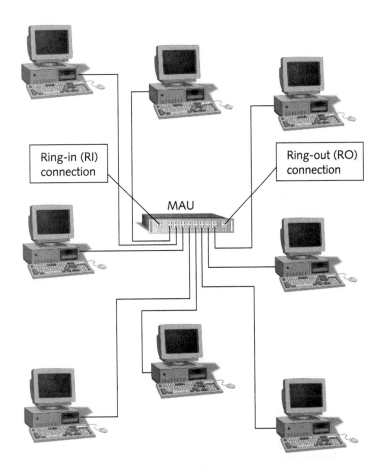

All MAUs have ring-in (RI) and ring-out (RO) connections to enable them to connect with additional MAUs in daisy-chain fashion. The RI and RO connections enable a token ring network to be expanded as there is a need for more workstations to join the network. When two or more MAUs are used, the RO port of the first MAU is connected to the second MAU's RI port, and so on, until all the MAUs are connected, as shown in Figure 6-2.

Up to 12 MAUs can be connected to a single ring on a token ring network.

Figure 6-2

MAUS
connected
using the RI
and RO ports

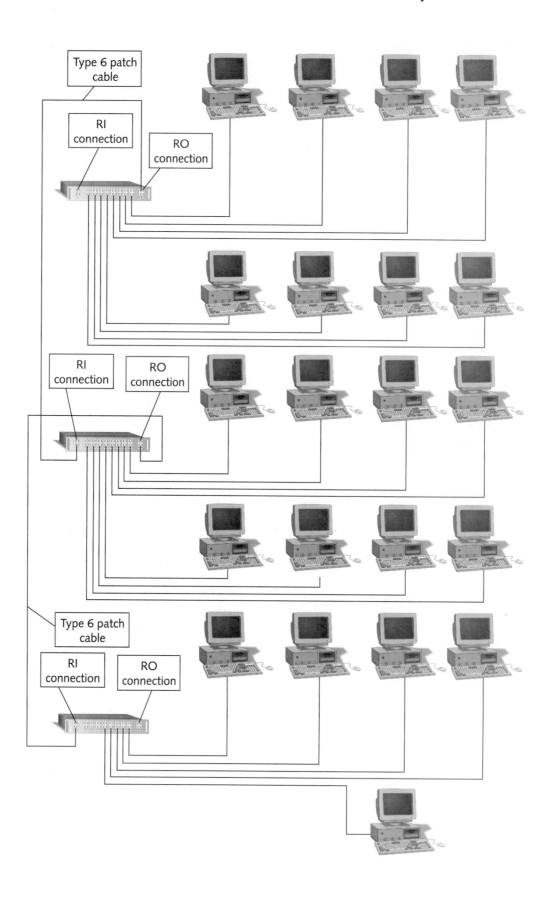

In this hands-on activity you have an opportunity to practice connecting workstations to a MAU on a simple token ring network. You will need a lab with two to four workstations, all with token ring NICs that have been configured for each workstation, and an 8-port MAU. You also will need twisted-pair cable, with attached connectors to connect the workstations to the MAU.

To set up the network:

1. For your own information, consult the MAU documentation to determine if the MAU is a passive or an active hub.

2. Connect one end of the first cable to the MAU.

3. Connect the other end of the cable to the first workstation's NIC.

4. Repeat steps 2 and 3 until all workstations are attached to the MAU.

5. Connect the MAU to power, if required in the MAU documentation.

6. Turn on the workstations and boot Windows 95 or Windows NT Workstation.

7. Double-click **Network Neighborhood** and look for all the workstations you attached.

 In this hands-on activity, you draw a representation of the token ring network you configured in the preceding hands-on activity. If you are unable to configure the token ring network because equipment is not available, draw a network diagram of four workstations connected to a MAU. Use Microsoft Paint from a computer running Windows 95 or Windows NT Workstation.

To draw the network diagram:

1. Click **Start**, **Programs**, **Accessories**, and **Paint.**

2. Click the **View** menu. If the Tool Box option has no check mark in front of it, click **Tool Box**. If the Tool Box option is already checked, press [ESC] to close the View menu. The Paint toolbar is displayed. If necessary, drag the toolbar to dock it away from the drawing area.

3. Click the **Edit** menu and **Paste From**. Open the **mau.bmp** clip art provided by your instructor.

4. Drag the MAU representation to the center of the drawing area.

5. Click the **Edit** menu and **Paste From**. Open the **PC.bmp** clip art provided by your instructor and place it on the drawing area, dragging it above and to the left of the MAU.

6. Press **[Ctrl]+[C]** to copy the clip art of a PC. Press **[Ctrl]+[V]** to paste it in the drawing area and drag the second PC to the upper right of the MAU.

7. Press **[Ctrl]+[V]** again and drag the third PC to the lower right under the MAU.

8. Press **[Ctrl]+[V]** one more time, dragging the fourth PC to the lower left under the MAU.

9. Click the Line button on the toolbar. Place the crosshair cursor on the screen and, while holding down the left mouse button, draw a line from the lower left PC to the port second from the left on the MAU, as in Figure 6-3 (the leftmost port is the RI port).

Figure 6-3

Drawing the
token ring
network in
Microsoft Paint

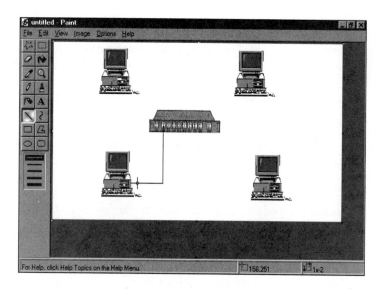

10. Repeat step 9 to connect the remaining three PCs to unused ports on the MAU. Make sure you do not use the leftmost or rightmost (RI or RO) ports.

11. If a printer is available, print the drawing.

12. Press **[Ctrl]+[S]** to save the drawing. Save it with the name **Token_Ring.bmp** to a floppy disk in drive A or to a location specified by your instructor.

MULTIPLEXERS

Multiplexers are network devices that can receive multiple inputs and transmit them to a shared network medium. Multiplexers simply are switches used in old and new technologies, such as the following:

- Telephone switching

- Switching telecommunications lines to create multiple channels on a single line (such as T1 lines)

- Serial communications to enable more than one terminal to communicate over a single line

- Fast Ethernet, X.25, ISDN, frame relay, ATM, and other networking technologies to create multiple communication channels over a single communications cable

 A **multiplexer** is a switch that divides a communication medium into multiple channels so several nodes can communicate at the same time. A signal that is multiplexed must be demultiplexed at the other end.

On networks, X.25, ISDN, and frame relay use multiplexers for packet-switched communications. In those technologies, the multiplexer acts as a packet-switching node to receive data from other nodes. The multiplexer is connected to a single cable, which is divided into channels or virtual circuits. The multiplexer stores the received packets until it can open the intended channel. The multiplexer simply switches from channel to channel. Each packet is stored until the multiplexer opens its channel for transmission. Figure 6-4 shows an example of how multiplexers are connected.

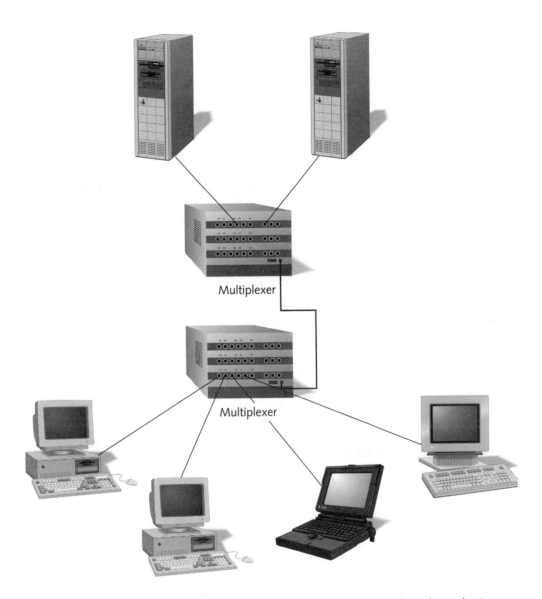

Figure 6-4

Multiplexers

Multiplexers work at the OSI physical level, switching from channel to channel using one of three different physical methods:

- Time division multiple access (TDMA)
- Frequency division multiple access (FDMA)
- Statistical multiple access

Time division multiple access (TDMA) divides the channels into distinct time slots. Each time slot is designated for a particular network node, as if it were a dedicated line. The multiplexer rotates from time slot to time slot for each channel. That is similar to 24-hour television programming, where the 6:00 p.m. time slot is for the news, 6:30 p.m. is for entertainment news, and 7:00 p.m. is for a family comedy. TDMA does not guarantee the most efficient use of the network medium, since transmission occurs on only one channel at a time. The timing of node transmission also is important, because a node may transmit at an interval that is out of synchronization with its time slot. (Also, by IEEE specifications a packet has a designated time by which it must travel the length of the network, to avoid a collision with the next packet sent.)

Time division multiple access (TDMA) multiplexing enables multiple devices to communicate over the same communications medium by creating time slots in which each device transmits.

Frequency division multiple access (FDMA) divides the channels into frequencies instead of time slots. Each channel has its own broadcast frequency and bandwidth. The multiplexer switches from frequency to frequency as it sends data, similar to four listeners with headsets sharing a radio modified to have four channels. The first listener might be listening to a classical station, the second to a talk show, the third to a baseball game, and the fourth to the news. Each listener is at a different frequency. The radio inputs to each channel so quickly that no one can tell it is switching from channel to channel as it receives the signal on each frequency.

Frequency division multiple access (FDMA) multiplexing creates separate channels on one communication medium by establishing different frequencies for each channel.

Statistical multiple access, or statistical multiplexing, is used by X.25, ISDN, and frame relay. This method is more efficient than TDMA or FDMA, because the physical medium bandwidth is dynamically allocated based on the application need. The multiplexer continuously monitors each channel to determine the communication requirements. For example, at one moment a channel may need to transmit a large graphics file, and then be quiet. Algorithms on the multiplexer determine the bandwidth needed to transmit the file. After the file has been transmitted, the multiplexer reallocates bandwidth to another channel. This can be equated to the way in which a workstation operating system automatically decides how much memory to give to three applications running at the same time. It might give 15 KB for an active word processing file, 7 MB for an image from a scanner, and 1.2 MB to print a graphic.

Statistical multiple access multiplexing allocates the communication resources according to what is needed for the task, such as providing more bandwidth for a video file and less for a small spreadsheet file.

REPEATERS

Sometimes the 500-meter limit for 10BASE5 or 185-meter limit for 10BASE2 is too restrictive to connect all nodes required for a **segment**. Operating at the OSI physical layer, a **repeater** is an inexpensive solution that enables a network to reach users in distant portions of a building that are beyond the IEEE specifications for a single cable run. The repeater amplifies an incoming signal, retimes it, and reproduces it on all cable runs, as shown in Figure 6-5. Retiming helps to avoid packet collisions once the signal is placed on the cable. Repeaters are used in the following ways:

- To extend a cable segment, such as beyond 185 meters for a 10BASE2 segment
- To increase the number of nodes beyond the limit of one segment, such as to over 30 nodes for Ethernet
- To sense a problem and shut down a cable segment
- As a component in other network devices, such as hubs, to amplify and retime a signal

A **repeater** amplifies and retimes a packet-carrying signal so it can be sent along all cable **segments**. As used in this context, a segment of cable is one cable run within the IEEE specifications, such as one run of 10BASE2 cable that is 185 meters long and that has 30 nodes or less (including terminators and network equipment).

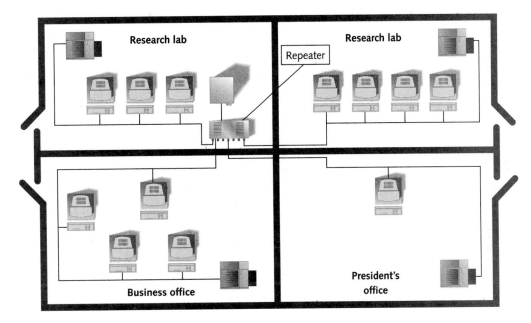

When a repeater retransmits a signal along more than one additional cable segment, it is called a multiport repeater. For example, one repeater may have ports for two to eight additional cable segments. The cable that is run from a port is treated by the network as a normal cable segment. For example, a 10BASE2 Ethernet multiport repeater can put a received signal on multiple cable runs 185 meters in length. Each cable run supports up to 29 connected nodes and a terminator at the end of the segment. According to IEEE specifications and depending on the network topology and media, a single packet can travel through up to four repeaters. However, because of the presence of other network equipment that amplifies and retimes a signal, a safer design is to ensure that the packet never travels to its destination through more than two repeaters.

Most repeaters have ports for several types of inbound cable connections, such as for thick or thin Ethernet cable. Many also have a specialized **attachment unit interface (AUI)** port to connect to a coaxial or fiber-optic backbone utilizing the appropriate transceiver. The outbound cable segments are typically for thin coaxial cabling.

An **attachment unit interface (AUI)** connects coax or fiber-optic backbone cable to a network node, such as a repeater. The interface consists of AUI standards for connectors, cable, interface circuits, and electrical characteristics.

Repeaters constantly check each outbound cable segment for problems, such as signal problems caused by a missing terminator or a break in the cable. If a problem is detected on a segment, the repeater halts the transmission of data to that segment. This method of closing down a segment is called **partitioning**. For example, a segment may be partitioned if a terminator is missing or a workstation's NIC is malfunctioning and sending excessive packet traffic. One segment on a multiport repeater can be partitioned without affecting the others. The segment also can be reset at the repeater for resumed transmission as soon as the network problem is fixed.

 A **partitioned** segment is one that has been shut down because a portion of the segment is malfunctioning.

Simple repeaters offer an inexpensive way to extend older bus topology coaxial-based networks. However, as a network grows, repeaters eventually limit your options for high-speed networking and can result in bottlenecks as the network expands. If you are designing a new network, design around more modern equipment with built-in repeater functionality, such as centralized hubs.

 When using a multiport repeater, design the network to place the minimum number of nodes on one segment. For example, on a network with 40 workstations, it is better to have four segments with 10 nodes each than to have two segments, with 12 nodes on one and 28 nodes on the other. That way, you minimize the number of computers affected when a segment is partitioned.

 In this hands-on activity you practice extending an Ethernet network using a repeater. You will need a lab with two Windows 95 or NT workstations, both already equipped with NICs having thin coax connectors. You also will need four terminators, T-connectors, and two sections of 10BASE2 cable with the ends already installed with connectors.

To attach a repeater to extend a network:

1. Attach a T-connector to one end of the first cable.

2. Attach one end of the T-connector to a workstation and place a terminator on the other end.

3. Attach the other end of the cable to the inbound port on the repeater; check the manufacturer's instructions to determine how to attach the cable (e.g., if you need a T-connector and a terminator on the workstation end).

4. Connect the other cable to one of the outbound ports on the repeater, following the manufacturer's instructions, as in step 3 (using a T-connector and a terminator).

5. Attach a T-connector to the opposite end of the cable coming out of the repeater from step 4.

6. Attach one end of the T-connector to the second workstation and place a terminator on the other end of the T-connector.

7. Plug the repeater into a wall outlet and turn it on.

8. Boot up both workstations.

9. Access **Network Neighborhood** on the workstations to verify that each is recognized on the network.

In this hands-on activity, you create a network drawing in Microsoft Paint to show how you would connect two large offices using a repeater.

To diagram the interoffice network:

1. Click **Start**, **Programs**, **Accessories**, and **Paint.**

2. Make sure the Paint toolbar appears on the screen. If it does not, use the **View** menu to check the **Tool Box** option.

3. Click the **Line** button on the toolbar.

4. Use the crosshair cursor to draw a large office at the top of the drawing area, including a door to the office, as shown in Figure 6-6.

5. Repeat step 4 to draw an adjoining office area under the one you just drew.

6. Click the **Edit** menu and **Paste From**. Open the **repeater.bmp** clip art provided by your instructor.

7. Drag the repeater representation to the lower-right corner of the top office.

8. Click the **Edit** menu and **Paste From**. Open the **pc.bmp** clip art provided by your instructor and drag it into the top office.

9. Press **[Ctrl]+[C]** to copy the art. Press **[Ctrl]+[V]** to paste it in the drawing area. Drag the second PC to a place of your choice in the office.

10. Press **[Ctrl]+[V]** and drag a PC to another location in the top office.

11. Repeat step 10 five more times until you have one more PC (four total) in the top office and four in the bottom office.

12. Click the **Edit** menu and **Paste From**. Open the **server.bmp** clip art provided by your instructor.

13. Drag the server close to the repeater in the top office.

14. Click the **Line** button on the toolbar.

15. Use the crosshair cursor to link all four workstation PCs in the top office to the repeater in one line.

16. Use the crosshair cursor to link the server to the repeater so it is on its own segment.

17. Use the crosshair cursor to link all four workstation PCs in the bottom office to the repeater in one line.

18. If a printer is available, print the completed drawing (Figure 6-6).

19. Press **[Ctrl]+[S]** to save the drawing. Save it with the name **Two_rooms.bmp** to a floppy disk in drive A or to a location specified by your instructor.

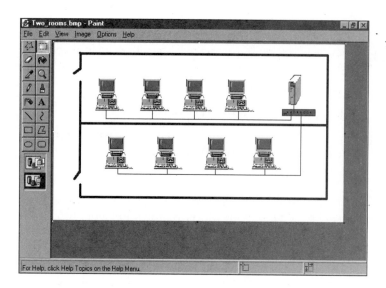

BRIDGES

A **bridge** is a network device that connects one LAN segment to another. Bridges are used in the following circumstances:

- To extend a LAN when the maximum connection limit has been reached, such as the 30-node limit on an Ethernet segment

- To extend a LAN beyond the length limit, such as 185 meters for thinnet Ethernet

- To segment LANs to reduce data traffic bottlenecks

- For security, to prevent unauthorized access to a LAN

A **bridge** connects different LAN segments using the same access method, such as one Ethernet LAN to another Ethernet LAN or a token ring LAN to another token ring LAN.

The first bridges were developed by DEC in the early 1980s. DEC's work on bridges was incorporated in the IEEE 802.1 standard. Today, bridges are popular on Ethernet/IEEE 802.3 networks. Because their implementation is unseen by users, the term *transparent bridge* is commonly used. Bridges are described as operating in **promiscuous mode,** which means they look at each frame's physical destination address before sending it on. That ability separates a bridge from a repeater, which does not have the ability to look at frame addresses. Figure 6-7 shows a bridge connecting two NetBEUI-based Ethernet LANs and a TCP/IP Ethernet LAN.

A network device that operates in **promiscuous mode** reads frame destination address information before sending a packet onto other connected segments of the network.

Figure 6-7

Bridged
network

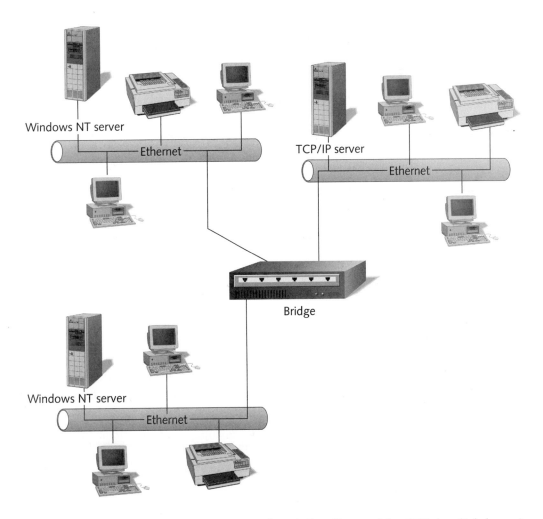

Bridges operate at the media access control (MAC) sublayer of the OSI data link layer. A bridge intercepts all network traffic and examines each packet as it is received. It reads the destination address on each packet and determines if the packet should be forwarded to the next network. If the packet is intended for a local node, the bridge filters the packet to that node on the originating LAN. A standard Ethernet bridge can filter over 30,000 packets per second and forward about 15,000 packets per second.

Bridges provide full network access because they are protocol independent. They look only at the MAC address. A single bridge can forward TCP/IP, IPX, and X.25 packets without regard to the frame structure. Bridges do not attempt to convert packets from one network protocol format to another.

There are two types of bridges: local and remote. A **local bridge** is used to directly connect two LANs in close proximity, such as two Ethernet LANs. It also is used to segment network traffic for the purpose of reducing bottlenecks. For example, in one agricultural research company a bridge was used to link the business department network with the research lab network to enable sharing of certain files and e-mail. The business department network created high-volume traffic due to the number of reports generated from a database server in a client/server software application system. Once the high-volume traffic to the database server was identified, the bridge was set to filter packets bound for that server so they would not be forwarded to the lab network.

A **local bridge** connects networks in close proximity and is used to segment a portion of a network to reduce problems caused by heavy traffic.

In a case like a college campus, mainframes, graphics workstations, diskless workstations, and PCs accessing file servers may share the same network. Performance on such a high-traffic network suffers unless the network is divided into separate strategic networks based on device and application use. Bridges can be placed on the network to isolate high-traffic areas into smaller network segments.

Remote bridges are used to join distant networks. To reduce costs, the bridges can be joined by a serial line. (This is one way to join networks in different cities or states and combine them into a single large network, but, as you learn later in this chapter, a router often is a better choice for that function.)

A **remote bridge** joins networks across the same city, between cities, and between states to create one network.

A bridge performs three important functions: learning, filtering, and forwarding. When it is turned on, a bridge learns the network topology and addresses of devices on all attached networks. The bridge learns what is on the network by examining the source and destination addresses in the frames it receives. Each bridge builds a bridging table so it knows the address of every network node. Most bridges can store a large range of addresses in their bridging tables.

The bridge uses its table as the basis for forwarding traffic. When a packet is received, the bridge reads the destination address and looks up the address in the bridging table. If an association is found, the bridge forwards the frame to a known destination (port). If no association exists, the frame can be flooded to all ports on the bridge, except the port from which the frame was sent.

A bridge also may contain instructions entered by the network administrator not to flood frames from specified source addresses, or it may have instructions to discard certain frames instead of forwarding them. Those instructions enable the bridge to filter network traffic. Such a filtering capability means that a bridge can be used for security, for example, to control who can access a server used for the company payroll.

Some bridges can link only two network segments. Such bridges are used to cascade network segments. For example, in Figure 6-8 bridge A connects LAN 1 and 2, and bridge B connects LAN 2 to LAN 3. A packet from LAN 1 will have to go through bridges A and B to reach LAN 3.

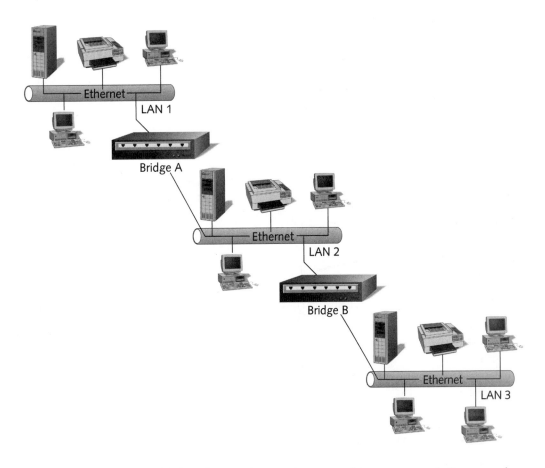

Figure 6-8

Cascaded
network
segments

There also are multiport bridges that can tie several segments into one network. Some vendors offer multiport bridges with up to 52 ports or interfaces. Using the example in Figure 6-8, if bridge A were a multiport bridge, it would have three ports to enable it to connect LANs 1, 2, and 3. A packet from any one of those LANs would travel through only one bridge to reach its destination; the bridge's table would contain addresses of all the nodes on each LAN.

On an Ethernet network, the total number of bridges in a linear path between two nodes is limited to eight. Exceeding eight bridges can result in packet timing problems for CSMA/CD algorithms. While that is not an official standard, it is followed by conscientious network administrators.

TOKEN RING BRIDGING

Token ring bridges use source routing to forward packets on the network. Originally proposed by IBM, source-route bridging has been incorporated into the 802.5 token ring LAN specification. Source-route bridges perform routing at the OSI network layer.

Source-route bridging (Figure 6-9) places the complete source-to-destination route into all inter-LAN frames sent by the source. The bridges store and forward frames as indicated by the route specified within the frame.

Figure 6-9

Source route
bridging

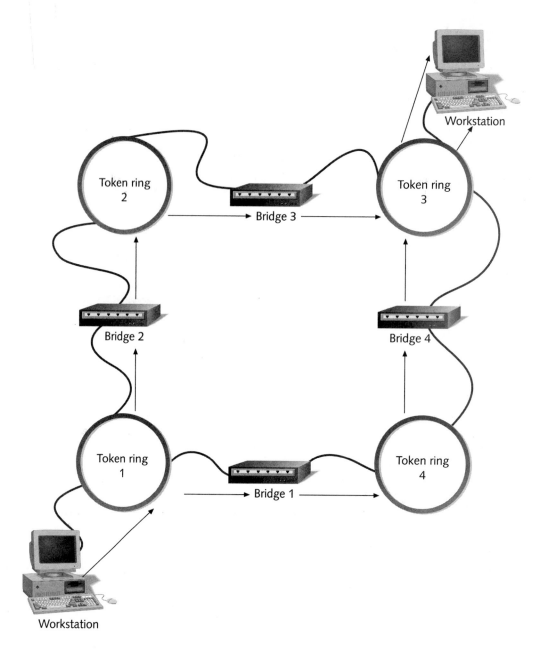

When a node anticipates sending a packet on a bridged network, it issues an explorer packet. Each bridge that receives the explorer packet copies it onto all outbound ports. Route information is appended to the data area of the explorer packets as they travel throughout the internetwork. When the sending node's explorer packets are received by the destination node, the destination node replies to the sending node using the accumulated route information. Then the sending node must select a path to the destination node. The path is determined by three factors: the route taken by the first packet received back, the minimum number of **hops** to the destination, and the path that will enable the largest packet size (4–Mbps network segments have 4,000-byte packets; 16 Mbps networks have 17,800-byte packets). After the path has been determined, the path information is placed in the routing information field (RIF) of the 802.5 packet. The presence of routing in the 802.5 packet is indicated by setting the routing information indicator (RII) in the packet. Token ring networks are limited to a maximum of seven bridges.

Hops are the number of times a packet travels point-to-point from one network to the next.

Another way to view a hop is the number of times the packet is regenerated, amplified, and placed onto another network by a source-route bridge or router. For example, a packet that has traveled through three routers has made three hops. Hop information can be included in frames retransmitted by source-route bridges or routers to help identify the fastest route to a particular destination and to detect frames that may be traveling through the network in an endless loop.

ROUTERS

A **router** performs functions similar to those of a bridge, such as learning, filtering, and forwarding. Unlike bridges, however, routers have built-in intelligence to direct frames to specific networks, to study network traffic, and to adapt quickly to changes detected in the network. Routers connect LANs at the network layer of the OSI model, which enables them to interpret more information from frame traffic than bridges. Figure 6-10 shows a router directing a frame to a specific network rather than unnecessarily broadcasting that frame to all networks connected to the router. In general, routers are used for the following:

- To efficiently direct packets from one network to another, reducing excessive traffic
- To join neighboring or distant networks
- To connect dissimilar networks
- To prevent network bottlenecks by isolating portions of a network
- To secure portions of a network from intruders

A **router** connects networks having the same or different access methods, such as Ethernet to token ring. It forwards packets to networks by using a decision-making process based on routing table data, discovery of the most efficient routes, and preprogrammed information from the network administrator.

Figure 6-10

A router
forwarding a
frame to the
right network

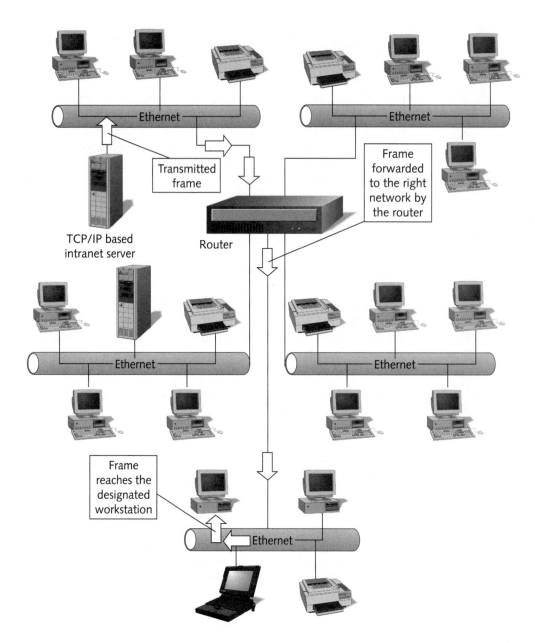

Routers can connect networks that have dissimilar data links. For example, an Ethernet network using the TCP/IP protocol can be connected to a packet-switched frame relay network that also uses IP. Some routers support only one protocol, such as TCP/IP or IPX.
Multiple-protocol routers offer protocol conversion between dissimilar networks, such as
TCP/IP on an Ethernet network and AppleTalk on a token ring network. When equipped
with the appropriate hardware and software, routers can connect to the following networks,
among others:

- Ethernet
- Fast Ethernet
- Token ring
- Fast token ring
- Frame relay

- Cell relay
- ATM
- ISDN
- X.25

Unlike bridges, which are transparent to the end node, routers are known to the end node. Nodes regularly communicate with a router to confirm their address and presence. Routers are designed to send packets along paths with the lowest volume of traffic and with the lowest cost in terms of using network resources. They also can isolate portions of a network to contain areas of heavy traffic from reaching the broader network system. That characteristic enables them to prevent network slowdowns and broadcast storms.

As a network grows in complexity, the need to ship packets along the shortest, most efficient path grows proportionally. Bridges often are replaced by routers to ensure that growing network traffic is handled efficiently and network congestion avoided. Also, when large networks must be joined, routers are more efficient than bridges in linking them.

 When you plan an upgrade to a network, consider the protocols in use. For example, some protocols, such as NetBEUI, *cannot* be routed, which means it is difficult to upgrade a bridge to a router where NetBEUI needs to pass from one network to the next.

STATIC AND DYNAMIC ROUTING

Routing is performed in one of two ways: static or dynamic routing. **Static routing** is accomplished by the network administrator setting up the routing tables so there are fixed paths between any two routers. The network administrator also intervenes to update routing tables when a network device fails. A static router can determine that a network link is down, but it cannot automatically reroute traffic without intervention from the network administrator. Because it is labor intensive, most network administrators do not commonly use static routing.

Dynamic routing occurs independently of the network administrator. Dynamic routers monitor the network for changes, update their own routing tables, and reconfigure network paths as needed. When a network link fails, a dynamic router automatically detects the failure and establishes the most efficient new paths. The new paths are configured based on the lowest cost as determined by network load, line type, and bandwidth.

 Static routing involves control of routing decisions by the network administrator through preset routing instructions.

 In **dynamic routing** the router constantly checks the network configuration, automatically updates routing tables, and makes its own decisions (often based on guidelines preset by the network administrator) about how to route frames.

ROUTING TABLES AND PROTOCOLS

Routers maintain information about node addresses and the network status in databases. The routing table database contains the addresses of other routers and of each end node. Dynamic routers automatically update the routing table by regularly exchanging address information with other routers and with network nodes.

Routers also regularly exchange information about network traffic, the network topology, and the status of network links. The information is kept in a network status database in each router. When a packet arrives, the router examines the protocol destination address. It decides how to forward the packet based on network status information and a calculation of the number of hops required for the packet to reach its destination.

Routers that use a single protocol (such as TCP/IP) maintain only one address database. A multiprotocol router has an address database for each protocol it recognizes (such as a database for TCP/IP nodes and a database for IPX/SPX nodes). Routers exchange information by using one or more routing protocols. For example, a router that handles only TCP/IP uses one or more routing protocols for communications between routers. A multiprotocol router, such as one that handles TCP/IP and IPX/SPX, requires specialized routing protocols between routers.

LOCAL AND REMOTE ROUTERS

Routers that join networks in the same building or that link adjacent networks on a campus are **local routers**. For example, a local router might join two Ethernet networks on the same floor of a building or two networks in separate buildings (Figure 6-11). One local router may handle 15 different network protocols, such as TCP/IP, IPX/SPX, and AppleTalk. Such routers continuously monitor their constituent networks so that routing tables can be updated to reflect network changes. They monitor changes in line speeds, network load, network addressing, and network topologies.

In the process of joining networks, local routers are used to segment network traffic and to enforce security. A local router can be used to limit certain types of packets from leaving a specific network segment. It can be used to control which network nodes are able to reach a segment that contains sensitive business information. When a router is employed for security, it acts like a **firewall** on the network, protecting the network from hackers and unwanted traffic.

 A **local router** is one that joins networks in the same building or between buildings in close proximity, for example, on the same business campus.

 A **firewall** is software, hardware, or both employed to restrict who has access to a network, to specific network segments, or to certain network resources (such as servers).

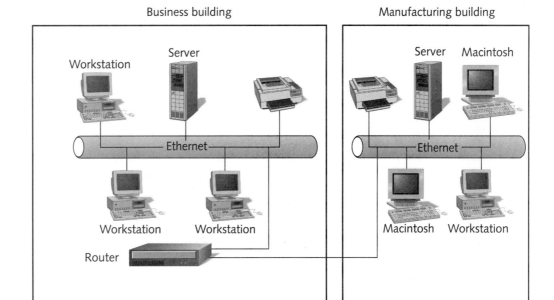

Figure 6-11

A local router connecting networks in adjacent buildings

A **remote router** enables networks to be connected over long distances, such as New York to Los Angeles. A single router in Los Angeles might connect a business in that city to remote business routers in Vancouver, Toronto, and New York. Another example is a remote router at a state university campus connecting with corresponding routers at satellite campuses throughout the state.

A **remote router** joins networks across large geographic areas, such as between cities, states, and countries.

Remote routers connect ATM, frame relay, high-speed serial, and X.25 networks. Similar to a local router, a remote router can support multiple protocols, enabling communication with many kinds of distant networks. Also similar to a local router, a remote router can be set up as a firewall to restrict access to particular network resources.

This hands-on activity takes you to the Web site of one router manufacturer to view the options that come with a router.

To view information about routers:

1. Open Internet Explorer by clicking its icon from the desktop or by clicking **Start**, **Programs**, and **Internet Explorer**.

2. Access the Cisco Systems Web site by entering **http://www.cisco.com/** in the address text box.

3. Click **Products & Ordering**.

4. Click the option to view **Cisco Products**.

5. Select one or more Cisco router products, such as the 7000 series or 4000 series routers.

6. Read the product literature or product overview.

7. Check out the pictures of routers so you can see what they look like, particularly the connections available in the back view.

8. Also check out the router features, such as the transport media and protocol support. (For example, the 7500 routers have interfaces for Ethernet, token ring, FDDI, ATM, and others.)

9. Create a document describing at least two different router models and their features.

BROUTERS

A **brouter** is a network device that acts like a bridge in one circumstance and like a router in another. Brouters are used in the following situations:

- For efficient packet handling on a multiprotocol network with some protocols that can be routed and some that cannot

- To isolate and direct network traffic to reduce congestion

- To join networks

- To secure a certain portion of a network by controlling who can access it

A brouter is used on networks that operate with several different protocols, such as NetBEUI, IPX/SPX, and TCP/IP, and for that reason is also called a multiprotocol router. Whether it bridges or routes a protocol can depend on (a) the instructions programmed in by the network administrator for handling a protocol and (b) if the incoming frame contains routing information (if it does not, the protocol typically is forwarded to all networks).

 A **brouter**, also called a multiprotocol router, acts like a bridge or a router, depending on how it is set up to forward a given protocol.

When a brouter is set to forward but not route a protocol, it forwards each frame using addressing information in the MAC sublayer of the data link layer, just like a bridge. That capability is important on a network where one of the protocols is NetBEUI (because it cannot be routed). For protocols that are routed, such as TCP/IP, the brouter forwards each frame based on address and routing information contained in the network layer.

HUBS

There are many types of network **hubs**. The simplest hubs provide central network connectivity by enabling a logical Ethernet bus network or a token ring network to be physically connected as a star. More complex hubs are used to replace bridges and routers to reduce network congestion. Most hubs function as active hubs, because they amplify and retime a signal whenever it passes through the hub. Advanced hubs provide very high speed connectivity for FDDI, Fast Ethernet, frame relay, and ATM networks. In general, hubs offer one or more of the following services:

- Provide a central unit from which to connect multiple nodes into one network

- Permit large numbers of computers to be connected on single or multiple LANs

- Reduce network congestion through centralizing network design

- Provide multiprotocol services, such as Ethernet-to-FDDI connectivity

- Consolidate the network backbone

- Enable high-speed communications

- Provide connections for several different media types (e.g., coax, twisted-pair, fiber)

- Enable centralized network management

 A **hub** is a central network device that connects network devices in a star topology. A hub also is referred to as a **concentrator** (or switch), which is a device that can have multiple inputs and outputs all active at one time.

You already have learned about one type of hub, the MAU. Four others that you learn about in the following sections are:

- 10BASE-T hubs

- Switching hubs

- 100BASE-X hubs

- Intelligent and modular hubs

10BASE-T HUBS

One of the simplest hubs is the 10BASE-T hub used on an Ethernet LAN. It also is one of the most popular ways to connect workgroups on small and large LANs. A 10BASE-T hub uses a physical star topology to connect PCs to the central hub. A physical star topology is easier to maintain than a physical bus, because only one or two nodes (usually one) are connected to each port on the hub. If a NIC on a single port malfunctions, you simply disable that port until the card can be replaced. Workstations on the other ports continue operation without interruption.

Additional hubs are added by connecting one hub to the next. For example, some manufacturers make stackable hubs that can be placed one on top of the other and daisy-chained together. Each hub in the stack has a designated number of ports, for example, 8 or 16. When stacked together there may be a total of nearly 100 ports in all the hubs, with the advantage that the stack of combined hubs represents only one repeater node.

 In this hands-on activity, you connect workstations to a small 10BASE-T hub. In a lab, you need an 8- or 16-port 10BASE-T hub, two to eight workstations equipped with 10BASE-T NICs (already configured), and two to eight sections of category 3 or 5 UTP cable with RJ-45 connectors.

To create a small 10BASE-T network:

1. Make sure the hub is not plugged into a wall outlet.

2. Examine each section of cable, checking the cable and the connectors for damage or loose cable-to-connector connections.

3. On the first cable, plug one end into a workstation NIC. Run the cable to the hub and connect it to the first port on the hub.

4. Repeat step 3 for all the workstations, to connect each workstation to the hub.

5. Plug the hub into a wall outlet and turn it on. (If the hub has no switch, it will have power as soon as you plug it in.)

6. Boot all the workstations.

7. Check the front or the back of the hub (depending on the manufacturer) for LEDs and make sure one is lit (normally green) for each workstation cable connection. (If one or more is not lit, check for a reset button and press it. Also, check to make sure you have completely plugged in the connectors on any segment that is not lit.)

8. Double-click **Network Neighborhood** on the desktop of one of the workstations and look for the name of each workstation you connected.

SWITCHING HUBS

Switching hubs permit you to increase significantly the throughput capability of an existing 4 Mbps, 10 Mbps, or 16 Mbps network by taking full advantage of existing bandwidth capabilities. On a standard Ethernet or token ring network, only one packet can be transmitted at a time. As more nodes are added, transmission delays and packet collisions (on Ethernet) become frequent. And even though the cable plant has greater bandwidth available, only a fraction of it is put to use.

Switching hubs allow an existing network to be separated into multiple smaller segments, each independent of the others and each able to support packet transmissions at regular network speeds. No additional network equipment is needed. That makes switched Ethernet a low-cost way to increase network throughput as demands on a LAN increase, particularly with the implementation of client/server applications and database servers.

Switching hubs can be installed on LANs in a WAN where specific LANs are experiencing increased network traffic. The switching hub can divide network bandwidth into two or more segments. That means network throughput is at least doubled and sometimes increased even more, depending on the capabilities of the switch.

100BASE-X HUBS

Fast Ethernet has gained broad acceptance in networking circles since it was proposed in the early 1990s. Multimedia, video, and GUI client/server applications have fostered the need for high-bandwidth, high-speed technologies. One answer to that demand is 100 Mbps Ethernet (Fast Ethernet), as long as category 5 cable is installed in the cable plant. Fast Ethernet is so prevalent now that many Ethernet NICs have 10 Mbps and 100 Mbps capability, and switching hubs have the same combined capability.

INTELLIGENT AND MODULAR HUBS

Many enterprise-wide networks have grown to include Ethernet, Fast Ethernet, token ring, FDDI, and ATM segments. Such growth often is accompanied by the presence of a variety of repeaters, bridges, routers, and switches. Network support is complex as the number of independent network devices grow and as those devices are spread over large geographic areas.

One solution to unifying network equipment needs is to implement a central **intelligent modular hub**. At the heart of the hub is a **backplane** circuit board. Some hubs come with redundant backplanes and redundant power supplies, in case one of the components malfunctions during live network operations. The hub backplane has multiple slots (multiple buses) for plug-in network cards. Each plug-in card may handle a different network function. For example, one card may perform bridge functions, one may act as a token ring hub, one may support a 10 Mbps Ethernet segment, and one may provide a 100 Mbps FDDI interface.

An **intelligent hub** is one that has network management and performance monitoring capabilities.

A **modular hub**, also called a chassis hub, is one that contains a backplane into which different modules, such as retiming, bridge, routing, and ATM modules, can be inserted.

A **backplane** is the main circuit board in modular equipment, containing slots as plug-ins for modular cards. The backplane provides connections between the modular boards, a power source, and grounding.

The hub represents a strategy to unify network equipment and to manage the network at single points of origin. That enables the network manager to gather and distill performance data close to the source. At the same time, the network is more easily scaled upward as expansion needs arise. For example, if a new Ethernet segment is required in a building wing, that growth is accommodated by adding a card in the hub.

The hub also functions as an intelligent hub, with the ability to gather network data and to control network functions. It collects, analyzes, and forms the raw data into meaningful information. The data is forwarded to a central network management station, where the network administrator can track network performance and control specific network segments.

In this hands-on activity, you create a network diagram for a building that has 10BASE-T star topology networks on two upper floors. The 10BASE-T hubs on the two floors are connected to a fiber-optic backbone that connects into an intelligent hub on the main floor. The servers for the building are connected to the intelligent hub on the first floor.

1. Click **Start**, **Programs**, **Accessories**, and **Paint**.

2. Make sure the Paint toolbar appears on the screen. If it does not, use the **View** menu to check the **Tool Box** option.

3. Click the **Edit** menu and **Paste From**. Open the **intellhub.bmp** clip art provided by your instructor and drag it to the lower center of the drawing area, as shown in Figure 6-12.

4. Click the **Edit** menu and **Paste From**. Open the **10basethub.bmp** clip art provided by your instructor and drag it to the center of the drawing area, directly above the intelligent hub.

5. Press **[Ctrl]+[C]** to copy the 10BASE-T hub.

6. Press **[Ctrl]+[V]** to paste another 10BASE-T hub onto the drawing area. Drag that hub to the upper center of the drawing area, directly above the 10BASE-T hub in the middle of the drawing area.

7. Click the **Text** button [A] and put the title **Intelligent hub** under the intelligent hub. Also, label the 10BASE-T hubs.

8. Click the **Line** button [\] on the toolbar. Just under the toolbar buttons, click the middle line to increase the thickness of the line to represent a fiber-optic backbone.

9. Use the crosshair cursor to draw a line between the intelligent hub and the middle 10BASE-T hub.

10. Draw another line between the intelligent hub and the top 10BASE-T hub.

11. Click the **Edit** menu and **Paste From**. Open the **pc.bmp** clip art and drag the first PC just to the left of the 10BASE-T hub in the top center of the drawing area.

12. Press **[Ctrl]+[C]** to copy the PC clip art.

13. Press **[Ctrl]+[V]** to paste another PC onto the drawing area. Drag that PC just to the left of the first PC.

14. Paste and drag six more PCs onto the drawing area until there are two PCs to the right and two PCs to the left of each 10BASE-T hub.

15. Click the **Line** button ◹ on the toolbar. Just under the toolbar buttons, click the top line so the lines you draw next, to represent the category 5 cable, are thinner than the lines in steps 8 and 9.

16. Connect each of the top four PCs, using a separate line for each, to the top center 10BASE-T hub.

17. Connect each of the middle four PCs, using a separate line for each, to the 10BASE-T hub in the middle of the drawing area.

18. Click the **Edit** menu and **Paste From**. Open the **server.bmp** clip art and drag it just to the right or the left of the intelligent hub.

19. Press **[Ctrl]+[C]** to copy the server. Press **[Ctrl]+[V]** to paste another server onto the drawing area. Drag that server next to the first one, near the intelligent hub.

20. Click the **Line** button and use the crosshair cursor to connect each server to the intelligent hub, using a separate line for each.

21. If a printer is available, print the completed drawing (Figure 6-12).

22. Press **[Ctrl]+[S]** to save the drawing. Save it with the name **Intelhub.bmp** to a floppy disk in drive A or to a location specified by your instructor.

Figure 6-12

Network diagram of 10BASE-T network segments connected to an intelligent hub

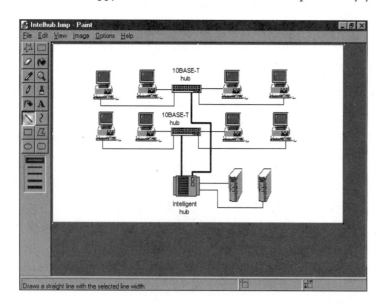

The network in Figure 6-12 has several important design advantages. One is that it is segmented into smaller networks by the hubs. If the top-floor 10BASE-T hub fails, the other portions of the network still can function. Each server is segmented so a malfunction in other network equipment (except the intelligent hub) does not affect access to a server. Also, it is easy to expand the network to other floors, simply by adding a 10BASE-T hub on the floor to be added and connecting that hub to the intelligent hub on the main floor. Another advantage is that the segments to the servers can be converted to 100BASE-TX for high-speed communications (using 10/100 Mbps NICs in the servers).

GATEWAYS

The term **gateway** is used in many contexts, but in general it refers to a software or hardware interface that enables two different types of networked systems or software to communicate. For example, you might use a gateway for the following purposes:

- To convert commonly used protocols (e.g., TCP/IP) to a specialized protocol (e.g., SNA)
- To convert message formats from one format to another
- To translate different addressing schemes
- To link a host computer to a LAN
- To provide terminal emulation for connections to a host computer
- To direct e-mail to the right network destination
- To connect networks with different architectures

Because there are so many broad applications of gateways, they can function at any of the OSI layers. You already have learned about Microsoft's Gateway Services for NetWare, which is software on a Windows NT server that enables workstations running Windows 3.x, 95, or NT to access file services on a NetWare file server.

A **gateway** enables communications between two different types of networked systems, such as between complex protocols or between different e-mail systems.

The most traditional concept of a gateway is a network device that translates one type of protocol to another having a very different structural composition. This type of gateway operates at the network layer of the OSI model. One of the best examples is a gateway that translates IBM's **Systems Network Architecture (SNA)** protocol for mainframe communications to another protocol, such as TCP/IP (Figure 6-13). The problem with that type of gateway is that it is relatively slow compared to other solutions. For that reason, use of traditional gateways is becoming more infrequent. For example, there are two better solutions for communicating with an IBM mainframe than using an SNA gateway. The less expensive solution when only workstations running Windows need to access an IBM mainframe is to use Microsoft's DLC protocol, as you learned in chapter 4. When other computers need to access the mainframe, such as those running UNIX, IBM has TCP/IP connectivity options, including TCP/IP interfaces for their mainframes.

Systems Network Architecture (SNA) is a layered communications protocol used by IBM for communications between IBM mainframe computers and terminals. SNA employs seven-layered communications that are similar to the OSI model, but there are differences in the way the services are grouped within the layers.

Figure 6-13

IBM mainframe connected through an SNA gateway

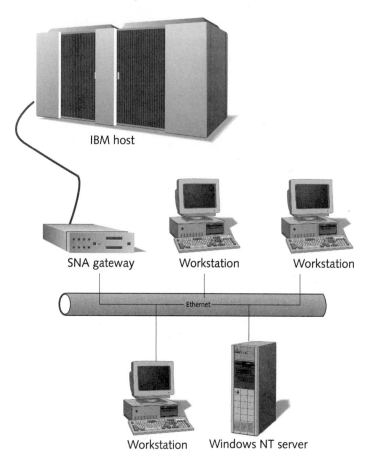

With the exploding use of e-mail, another common meaning of the term gateway is software that converts e-mail messages from one format to another. That type of gateway functions at the application layer of the OSI model. E-mail gateways such as Microsoft Mail Services, Mercury Mail, and CC:Mail are in use on mail servers throughout the world.

ATM SWITCHES

An **ATM switch** offers high-speed cell switching at 155 Mbps to more than 1.2 Gbps. ATM switches enable voice, video, and data to be transmitted over a network using existing category 5 UTP or fiber-optic cabling. ATM switches have the following capabilities:

- Providing high-speed communications on a network backbone
- Providing cell transmissions directly to the desktop
- Enabling high-speed communication between network hubs
- Centralizing network design for better management

- Connecting to very high speed networks, such as SONET

- Enabling network design around workgroup members at dissimilar locations (virtual LANs)

- Reducing network bottlenecks through high-speed communications and efficient traffic management through workgroups

 An **ATM switch** determines the network channel used to transmit an ATM cell received from a node, taking into account the type of information in the cell (voice, video, data) and the transmission speed needed.

The ATM switch provides high-speed communications with dedicated bandwidth by means of fast data link MAC sublayer transport. Some ATM switches can operate at either the data link or the network layer. Virtually any type of data can be transmitted directly from one node to another through the MAC layer (Figure 6-14).

Figure 6-14

ATM switch

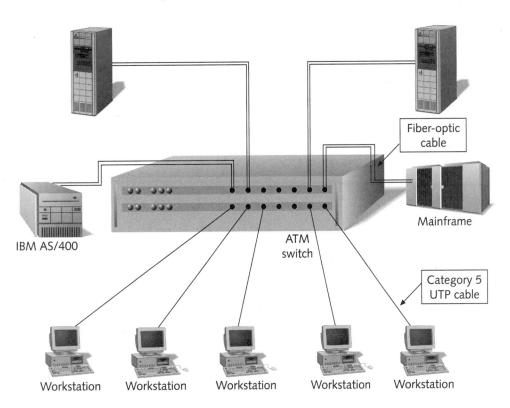

IBM AS/400 — ATM switch — Fiber-optic cable — Mainframe — Category 5 UTP cable — Workstation — Workstation — Workstation — Workstation — Workstation

VIRTUAL LANS (VLANS)

ATM switches, along with internetworking software, have made **virtual LANs (VLANs)** possible. A VLAN arranges the logical network topology by workgroup instead of by physical location. For example, assume that a company occupies a 10-story building, with all stories networked. Also assume the people in the company work in teams, such as marketing teams, business accounting teams, computer support teams, management teams, and so on. One marketing team has 20 members whose offices are spread out on the second, fourth, seventh, and eighth floors. The physical topology shows them spread among four different networks. However, if the network employs ATM switches, routers, and VLAN internetworking software, the network can be configured logically through the software so that all 20 team members appear in one segment or VLAN.

A **virtual LAN (VLAN)** uses switches, routers, and internetworking software to configure a network into subnetworks of logical workgroups, independent of the physical network topology.

Besides ATM, vendors are now incorporating VLAN technology into other kinds of network equipment, such as intelligent hubs and routers.

In a large networking operation, VLANs can have a significant impact. The most obvious is that network resources can be managed based on the actual work groupings of users. For example, a marketing group may need more bandwidth resources because they create graphics, brochures, and other marketing aids that require huge files to be transmitted back and forth. Another grouping of office assistants may need only enough bandwidth for small word processing files. VLANs enable the network administrator to allocate resources based on the needs of each group. The result is greater productivity for each user and a more economical application of resources.

Another advantage of VLANs is that when a user takes on a different function in the organization, there is less need to move that user's office and workstation next to members of a new workgroup. The VLAN simply is reconfigured to move the user from the old workgroup to the new one. With the VLAN internetworking software, that can be accomplished by a simple point, click, and drag software operation on the part of the network administrator. That saves time and money over moving a workstation and cable and reprogramming a network device port.

The most important advantage is that VLANs enable a network to operate at the most efficient level. It is no longer limited by the physical topology. When VLANs are set up, they redirect network traffic along the most desirable routes throughout the enterprise, reducing heavy network traffic and bottlenecks. The routing tables are adjusted for the most efficient frame transfer, and ATM switching enables the frame to go directly from source to destination. The frame is sent directly to the destination node and is never flooded to other nodes. That is much more efficient than using routers alone, where the frame is sent to the destination router and then flooded onto the network where the receiving workstation is connected. Figure 6-15 illustrates how ATM switches can be used to set up VLAN workgroups.

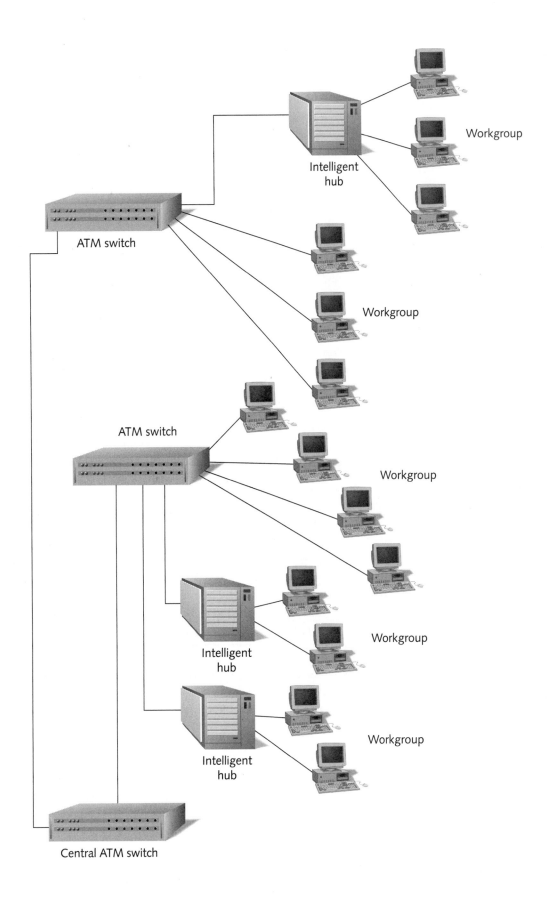

Figure 6-15

VLAN
workgroups
through ATM
switching

CHAPTER SUMMARY

Networking devices are the nerve centers of a network. Some devices, such as MAUs and 10BASE-T hubs, provide central connectivity at the grassroots level of the workstation. Other devices, like repeaters, bridges, and routers are used to extend the reach of a network. Bridges and routers also connect networks and forward frames to other networks, and routers direct frames to specific network locations.

Sometimes special translation is required to communicate with a mainframe or to convert e-mail messages from one system to another. Those duties are handled by gateways, which can operate at any level of the OSI layered model. Multiplexers and switches can turn single communications channels into many, greatly increasing the capacity of a network.

Modular hubs are jacks of all trades because they may contain cards to act as hubs, bridges, routers, switches, and other network devices. Intelligent hubs bring network management capabilities, giving the network administrator tools to make adjustments or to identify problems.

ATM switches have increased the high-speed capacity of networks and have made VLANs possible. The combined capabilities have enabled medium and large networks to operate efficiently, bringing productivity improvements to workstation users and to network administrators. ATM switching brings quality of service (QOS) to networks, which guarantees bandwidth to time-sensitive applications, such as voice and video.

Most of the devices described in this chapter have a relationship to one or more layers of the OSI model. Some operate at only one layer, while others operate at many. Table 6-1 summarizes the relationship between the devices and the OSI model.

Table 6-1

Networking devices and the OSI model

OSI Layer	Network Device
Application	Gateways
Presentation	Gateways
Session	Gateways
Transport	Gateways
Network	Gateways, routers, source-route bridges, brouters, ATM switches
Data link	MAUs, intelligent hubs, bridges, gateways, brouters, ATM switches
Physical	MAUs, multiplexers, passive and active hubs, repeaters, gateways

In chapter 7 you put together what you have learned about networks as you discover how to plan actual networks. You look at scenarios as you learn to plan for topology, network equipment, network setup, and network security.

REVIEW QUESTIONS

1. Frequency division multiple access (FDMA) is a method of
   a. multiplexing.
   b. bridging.
   c. repeating.
   d. error detection.

2. A multistation access unit (MAU) that does not amplify a data signal before it goes to the next node is an example of a(n)

   a. repeater.

   b. passive hub.

   c. active hub.

   d. sole source signal regenerator.

3. You need to connect two separate 10BASE-T networks that have Windows NT servers using NetBEUI. Which of the following would you use?

   a. repeater

   b. bridge

   c. router

   d. multiplexer

4. Virtual LANs (VLANs) are possible because of

   a. VLAN internetworking software.

   b. ATM switches.

   c. 10BASE2 networking.

   d. all of the above

   e. only a and b

5. Which of the following can act as a firewall?

   a. bridge

   b. router

   c. brouter

   d. all of the above

   e. only a and c

6. A bridge operates at which OSI layer?

   a. network layer

   b. LLC sublayer of the presentation layer

   c. application layer

   d. MAC sublayer of the data link layer

7. Which of the following might you use to connect an Ethernet network to a token ring network?

   a. repeater

   b. multiplexer

   c. router

   d. bridge

8. Gateways operate at which OSI layer?

   a. network

   b. application

   c. data link

   d. all OSI layers

   e. They do not operate at the OSI layers.

9. Which network device might be a router, a hub, a bridge, and a switch in one box?

   a. multiprotocol router

   b. modular hub

   c. source router

   d. multiplexer

10. When a segment on a hub is shut down because it is malfunctioning it is said to be

   a. restricted.

   b. errored out.

   c. partitioned.

   d. overheated.

ASPEN CONSULTING PROJECT: A WEEK OF VARIED ASSIGNMENTS

Again this week, Mark Arnez has a variety of assignments for you to tackle. The first is to help a firm of investment advisors set up a network in a small office. Next, Mark asks you to explain networking devices to a new consultant. You also are working with a company that prints coupons to help them extend a network, and you need to provide some networking advice to a college network administrator.

 ## ASSIGNMENT 6-1

You have been working with a group of 12 investment advisors who are partners in a company called Plains Investments. Each advisor has a PC, and the firm has purchased a computer for a server. The company occupies a one-story office in the downtown area, with separate small offices for each partner. What network device would you recommend to connect the PCs in each office and the server?

Use the following space to explain what you would use and why. Then, draw a simple network diagram to illustrate how the PCs and the server would connect to the device.

ASSIGNMENT 6-2

Mark Arnez has assigned you to train a new consultant, Sheila Markovski, who has just completed her bachelor's degree. She has some questions about bridges and routers. Use the following area to explain how the devices are similar and how they are different.

ASSIGNMENT 6-3

Your new customer, Discount Coupons, prints coupon books for local merchants such as grocery and drug stores. Discount Coupons has been in the same building for 10 years and has an older 10BASE2 network, which has reached the limit in terms of nodes and distance. Five newly hired people will have offices just at the end of where the network currently reaches in the building. Discount Coupons wants to provide PCs and network access to the new employees while retaining the 10BASE2 network. Explain in the space below what equipment you recommend to extend their network and why you recommend it. Include the advantages and the disadvantages. As part of your consulting assignment, draw a network diagram illustrating how the equipment is used to extend a network.

ASSIGNMENT 6-4

In a lab at Aspen Consulting, you practice connecting PCs to a 10BASE-T hub or a MAU. Explain in the following table the steps to connect the hub.

Steps to Connect PCs to the Hub or MAU
Step 1:
Step 2:
Step 3:
Step 4:
Step 5:
Step 6:
Step 7:
Step 8:

ASSIGNMENT 6-5

Fully examine the features of the 10BASE-T hub or MAU you worked with in Assignment 6-4, such as LEDs, redundant power source, reset options, and so on. Describe the features in the following table.

Hub or MAU Features and Options

ASSIGNMENT 6-6

You have a client who uses an older IBM mainframe and Systems Network Architecture (SNA). All the mainframe users have or will have networked PCs running Windows 95 or Windows NT Workstation. No other types of workstations will connect to the mainframe. Use the following space to explain the options available for accessing the mainframe from the network, using the PC workstations.

ASSIGNMENT 6-7

You and a consulting associate, Jim Ramirez, have been discussing networking devices and the OSI layers at which those devices work. List five commonly used network devices and record their relationship to the OSI model in the following table. Also make a note in the table about the function of each device.

Network Device	OSI Layers	Functions

ASSIGNMENT 6-8

One of the network administrators on a college campus with 4,000 students has stopped by for your advice. Her campus administrative users (about 100) access seven Windows NT servers housed in one of the administration buildings. They are set up to use NetBEUI. The users are located in two administrative buildings and in academic department offices in three other buildings. The network administrator is looking for a way to enable access to the NT servers from networks in each of the seven buildings, but to limit access to only the administrative building networks for sensitive grade information that is processed on a mainframe using TCP/IP communications. The campus network is entirely Ethernet based. What network device or devices would you recommend for placement in the buildings to connect the networks? Use the space that follows for your answer, explaining your recommendations. Then, draw a generic network diagram showing the equipment you would use and how you would connect it.

OPTIONAL CASE STUDIES FOR TEAMS

 Team Case 1

One of your largest clients, a manufacturing company that employs 1,200 people and that has over 1,000 networked computers, has been complaining that the network seems sluggish at times. Also, their network administration costs are high because the company has gone through two major reorganizations in the last year and a half, with people moving from office to office and new work teams constantly being formed. Form a group with two or three other consultants and suggest some general ways to help design a network to ease the administration costs and improve network performance.

 Team Case 2

Discount Coupons, the company you worked with in Assignment 6-3, has been purchased by a large printing company that wants to expand the current building and bring in 30 or more new employees. They want your advice on whether they should keep the current network or install a new one. Form a team to examine the possibilities. What network equipment would your group recommend if the new parent company simply expands the network? What network equipment would you recommend to go with a new network?

 Team Case 3

Mark Arnez has assigned you to head a team to investigate some of the latest options in modular hubs. He would like your team to use the Internet for your research. Check out sites such as *www.baynetworks.com* and *www.3com.com* and write a report for Mark on the options.

CHAPTER SEVEN

PLANNING A NETWORK

Planning is the best tool in your arsenal of networking knowledge. There is no better way to succeed as a network administrator than to thoroughly plan each step of the way. If you plan well, you will prevent 80–90% of the problems experienced in networking, and the problems you cannot prevent will be easier to solve. Planning a network involves applying your knowledge of computers, topologies, communications media, protocols, and networking devices to the organizational needs of those who depend on your services.

Your knowledge of the devices presented in chapter 6 is critical to becoming a successful network planner and administrator. You need to make many choices in planning. Do you design your network around twisted-pair cable and hubs or coaxial cable and repeaters? Is it better to use a bridge, a router, or a hub to connect buildings? Can you afford ATM for backbone communications? Do the needs of your organization *require* ATM implementation? If security is important to your organization, should you install bridges, routers, or some other type of firewall?

AFTER READING THIS CHAPTER AND COMPLETING THE EXERCISES YOU WILL BE ABLE TO:

- ASSESS THE NETWORK NEEDS OF AN ORGANIZATION
- DEVELOP A NETWORK PLAN
- SELECT THE APPROPRIATE NETWORK MEDIA AND TOPOLOGY FOR DIFFERENT SITUATIONS
- ESTIMATE NETWORK COSTS FOR EQUIPMENT AND HUMAN RESOURCES
- EXPLAIN MANAGEMENT OF NETWORK PERFORMANCE THROUGH CENTRALIZED PLANNING AND NETWORK SEGMENTING
- PLAN ACCOUNT MANAGEMENT
- PLAN NETWORK SECURITY

Here are some examples of insufficient planning. An engineering department on a college campus first networked its building by running thinnet coaxial cable through some walls near offices and labs. As the network grew, individual members of the department purchased more cable at a local electronics outlet. Because of its low budget, the department purchased an inexpensive repeater that was not consistent in partitioning segments when network problems arose. Eventually the network became unreliable because no one kept track of how the network was expanding. In another case, a clothing manufacturer remodeled several offices and decided to install an Ethernet network after most of the remodeling was finished. To cut costs, the company ran cable through the false ceiling, dropping it down from holes in the removable ceiling tile. Planning for the network was not well coordinated, so there were some cable runs of STP and others with UTP but no category 5 cable. Hubs were purchased but were not compatible with both kinds of cable. Some cable running through the doorways of adjoining offices was crushed each time the doors closed. The network was unreliable from the start: parts of the network did not work because of the incompatibility between the hubs and cable, and the cable runs through the doorways either did not work or worked intermittently. The network had to be reinstalled by an experienced networking firm.

Those examples are extreme but not uncommon. At the other end of the spectrum is this example of planning ahead. An art museum contacted its network administrator at the beginning of planning for a new building. The network administrator provided advice on the topology, the communications cable, the network devices, and the installation of the network throughout the building. Wiring closets were designed and located to protect network equipment and wiring and to provide the most favorable distances from which to run cable to each area (including between floors). The network administrator monitored the installation at every phase, to make sure the installation went well. The administrator also worked to design a network that could be expanded easily for new workstations and that was well positioned to take advantage of future networking options.

This chapter teaches you about planning a network. It is impossible to cover all the possibilities, but you learn about setting up a network for high performance, security, and effective management. Most important, you learn to set up a network to match the needs of those who must use it.

ASSESSING NETWORK NEEDS

The first step in network planning is to assess the business or organizational needs for which the network is to be used, including the following:

- The size and the purpose of the organization
- The potential growth of the organization in terms of people and services
- The number of mission-critical applications on the network
- Important cycles for the business or organization
- The relationship of the network resources to the mission of the business or organization
- Security needs
- The amount budgeted for network and computer resources

There are many other considerations, but the preceding list provides a good start. For example, if you are working with a large organization that is likely to grow, the emphasis will be on planning for high-capacity options such as Fast Ethernet, ATM, VLANs, and SONET. For a small network, such as a 15-person dental office, the network needs to be reliable and easy to manage on a small budget.

Some organizations, such as accounting and payroll departments or banks, work with sensitive financial information and require a high degree of reliability, security, and fault tolerance. Such organizations also have especially urgent business cycles, including daily electronic transmission of money transactions, daily account balancing, month-end and year-end accounting cycles, income tax reporting, and regular audits from independent financial auditors. Your network planning and management must take into account those important cycles. For example, you do not want to upgrade the accounting server in the middle of year-end processing or replace the ISDN equipment just before an electronic transmission to the Federal Reserve.

In many cases the network and computing resources are a cornerstone in the business strategy of an organization. A subscription company that markets collectible items regards its computer capabilities as the key reason the company stays ahead of the competition. Computing resources enable that company to provide the fastest customer service and delivery of products. When a customer places an order, a series of inventory, billing, customer profiling, promotional, manufacturing, and product shipping events occur automatically through the computer systems. For colleges, computer systems play an important role in attracting and retaining students, such as recruiting, admitting, and registering students and providing grade and degree progress information.

At one time, security was not a priority on many computers and networks, because few people knew how to intrude into such systems. Times have changed, and responsible network planning always includes a blueprint for security. Besides guarding against intrusions, security also includes backing up data, planning for computer failures, and having a disaster recovery plan.

Organizations rarely have all the budget they want for computer and network resources. As a responsible network administrator, you can plan a network in which the investment is retained for many years. For example, installing a new 10BASE2 network in a building that does not have an existing network will not help your organization retain its investment. 10BASE2 has limited options for expansion and high-speed networking and is expensive to manage and maintain. Installing a 10BASE-T network using category 5 cable is a better option. Compared to 10BASE2, 10BASE-T is cheaper to install, easier to manage, easier to expand, and easier to convert to high-speed networking.

 From the start, learn how the network is related to the needs of its users, determine what resources already exist, and plan a secure network positioned for growth. A given in networking is that once a network is successfully implemented and managed, the requests to expand its capabilities start immediately. Like it or not, this is a wired society.

DEVELOPING A PLAN

Most organizations have a business plan, a long-range plan, or a mission statement. Incorporate that information into your planning process. Develop your own network plan to describe the organization's current resources and what it needs for the future. An important part of documenting the current resources is to make a diagram of the existing network. If you are planning a new network, a network diagram is vital for visualizing the network and making improvements to the plan. Besides a diagram of the network, include the following information in your planning document:

- Number and kinds of workstations

- Number and kinds of server and host computers

- Network topology

- Network communications media

- Types of network devices

- Telecommunications services

- Current network performance statistics (chapter 10 describes how to determine such statistics)

Many organizations that are planning a new network or a major expansion write planning documents to send to vendors. Those documents are a **request for information (RFI)** and a **request for proposal (RFP)**. An RFI is an initial attempt to define in general terms what is needed. It usually describes the organization, its existing resources, and the type of services sought from the vendor. The description of services may be as general as this: "The vendor will install network cable and equipment in every room of the building." The RFI is sent to vendors, who respond with information about their products and how they meet the needs as set forth in the RFI. The organization may choose to select a vendor based on the vendor's response to the RFI, or it may choose to send out a follow-up RFP. An RFP takes cumulative information from the returned RFIs to establish exact specifications that later may be in a contract. An example specification might be the following: "The vendor will install category 5 cable for a 10BASE-T network to every room with two connections per room. The vendor will test every connection after the installation is complete and sign a verification that each connection is working."

 A **request for information (RFI)** is a general planning document sent to vendors to obtain information about what services and products each vendor can offer.

 A **request for proposal (RFP)** is a detailed planning document, often written from information received in RFIs, that is sent to vendors with exact specifications for services and products an organization intends to purchase.

In this hands-on activity you have an opportunity to view an organization's planning document.

To see a planning document:

1. Schedule an appointment with the computer center director, network administrator, or planning director of your school or a local business that is networked.

2. Ask to see the organization's network planning document, computer systems short- or long-range plan, or business plan.

3. Ask to see a diagram of the network, if one is available.

4. Ask the person you visit about the process he or she uses for planning.

SELECTING THE RIGHT NETWORK MEDIA AND TOPOLOGY

To plan a network for the best performance and management characteristics, as well as reasonable cost and future expandability, you should follow several general guidelines. By now you already know many of those guidelines:

- Use an Ethernet physical star, logical bus topology under most circumstances. Such a topology offers the most equipment, expansion, and support options. You also will have more networking colleagues with whom to consult.

- Install category 5 UTP cable for flexibility in most cable installations. That gives you the ability also to install high-speed communications immediately or to convert to high-speed communications later.

- Install fiber-optic cable on backbones and between buildings to give you the highest bandwidth and to adhere to the IEEE and EIA/TIA-568 specifications for interbuilding connections.

- Check for significant sources of EMI or RFI, for example, from equipment in a manufacturing plant or a machine shop. Install STP in those conditions to help minimize interference.

- Always install more cable and cable runs than you need immediately. Network growth happens quickly, so in the long run it is cheaper to install extra cable and wall outlets in the beginning than to add them later. That also ensures that all components are compatible from the start. From the beginning, increase your estimates of cable and outlets by 25% to 50% to accommodate expected and unexpected growth.

- Check the local building codes and install plenum cable where mandated by the codes.

- Follow 100% of the IEEE and EIA/TIA guidelines for commercial building telecommunications cabling.

- For new buildings or remodeled buildings, ask to participate in the early planning stages. Besides making recommendations concerning wire installation, work to locate computer machine rooms, equipment rooms, and wiring closets in central locations for the most flexibility in wiring. Also, the wiring configuration in wiring closets is important as to whether patch panels or "home-run" cabling schemes are used. Follow the EIA/TIA-569 specifications for wiring and telecommunications closets.

The next three sections use examples to describe how to apply these guidelines.

EXAMPLE 1: IMPLEMENTING A NETWORK ON A SINGLE FLOOR OF A BUILDING

Assume you are working with a title insurance company that employs 28 people in a one-story building. The building is 10 years old and has never been networked, although each employee has a desktop PC. There is no central computer; office members carry floppy disks to one another when they want to share files. Each title insurance representative keeps individual client records on his or her own PC. Information for billings is carried by floppy disk to an office assistant, who compiles the information for all representatives and sends out bills. The company has decided to install a network and has hired you as a consultant.

Before the wiring is installed, a good place to start is to obtain a floor plan or make your own using a tool such as Microsoft Paint or Visio. Next, inspect the entire location and the physical layout. Discuss with management personnel how the network is to be used and develop a planning document that can be revised as the project proceeds.

In this situation a Windows NT file server would enable the firm to take full advantage of a network and to manage network resources centrally from the server, such as shared files, user accounts, printers, and security. Network traffic also can be monitored through the server. An Ethernet physical star, logical bus network would give the firm options to grow while reducing the cost of network management by centralizing network communications. Problems with a node can be quickly identified and fixed through such a central design and network segments isolated so problems on one segment do not take down the entire network.

The physical connectivity can be accomplished by installing category 5 UTP cable (after you first have checked plenum requirements) connected to stackable hubs. Because the firm does not plan to transmit large files or graphics at this time, a 10BASE-T network with 10 Mbps hubs is likely to be sufficient. Also, combination 10 Mbps and 100 Mbps NICs are a good choice, providing easy conversion to a 100BASE-T network in the future, if needed. Figure 7-1 illustrates how the network can be implemented.

 If this were a publishing or engineering firm with a need to transmit large graphic files, 100 Mbps switching hubs would be the best choice for higher bandwidth and less network congestion. Also, a 100 Mbps network is an option in this situation, if the firm has a budget to purchase the more expensive hubs.

Figure 7-1

Single-floor
implementation

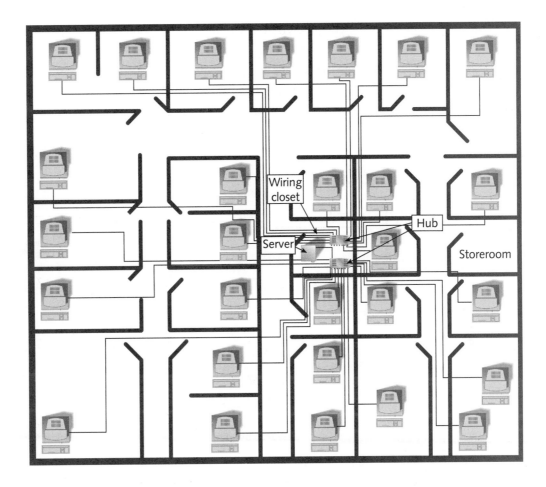

EXAMPLE 2: IMPLEMENTING A NETWORK ON MULTIPLE FLOORS IN TWO BUILDINGS

In this example, assume you are planning a network for a small chemical company with offices in two buildings, each with four floors. The business office building is to have two Windows NT file servers and a DEC minicomputer in a computer room on the first floor. The building containing research labs will have two Windows NT file servers on the first floor and workstations on the other three floors.

Again you would use an Ethernet physical star, logical bus design. The cabling on each floor would be category 5 UTP, connected to an intelligent hub at 10 Mbps or 100 Mbps (depending on the type of network traffic). The communications cable between floors would be fiber-optic. Also, fiber-optic cable would be used to connect the buildings. The hubs on each floor could be connected to a main intelligent hub on the first floor or to ATM switches on the first floor of each building (Figure 7-2). The advantage of using ATM switches are as follows:

- High-speed communications on the backbone between each floor and the ATM switch
- High-speed communications on the backbone between buildings
- High-speed communications to the minicomputer and the servers
- The ability to isolate each server on its own segment
- The ability to implement VLANs

- High-speed connectivity to an ISP or other outside telecommunications connection for future expansion

- The option of putting voice and video traffic between buildings, reducing additional costs of phone lines or third-party connections

Figure 7-2

Implementing a network for two buildings

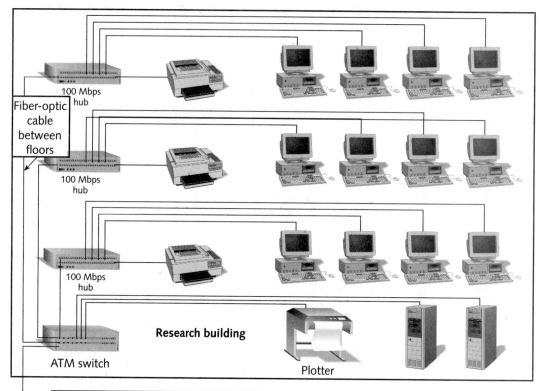

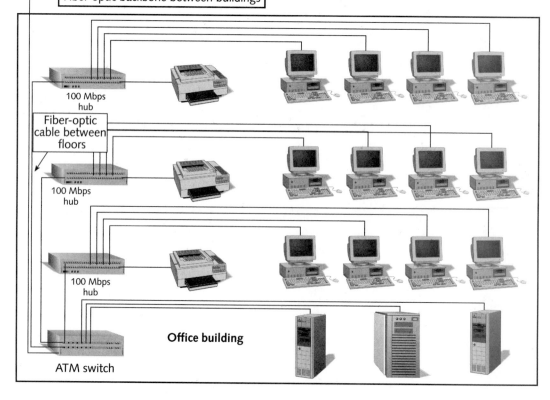

EXAMPLE 3: BUILDING A WAN BETWEEN CITIES

In this third example, assume you are designing a network to connect three atmospheric science research centers for a consortium of U.S. universities. Each center has more than a hundred networked users, mostly scientists and technicians. The researchers work with huge data files and share a supercomputer at the California research site. They need high-speed communications between the sites, which are located in Minnesota, Colorado, and California. Two of the centers have an Ethernet network and one has a combined FDDI and token ring network.

One way to build a WAN linking all three sites is to connect them using T1/T3 or satellite communications between router modules in intelligent modular hubs, as shown in Figure 7-3. When a router is connected to telecommunications services, such as to a T1 or T3 line, two devices are used to connect each router to the line: a **channel service unit (CSU)** and a **data service unit (DSU)**. The CSU is a physical interface to connect the router to the communications line. The DSU converts data so it can be sent over the line and converts received data to be forwarded onto the network. Both devices are combined into one unit (or are incorporated into the connecting device, i.e., router, hub, or switch) and work on a principle similar to a high-speed modem that converts and compresses or decompresses data transmitted over telephone lines.

A **channel service unit (CSU)** is a physical interface between a network device, such as a router, and a telecommunications line.

A **data service unit (DSU)** is used with a CSU for communications over a telecommunications line. The DSU converts data to be sent over the line and converts data received from the line into a readable digital format.

Using routers has the advantage that different kinds of transport systems and protocols can be connected over long distances. The intelligent modular hubs containing the routers have the advantages that network traffic can be monitored and controlled through network management software (see chapters 10 and 11) and that the hubs can be expanded later with modules for high-speed network connectivity. A disadvantage is that incorporating all network functions into one unit creates a single point of failure if a total meltdown occurs in that unit, such as a power supply or backplane failure.

Figure 7-3

Connecting
remote
research sites
using modular
intelligent
hubs

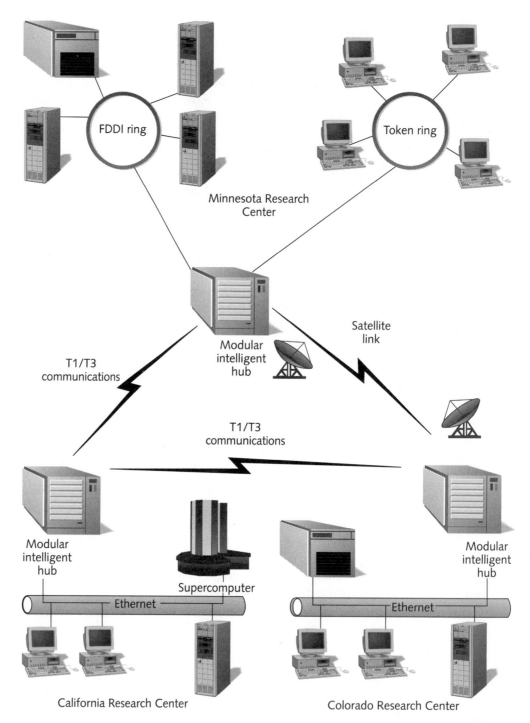

Another way to set up this network is to use an ATM switching module in the intelligent hub or to connect an ATM switch to the hub. The ATM switch can be connected to the SONET services (if available) of a telecommunications provider (Figure 7-4). The combined SONET and ATM switching capabilities yield the best high-speed communications solution between sites, with speeds of at least 155 Mbps.

Figure 7-4

Connecting remote research sites using ATM switches and SONET

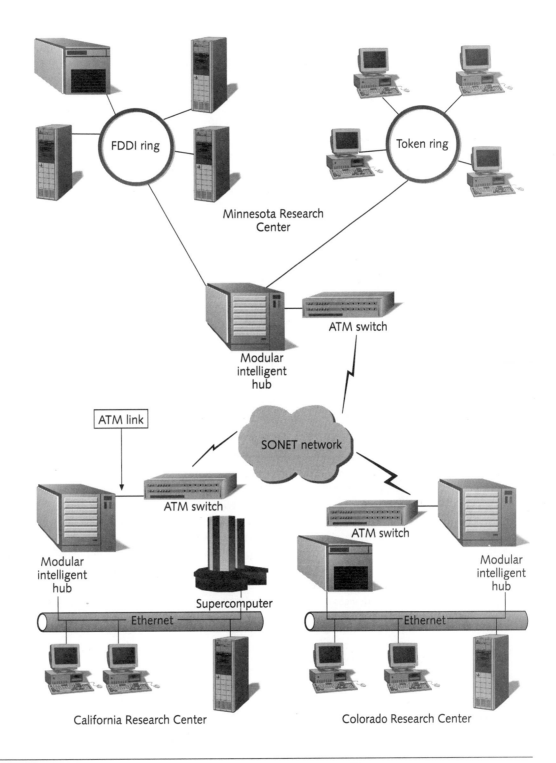

ESTIMATING NETWORKING COSTS

As you plan a network, you need to develop cost estimates and select network equipment based on what the organization can afford. You should calculate networking costs in terms of two factors: component costs and human resource costs. In most cases, a star topology using UTP cable and hubs is the least expensive solution. Category 5 cable is slightly more expensive than category 3 cable, but the option to upgrade to high-speed networking makes the extra expense worthwhile. (In chapter 3 you compared coaxial costs to UTP costs and found that UTP is less expensive than coax.)

Networking costs start to go up as you employ more complex equipment, such as Fast Ethernet switches, routers, hubs, and ATM switches. A Fast Ethernet switch with backbone connectivity may cost more than a 10BASE-T switch and require more expensive NICs than 10 Mbps networking. Routers, intelligent modular hubs, and ATM switches cost much more.

As you plan and design a network, consider the human resource costs, too. For example, a physical star, logical bus topology with network monitoring built into the hubs can make a network much easier to manage and troubleshoot than other alternatives. That translates into a savings in time for the network administrator, enabling him or her to be more productive. It also translates into a reliable network, reducing the amount of time that users experience work interruptions. Smart network devices also give the network administrator the ability to proactively solve network problems before they affect the entire network.

 One human resource cost that is often overlooked during planning is the cost to train personnel to install and operate additional network software. Modern hubs, routers, and other network devices come with complex software that requires initial training to make sure the software is installed and used correctly. Even though the software is advertised to be "user friendly," training often is needed to ensure it is used optimally.

Another human resource cost is the waiting time users spend on a slow or inefficient network. If you are an Internet user, you are familiar with painfully slow response times. You can increase the productivity of users if you plan for efficient and high-speed network options in areas where there is heavy network load. The extra expense of bridges, routers, intelligent modular hubs, Fast Ethernet switches, and ATM switches is offset by the productivity gains of enterprise network users. Thus, when you calculate costs in the planning stage, calculate the impact of network resources on user productivity.

 When you purchase network devices, consider purchasing maintenance contracts for hardware, software, and technical support. All intelligent network devices have their own software that is frequently upgraded to provide additional features. Also, it takes time to replace or repair a device that has failed. With a maintenance contract, the repair or replacement delay is reduced considerably. A technical support contract enables you to get telephone or on-site support for problems you cannot resolve. For a large network (or one with a healthy budget), consider purchasing spare equipment for critical network devices.

 In this hands-on activity you approximate the cost of two 100BASE-TX Fast Ethernet switches that can be connected to a fiber-optic backbone between floors to link 24 graphic artists.

To find the price of a Fast Ethernet switch:

1. Open Internet Explorer by clicking its icon from the desktop or by clicking **Start**, **Programs**, and **Internet Explorer**.

2. Access the Web site of a company that sells networking products, for example, CompUSA (*www.compusa.com*) or Computer Discount Warehouse (*www.cdw.com*).

3. Find the cost of three 8-port or two 12-port 100BASE-TX switching hubs with an AUI connection. Manufacturers include 3Com, Bay Networks, Cabletron, and Cisco. Prices likely will range from $700 to $3,000 per hub, depending on the features and the number of ports.

4. Find the cost of a 100 Mbps NIC (probably about $100).

5. Determine the combined cost of hubs and NICs to provide Fast Ethernet services to the 24 graphic artists.

6. Create a document that summarizes your findings.

 This hands-on activity gives you the opportunity to estimate user productivity costs of 100BASE-TX networking compared to 10BASE-TX networking for the 24 graphic artists.

To calculate productivity costs:

1. Assume that 10 of the graphic artists make $35,000 per year, 10 make $37,000 per year, and 4 make $40,000 (all conservative salaries).

2. Find the total expenses in terms of salaries: $(35,000 \times 10) + (37,000 \times 10) + (40,000 \times 4)$.

3. Assume that the slower 10BASE-TX network causes each artist to spend at least 2% of her or his time waiting, waiting time that 100BASE-TX equipment would eliminate. Multiply the amount from step 2 by 0.02.

4. Compare the amount from step 3 to the expense of 100BASE-TX equipment from the previous hands-on exercise. You likely will find that the human expense in waiting is several thousand dollars more than the equipment expense, making the 100BASE-TX equipment a good investment for the organization.

MANAGING NETWORK PERFORMANCE THROUGH CENTRALIZED PLANNING

Planning a network that uses a hub- and star-based design makes centralized network management possible. Centralized network management means that central points are established for critical network functions. For example, network monitoring can be performed at a dedicated network management station that gathers information about network performance from hubs and other equipment located throughout the network at central points. (Chapters 10 and 11 discuss network management and remote network monitoring in more detail.)

Besides hubs, another way to centralize network management is through computer equipment rooms and through the placement and design of wiring closets. For example, having a central computer room with servers, mainframes, and other equipment simplifies maintenance of those computers. Backups and software upgrades can be performed in one location instead of many. The computers share one protected and conditioned power source and a controlled environment (air conditioning and humidification), saving the cost of multiplying those resources at several locations. With centralized network management, much of the network, server, and host computer maintenance can be done from a central area, reducing the need to travel to multiple geographic locations. That is especially important on large networks.

 Servers, hosts, and other central computers can be located in one area, but they should be set up logically on the network to reduce bottlenecks. One way to do that is to put each device on its own segment coming out from a Fast Ethernet or ATM switch, as shown in Figure 7-2, with high-speed connectivity to each server or host.

Well-planned wiring closets are another way to centralize and improve network management. A **wiring closet** is a central location from which all network cabling runs to each distant location, such as out to workstations and servers. The network backbone cable is run into the wiring closet, and individual cable segments are run out to each workstation and server area. Hubs, repeaters, bridges, and routers are located in wiring closets, as are telephone and video cabling. Having the wiring and equipment centralized makes it easier to troubleshoot problems, to expand services, and to protect valuable equipment. Providing a clean and temperate wiring closest environment with power protection helps protect equipment and wiring from wear and damage. The locations of the wiring closets are critical, because they affect the kind of network equipment that can be used and the ability to reach all proposed network nodes. If a new building is proposed, it is important to locate the wiring closets so they are directly over one another on each floor. That reduces wiring costs and increases the total reach of the network.

A **wiring closet** is a centrally located enclosed room dedicated to house network, telephone, and video cable and associated equipment.

Security for wiring closets also is important. On all networks, security needs mount as the number of nodes increases. Access to wiring closets should be kept to a minimum, to prevent the connection of unauthorized snooping equipment and to prevent unauthorized changes to the physical configuration of the network.

To limit problems caused by someone accidentally turning off or damaging equipment, wiring closets should not be used for other purposes, such as storage.

Wiring closets should be kept cool and dry, to prevent humidity from damaging network equipment. Also, wiring closets should be kept clean. Equipment that becomes excessively dirty will overheat and be subject to extra wear or damage.

Patch panels (the cable wiring panels) should be built by professionals following the EIA/TIA 568 and 569 specifications. Patch cords should follow all distance limitations.

MANAGING PERFORMANCE THROUGH NETWORK SEGMENTING

Your network planning should take network traffic patterns into account, placing network equipment such as bridges, routers, hubs, and ATM switches to control network traffic. That includes the ability to use the equipment to **segment** a network to direct traffic along the most efficient routes while reducing the total traffic flow across each node. One way to segment a network is to use a bridge to filter packets with certain addresses so they do not enter portions of a network where there are no nodes that would receive the packets. For example, consider a network used by students who have meal cards for the cafeteria. Each time a card is read, information is automatically updated on the student's meal account on a server. Teachers share the same network to reach a server with student information, and administrators use the network for the financial systems at the school. There is no need to flood the network with meal account information, which needs to go only from the cafeteria card-reading machines to the meal accounting server. The network could be planned so a bridge or router would segment the meal-plan activity from the teachers' and the business office's network activities.

Segmenting a network involves isolating and directing network traffic to reduce bottlenecks and to reduce the impact of a network malfunction on other portions of the network.

Keep a record of the types of filters you create and where they are on the network; otherwise, the filters may cause difficulties in quickly identifying the source of network problems.

On a TCP/IP network, for example, you can create subnetworks, or subnets, using a special addressing scheme (see chapter 4). The cafeteria subnet might be 122.22.1.xxx, the teachers subnet 122.22.2.xxx, and the administration subnet 122.22.3.xxx. The servers and the host computers would be in a central location designated as subnet 122.22.4.xxx. A router could use the subnet information to direct traffic, so that traffic from the 122.22.1.xxx subnet would not enter the 122.22.2.xxx and 122.22.3.xxx subnets (Figure 7-5). For example, traffic from 122.22.1.xxx would go directly to subnet 122.22.4.xxx.

Figure 7-5

Using subnets to segment a network

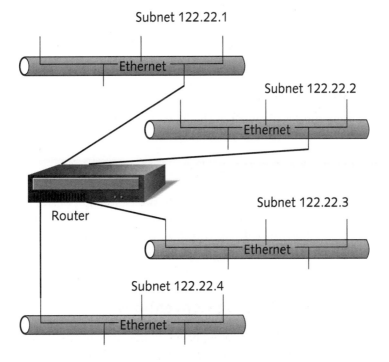

VLANs are another way to manage a network for best performance. As you discovered in chapter 6, hubs, routers, and ATM switches combined with VLAN administration software make it possible to divide a network into VLAN segments containing designated workgroup members. That is accomplished despite the physical layout of nodes on the network. Using VLANs not only enables workgroups, it improves network performance because frames follow the most direct route from the source to the destination.

Some guidelines for segmenting a network for optimal performance are as follows:

- Isolate each server and host on its own segment. That ensures that access to servers or hosts is not affected when another node on the same segment has malfunctioned. Figure 7-2 illustrated how servers and hosts can be isolated via an ATM switch with separate high-speed links to individual machines.

- Use bridges, routers, hubs, and ATM switches to segment network traffic, so a frame is not flooded onto networks unnecessarily.

- Design networks for easy segmentation through the placement of hubs and switches (see Figure 7-2).

PLANNING ACCOUNT MANAGEMENT

On many networks, management is simplified through the creation of user accounts on a centralized server. The setup of accounts can be standardized for each user so users have consistent account names, controlled access to network resources, and security to protect each account from intruders. Another advantage of centralizing user accounts is that it saves time on account management. It is easier to have a set of account management procedures automatically in place than to have to manually set up the same procedures for each account.

Microsoft Windows NT Server account management tools are one example of how accounts can be centrally managed at the server. Those tools enable account management by the following means:

- Account policies
- User home directories
- Group policies
- Account auditing

Each of those tools is discussed in the following sections.

SETTING ACCOUNT POLICIES

Part of your network planning should address establishing policies for accounts that access network resources, such as servers and printers. Many network administrators consult with a management or advisory group within an organization for direction on how to manage accounts. That includes direction on establishing account names and account security and providing users with home directory disk space on a server.

Setting Account Naming Conventions

Organizations set up account names based on the account users' actual names or functions within the organization. For example, if the organization uses actual names, it will adopt a particular naming convention, because it is clumsy to use full names and because server storage for account names is limited by the operating system. Some IBM mainframe operating systems limit the length of account names to eight characters. Windows NT Server limits account names to 20 characters. Some examples of conventions for account names based on the users' actual names are as follows:

- Last name followed by the first initial (e.g., PalmerM)
- First initial followed by the last name (e.g., MPalmer)
- First initial, middle initial, and last name (e.g., MJPalmer)

When an organization creates account names by position or function, it often is based on using descriptive names. For example, the payroll office may use the names Paysuper (payroll supervisor), Payclerk (payroll clerk), and Payassist (payroll assistant). Another example is how schools name accounts in student labs, such as Lab1, Lab2, Lab3, and so on. The advantage of naming accounts by function is that an account does not have to be purged when the account holder leaves or changes positions. The network administrator simply changes the account password and gives it to the new person in that position. The advantage of having accounts based on users' names is that it is easier to know who is logged onto a server (if the naming convention is well designed).

If you work in a large organization where computer systems and software are audited by independent financial auditors once a year, the auditors often prefer to have accounts named for individual users. That provides the best audit tracking of who has made what changes to data during the year.

Setting Account Policies in Microsoft Windows NT Server

The User Manager for Domains tool in Windows NT Server is used to set account policies. Once set up, the account policies are applied automatically to each newly created account. The account policies that can be set up are the following:

- Password expiration
- Password length
- Password history
- Account lockout

Password expiration is the option to require account holders to change their passwords at regular intervals. That practice guards against situations in which passwords have been compromised, such as when a user reveals his or her password to someone else or uses an easily guessed password. Some users may keep the same password for years if they are not required to change it periodically. A recommended interval to require users to change their passwords is every 30 to 90 days. Another policy option is to require that passwords be five or more characters in length, which makes them more difficult to guess.

Some operating systems keep a record of recently used passwords, to ensure an interval of time before a password is reused. Windows NT Server has the ability to remember a specified number of previously used passwords, as determined by the network administrator.

Account lockout is a mechanism that prevents access to an account after a certain number of unsuccessful logon attempts. Access may be denied for a specified period of time, such as 15 minutes, or until the account is unlocked by the network administrator. The lockout helps prevent a situation in which someone knows the account name and attempts to guess the password. Some organizations set a 30-minute lockout, so the wait is not excessive but accounts still are protected. A 30-minute lockout helps discourage a situation in which someone is in an office for a short time, attempting to access a user's account without that user's permission. If the account holder has just set a new password and is locked out because she or he does not remember it immediately, the 30-minute interval provides a reasonable time in which to try again. Of course, the network administrator always can unlock the account immediately or change the password at the user's request.

Account lockout is a security measure that prohibits logging on to an NT server account after a specified number of unsuccessful attempts.

In this hands-on activity, you practice setting the account policies on a Windows NT server. You need access to the Administrator's account or a practice account with Administrator security privileges.

To set account policies in Windows NT:

1. Log on to the server, click the **Start** button and then **Programs**.

2. From the Programs menu, click **Administrative Tools (Common)** and then **User Manager for Domains** (Figure 7-6). The User Manager is a tool for managing user accounts, user groups, and account policies.

Figure 7-6

Accessing the
User Manager
for Domains

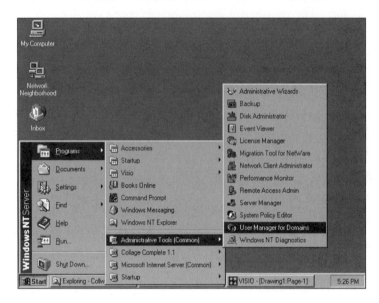

3. Click the **Policies** menu and the **Account** option, as shown in Figure 7-7. The Account Policy dialog box opens, which contains options to set the password security and account lockout policies (Figure 7-8).

Figure 7-7

Accessing the
Account Policy
dialog box

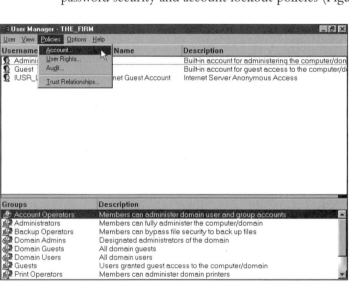

Figure 7-8

Setting account
policies

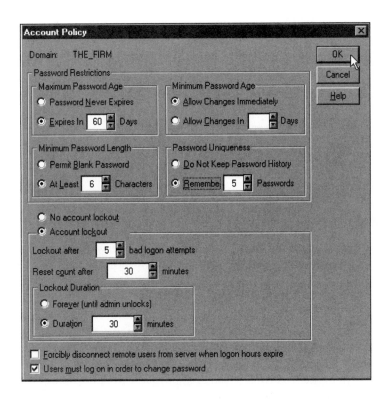

4. Under Maximum Password Age, click **Expires in _____ Days** and enter **60**, so users must change their passwords every 60 days.

5. Under Minimum Password Age, click **Allow Changes Immediately**, so account holders can use new passwords the next time they log on.

6. Under Minimum Password Length, click **At Least _____ Characters** and enter **6** to specify that users must have passwords six characters or more in length.

7. Under Password Uniqueness, click **Remember ___ Passwords** and enter **5** to prevent the last five passwords from being reused.

8. Click the **Account lockout** radio button.

9. Enter **5** in the Lockout after __ bad logon attempts scroll box. That means the account is locked after someone enters the wrong password five times in a row in the amount of time specified in the next line.

10. Enter **30** in the Reset count after _____ minutes scroll box.

11. Under Lockout Duration, click **Duration _____ minutes** and enter **30** as the number of minutes the account will remain locked until it can be accessed again.

12. At the bottom of the screen, check **Users must log on in order to change password**, which means a user must be able to log on to change a password. A user who does not change his or her password by the expiration date will have to ask the network administrator to change it.

13. Click **OK** to confirm the settings and exit the Account Policy dialog box.

14. Close the User Manager for Domains.

CREATING HOME DIRECTORIES

One way to manage where users place files on the network is through the creation of home directories. A **home directory** is a specified location where an account holder can store files, such as on a file server. In Windows NT Server, the location of an account's home directory is set at the time the account is created. Some organizations do not permit users to store files on a file server. In those instances the home directory is located in a folder on the account holder's workstation. Other organizations set aside a specific folder on a file server for each user's home directory.

 A **home directory** is a dedicated location on a file server or a workstation for a designated account holder to store files.

The advantage of having home directories on a file server is that it reduces expenditures for hard disk space on individual workstations. It is more expensive to upgrade workstations one at a time than to upgrade a server for mass disk storage. Also, each user's files are centrally located so file access can be managed centrally by the network administrator or individually by users. Placing home directories on a server makes it easier to back up files from one computer instead of from all computers on the network. The disadvantage is that Windows NT Server does not have a built-in utility to allocate a given amount of disk space to each user. The network administrator must watch closely to make sure home directories do not grow too large. Another approach is to purchase software to limit space allocations for home directories.

 Even with space allocation software, it does not take long for account holders to fill up home directories on a server and request more space. That can be a significant management problem, unless the network administrator plans ahead to set forth specific guidelines for home directories, including purging of old files.

SETTING GROUP POLICIES

Windows NT Server enables user accounts to be managed through the establishment of groups. That particularly applies to setting access rights and permissions. **Rights** enable an account or a predefined group to have high-level access capabilities, such as the right to access a server or to access advanced functions on a server. **Permissions** are associated with access to files and folders on a server, controlling the way an account or a group accesses information. For example, access can range from no permission to view files in a folder to full permission to add or change files.

 Rights in Windows NT Server are high-level access privileges for activities such as to log on to a server, to shut down a server, and to create user accounts.

 Permissions in Windows NT Server control account or group access capabilities for reading, viewing, and changing files or folders.

Managing rights and permissions by individual user accounts is far more labor intensive than managing by groupings of users. **Groups** are used on Windows NT Server computers to help reduce the effort required to manage accounts. Accounts having the same security and access needs can be assigned as members of a group. Then security access is set up for the group instead of for each account. User groupings can save a significant amount of time when there are tens or hundreds of accounts to manage. For example, all users who need access to scientific research files can be in a group called Research, with rights and permissions to access a research server and specific folders on that server. In the same organization, the payroll office members can have accounts in a group, such as Payroll, in which only they have access to payroll and human resources files on an administrative server.

 In Windows NT Server, a **group** is a common entity that contains user accounts and network resources, such as file and print servers.

Windows NT Server defines two types of groups: local and global. A **local group** consists of user accounts, network resources (servers, workstations, and network printers), and global groups. A local group is used to define rights and privileges in a single Microsoft domain. As you learned in chapter 1, a domain is a collection of network resources, managed by one or more Windows NT servers on a network. For example, a college with branch campuses in two cities might have three domains, one for the main campus and one for each branch campus. A **global group** is used to provide access rights across Microsoft domains, such as providing access from the main campus to the branch campuses. By using a combination of local and global groups, an enterprise network can be set up so that one network manager can manage server, workstation, and printing resources from one NT Server, even if the resources are spread out among networks in different geographic locations (and domains). Local and global group memberships and policies are set through the User Manager for Domains utility in Windows NT Server.

 A **local group** in NT Server consists of accounts, network resources, and global groups. It is used to manage accounts and resources in a single domain.

 A **global group** is used to make one Microsoft domain accessible to another, so resources can be shared and managed across two or more domains.

 This hands-on activity gives you an opportunity to practice setting a group management policy in Windows NT Server. You need access to the Administrator account or to an account with the same access privileges on a computer running Windows NT Server. The computer running NT Server should be intended for practice and have no one logged on when you perform this activity.

To set the group policy in Windows NT:

1. Log on to the server, click **Start**, **Programs**, **Administrative Tools (Common)**, and **User Manager for Domains** (see Figure 7-6).

2. Click the **Policies** menu and the **User Rights** option (see Figure 7-7). The User Rights Policy dialog box opens.

3. Click the down arrow in the Right: scroll box. Observe the possible rights, such as Add workstations to domain and Back up files and directories (Figure 7-9). Use the scroll bar on the right side of the scroll box to view all the rights.

Figure 7-9

Viewing rights

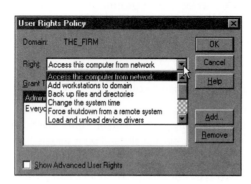

4. Click the right **Access this computer from network** and make sure that the Everyone group is in the Grant To: text box. Everyone is a local group of all server users. That right enables all users to log on to the server from a workstation connected to the network.

5. Highlight the **Everyone** group and click the **Remove** button (Figure 7-10). This action removes the right for anyone to access the server over the network, except for those who belong to the Administrators group. A network administrator might remove this right when he or she needs to work on a server and wants to make sure no one can access it until the work is finished. (If you do this in a live situation, give users prior warning and make sure they have saved their work and are logged off.)

Figure 7-10

Removing a
right

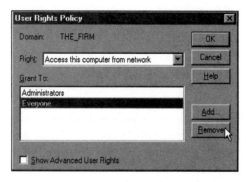

6. Next, give back access rights to Everyone. In the Right: scroll box, click the down arrow and again click **Access this computer from network**.

7. Click the **Add** button on the User Rights Policy dialog box.

8. Click the **Everyone** group in the Names: scroll box on the Add Users and Groups dialog box. Click the **Add** button (Figure 7-11).

Figure 7-11

Adding a right

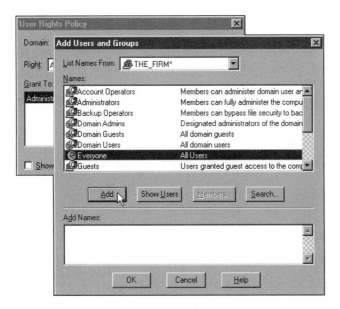

9. Notice that the Everyone group is now displayed in the Add Names: scroll box. Click **OK** on the Add Users and Groups dialog box.

10. Make sure the Everyone group is displayed in the Grant To: text box on the User Rights Policy dialog box for the right Access this computer from network.

11. Click **OK** to finish.

AUDITING ACCOUNT ACTIVITY

Windows NT Server has an option to track activity on accounts, which is called **auditing**. Records can be kept on the following:

- Account logon and logoff activity

- Successful and unsuccessful access of files and folders

- Successful and unsuccessful use of rights and permissions

- Significant changes to an account, such as adding it to a group

Auditing is the ability to track past activities as a means to help identify and solve problems.

The option to audit accounts enables the network administrator to trace problems. For example, if an account cannot access certain files, it may not have the appropriate permissions. Checking the audit information helps the administrator to determine if permissions are set correctly. Another reason for account auditing is to identify situations in which an intruder is attempting to access an account. In that case, the audit information shows a high number of unsuccessful logon attempts.

PLANNING NETWORK SECURITY

Developing a comprehensive plan to protect network resources is vital. All networks contain resources and information on which users depend. An interruption of network service or loss of data can be costly. A network security plan protects data and minimizes downtime resulting from natural hazards and human error. The security plan should address the following areas:

- Passwords and password maintenance
- Access privilege management
- Encryption
- Power protection
- System and data backups
- System fault tolerance and redundancy
- Firewalls
- Virus monitoring
- Disaster recovery

Passwords, access privileges, encryption, firewalls, and virus monitoring are discussed in the following sections. Chapter 8 examines power protection, backups, fault tolerance, and disaster recovery.

SETTING PASSWORDS

Passwords are a critical defense against intrusions. All network accounts should have a password that is changed on a regular schedule. Accounts such as the NT Server Administrator account should have a long password that is difficult to guess and that is changed every 30 to 60 days. A Guest account on computers running Windows NT Server or Workstation should be checked to make sure it is disabled or has a password, and permissions should be applied to control access to files and folders.

 Many operating systems create a default Guest account or its equivalent. Such an account can be an open "back door" into a system and should have a password or be disabled.

 This hands-on activity gives you practice in disabling the Guest account on an NT Server. Again you need access to the Administrator account or one with the same access.

To disable the Guest account:

1. Log on to the server, then click the **Start** button and **Programs**.

2. Click **Administrative Tools (Common)** and then **User Manager for Domains** (see Figure 7-6).

3. Double-click **Guest** under the Username column.

4. On the User Properties dialog box, enter a password in the Password: text box if none is present. Enter the password again in the Confirm Password: text box.

5. Check the **Account Disabled** box (Figure 7-12).

6. Click **OK** on the User Properties dialog box.

7. Close the User Manager.

Figure 7-12

Disabling the
Guest account

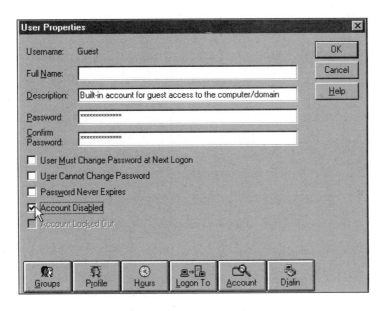

MANAGING ACCESS PRIVILEGES

Windows NT servers have file and folder permissions security that should be planned and set before a server is made available to the network. Permissions can be set in two ways. One way is to set permissions on shared resources such as folders or printers (Table 7-1). Those permissions are limited in scope but provide basic security.

Table 7-1

Windows NT
permissions on a
shared folder

Permission	Access Capability
No access	Prevents access to the shared drive for the specified group
Read	Permits groups or users to read and execute files
Change	Enables users to read, add, modify, execute, and delete files
Full Control	Provides full access to the directory, including the ability to take ownership or change permissions

The NT file system on Windows NT Server and Workstation comes with a more in-depth level of security that can be applied to individual folders and files (Table 7-2). Such security is part of Windows NT's government certification at the C2, or top-secret, level. Information on a server can be thoroughly protected using the NT file system security.

Table 7-2

NT file system folder and file permissions

Permission	Access and Abbreviation	Description	Applies to...
No Access	None	No access to the directory for any users other than the owner	Folders and files
List	Read and execute files	Can list files in the directory or switch to a subdirectory but cannot access file contents	Folders only
Read	Read and execute files	For existing and new files, can read their contents and can execute program files	Folders and files
Add	Write and execute files	Can write new files in the directory and execute program files but cannot view directory files	Folders only
Add & Read	Read, write, and execute files	Can read files, add new files, and execute program files but cannot modify file contents	Folders only
Change	Read, write, execute, and delete files	Can read, add, delete, execute, and modify files	Folders and files
Full Control	All directory and file permissions	Can read, add, delete, execute, and modify files plus change permissions and take ownership of directories	Folders and files

Microsoft provides the following guidelines for setting permissions:

- Protect the Winnt folder that contains operating system files on NT servers and workstations and its subfolders from general users through No Access, but give the Administrators group Full Control access.

- Protect utility folders with access permissions only for Administrators.

- Protect software application folders with Add & Read to enable users to run applications and write temporary files but not to alter files.

- Create publicly used folders to have Change access, so users have broad access except to take ownership and set permissions.

- Provide users Full Control of their own home directories.

- Remove the group Everyone from confidential folders, such as those used for personal mail or for software development projects.

This hands-on activity enables you to give the Administrators group Full Control of the system files in the Winnt folder on a Windows NT server.

To set file permissions:

1. Log on to the server and double-click **My Computer** on the desktop.

2. Double-click drive **C:** (or the drive where the Winnt folder is located) in the My Computer dialog box.

3. Right-click the **Winnt** folder and click **Properties** (Figure 7-13).

Figure 7-13

Selecting Winnt properties

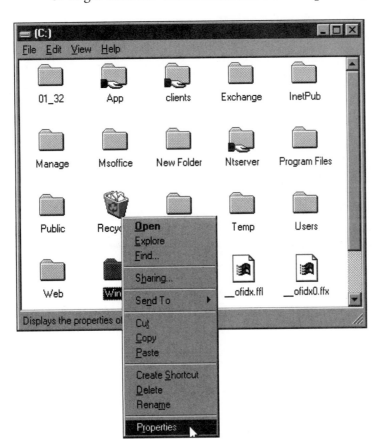

4. Click the **Security** tab on the Winnt Properties dialog box (Figure 7-14).

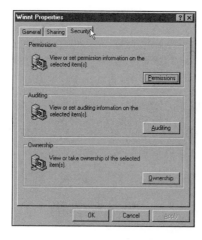

Figure 7-14

Clicking the
Security tab

5. Click the **Permissions** button.

6. Click the **Add** button and click the **Administrators** group on the Add Users and Groups dialog box. Set Type of Access: to **Full Control** (Figure 7-15).

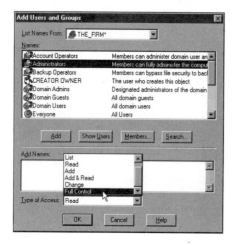

Figure 7-15

Giving the
Administrators
group Full
Control
permission

7. Click **OK** on the Add Users and Groups dialog box.

8. Click **OK** on the Directory Permissions dialog box.

9. Click **OK** on the Winnt Properties dialog box.

Similar to Windows NT Server, most network servers and host operating systems come with security capabilities, although capabilities can vary. Not all systems are certified at the C2 level, which means that some systems may not pass a financial or security auditor's inspection. If your organization handles money transactions, confidential human resources information, medical records, or other data that must be protected, plan to use network operating systems that can provide the needed security. If an existing system does not have built-in security, it may be necessary to purchase a security system from the original vendor or a third party. For example, the IBM mainframe operating system MVS does not have a native security package. Many IBM customers opt to purchase a security add-on from IBM or another vendor.

DATABASE SECURITY

Modern relational databases come with security capabilities. Oracle, Sybase, Microsoft SQL Server, Informix, and DB2 are some examples of database systems that have built-in security. Those systems enable the network or database administrator to establish security based on the database characteristics such as the entire database or by table, view, stored procedure, trigger, row, and column within the database.

Client/server systems employ security through the client/server programs, so that database access via a program is secure. Those same systems may leave open direct access to the database through report writers and database utilities, making the database unsecured. Besides program security, make sure the database security options are used to protect a client/server database.

DATA ENCRYPTION

It is relatively easy for an enterprising hacker to build a network interface and software to capture frames on the network. With that capability, someone could intercept user IDs and passwords. A hacker also might extract confidential data, such as credit card or bank account numbers.

Data **encryption** techniques have become increasing important to protect critical information from interception on networks. For example, if you make purchases through the Internet, you already may use a secure browser.

Encryption involves turning data into an unintelligible sequence of characters. A key is used to translate the nonsense into the original information.

A common method for encrypting data is to require one or more "keys." The **encryption key** is a digital code or password that must be known to both the sending node and the receiving node. Some security schemes use keys with up to 512 digits.

An **encryption key** is a digital password known to the sending node and the receiving node on a network.

One method that employs keys is the public-key encryption technique. In that technique, the key is divided into two parts. One part is published in a directory that is available to all network nodes. The second part is kept private by the sending and receiving nodes. Both portions of the key must be known by the receiving node before data packets can be decrypted.

The National Institute of Standards and Technology (NIST) and IBM have created a public-key encryption method called **Data Encryption Standard (DES)**. DES uses keys that contain either 56 digits or 112 digits. Half of the key is used to encrypt information, and the rest of the key is used for decrypting the received data. For example, Microsoft Internet Information Server (IIS) employs DES-compatible data encryption as a Web server.

The **Data Encryption Standard (DES)** is a network encryption standard developed by the National Institute of Standards and Technology (NIST) and IBM.

Some vendors have designed private-key encryption methods that give unique keys to the sending and receiving nodes. No portion of a key is published in a common directory. Keys are generated by a specialized encryption computer that verifies each node's authorization to transmit data. The specialized computer contains a database of information on each node such as IP address, user ID, user name, time, date, and so on. The key codes for the sender and the receiver must be known before information can be decrypted.

The public-key and private-key techniques both incorporate an additional encryption step for each frame that is sent. The additional step includes a message authentication code (MAC), an encrypted checksum attached to the stream of data. The checksum enables the recipient to determine if data is sent without error. It also provides a second level of data security, because both the sending and the receiving nodes must be able to compute the MAC.

CREATING FIREWALLS

Firewalls protect a network from intruders and reduce unwanted traffic. As network administrator, for example, you might be required to protect the accounting system and payroll file server from being accessed by individuals outside the accounting department. You could restrict access by installing a firewall between the accounting office network segment and the rest of the network.

Routers frequently are used as firewalls, because they examine every packet before sending it on. The path through a router can be limited based on the local network address, subnet address, and other IP addressing information.

If your network spans a large campus or is connected to the Internet, router security may not be enough. For example, you might not be able to fine tune your router for adequate control over TCP-type protocols, such as file transfer protocol (FTP). An effective solution is to install a device designed specifically to operate as a firewall. A dedicated firewall adds security options such as network address translation, logging, FTP management, simple mail transfer protocol (SMTP) proxy, hypertext transport protocol (HTTP) proxy, network encryption, and virtual network encryption.

A **firewall** is hardware and software that protect portions of a network in two ways. One is by securing access to data and resources from outside intruders. The second is by preventing data from leaving the network through an inside source.

Network address translation is used to hide internal networks from view of the Internet. Knowledge of how to reach a particular node on a network is kept secret from Internet intruders. But communication from the internal network nodes to the Internet is unrestricted (or can be restricted if necessary).

The firewall logging capability produces reports of intrusions so you can trace their origin. Some firewalls provide instant notification of intrusions.

A firewall can monitor all FTP sessions and the port number designated for a session. It can foil intruders who attempt to exploit FTP access by going through a port where they are not authorized. Firewalls also have FTP proxy, which enables the firewall to check an FTP session for Gets and Puts (whether a file has been sent or received). For example, FTP proxy can be used to allow employees—but no one else—to transmit a file to a server from the Internet.

A disadvantage of e-mail is that header data often reveals information about the sender's network. When a message is sent, an intruder may intercept it and obtain sensitive network information. The SMTP proxy option enables you to remove header data before the message leaves the firewall.

Some firewalls have an HTTP proxy to protect Web applications. Through the HTTP proxy, only given users may access a specified Web page. If you work for a company that provides executive information reporting on the Web or through an intranet, HTTP proxy ensures that only the managers you designate can view the reports.

Firewalls offer DES, proprietary, and other forms of data encryption for networkwide communications. Firewalls also can offer virtual or private network encryption. Virtual network encryption enables you to designate certain parts of the network for private communication exchanges. For example, say you are the network administrator at a college where the payroll office is across campus from the personnel office. The two offices frequently need to share confidential information and common database files. The network locations could be designated as a private network using specialized encryption not available to the wider network.

VIRUS PROTECTION

The term **computer virus** relates to several types of software programs that damage files on a server or a workstation: viruses, Trojan horses, and worms. Viruses are program code that spreads into executable files, partition tables, system files, and other sensitive areas. As they spread, they corrupt files, delete data, and even prevent systems from booting. A virus can be carried by an executable program, e-mail, a macro (such as in a word processor or a spreadsheet), a downloaded file, and other sources. For example, in 1987 the Christmas Virus painted a Christmas tree on the user's monitor while it searched that user's e-mail files for names and network addresses. It then sent itself on to other users of WANs throughout the United States, slowing down BITNET (a predecessor of the Internet) and crippling other networks.

A **computer virus** is software that can spread throughout a computer, damaging files, file allocation tables, and other software components.

A Trojan horse is program code hidden in software and set to strike on a given date or event, such as Halloween. It also damages files, data, and programs. A Trojan horse usually is packaged with a program that seems harmless, such as a computer utility or even a virus checker. Worms search for vulnerable entry points in a computer operating system, such as a Guest account that is not protected with a password. Once in, the worm grows in the operating system or duplicates files until the system fails.

The best precaution against viruses is to purchase software from reliable vendors and to avoid free utilities or disks that have passed among several people. Always use virus-scanning software to check for viruses in software downloaded from the Internet. Even software from a vendor may be infected when disks are returned and reused.

Develop a plan to prevent and detect viruses as you implement a network. Careful network administrators run a virus scanner on all software before loading it on the server. You can use the following measures in network planning to protect against viruses:

- Purchase reliable scanning software, obtaining a site license for all servers and workstations on the network.

- Have the virus scanner running in the background on servers so it can immediately detect a virus.

- Set the scanner to run a full scan on a regular basis, such as every night before or after file backups.

- Scan all software for viruses before installing the software on a network server or workstation (use a workstation that is not connected to the network).

- Unzip or decompress compressed files before scanning, because a scanner may not find a virus in that type of files.

- Do not use software that has been handed from person to person, including macros.

- Educate users to be careful about where they obtain software and to scan for viruses as soon as they install the software on a workstation.

Also in the planning stage, consider purchasing scanning software that meets the following criteria:

- Is easy to use

- Tests memory as well as disk drives

- Is compatible with Windows NT, Windows 95, and Windows 3.x

- Is designed for network workstations and servers

- Is updated frequently, with scanning for new viruses

- Is recommended by other network administrators

CHAPTER SUMMARY

The network you end up with is a direct product of your advance planning. While you cannot plan for every contingency, you can plan for most. Planning starts with assessing why the network is needed and how it will be used. That phase of the planning helps you tie the end result into what your users need from their network. Writing an RFI (request for information), RFP (request for proposal), or both gives you an opportunity to pull together all your planning into one document that serves as a reference point.

Part of the network planning process is to select the right network media and topology for your situation. General guidelines can help you plan for the present and lay a foundation for the future. Those guidelines include using a modular logical star, physical bus topology with ample cabling for growth. Also, category 5 cable is a good choice for connectivity to desktops, and fiber-optic cable is the best choice for backbone connectivity. Small and large networking situations were presented as examples to show you how to plan media and topology.

Another part of the planning is for management of network performance. Centralized network design using intelligent hubs and switches is one way to design for top performance. Another is to use segmenting techniques available through bridges, routers, and switches. Examples of those techniques are subnets and VLANs. Also, as you will discover in chapters 10 and 11, centralized and dedicated network management on a high-performance network management station is important for medium to large networks, enabling the network administrator to proactively resolve problems before they become networkwide dilemmas.

Account and group management is another important aspect of network planning. Windows NT Server has tools available through the User Manager for Domains that let you set up the account and group policies you have planned. Establishing plans for home directories and account auditing are other ways you can manage accounts.

A security management plan involves establishing methods to protect your network and data. That plan includes securing the network through passwords, file and folder access controls, data encryption, firewalls, and virus protection.

The next chapter explains other ways to secure your network through building in redundancy and establishing sound backup techniques. It discusses creating reserve disk storage and power sources and different backup techniques that provide a line of defense against equipment failures and natural disasters.

REVIEW QUESTIONS

1. Microsoft Windows NT Server account policies include
   a. account lockout.
   b. password requirements.
   c. DES data encryption.
   d. all of the above
   e. only a and b

2. Permissions are part of a security plan to
   a. obtain written verification that a user can have an account.
   b. control who can access folders and files on a Windows NT Server.
   c. implement HTTP proxy on a network.
   d. limit account access on a workstation running Windows 95.

3. DES (Data Encryption Standard) uses
   a. encryption keys.
   b. SMTP proxy.
   c. account testing.
   d. routing encryption.

4. Using subnets to segment a network is possible through
   a. using the NetBEUI protocol.
   b. using the TCP/IP protocol with IP addressing.
   c. deploying bridges.
   d. 10BASE-T networks but not 10BASE2 networks.

5. Viruses can be spread through
   a. macros.
   b. e-mail.
   c. downloaded files.
   d. all of the above
   e. only a and c

6. From where would you set up account policies on a Microsoft NT Server?
   a. User Manager for Domains
   b. through establishment of network bindings to the server
   c. Network Neighborhood
   d. My Computer

7. From where would you set up permissions on a Microsoft NT Server?
   a. User Manager for Domains
   b. Network Neighborhood
   c. My Computer
   d. Settings option on the Programs menu

8. Which of the following might you accomplish using a firewall?
   a. logging intrusion attempts
   b. controlling access to FTP services
   c. rejecting e-mail sent from designated gateways
   d. all of the above
   e. only a and b

9. Which of the following would provide the highest-speed connectivity for networks joined between two cities on the East Coast?
   a. Connect each location using bridges and microwave links.
   b. Connect each location using ATM switches and SONET.
   c. Connect each location using routers and T1 lines.
   d. Connect each location using repeaters and T3 lines.

10. When planning security, you should take into account
    a. use of passwords.
    b. file and folder access.
    c. a means for the network administrator to access all files and programs.
    d. all of the above
    e. only a and b

ASPEN CONSULTING PROJECT: DEVELOPING A PLAN FOR THE PHYSICIANS GROUP

This is your week to work more with Gary Sharma from the Physicians Group. You now are working to develop a concrete network plan for the new two-story Physicians Group building. In the plan you must specify how to network the 60-plus workstations, with 30 or more on each floor. Also, you need to help develop plans for effective network performance, account management on the Windows NT Server, and security.

ASSIGNMENT 7-1

Using the space that follows, explain to Gary the factors you want to cover in assessing the needs of the Physicians Group as they relate to your planning process.

What information do you need to determine if the Physicians Group requires high-speed networking immediately? At what point should you request to be in on the planning for the building? Why is that important?

ASSIGNMENT 7-2

What communications media and network equipment would you use to connect work-stations on each floor of the building? What communications media would you use to connect the two floors? Explain the topology you would use and how that might affect network performance. Present your answers in the form of a plan for Gary.

ASSIGNMENT 7-3

Use Microsoft Paint or another drawing package to produce a sample network diagram to help illustrate the plan you made in Assignment 7-2. Label the communications media and network equipment.

ASSIGNMENT 7-4

Gary has explained to you that each physician keeps confidential records on her or his patients. The group has decided to centralize those records on the Windows NT server, with each physician having a protected folder. Sometimes a physician needs to share a patient's file with another physician in the group. All physicians need their own server accounts. And each physician's nurse needs an account that can access the same files as the physician for whom the nurse works. In the space below, develop a plan for setting up account and group policies.

ASSIGNMENT 7-5

After you have developed the plan for account policies, practice setting up the policies on a Windows NT Server in a lab your instructor has provided. Use the following table to briefly explain the steps you used to set up the account policies.

Steps to Set Up Account Policies
Step 1:
Step 2:
Step 3:
Step 4:
Step 5:
Step 6:
Step 7:
Step 8:

ASSIGNMENT 7-6

Develop a security plan that covers access to each physician's folder on the server (Assignment 7-4). Include in the plan how you would use the NT file system security options.

 ASSIGNMENT 7-7

As you discovered in the case study for chapter 4, the Physicians Group network will be connected to the hospital network. Gary has explained that the Physicians Group will exchange e-mail with the hospital and will access certain forms and records directly on the hospital's AS/400 minicomputer and NetWare file servers. However, the hospital will not have access to the workstations and the server on the Physicians Group network, due to the confidential nature of the information. Explain in the following space the security measures you would include in your planning for this situation.

OPTIONAL CASE STUDIES FOR TEAMS

 TEAM CASE 1

Mark Arnez wants you to form a team to select a virus-scanning software package that Aspen Consulting will recommend to its clients. Develop a set of criteria for the software. Next, use the Internet to find two or more software packages that meet your criteria.

 TEAM CASE 2

Mark has asked that you keep your team together from the last assignment and develop a set of desired features for a dedicated firewall. Use the Internet to find one or more products that match your criteria. Create a report for Mark recording the results of your work.

 TEAM CASE 3

You are on a team to develop a plan for network communications media and equipment for a law firm with two offices, one in Toronto and one in Ontario. There are 40 people in the three-story building in Toronto and 22 people in the single-story building in Ontario. Describe in general terms the factors you would take into account to develop a network plan. Would you write an RFI or an RFP? Explain.

 TEAM CASE 4

One of the community colleges in your city has contacted you for consulting advice on developing an account-naming plan for the student labs. There will be 12 new labs, each with 30 to 40 computers. Form a team to work on the recommendations. Each lab provides access to Microsoft Office products, e-mail, Lotus Notes, math software, and other software used by specific classes. Four central Windows NT servers provide services to the labs. Write a set of recommendations explaining how to name accounts in the labs.

FAULT-TOLERANCE TECHNIQUES

Developing a plan for network performance, account management, and security, topics covered in chapter 7, addresses areas of networking over which you have some control. If you plan a network with modular hubs, switches, and central points for management, you have design opportunities to segment and manage network traffic for the best performance. If you develop account policies and set up groups, you can make a network easier to manage. If you set up a thorough security plan, you can minimize data and network problems caused by human actions.

Other events can be unpredictable, such as natural hazards and equipment failures. You don't know when such events will occur, but you know they can occur. Power failures and fluctuations are the most common problems for a network administrator, but there are many other unpredictable hazards to your network. For example, before dawn one Saturday morning, more than 20 computers and a file server in a community college computer lab were destroyed when lightning struck a telephone line. The lightning followed a telephone cable into the server's modem, jumped to the network cable, and damaged nearly all the computers in that lab. In another example, a university computer room housing servers and external disk drives connected to those servers had a totally unexpected problem. A large overhead light fixture came loose and fell from the plaster ceiling onto a server and the hard drives connected to that server and to a server nearby. The server had some slight damage, but the hard drives had to be replaced. The disk drives were packed with important data necessary to the work of several hundred users.

AFTER READING THIS CHAPTER AND COMPLETING THE EXERCISES YOU WILL BE ABLE TO:

- DESCRIBE DIFFERENT TYPES OF HARDWARE FAILURES
- PLAN AND SET UP FAULT-TOLERANCE METHODS FOR DISK STORAGE
- DESCRIBE THE BUILT-IN FAULT-TOLERANCE FEATURES OF SOME OPERATING SYSTEMS
- EXPLAIN AND SET UP UPS FAULT-TOLERANCE OPTIONS
- DEVELOP AND IMPLEMENT A TAPE BACKUP PLAN AND ROTATION METHOD
- DEVELOP A DISASTER RECOVERY PLAN

In a third example, a small business that keeps servers and network equipment in an empty office experienced occasional brief power failures to that office and a couple of adjoining offices, causing interruption of all network functions. One day there were several power failures, and because the business did not have the computer equipment on power protection devices, one of the server disk drives failed to boot. A staff member discovered that a power failure occurred each time someone closed the door to the office containing the computers. An electrician determined the power problems were related to a bad circuit in the main circuit box, which was next to the door of the office containing the computer equipment.

As you plan and implement a network, you have many options to reduce the consequences of unforeseen hazards. The two simplest ways to guard against unexpected failures are to implement protection against power problems and to develop thorough data-backup procedures. Another option is to protect data by duplicating it on extra disk drives. Those and other solutions can be incorporated into a disaster recovery plan to protect data and network resources.

COMPONENT FAILURES

Hardware components can and do fail, including the components in the following devices:

- Workstations
- Servers
- Switches
- Repeaters
- Bridges
- Routers
- Hubs
- Connectors
- Terminators

The hardware components most likely to fail are those with moving parts, such as disk drives and tape drives. Disk drives are particularly vulnerable to failure. That is partly because the read heads on disk drives are located as close as possible to the disk platters without physically touching them. Each time the disk drive is powered down, the read head is moved away from the platter as the drive spins down. The mechanical movement of spinning down a drive results in extra wear on the read head mechanism. Power failures, sudden surges of power, and power brownouts are especially hard on disk drives, because they cause extra read head movement as the disk spins down and up.

Disk drives that are over 80% full also are subject to increased mechanical wear. Extensive fragmentation of files on a disk is another cause of extra wear. **Disk fragmentation** exists when the files on a disk gradually become spread throughout the hard drive, with empty pockets of space scattered throughout. Fragmentation occurs normally over time, the result of creating new files and deleting old files. Full and fragmented drives cause the read head to move across the disk more extensively than when disks are maintained regularly. Regular maintenance of disks involves moving files to less-full disks and defragmenting disks. **Defragmenting** a disk is a process used to reorganize files to reduce the number of empty spaces between files. Some operating systems come with software to defragment disks, but many do not. Disk-defragmenting software is a sound investment to extend the life of disk drives.

Disk fragmentation is a normal and gradual process in which files become spread throughout a disk and empty spaces develop between files.

Defragmentation is a software process that rearranges data to fill in the spaces that develop on disks and makes data easier to obtain.

On a busy server, defragment the drives every one to two weeks. On less busy servers, defragment the drives at least once a month. Encourage users to defragment workstation drives once a month.

When a disk-drive failure occurs, it is most likely to be a read head that has physically touched the disk platter. That causes damage to the platter, sometimes resulting in the release of metal fragments within the sealed module of the disk unit.

Because they have moving parts, tape drives also are subject to failure. Their failure rate, however, is lower than that of disk drives, because the tape-drive read heads and moving parts do not require such exacting tolerances or a 100% clean environment.

Other critical network components also can fail, for example, disk controllers and adapters that enable a disk to communicate with the CPU of a computer. That type of failure can be difficult to diagnose, because the failure may be intermittent. A disk controller that is failing intermittently may cause a disk drive to fail completely, falsely indicating that the problem is in the drive and not the controller.

A **power supply** and a **backplane** also can fail. Sometimes you can detect a faulty power supply by monitoring the power supply output. A bad power supply also can burn out completely. A faulty backplane is more difficult to detect, because damage may occur to the plugged-in boards before the problem can be diagnosed correctly.

A **power supply** is the component in an electrical device that converts power from the wall outlet to the type and level of power required by the electrical device.

A **backplane** is a main circuit board in a modular computer or network device with plug-in connectors for the modular boards. For example, bridge, router, and other modular boards in a hub plug into a common backplane. The backplane provides connections between the modular boards, power to the modular boards, and grounding.

The CPU is another vital component that can fail, although such failure is infrequent. CPU failure may be indicated by a system that will not boot, CPU clock timing errors, or a general protection fault (GPF) message on the computer. RAM also can fail or suffer damage from power brownouts and surges and is usually indicated by memory errors or system aborts.

This hands-on activity gives you an opportunity to view the backplane of a modular hub. You need access to an unused hub in a lab.

To view the backplane:

1. Consult the manual for the hub to determine how to remove the cabinet front or back to view the backplane.

2. Open the hub and notice how the internal cards plug into slots on the backplane.

3. Check to determine the total number of slots and the number of empty slots.

4. Determine the location of the power supply. Is there a redundant power supply in this hub model?

FAULT TOLERANCE

The best defense against hardware failure is to implement fault tolerance. **Fault tolerance** is hardware or software designed to provide redundancy in the event a failure occurs. As you plan for securing data on a network and providing uninterrupted service, include fault tolerance features, such as the following:

- Redundant disk drives

- Server fault tolerance

- Power conditioning and protection

- Redundant networking devices and network paths

- Transaction tracking

- Data backups

- Disaster recovery options

Fault tolerance is using hardware and software to ensure against equipment failures, computer service interruptions, and data loss.

DISK-STORAGE FAULT TOLERANCE

Because hard disk drives are prone to failure, one of the best data security measures is to plan for disk redundancy in servers and host computers. That is accomplished in two ways: by installing backup disks and by installing RAID drives.

One fault-tolerance option common to many server and host computer operating systems is **disk mirroring** to store redundant data. With disk mirroring, there are two separate drives for each disk volume of data. The main drive handles the users' requests to access or write data. The second drive contains a mirror image of the data on the first. All updates and deletions are made on the main drive and replicated on the second. If the main drive fails, the mirror drive takes over with no data loss. In disk mirroring, both drives are attached to the same disk controller or **small computer system interface (SCSI) adapter** (Figure 8-1). A SCSI ("scuzzy") adapter is a 32-bit or larger fast interface to which one or more computer devices, such as hard disks and tape drives, can be attached. For example, one SCSI adapter plugged into a slot on the computer's main board might have two disk drives and one tape drive daisy-chained to a cable attached to the adapter. Each disk drive and the tape drive has its own controller.

Disk mirroring is a fault-tolerance method that prevents data loss by duplicating data from a main disk to a backup disk. Some operating systems refer to it as disk shadowing.

A **small computer system interface (SCSI) adapter** is a 32- or 64-bit computer adapter that transports data between the computer and one or more attached devices, such as hard disks. There are several types of SCSI adapters, including SCSI, SCSI-2, SCSI-3, SCSI wide, SCSI narrow, and UltraSCSI. All are used to provide high-speed data transfer to reduce bottlenecks in the computer.

Figure 8-1

Disk mirroring

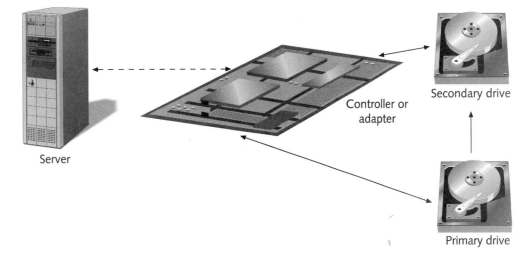

Server

Controller or adapter

Secondary drive

Primary drive

Disk mirroring has a weakness in that the data is inaccessible if it is the controller or the adapter that fails. To compensate for that weakness, another fault-tolerance method, **disk duplexing**, combines disk mirroring with redundant adapters or controllers. Each disk is still mirrored by a second disk, but the backup disk is placed on a controller or an adapter separate from that used by the main disk (Figure 8-2). If the main disk, controller, or adapter fails, users can continue their work on the redundant device. Some operating systems can switch from the main to the backup disk without interruption in service to the users, while other systems require that the server or host computer be rebooted to use the mirror drive instead of the failed main drive.

Disk duplexing is a fault-tolerance method similar to disk mirroring in that it prevents data loss by duplicating data from a main disk to a backup disk; disk duplexing, however, places the backup disk on a controller or adapter different from the one used by the main disk.

Figure 8-2

Disk duplexing

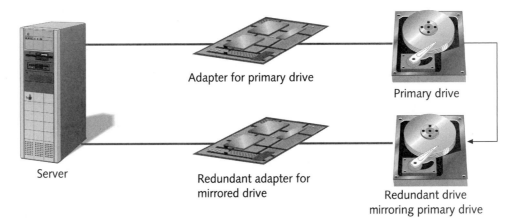

Server

Adapter for primary drive

Redundant adapter for mirrored drive

Primary drive

Redundant drive mirroring primary drive

Another approach to disk redundancy is the use of a **redundant array of inexpensive disks (RAID)**. RAID is a set of standards for lengthening disk life and preventing data loss. There are eight levels of RAID, beginning with the use of disk striping. **Striping** is the process of spreading data over multiple disk volumes. For example, part of a large file may be written to one volume and part to another. The goal is to spread disk activity equally across all volumes, thus preventing wear from being concentrated on a single volume in a set.

 Redundant array of inexpensive disks (RAID) is a set of standards to extend the life of hard disk drives and to prevent data loss from a hard disk failure.

 Striping is a data storage method that breaks up data files across all volumes of a disk set to minimize wear on a single volume.

The eight RAID levels are as follows:

- *RAID level 0.* Striping with no other redundancy features is RAID level 0. For example, Windows NT Server supports RAID level 0 to extend disk life and to improve performance. Data access on striped volumes is fast on an NT server because of the way the data is divided into blocks, which are quickly accessed through multiple disk reads and data paths. NT Server can stripe data across 3 to 32 disks. A significant disadvantage to using level 0 striping is that if one disk fails, you can expect a large data loss on all volumes.

- *RAID level 1.* This level employs simple disk mirroring and is used on smaller networks. Windows NT Server also supports level 1 but includes disk duplexing as well as mirroring. If three or more volumes are to be mirrored or duplexed, RAID level 1 is more expensive than the other levels. However, this option is sometimes preferred by network administrators because disk mirroring has better read and write performance than RAID methods other than level 0. Also, disk mirroring and disk duplexing offer the best guarantee of data recovery when there is a disk failure.

- *RAID level 2.* This level uses an array of disks in which the data is striped across all disks in the array. Also, in this method all disks store error-correction information that enables the array to reconstruct data from a failed disk. The advantages of RAID level 2 are that disk wear is reduced and data is reconstructed if a disk fails.

- *RAID level 3.* Like level 2, RAID level 3 uses disk striping and stores error-correcting information, but the information is written to only one disk in the array. If that disk fails, the array cannot rebuild its contents.

- *RAID level 4.* This level stripes data and stores error-correcting information on all drives, in a manner similar to level 2. An added feature of RAID level 4 is its ability to perform checksum verification. The checksum is a sum of bits in a file. When a file is re-created after a disk failure, the checksum previously stored for that file is checked against the actual file after it is reconstructed. If the two do not match, the network administrator will know that the file may be corrupted. RAID levels 2 through 4 are not supported by Windows NT Server because they do not offer the full protection found in level 5.

- *RAID level 5.* Level 5 combines the best features of RAID, including striping, error correction, and checksum verification. NT Server supports level 5, calling it "stripe sets with parity." Whereas level 4 stores checksum data on only one disk, level 5 spreads both error-correction and checksum data over all the disks, so there is no single point of failure. An added feature of level 5 is that a network administrator can replace a failed disk without shutting down the other drives. RAID level 5 uses more memory than other RAID levels, with 16 MB recommended as additional memory for system functions. In addition, level 5 requires at least three disks in the RAID array. Level 5 guarantees roughly the same recovery from a failed disk as disk mirroring, but it takes longer.

- *RAID level 6.* This level is similar to level 5, but it creates two sets of error-correction and checksum data on all the disks in the array. In level 6 two disks in the array can fail simultaneously without loss of data.

- *RAID level 10.* Level 10 performs disk mirroring, as in level 1, and also stripes the disks when there are multiple sets of main and mirrored disks (similar to level 0).

On a Windows NT server, mirrored disks or RAID drives are set up using the Disk Administrator, a central tool for managing the server disk and CD-ROM drives. The Disk Administrator offers several disk management options:

- Viewing status information about drives, including file system information

- Creating an NTFS (NT file system) partition on a new disk drive

- Combining two physical drives into one logical drive

- Changing drive letter assignments

- Formatting drives

- Extending a partitioned drive to include any free space not already partitioned

- Creating a mirrored drive set

- Creating a striped drive set

 In this hands-on activity, you have an opportunity to set up disk mirroring. You need a computer running Windows NT Server or NT Workstation. The computer should have two installed disk drives, with the second drive having as much or more unpartitioned free space as the main drive.

To mirror a drive:

1. Click **Start**, **Programs**, **Administrative Tools (Common)**, and **Disk Administrator**, as shown in Figure 8-3.

Figure 8-3

Opening the Disk Administrator

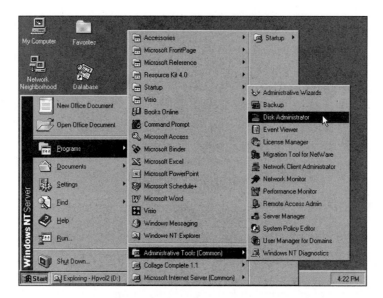

2. In the Disk Administrator, click the **View** menu and select **Disk Configuration** to view the amount of free space on all drives.

3. Click the main drive partition, such as drive **C:** A black border appears around the box containing the drive information.

4. Press **[Ctrl]** and simultaneously click a free area on another disk, such as drive **D:**. The free area must be at least as large as the volume to be mirrored. This is disk space that is not partitioned until it is designated as a mirror volume and partitioned for that purpose.

5. Click the **Fault Tolerance** menu and **Establish Mirror** (Figure 8-4).

6. Click **OK** to confirm that you want to establish the mirror.

7. Close the Disk Administrator.

8. Click **Yes** to restart the computer for the new mirroring to go into effect.

Figure 8-4

Setting up a mirrored set

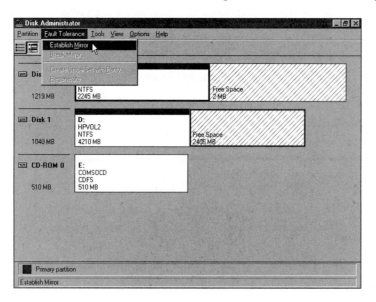

SERVER FAULT TOLERANCE

Selecting a server operating system with built-in fault-tolerance capabilities, such as Microsoft Windows NT Server or Novell NetWare, is another way to ensure the security of network resources. Besides the use of mirroring, duplexing, and RAID (through striping) disk fault tolerance, other fault-tolerance capabilities include the following:

- Hard disk hot-fix methods
- Transaction tracking
- Directory replication
- User account and security replication
- Protection of the operating system from application software errors
- Record locking

HOT-FIX CAPABILITIES

One of the most important fault-tolerance features is the ability to perform a hot fix for data when a bad spot is located on a disk. In a **hot fix**, the operating system temporarily stores data that cannot be written immediately because of a disk problem at that location, such as damage to the disk surface. The operating system then locates another disk area that is free from damage and writes the stored data there. Many server operating systems perform hot-fix operations instantaneously and without intervention from the network administrator. The instantaneous action prevents users from experiencing an interruption in service, guarantees that data is not lost, and prevents error messages such as "I/O Error" and "Abort, Retry, Fail?"

 A **hot fix** is a data-recovery method that automatically stores data when a damaged area of a disk prevents the data from being written. The computer operating system finds another undamaged area on which to write the stored data.

The Windows NT file system on an NT server performs hot fixes in one of two ways: sector sparing and cluster remapping. **Sector sparing** is available only on disk drives connected to a SCSI adapter. It also requires that mirrored disks or a striped RAID array are set up through the Disk Administrator. In sector sparing, the operating system designates certain sectors as reserved or as spares to be used when a disk write problem occurs. Information about which sectors are spares is kept by the hard disk's device driver. When a bad disk sector is discovered, the operating system obtains a copy of the data to be written from the mirrored or RAID backup drives and writes it to a spare sector on the drive to which it originally tried to write. It also keeps a record of the bad sector so there are no further attempts to write to that sector.

 In **sector sparing**, available in Windows NT Server and NT Workstation for SCSI drives, certain hard disk sectors are reserved so they can be used when a bad sector is discovered.

On non-SCSI drives, Windows NT uses a technique called **cluster remapping**. When a damaged disk area is discovered, the operating system designates the disk cluster with the bad sector as damaged. It then finds an undamaged cluster and writes the information there. The locations of bad clusters are recorded into the operating system file $BadClus.

Cluster remapping is a fault-tolerance technique used by Windows NT to flag a damaged cluster and find an undamaged cluster on which to write data.

A sector is the smallest storage unit on a hard disk. A cluster may contain one or more sectors, depending on how disk resources are allocated by the operating system. Windows NT keeps information about how the sectors are allocated into clusters in the file $Bitmap.

TRANSACTION TRACKING

Another fault-tolerance method that may be available through an operating system is transaction tracking or logging. **Transaction tracking** involves the keeping of a log, sometimes called a journal, of transactions until they are written to disk. On some systems the log is kept in memory or disk cache, while on others it is stored on hard disk or tape. Some systems store the transaction information in virtual memory, which is a designated area of the hard disk that acts as an extension of memory. When a system problem occurs, such as a bad disk sector or a system crash, the transactions can be recovered from the transaction log. Some network operating systems, such as Microsoft Windows NT Server and Novell NetWare, have transaction tracking.

Transaction tracking, also called transaction logging or journaling, is a fault-tolerance method in which a log is kept of all recent transactions until they are written to disk. If a hard disk or system failure occurs, unwritten transactions are recovered from the log.

Database systems also may have transaction tracking capabilities, to ensure that (a) data is not lost after a system failure and (b) databases and tables can be resynchronized in case a failure occurs after data is written in one place but before it is written in another place. As you plan network data security, make sure newly purchased databases have transaction tracking, such as for client/server systems.

The NT file system on an NT server uses transaction logging to recover data in the event of a hard disk failure or a full system failure. If such a failure occurs, the system can recover the data from the transaction log, which is contained in the file $LogFile.

DIRECTORY REPLICATION

When a network contains multiple servers, it is possible to regularly back up designated files or folders at certain intervals. If the main server malfunctions, the secondary server has a copy of the information. Another use for directory replication is to make duplicate copies of database information so database reports can be generated on the secondary server without slowing down updates on the primary server.

Microsoft NT servers have directory-replication fault tolerance through the Microsoft Directory Replicator services. The Directory Replicator copies folders and files from one server to another or from a server to a workstation. For example, the Directory Replicator can be used to copy logon scripts from a primary server to a secondary server. If the primary server is down, the secondary server can provide users with the same logon sequences they are used to having on the primary server. Also, when a database is replicated, users still can access it on a secondary server, even though the primary server is down.

USER ACCOUNT AND SECURITY REPLICATION

Network operating systems keep files, a database, or both containing vital information about each account, account groupings, and the access privileges given to each account holder. That information needs to be protected through fault-tolerance methods to make sure it never is lost. On a large network such information might take several days to reconstruct accurately. Users cannot access their accounts until the information is reconstructed, resulting in a costly loss in productivity. Two approaches to protecting the data are to regularly duplicate it on another server in a multiserver network and to back up the data onto tape regularly. User account and security data on a Novell NetWare system are stored in a grouping of files called the Bindery (in versions below 4.0) and in the NetWare Directory Services (version 4.0 and higher). The information is stored in Microsoft NT Server as the **security accounts manager (SAM) database**, which is part of a larger system of files and databases called the **Registry**.

 The **security accounts manager (SAM) database**, also called the directory services database, stores information about user accounts, groups, and access privileges on a Microsoft Windows NT server.

 The **Registry** is a database used to store information about the configuration, program setup, devices, drivers, and other data important to the setup of a computer running Windows NT or Windows 95.

One way to provide fault tolerance for an NT server's SAM is to implement two or more servers within a Microsoft domain. The first server placed in the domain is the primary domain controller. The **primary domain controller (PDC)** keeps and maintains the master copy of the SAM for all servers in that domain. Other servers can be designated as backup domain controllers or as standalone servers. Each **backup domain controller (BDC)** has a regularly updated copy of the SAM from the PDC (Figure 8-5). If the PDC server malfunctions, any of the BDC servers can be promoted to act as the PDC, so users can access their accounts with their normal privileges. A **standalone server** is a special-function NT server, such as a database server, that does not have a copy of the SAM and that does not handle security validations.

 A **primary domain controller (PDC)** is an NT server that acts as the master server when there are two or more NT servers on a network. It holds the master database of user accounts and access privileges.

 A **backup domain controller (BDC)** is an NT server that acts as a backup to the primary domain controller. It has a copy of the security accounts manager database that contains information about user accounts and access privileges.

Figure 8-5

Backing up the
PDC with
BDCs

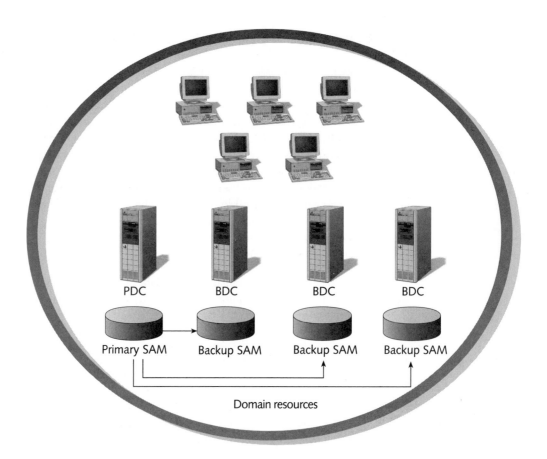

PDC   BDC   BDC   BDC

Primary SAM   Backup SAM   Backup SAM   Backup SAM

Domain resources

 A **standalone server** is an NT server that is used as a special-purpose server, such as to store databases. It does no account logon verification.

 This hands-on activity shows you how to manually synchronize the BDCs with the PDC on a Microsoft network. Normally, the PDC SAM is backed up automatically to the BDCs, but you can have the system do that manually, for example, just after you have created new accounts on a server. You need access to the Administrator account or equivalent on a computer running Windows NT Server and designated as a PDC. You can simulate the process, even if there are no BDC computers on the network.

To manually synchronize the PDC and BDC SAM databases:

1. Click **Start**, **Programs**, **Administrative Tools (Common)**, and **Server Manager.**

2. Click **Computer** on the Server Manager menu bar, then **Synchronize Entire Domain** (Figure 8-6).

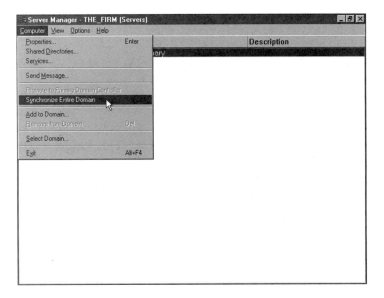

Figure 8-6

Synchronizing
the BDCs with
the PDC

3. A warning message may appear to let you know that resynchronizing the domain may take several minutes. Click **Yes**.

4. Next an informational message announces that the PDC has contacted all BDCs to start the synchronizing process. (An entry is made in the Event Log of the PDC to indicate if the process was successful.)

5. Close the Server Manager.

PROTECTING THE OPERATING SYSTEM

Some network operating systems can crash because of the activities of a program running on the server. The program may make an illegal call to a serial port or to the CPU, causing the entire computer to crash. A protected operating system is one that runs in a separate area of memory from other programs. Software program calls to the computer hardware, such as to the CPU, are filtered through the operating system instead of made directly from the program to the hardware. For example, the Windows NT Server operating system runs in **privileged mode**, which protects it from problems created by a malfunctioning program. The NT Server operating system runs in a designated memory area that is not accessed by other programs. Programs make calls to the computer's hardware by sending requests to the operating system. A program may crash due to a bug or poorly written code, but it cannot crash the Windows NT operating system.

The Windows NT **privileged mode** is a protected area from which the operating system runs. Direct access to the computer's memory or hardware is allowed only from this mode. Application programs that need to access memory and hardware issue requests to an operating system service rather than issuing direct memory or hardware instructions.

FILE AND RECORD LOCKING

When two or more users have access to a file or a record in a file, they can corrupt the data if they update the data at the same time. For example, if a bank teller accesses a customer's record to add a deposit and the bank credit officer accesses the same record to post the monthly interest, the record may be corrupted if the updates are simultaneous.

Locking is the process in an operating system that prevents two users from accessing and updating the same information at the same time. Some operating systems lock data so that the first person accessing the data has the authority to update it; other users can only view the file or record until the first person is finished. Other systems simply lock the file or record so only one person at a time can view and update it. Some operating systems lock data at the file level, which means that all records in the file are locked, even though only one record is in use. Modern operating systems lock to the record level, enabling many users to access and update the same file but not the same record in that file. Windows NT Server has file and record locking: while one person is updating a record, others can view but not update it.

 Locking is an operating system process that prevents more than one user from updating a file or a record in a file at the same time.

USING AN UNINTERRUPTIBLE POWER SUPPLY FOR FAULT TOLERANCE

One of the best fault-tolerance investments is protecting the power to essential computer equipment by attaching it to an **uninterruptible power supply (UPS)**. UPSs come with an array of features, but their main purpose is to shield electrical equipment from power failures and fluctuations. A UPS is primarily a box of rechargeable batteries that provide temporary power until electrical equipment can be shut down safely. A UPS is particularly important for computer equipment, especially servers, that are subject to software and hardware damage when a power failure or fluctuation strikes. For example, if software is not properly shut down, data may be lost, data files may get out of synchronization, or a boot file may be damaged. Hardware is susceptible, too, with disk drives especially at risk because they may be at full spin or seeking data at the time power fluctuates or is suddenly lost. Each power failure exacts wear as the disk drives experience a sudden stop and start when the power goes off and on. When a power failure is about to occur, there may be a steady drop in power, called a brownout or sag, which often is visible as surrounding lights dim. RAM and disk drives are more vulnerable to damage during the brownout leading up to a power failure than they are to the power failure itself.

 An **uninterruptible power supply (UPS)** is a device built into electrical equipment or a separate device that provides immediate battery power to equipment during a power failure or brownout.

Two kinds of UPS systems commonly are marketed: online and offline. Online systems provide electrical power to equipment directly from their batteries. The batteries always are charging from municipal power, until a power failure strikes. An offline UPS connects municipal power directly to the electrical equipment until it senses a sudden reduction in power, at which time it switches over to batteries. The advantage of an offline UPS is that it is less expensive than the online variety, and batteries often last longer. The disadvantage is that it may not switch to battery power in time to fully protect equipment during a sudden power failure. For that reason, many network administrators prefer online systems for more guaranteed protection.

UPS systems are designed to provide power for a limited time period, say, 10 to 20 minutes, so it can be determined how long the power failure will last and a decision made whether to shut down computers immediately. Of course, the amount of time the batteries can provide power depends on how much and what equipment is attached to the UPS. For that reason, most network administrators attach only critical equipment to a UPS, such as computers, monitors, external disk arrays, and tape drives. Some manufacturers recommend against plugging laser printers into a UPS, because they draw excessive power when turned on, risking damage to the UPS.

For an extra cost, a UPS system may include circuitry to guard against power surges. During a power surge, power traveling through the electrical lines may damage motors, power supplies, or electronic components. Additional circuits in some offline UPSs protect against power brownouts or sags where not enough power is available. Online UPSs normally regulate power to ensure against damage during brownouts as well as outages. Many systems also protect modem lines in case lightning strikes telephone lines. Another feature of modern UPS systems is their ability to communicate information to the computers they support, such as a warning that the power is out or that the UPS batteries are low. Some UPS systems also have a module that can alert a network administrator's management station that there are power problems.

This hands-on activity enables you to practice setting up a UPS for use with Windows NT Server. You need access to an account with Administrator privileges on a computer running Windows NT Server (or NT Workstation). You can set up the UPS parameters, even if the computer is not connected to a UPS.

To set the UPS interface parameters:

1. Click **Start**, **Settings**, and **Control Panel**.

2. Double-click the **UPS** icon (Figure 8-7).

Figure 8-7

Selecting the
UPS icon on
the Control
Panel

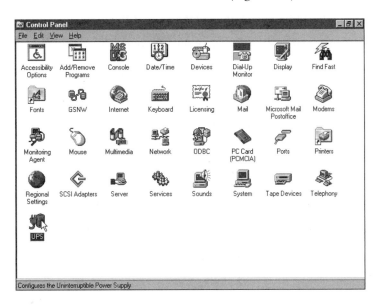

3. In the UPS dialog box, click the check box **Uninterruptible Power Supply is installed on:** (Figure 8-8).

Figure 8-8

Configuring
the UPS setup
interface

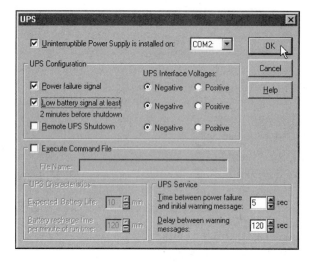

4. Click the scroll box arrow and select **COM2:** or another unused port.

5. Check the **Power failure signal** box in the UPS Configuration area to have the UPS send the NT server a message when the UPS has detected a power failure.

6. Click the **Negative** radio button to indicate that the UPS interface is to send a negative voltage to signal a power failure.

7. Under UPS Characteristics, enter **10** in the scroll box for Expected Battery Life.

8. Enter **120** in the scroll box for Battery recharge time per minute of run time (the recharge time after the battery power has been completely used up).

9. In the UPS Service area, enter **5** seconds as the time to wait before issuing a notification through the computer that the power is out.

10. Enter **120** as the number of seconds between warning broadcasts to users that there is a power failure.

11. Check **Low battery signal at least 2 minutes before shutdown** to provide advance warning when the UPS batteries are low.

12. Click the **Negative** radio button to show that the interface is to send a negative voltage to indicate that the batteries are low.

13. Leave the Remote UPS Shutdown and Execute Command File boxes unchecked. Assume you do not have the capability to remotely shut down the UPS (the UPS can receive a signal from the computer to instruct it to shut down) and that you do not have a file of commands to execute at shutdown.

14. Click **OK** to finish.

To use the UPS capabilities in NT Server, the UPS software service must be running, which you can start from the Services icon on the Control Panel. This hands-on activity shows you how to start the UPS service.

To start the UPS service:

1. Double-click the **Services** icon in the Control Panel (see Figure 8-7).

2. In the Services dialog box, scroll to the **UPS** service and highlight that service.

3. Click the **Startup** button.

4. In the Service dialog box, click **Automatic** as the Startup Type, which causes the UPS service to automatically start when the server is booted (Figure 8-9). Click **OK**.

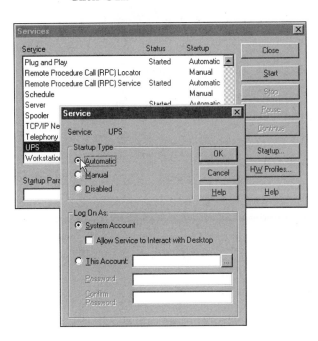

Figure 8-9

Setting the UPS service to start automatically

5. Click the **Start** button in the Services dialog box to start the service now, since the server is already booted.

6. Click **Close**.

DEVELOPING A BACKUP PLAN

With even the best-laid plans, components fail and data is lost. There is no better protection than to have a solid data backup plan. That plan should include purchase of a reliable tape system and development of a regular backup schedule for network servers, hosts, and workstations. For example, a tape drive used to back up NT servers on a network can be mounted inside a server, or it can be an external unit. For best server response, consider purchasing a SCSI-based tape drive, making it the only device connected to the SCSI adapter (Figure 8-10).

 If hard disks also are on the SCSI interface, server access to the disks may be slowed due to the high traffic through that SCSI adapter during backups.

Figure 8-10

Connecting a
tape drive to a
separate SCSI
adapter

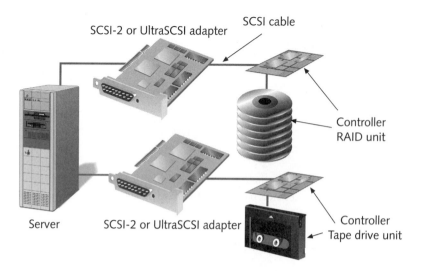

Windows NT servers typically use quarter-inch cartridge (QIC) cassette, digital audio tape (DAT), or digital linear tape (DLT) backup. Cassette backup systems have the smallest storage capability, in the range of 2 to 4 GB. Use of QIC tapes for backups has decreased over the past several years because the storage capacity is limited.

Much more popular among network administrators is DAT technology, which stores data in the medium gigabyte range. Most administrators have moved from the initial 4 mm tape, which holds 2 to 9 GB per tape, to the newer 8 mm format, which holds 4 to 25 GB.

Network administrators with high-capacity backup needs also are moving to the DLT systems, which store data in the range of 10 to 40 GB. DLTs are more resistant to damage than DATs or QIC tapes and have a longer shelf life, up to 30 years. DLT systems write information to tape about three times faster than DAT systems.

To help you plan for tape systems on different types of networks, consider two situations. In the first example, an independent insurance agency uses three Windows NT servers, each with 8 to 12 GB of disk storage. The agency is very active during the day, but there is little network activity in the evening. In this situation, you can use one tape drive for all the NT servers. The network traffic will be greater than if you install one tape drive per server, but because the network hardly is used at night, you can run tape backups in the evening. The traffic is greater with one tape drive because backups on the servers to which the drive is not attached must go over the network to the server that has the drive. A high-capacity 8 mm DAT or a DLT system is a reliable choice in this case. For example, using a 40 GB DLT system would enable you to back up all servers to one tape. You would be able to insert the backup tape and have the built-in NT scheduler start the backup any time during the night, freeing you from staying late to start the backups manually.

For the second example, assume you are planning a network that will have 10 NT servers for a liberal arts college. Each server has 20 to 25 GB of disk storage. Three of the servers are used by college administrators and faculty; the remaining servers are used for student labs. On some evenings, particularly before midterm and final exams, the servers are busy until 1:00 a.m., which is when the labs are closed. In this situation, you might equip each of the three administrative and faculty servers with its own tape drive, to reduce the network load during their backups. Backups on the servers might be started after 9:00 p.m., depending on the work patterns of the faculty members and the administrators. You also might purchase two or three tape drives to be used for the student lab computers. Backups for those computers would start after 1:00 a.m. DLT systems are a good choice in this situation, because of their reliability and tape capacity.

Reliable tape systems and tapes are one of the best investments you can make. When data is lost, the money spent on tape backup equipment and tapes is small compared to the cost of the human resources needed to reconstruct data.

There are several types of backups from which to choose. Most popular is a **full backup**, in which all volumes, directories, and files are backed up. One form of the full backup is to create an exact image of the disk files on tape. Image backups are performed in binary format, storing the information bit by bit. Image backups are fast, but have the disadvantage that if only a few files on the hard disk are accidentally deleted or corrupted, all files must be restored from tape. There is no option to restore only selected files or directories. A more widely used full backup is the file-by-file procedure, in which data is stored as files on tape. In the file-by-file format, the network administrator and backup operators can restore single files or selected directories as needed. The backup software that accompanies NT Server has file-by-file backup options but no image backup capabilities. Backup software from tape system vendors may come with image backup options.

A **full backup** is a backup of an entire system, including all system files, programs, and data files.

Another method is the **incremental backup,** which backs up only those files that have changed since the previous backup, as indicated by the archive attribute on the file. Many organizations combine full and incremental backups because there is not enough time to back up all files after each workday. For example, a full file-by-file backup is performed on a Friday night or a weekend day, when there is less activity on servers. During the week, an incremental backup is performed at the end of each workday. If a disk fails on Wednesday, the procedure would be first to restore the volume from the weekend full backup, then to restore from Monday's incremental backup, followed by Tuesday's incremental backup.

An **incremental backup** is a backup of new or changed files.

The NT Server backup software recognizes five backup options, which are variations of full or incremental backups. The first is the normal backup, which is the same as a full file-by-file backup. The advantage of performing a full backup each night is that all files are on one tape or tape set. Another NT option is the copy backup, which backs up only selected files or directories. The archive attribute, which shows that a file is new or updated, is left unchanged. For example, if the archive attribute is present on a file, the copy backup does not remove it. Copy backups are used in exceptional cases: a backup is performed on certain files, but the regular backup routines are unaffected because the copy backup does not alter the archive bit.

NT has an incremental option that backs up only files that have the archive attribute. When it backs up a file, the incremental backup removes the archive attribute. A differential backup is the same as an incremental backup, except that it does not remove the archive attribute. Incremental or differential backups often are mixed with full backups. The advantage of the differential backup is that only the most recent full backup and the most recent differential backup are required to restore data. That saves time over incremental restores, which require the full backup and all incrementals after the last full backup.

The daily backup option backs up only files that have been changed or updated on the day the backup is made. It leaves the archive attribute unchanged, so regular backups are not affected. A daily backup is valuable when there is a failing hard disk and little time to save the day's work to that point. It enables the Administrator to save only that day's work, instead of all changed files, which may span more than a day.

Many network administrators plan a tape rotation method to ensure alternatives in case there is a bad or worn tape. One common tape rotation method is the so-called Tower of Hanoi procedure, which rotates tapes so that some are used more frequently than others. If one of the frequently used tapes is bad, a less frequently used tape is likely to be intact (although some recent data cannot be restored). In a given week the tapes are rotated Monday through Saturday, as shown in Figure 8-11, which is an example rotation scheme for one server that requires one tape for the backup and in which a full backup is taken each day.

Figure 8-11

A sample tape rotation schedule

Sunday	Monday	Tuesday	Wednesday	Thursday	Friday	Saturday
1	2 Tape 1, set 1 (Set 2 in bank)	3 Tape 2, set 1	4 Tape 1, set 1	5 Tape 3, set 1	6 Tape 2, set 1	7 Tape 4, set 1
8	9 Tape 1, set 2 (Set 1 in bank)	10 Tape 2, set 2	11 Tape 1, set 2	12 Tape 3, set 2	13 Tape 2, set 2	14 Tape 4, set 2
15	16 Tape 1, set 1 (Set 2 in bank)	17 Tape 2, set 1	18 Tape 1, set 1	19 Tape 3, set 1	20 Tape 2, set 1	21 Tape 4, set 1
22	23 Tape 1, set 2 (Set 1 in bank)	24 Tape 2, set 2	25 Tape 1, set 2	26 Tape 3, set 2	27 Tape 2, set 2	28 Tape 4, set 1
29	30 Tape 1, set 1 (Set 2 in bank)					

The rotation schedule in Figure 8-11 has two sets of tapes with four tapes in each set. The complete sets are rotated every week, and the four tapes within a set are rotated each day of the week. For instance, during the first week of the month, set 1 is used while set 2 is stored in a bank vault or safe deposit box. During the second week, set 1 is vaulted and set 2 is put to use. On Monday of the first week, the first tape in set 1 is used. On Tuesday, the second tape in set 1 is used, and so on. Tapes 1 through 4 are rotated throughout the week, but some tapes are used more than others. This method has several advantages. First, tapes 3 and 4 in each set are used half as much as tapes 1 and 2. If there is a problem with tapes 1 or 2, tapes 3 and 4 likely are usable. If any one of the tapes in the set is bad, it is unlikely that you will lose more than a single day of work. By having one complete set in a bank vault, you are protected if there is a fire, flood, or theft at the office. The most you would lose is a week of work. Tape vaulting is one example of planning for disaster recovery.

 This hands-on activity gives you practice backing up a hard drive on a Windows NT server from the Administrator's account or equivalent. You need a server with the tape drive already set up.

To back up a drive to tape:

1. Make sure a formatted tape is in the tape drive and the drive is turned on.

2. Click **Start**, **Programs**, **Administrative Tools (Common)**, and **Backup**. The Backup option automatically detects a previously installed tape drive each time it starts.

3. Highlight one of the drives on the screen, such as drive **C:**, click the **Select** option on the menu bar, and click **Check** to check the box in front of the drive, as shown in Figure 8-12.

Figure 8-12

Backing up a
server hard disk

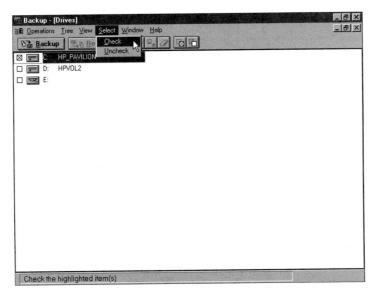

4. Click the **Backup** button under the menu bar (the Backup option also is available from the Operations menu). The Backup Information dialog box opens.

5. Check the box to **Backup Registry**.

6. Enter a description of the backup, such as **Drive C backup**.

7. Enter **Normal** as the Backup Type.

8. Click **OK** to start the backup.

Before starting a backup it may be necessary to format a new tape or to retension new and used tapes. Both tasks can be performed from the Operations menu. Formatting deletes existing information and automatically retensions a tape. Retensioning makes sure the tape starts from the beginning of the reel.

BACKING UP WORKSTATIONS

You also can back up workstations over the network, backing up to a server or workstation equipped with a tape drive. For example, for workstations running Windows NT or Windows 95, you would leave the workstation turned on and share the entire drive.

Before you make plans to back up workstations, consider the network traffic that will create. Backing up workstations on a small network of 10 or 15 may be acceptable, particularly if the backups are performed at night or during low-activity periods, such as during lunch. Backing up workstations on a large network of several hundred likely will cause too much network traffic. For those networks, it often is better to purchase several tape drives that can be rotated from workstation to workstation and to make workstation backups the responsibility of workstation users.

KEEPING SPARE EQUIPMENT ON HAND

Stocking equipment spares is a good way to reduce interruptions to network computing. A spare equipment list might include PCs, NICs, prebuilt cables, connectors, terminators, disk drives, tape drives, SCSI adapters, bridges, routers, hub modules, and switch modules. Purchase spares to help ensure that your critical business or organizational functions suffer only brief interruptions due to equipment failure.

DEVELOPING A DISASTER RECOVERY PLAN

Disasters don't happen often, but they do happen. Floods can damage computer rooms and onsite tape vaults have flooded; fires can destroy servers and workstations. At one business where the main computer room had a large picture window, vandals fired a rifle and destroyed a host computer.

The network administrator is responsible for having contingency plans in place should disaster strike. Such plans should include the security-planning and fault-tolerance options you have learned in this chapter, including the following fault-tolerance procedures:

- Purchase of computer operating systems with built-in fault tolerance
- Implementation of a tape backup scheme with tape rotation
- Storage of recent full backups at an offsite location, such as a bank safe deposit box or at a branch office
- Implementation of disk storage redundancy, such as mirrored or RAID drives
- Installation of a UPS
- Purchase of spare equipment
- Installation of additional cable in the network cable plant to have backup cable and to enable network redesign for routing

Another important step is the formulation of a written disaster recovery plan. The plan should outline both onsite and offsite recovery options. On a college campus or in a business park, other onsite departments or businesses may have similar equipment. For example, if your Windows NT order-entry server is damaged, you may be able to temporarily place applications on a neighbor's Windows NT server. However, if the entire campus or business park is destroyed by flooding, your disaster recovery plan should include the ability to continue operations offsite. If you are the network administrator at a state university and state government offices are in a nearby town, you might form a mutual arrangement to use each other's facilities in case a disaster strikes. If you work for a small- or medium-size business, you might contact a vendor who can provide equipment and disaster recovery services.

Your disaster recovery plan should take into account the following possibilities:

- A damaged tape system that prevents making backups and restores
- Operating system problems that cannot be fixed immediately
- One or more damaged CPUs
- Multiple disks that cannot function

- Downed telecommunications systems

- A series of damaged backup tapes

- Regional power outages that can last for days

- Extensive electrical damage

- Major portions of a network that have been damaged or destroyed

- Malfunctioning UPS systems

- Flooded tape vaults

- Natural disasters

If you do not have the resources in your organization for disaster recovery, consider hiring a company that specializes in that area. Disaster recovery specialists have computers, backup systems, networks, and Internet access you can use to keep your operation going after a disaster.

After you have formulated a disaster recovery plan, have key people in your organization review it, to ensure that the plan matches the needs and goals of the organization. Some organizations have their financial auditors review the disaster recovery plan as part of the regular audit. The plan also should be tested, to identify weaknesses or contingencies that have been missed. If your plan calls for help from a business neighbor or from a recovery specialist, go through a dry run as part of your test.

 In this hands-on activity you have an opportunity to view a disaster recovery plan.

To see the plan:

1. Make an appointment with the computer center director or network administrator at a local business or at your school.

2. Ask to view the disaster recovery plan or to discuss the disaster recovery measures that are in place.

CHAPTER SUMMARY

Preparing for problems in advance will help you deliver reliable network services to your constituents. Fault-tolerance methods are an effective way to protect network resources from human error, equipment problems, and natural disasters. Network administrators use disk mirroring, disk duplexing, and RAID technologies to guarantee the safety of data and to reduce the time systems are down due to a failed hard drive.

Modern network operating systems have built-in fault tolerance to hot-fix hard disk drives while a server is running. Transaction tracking and automated data replication techniques are additional examples of operating system fault tolerance. Another way to keep a system running is by implementation of a UPS. Many UPS systems have the ability to communicate with servers and host computers to provide alerts that the power is out or that the UPS batteries are low.

Developing sound backup practices is one of the best ways to protect data. Many reliable tape drives and tapes are available for systems such as Windows NT Server. One of the first steps a network administrator must take before releasing a server for production use is to plan and implement a backup system, including a means to rotate tapes to reduce wear.

Disaster recovery incorporates fault-tolerance security methods with a plan of action in case of flood, fire, or some other type of disaster. One example of disaster planning is the storage of designated backup tapes offsite. Another is a plan to use equipment at another site in case your own is damaged.

In chapter 9, you learn how to set up a network so users can access it from their homes or from other cities. More and more computer users work from home using computer resources on networks at their businesses or schools. Remote network access is opening up new possibilities for work and for leisure activities.

REVIEW QUESTIONS

1. Which of the following provides fault tolerance for hard disk access problems due to a failed hard disk or a failed disk adapter?

    a. hot fix

    b. cluster repairing

    c. duplexing

    d. mirroring

2. Which Windows NT Server tool would you use to synchronize a BDC with a PDC?

    a. Server Manager

    b. Disk Administrator

    c. Backup option on the Administrative Tools (Common) menu

    d. Disk adapter driver

3. A disaster recovery plan should include

    a. tape vaulting.

    b. a contingency plan in case the server CPU cannot function.

    c. a way to continue working regardless of a flood or fire.

    d. all of the above

    e. only b and c

4. Disk _____ is used as a way to prepare RAID drives for fault tolerance.

    a. fragmenting

    b. striping

    c. seeking

    d. sectoring

5. _____ is (are) used on Windows NT Server to perform a hot fix.

    a. Track partitioning

    b. Cluster remapping

    c. Sector sparing

    d. all of the above

    e. only b and c

6. Which of the following is used to keep a record from being updated by two users at the same time?

    a. rerouting

    b. locking

    c. block enabling

    d. simultaneous updates like this are not a problem

7. A(n) _____ UPS ensures there is no delay between the onset of a power failure and when the UPS kicks in.

    a. online

    b. offline

    c. recharging

    d. conditioning

8. In Windows NT Server the _____ backup option is equivalent to a full backup.

    a. incremental

    b. differential

    c. daily

    d. normal

9. Keeping a log or a journal so data can be restored due to a computer problem is an example of

    a. data warehousing.

    b. data normalization.

    c. transaction tracking.

    d. account auditing.

10. From where would you start the UPS service on a Windows NT server?

    a. Disk Administrator

    b. Services icon on the Control Panel

    c. UPS icon on the Programs menu

    d. Event icon on the Settings menu

ASPEN CONSULTING PROJECT: FAULT TOLERANCE AND DISASTER PLANNING

This week you are working more with the Physicians Group and with Easton Car Parts. You also are preparing a presentation for other consultants at your company. In the following assignments, you work on fault-tolerance methods and disaster planning.

ASSIGNMENT 8-1

As you know, the Physicians Group is installing a Windows NT server. Once the server is installed, about 60 workstations will be using the network and server resources. Design a backup plan for the server, using the Windows NT Server backup capabilities. Outline your plan in the space that follows.

Would you back up the network workstations onto a tape drive located at the server? Explain why or why not.

ASSIGNMENT 8-2

What UPS options would you recommend to the Physicians Group? Use the following table to list and explain the options.

UPS Options You Recommend for Physicians Groups
Option 1:
Option 2:
Option 3:
Option 4:
Option 5:
Option 6:
Option 7:
Option 8:

ASSIGNMENT 8-3

Gary Sharma has asked your advice on what spare equipment to purchase for the Physicians Group. What would you recommend and why?

ASSIGNMENT 8-4

Mark Arnez has asked you to give a presentation on disk mirroring and RAID. Describe this type of fault tolerance in the space that follows. Explain what method you recommend for the Physicians Group and why.

 ASSIGNMENT 8-5

As part of your presentation for Assignment 8-4, discuss the steps used to set up disk mirroring. Practice the steps in a lab, then describe each step in the following table.

Steps to Mirror Two Disk Drives Using Windows NT
Step 1:
Step 2:
Step 3:
Step 4:
Step 5:
Step 6:
Step 7:
Step 8:

ASSIGNMENT 8-6

After you have given the presentations in Assignments 8-4 and 8-5, the attendees have asked you to prepare a table showing different types of fault tolerance and where to access them in Windows NT. Complete the following table for your colleagues.

Task	Where Accomplished in Windows NT
Mirror a drive	
Resynchronize domain controllers	
Start UPS services	
Set up communications with a UPS	
Determine what type of hot-fix method the operating system is using	

ASSIGNMENT 8-7

One of your clients from chapter 5, Easton Car Parts, has hired you to help them develop a disaster plan for operations at both of their plants, which are several hundred miles apart in Wisconsin. Each plant has more than 100 networked PCs. One plant has two Microsoft NT servers and a Novell NetWare server. The other plant has two Microsoft NT servers and a DEC minicomputer. The company needs a plan that will enable either plant to access information from servers or minicomputer data files within 48 hours of a disaster and a plan that will minimize down time from failed disks, power problems, or other similar interruptions. Use the space that follows to outline your plan.

ASSIGNMENT 8-8

Easton Car Parts is upgrading its tape backup system for the NT servers from an older QIC-type system with 150 MB tapes. What tape system would you recommend and why? How many tape drives would you recommend for each site, keeping in mind that operations run 24 hours a day? Why?

OPTIONAL CASE STUDIES FOR TEAMS

TEAM CASE 1

One afternoon at lunch, you and a couple of consultants start a discussion about fault tolerance in network operating systems. Describe the fault-tolerance options available through Windows NT Server. Compare those to what is available in another system you know about, such as Windows 95 or Novell NetWare. What new fault-tolerance features would you build into an operating system?

TEAM CASE 2

Your discussion group in team case 1 has turned to another question. You are discussing what two fault-tolerance methods you would recommend to a startup company on a limited budget. The company has 32 employees and an Ethernet network but has not yet purchased the two file servers that are in the budget. The company also has not yet purchased the network operating system for the file servers. What fault-tolerance methods would you recommend?

TEAM CASE 3

One of Aspen Consulting's clients with whom you have worked is Winston Research Labs, which has large medical research centers in Boston, Atlanta, Houston, and Phoenix. The centers have more than 1,100 total users, and all the sites are now networked, thanks to your help. Winston wants you to help them develop a disaster recovery plan. Form a team and come up with a list of questions you need to have answered before you can start the plan. Also, explain some preliminary recommendations you have that the client can begin thinking about.

 TEAM CASE 4

As is true in many organizations, most of the users at Winston Research Labs do not back up their workstations on a regular basis. Use your team from Team Case 3 to develop a workstation backup plan that can be a model for a large organization.

REMOTE NETWORK ACCESS

In chapter 8, you learned how to build fault tolerance into your network to maximize the amount of time network resources are available to users. You learned about redundant disk storage and backup strategies, fault-tolerant operating systems such as Windows NT Server, and using an uninterruptible power supply (UPS). All those techniques help make network and computer problems invisible to the users, giving them confidence in the network administrator's management practices. That is vital in today's business climate, when the network and computer resources are expected to be working 24 hours a day, 7 days a week.

Another way network users want to extend the full-time capabilities of the network is by accessing it from home or while they are traveling. For example, a salesperson needs remote access to her network to place orders or to obtain more information on a product. A news reporter uses remote access to file a story from Vancouver with his newspaper in Toronto. A physician wants to access medical research records on her office network while she prepares a research presentation from home.

More people are remotely accessing networks than ever before. Vendors have responded quickly by offering improved hardware and software for that purpose. In this chapter, you learn how to make a network available to remote users. You learn about modems and how to connect a bank of modems so many users have access at the same time. You also learn about remote computing protocols and how to set up remote access services on a server and a workstation.

AFTER READING THIS CHAPTER AND COMPLETING THE EXERCISES YOU WILL BE ABLE TO:

- EXPLAIN THE HISTORY OF REMOTE ACCESS TECHNIQUES
- DESCRIBE MODEM STANDARDS AND HOW MODEM SPEEDS ARE MEASURED
- EXPLAIN DIAL-UP AND LEASED TELEPHONE LINES
- DESCRIBE THE DIFFERENT TYPES OF MODEMS
- DESCRIBE HOW TO CONNECT MODEMS TO A NETWORK
- EXPLAIN REMOTE ACCESS PROTOCOLS
- EXPLAIN AND SET UP MICROSOFT REMOTE ACCESS SERVICES ON A SERVER AND A WORKSTATION
- DESCRIBE HOW TO SET UP REMOTE ACCESS SECURITY

A BRIEF HISTORY OF REMOTE ACCESS

A few years ago, the most common way to remotely access a network was to dial into a workstation on the network running remote access software, such as pcANYWHERE or Carbon Copy. That workstation would be left running most of the time so a single user could dial into it from a remote computer, such as from the user's home (Figure 9-1). Access was frustrating because modems were slow, and sometimes the computer connected to the network was inadvertently turned off. Also, there was no way to use a mouse over the remote connection.

Figure 9-1

Remotely accessing a workstation on the network

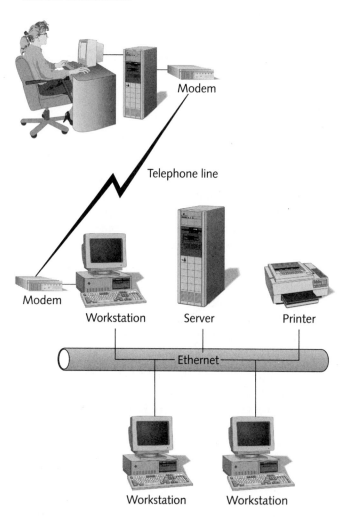

Modem

Telephone line

Modem   Workstation   Server   Printer

Ethernet

Workstation   Workstation

In the early 1990s, Novell improved on the technology by introducing the NetWare Access Server (NAS). The original concept of NAS was to make one node connected to the network act as many workstations in the same unit. For example, a network computer running NAS might contain five modem cards, enabling that number of users to dial in. Each user would have a specific portion of the computer to use, including CPU and hard disk space, with the NAS acting like five small computers in one (Figure 9-2).

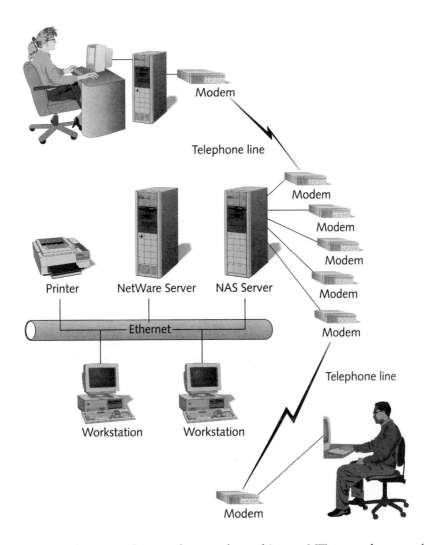

Figure 9-2

Remotely accessing a network through a NetWare Access Server

Microsoft improved network access by making an NT network server double as a remote access server. A Windows NT server (or workstation) can be installed with **remote access services (RAS)** to turn it into a RAS server capable of handling hundreds of simultaneous connections. The NT Server performs its normal functions as a server but serves remote access needs at the same time. A user dials into the RAS server, providing his or her NT Server account name and password. If NWLink is set up at the user's workstation and IPX is set up in the RAS server, the user also can provide a password to log on to a NetWare server at the same time.

Remote access services (RAS) are software services that enable off-site workstations to access an NT server through modems and analog telephone or digital ISDN telecommunication lines.

Improvements in remote access also have involved dramatic improvements in remote communications devices such as modems. Like remote access software, modem capabilities continue to mature.

MODEMS

Modems are a key piece in making remote access possible and worthwhile. The term **modem** is a shortened version of modulator/demodulator. A modem is a device that converts a computer's outgoing digital signal to an analog signal, which then can be transmitted over a telephone line. It also converts the incoming analog signal to a digital signal, which the computer can understand. A modem is attached to a computer in one of two ways: internally or externally. An internal modem is installed inside the computer using an empty expansion slot on the main board. An external modem is a separate device that connects to a serial port on the computer. (Serial communications are explained later in this chapter.) An external modem is attached by a cable designed for modem communications that matches the serial port connector on the computer. There are three types of connectors: (a) an older-style DB-25 connector that has 25 pins and resembles a parallel port for a printer (but does not use parallel communications), (b) a DB-9 connector with nine pins, and (c) a round PS/2 connector for serial communications on an IBM PC. Both internal and external modems connect to a telephone outlet through a regular telephone cable with RJ-11 connectors at each end.

 A **modem** is a modulator/demodulator that converts a transmitted digital signal to an analog signal for a telephone line and converts a received analog signal to a digital signal for use by a computer.

The modem data transfer rate is measured in two similar, but not identical, ways: baud rate and bits per second (bps). **Baud rate** is the number of changes per second in the wavelength of the signal transmitting the data. Baud rate was an appropriate way to measure the modem transmission rates when modems were first developed and could transmit only one data bit per signal change. Early modems were painfully slow at 300 and 1200 baud; 9600-baud modems were available but at great expense. Modem technology has advanced rapidly, requiring a different measurement of modem transfer rates. Vendors have developed technologies to send multiple bits of data per each change in the signal. Because of new technologies, modem rates are now measured in **bits per second (bps)**. Modems currently are capable of rates of up to 56 Kbps.

 Baud rate is the speed measurement used for early modems, reflecting that one data bit is sent per each signal oscillation. For example, an early 300-baud modem could make a maximum of 300 signal changes per second, thus sending 300 bits per second.

 Like network speeds, modem speeds now are measured in **bits per second (bps)**, which is the number of binary bits (0s or 1s) sent per second.

Modem speeds soon are expected to reach over 100 Kbps. A main influence on modem technology has been Microcom, the company that pioneered the **Microcom Network Protocol (MNP)** for modems. MNP consists of communication service classes (MNP classes 2 through 6; a newer class 10 provides for cell phone transmission), providing efficient communications, error-correction techniques, and data compression.

Microcom Network Protocol (MNP) is a set of modem service classes that provide efficient communications, error correction, data compression, and high-throughput capabilities.

The International Telecommunications Union (ITU) also has developed standards for modem communications with many of the MNP service classes included in its V.42 standard. Table 9-1 lists the ITU-T modem standards.

Table 9-1

ITU-T modem standards

ITU-T Modem Standard	Description
V.17	14400 bps fax transmissions for dial-up lines
V.21	300 bps data transmission for dial-up lines
V.22	1200 bps data transmission for dial-up and leased lines
V.22bis	2400 bps data transmission for dial-up leased lines
V.23	600/1200 bps data transmission for dial-up and leased lines
V.25	Standards for automatic calling and answering
V.26	2400 bps data transmission for leased lines
V.26bis	1200/2400 bps data transmission for dial-up lines
V.26ter	2400 bps data transmission for dial-up and leased lines
V.27	4800 bps data transmission on leased lines
V.27bis	2400/4800 bps data transmission on leased lines
V.27ter	2400/4800 bps data transmission on dial-up lines
V.29	9600 bps data transmission on leased lines
V.32	9600 bps data transmission on dial-up lines
V.32bis	14400 bps data transmission on dial-up lines using synchronous communications
V.33	14400 bps data transmission on leased lines
V.34	28800 bps data transmission on dial-up lines with the ability to drop to slower speeds when there are line problems
V.35	48000 bps data transmission on leased lines
V.42	Error detection and correction on noisy telephone lines
V.42bis	4:1 data compression for high-capacity transfer

 At this writing, a standard for 56 Kbps modem transmissions has not been formalized. Two incompatible approaches exist for 56 Kbps modems, one developed by U.S. Robotics and one by Rockwell Semiconductor Systems and Lucent Technologies. There are also some references to V.FC (V. FastClass) as a modem "standard" for 28000 bps. V.FC is really a proprietary specification that was replaced by the more universal V.34 standard.

When a PC is connected to a modem, the data transfer speed of the PC is the data terminal equipment (DTE) communications rate. The speed of the modem is called the data communications equipment (DCE) communications rate. The PC port setup for the modem (DTE rate) should be the same as or higher than the DCE rate of the modem. (DTE and DCE were covered in chapter 5.) For example, if you have a 56 Kbps modem, select a maximum speed of 57600 (the closest setting) in Windows 95 or NT when you configure the PC for that modem.

When two modems are communicating over a telephone line, such as the modem on a PC communicating with a modem on a network, they may not truly communicate at the maximum speed for both modems. For example, two V.34 or V.42 modems may negotiate to transmit at 14400 bps instead of 28800 bps because of the noise detected on the line.

 Sometimes modems will not communicate because of how they are set. For example, a 2400/4800 bps V.27ter modem cannot establish communications with a 36600 bps V.42 modem if the 36600 bps modem is not set to negotiate down to a slower speed. Also, when telephone lines are very noisy, some V.42bis modems attempt to step down to MNP-5 for data compression. If one of the communicating modems does not have MNP-5 capability, they may not be able to establish a link-up. Keep these cautions in mind when you set up network modems and work with users to solve modem communication problems.

 In this hands-on activity, you view the modem setup for a workstation running Windows 95 or Windows NT 4.0 Workstation. You need a workstation with a modem.

To view the modem setup:

1. Click **Start**, **Settings**, and **Control Panel**.

2. Double-click the **Modems** icon.

3. View the type of modem installed and set as the default by looking at the highlighted modem in the box titled The following modems are set up on this computer (Figure 9-3).

Figure 9-3

Viewing installed modems

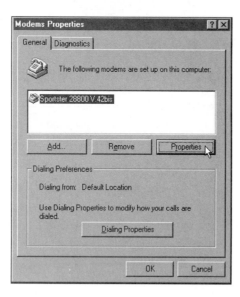

4. Click the **Properties** button to see what modem speed is set up.

5. If the speed is less than the maximum speed of the modem (the maximum speed is often part of the modem description in the title bar of the dialog box), click the **Maximum speed** drop-down box and select a speed as high as or higher than that of the modem (Figure 9-4).

Figure 9-4

Determining the modem speed setup

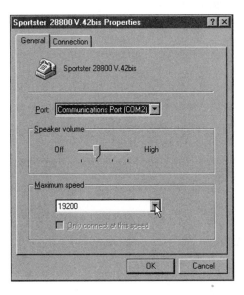

6. Click **OK** on the Modems Properties dialog box.

7. Click **Close** on the Modems Properties dialog box.

DIAL-UP AND LEASED TELEPHONE LINES

Most communications by modem still use **public dial-up lines**, which are the voice-grade lines you use to make telephone calls. A public dial-up line offers a temporary connection that lasts as long as your session on the modem. In some areas, the lines are subject to noise from other callers using portions of the line bandwidth for their calls and from EMI and RFI.

A **leased telephone line** is one that is used exclusively for your data transmissions and is a permanent connection between two sites. It bypasses the need to dial and select a circuit for a connection each time you send data and provides a high-quality signal. Another advantage of a leased line is that it is conditioned to reduce noise and provide reliable transmissions. Low-cost lease lines provide 56 Kbps transmission rates. More expensive fractional T1 and T1-based lines offer higher transmission speeds and more bandwidth for data communications.

A **public dial-up line** is an ordinary telephone connection that is temporarily switched for the duration of the network communication session, with the connection dropped as soon as you hang up.

A **leased telephone line** is one that is conditioned for high-quality transmissions and is a permanent connection without going through a telephone switch. There are different levels of conditioning, depending on the cost and the type of line.

Public telephone dial-up and leased lines are analog based and require the use of asynchronous or synchronous modems (to connect PCs) or DSU/CSUs (to connect network devices such as routers or switches) for data transmissions from point to point. A popular alternative, where service is available, is to use ISDN links available from the local telephone company. ISDN provides a digital line for fast, high-quality data transmissions. ISDN requires using a digital modem (a **terminal adapter**, or **TA**) to connect a PC to an ISDN line. ISDN digital modems are available for about the same cost as a high-quality asynchronous or synchronous modem but with higher data-transfer capabilities (e.g., 128 Kbps to 512 Kbps). (Synchronous and asynchronous communications and ISDN lines were introduced in chapter 5.) Another alternative is to connect some or all of those devices using an access server (discussed later in this chapter).

A **terminal adapter (TA)**, popularly called a digital modem, connects a computer or a fax machine to an ISDN line. A digital modem does not truly convert a signal between digital and analog circuits (modulate and demodulate). It simply converts a digital signal to a protocol that can be sent over a digital telephone line.

TYPES OF MODEMS

When you purchase modems for remote communications, you likely will use asynchronous modems. An asynchronous modem sends information a bit at a time, in byte-sized packages. One byte represents a character, such as the uppercase letter *B* or the lowercase letter *t*. There is a start bit in front of each byte package and a stop bit at the end, showing where each package of bits begins and ends. Asynchronous modems transmit at rates from 300 bps to 56 Kbps, depending on the modem you purchase.

Synchronous modems package data in streams. One data stream may contain several bytes of data, each contained in a single-byte unit within the stream. Each data stream is sent based on a timing or synchronized interval established by the communicating modems, called the clocking interval. Data streams are clocked continuously onto the line so that the streams are sent by one modem and received by the other at the preestablished synchronized intervals. A synchronous modem potentially can send and receive more data in a given time than an asynchronous modem, because a start and a stop bit do not have to be placed at the beginning and the end of each byte (although with some methods there is a start and a stop indicator for each stream).

Synchronous modems are more expensive than asynchronous and are not of real advantage to the single user working remotely from home. They are used more commonly for remote communications between a site with multiple users and a host computer. For example, before networks were widely used, 10 researchers studying water quality in the Adirondack Mountains remotely connected to a mainframe computer at their city university through synchronous modems at each end. They connected 5 terminals to a multiplexer, which was connected to a synchronous modem. The synchronous modem connected over a telephone line to another synchronous modem at the city university, also connected to a multiplexer. The multiplexer was connected to the mainframe, providing a channel for each terminal connected at the other end.

CONNECTING DIAL-IN MODEMS TO THE NETWORK

When you plan for remote network connections, find out how many people want to use the service on a regular basis. If there are only a few users, say, 10 or 20, and intermittent demand, one modem card in the server may be enough. More users require more modems and a telephone line for each modem. An organization of 100 users may need 10 modems for remote access to the network, while a group of 500 users may need 40 modems. One problem is that there is a limited number of expansion slots within a server for multiple modem cards. A common solution is to purchase a communications server to attach to the network.

A **communications server** is used to connect devices to the network that use asynchronous **serial communications** such as modems and terminals. The server contains a NIC with which to attach to the network and serial ports to connect the serial devices to the network. Communications servers can provide asynchronous routing for protocols such as IP and IPX. Figure 9-5 shows a small communications server connecting seven modems to the network for RAS communications through an NT server.

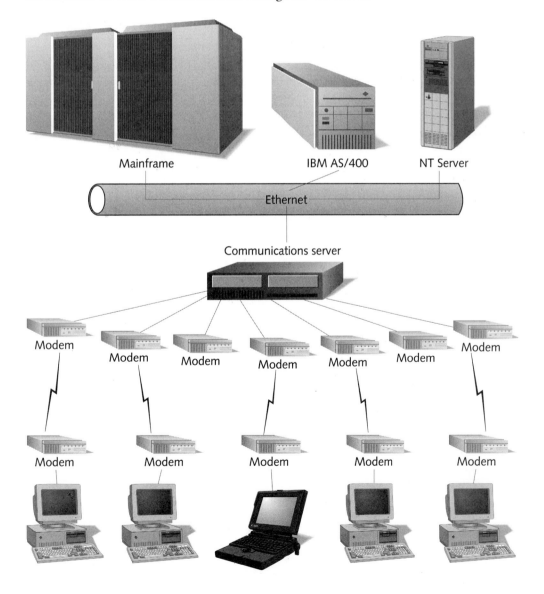

Figure 9-5

Communications server connecting modems to a network

Mainframe   IBM AS/400   NT Server

Ethernet

Communications server

Modem   Modem   Modem   Modem   Modem   Modem   Modem

Modem   Modem   Modem   Modem   Modem

A **communications server** connects asynchronous serial devices to a network.

 Serial communications are data transmissions that use one channel to send data bits one at a time. Terminals and modems use serial communications. The serial communications port on a PC conforms to the EIA/TIA-232 (formerly RS-232) standard for communications up to 64 Kbps.

Newer devices for serial connectivity are called **access servers**. An access server connects synchronous and asynchronous devices, providing routing for both types of communications. That enables communications via X.25, T1, and ISDN. Some access servers are designed for small to mid-size applications. Those servers have one Ethernet or token ring NIC to connect to the network. They also have a combination of synchronous and asynchronous ports, for terminal, modem, public telephone, ISDN, and X.25 connectivity. Smaller access servers typically have 8 or 16 asynchronous ports and one or two synchronous ports. Larger access servers are modular with slots (e.g., 10 to 20) for communications cards (Figure 9-6). For example, one card may have 8 asynchronous ports and 1 synchronous port. Another card may be for T1 communications. There also may be modular cards with built-in modems, such as 4 modems per card. Some modular access servers can have nearly 70 modems and may have redundant power supplies for fault tolerance.

 An **access server** is a device that connects synchronous and asynchronous devices to a network, providing routing for both types of communications.

Figure 9-6

Modular
access servers
connecting
remote PCs and
telecommunication
lines to a network

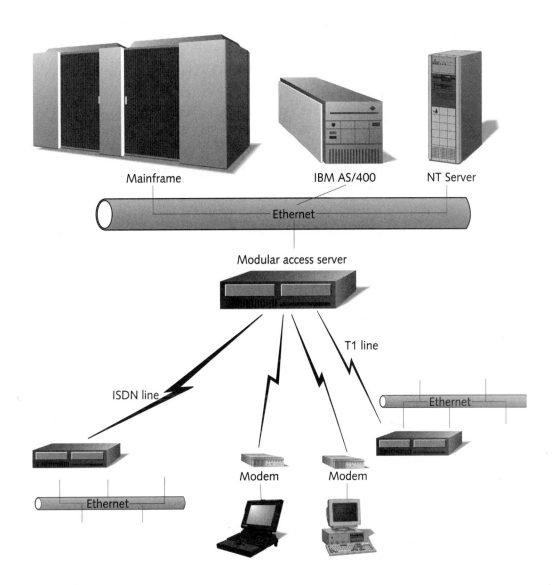

Mainframe
IBM AS/400
NT Server
Ethernet
Modular access server
T1 line
ISDN line
Ethernet
Ethernet
Modem
Modem

REMOTE ACCESS PROTOCOLS

Two protocols are used most frequently in remote communications: Serial Line Internet Protocol (SLIP) and Point-to-Point Protocol (PPP). **Serial Line Internet Protocol (SLIP)** was originally designed for UNIX environments for point-to-point communications between computers, servers, and hosts using TCP/IP. SLIP is an older remote communications protocol with more overhead than PPP. **Compressed Serial Line Internet Protocol (CSLIP)** is a newly developed extension of SLIP that compresses header information in each packet sent across a remote link. CSLIP reduces the overhead of a SLIP connection by decreasing the header size and thus increasing the speed of communications. However, the header still must be decompressed at the receiving end. Both SLIP and CSLIP are limited in that they do not support network connection authentication to prevent someone from intercepting a communication. They also do not support automatic negotiation of the network connection through multiple OSI layers at the same time. Another disadvantage is that SLIP and CSLIP are intended for asynchronous communications, such as through a modem–to–modem type of connection.

Serial Line Internet Protocol (SLIP) is an older remote communications protocol used by UNIX computers.

Compressed Serial Line Internet Protocol (CSLIP) is an extension of the SLIP remote communications protocol that provides faster throughput than SLIP.

Point-to-Point Protocol (PPP) is used more commonly than SLIP or CSLIP for remote communications because it has lower overhead and more capability. PPP supports more network protocols, such as IPX/SPX, NetBEUI, and TCP/IP. It can automatically negotiate communications with several layers of the OSI model at once, and it supports connection authentication. PPP is supplemented by the newer **Point-to-Point Tunneling Protocol (PPTP)**, which enables remote communications to intranets by way of the Internet. Through PPTP, a company manager can access a report on the company's in-house intranet by dialing into the Internet from home. As you learned in chapter 1, an intranet is a private virtual network that is highly restricted from public access.

Point-to-Point Protocol (PPP) is a widely used remote communications protocol that supports IPX/SPX, NetBEUI, and TCP/IP communications (such as between a remote PC and an NT server on a network).

Point-to-Point Tunneling Protocol (PPTP) is a remote communications protocol that enables connectivity to intranets (private virtual networks) through the Internet.

Both PPP and PPTP support synchronous and asynchronous communications, enabling connectivity through modems, dial-up telephone lines, leased lines, ISDN, and X.25 telecommunications. PPP is available in Windows 95 and Windows NT (3.5, 3.51, and 4.0). PPTP is available in Windows NT 4.0. When a Windows NT 4.0 server is also configured as a RAS server, it can be configured to accept remote connections through SLIP or PPP. PPP configuration is necessary where users running Windows 95 or NT remotely access networks using NetBEUI or IPX/SPX. Table 9-2 compares SLIP to PPP.

Table 9-2

Comparison of SLIP and PPP

Feature	SLIP	PPP
Network protocol support	TCP/IP	TCP/IP, IPX/SPX, and NetBEUI
Asynchronous communications support	Yes	Yes
Synchronous communications support	No	Yes
Simultaneous network configuration negotiation and automatic connection with multiple levels of the OSI model between the communicating nodes	No	Yes
Support for connection authentication to guard against eavesdroppers	No	Yes

In this hands-on activity, you learn where to check to determine that a computer running Windows NT 4.0 is using PPP remotely to communicate with an NT server also configured as a RAS server using PPP. You need a computer already set up for dial-up networking. If you cannot find a workstation already configured for dial-up access, go through the hands-on activity, "Installing Remote Access Services at the Workstation" later in this chapter, and then come back to this one.

To check the remote protocol setup in Windows NT 4.0:

1. Double-click **My Computer** on the desktop.

2. Double-click the **Dial-Up Networking** icon.

3. In the Dial-Up Networking dialog box, click the **More** button (Figure 9-7).

Figure 9-7

Clicking More on the Dial-Up Networking dialog box

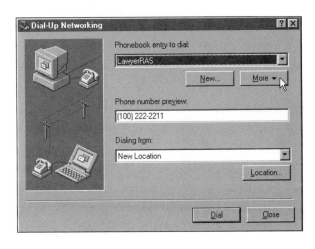

4. Click the menu option to **Edit entry and modem properties**.

5. Click the **Server** tab in the Edit Phonebook Entry dialog box (Figure 9-8).

Figure 9-8

Checking the remote networking protocol setup for PPP

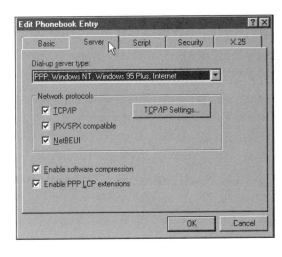

6. Observe the entry in the Dial-up server type: drop-down box, which should be **PPP: Windows NT, Windows 95 Plus, Internet**. If it is not, click the drop-down box arrow and select this option.

7. Also observe what network protocols are checked for dial-up networking under Network protocols (such as TCP/IP, IPX/SPX, and NetBEUI).

8. Click **OK** when you are finished with the Edit Phonebook Entry dialog box.

9. Click **Close** on the Dial-Up Networking dialog box.

In this hands-on activity you check the remote access protocol in use by a workstation running Windows 95. You need a workstation already configured for dial-up networking, such as for a RAS server, America Online, or The Microsoft Network.

To check the remote access protocol setup:

1. Double-click **My Computer** on the desktop.

2. Double-click the **Dial-Up Networking** icon.

3. Right-click an existing dial-up networking icon, such The Microsoft Network.

4. Click **Properties**.

5. Click the **Server Type** button (Figure 9-9).

Figure 9-9

Selecting to view the Server Type information

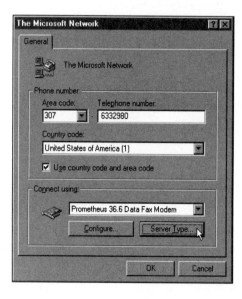

6. Click the arrow on the **Type of Dial-Up Server:** drop-down box to view the remote network protocol options (Figure 9-10).

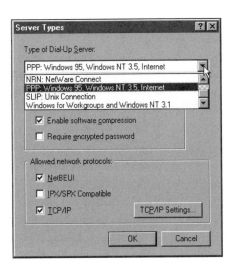

Figure 9-10

Viewing
the remote
protocol setup

7. Make sure the option **PPP: Windows 95, Windows NT 3.5, Internet** option is selected.

8. Also notice the network protocols that are checked to be used over the PPP–based connection.

9. Click **OK** in the Server Types dialog box.

10. Click **OK**.

MICROSOFT REMOTE ACCESS SERVICES

Microsoft offers an effective way to connect multiple users to one network through Microsoft's RAS. Using RAS on a Microsoft-based network requires three important pieces:

- Making a Microsoft NT server a network's RAS server

- Installing RAS on workstations

- Installing dial-up networking on workstations

CREATING A RAS SERVER

There are two components to making an NT server double as a RAS server. You have learned the first component, which is to implement a way to connect multiple modems to a network. On a very small network, you may need only to install one or two modems directly into an existing networked computer running Microsoft NT Server. For a larger network, you can install an access server with enough modems, T1, and ISDN connections for the type of communications required by users.

 Choose an access server that is designed to be compatible with Microsoft NT Server. A compatible access server includes software and drivers that can be used to coordinate communications between the NT server and the access server.

The second component is to install the software needed to turn the NT server into a RAS server.

The software is included with Windows NT Server versions 3.51 and higher. Version 4.0 enables up to 256 remote callers to connect at the same time. Designed to work with RAS installed on computers running Windows 95 or NT, a RAS server supports the following types of connections:

- Asynchronous modems
- Synchronous modems
- Regular dial-up telephone lines
- Leased lines
- ISDN lines (and digital modems)
- X.25 lines

 In this hands-on activity, you practice installing the RAS Server software on a computer already running Windows NT 4.0 Server and with a modem that is already installed. You need access to the Administrator account or its equivalent to install the software. Also, you need the Windows NT 4.0 CD-ROM.

To install the RAS server software:

1. Double-click the **Network icon** from the Control Panel.

2. Click the **Services** tab and click the **Add** button.

3. Scroll to the **Remote Access Service** in the Select Network Service dialog box and highlight it (Figure 9-11).

Figure 9-11

Selecting to install the Remote Access Service on the server

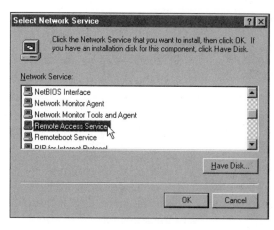

4. Insert the Microsoft Windows NT 4.0 Server CD-ROM.

5. Click **OK** on the Select Network Service tab.

6. Make sure the confirmation box contains the drive letter for the CD-ROM drive and the path **\i386**. Click **Continue** (Figure 9-12). The setup process now loads files onto the server.

Figure 9-12

Entering the
path on the
Microsoft
Windows NT
Server
CD-ROM

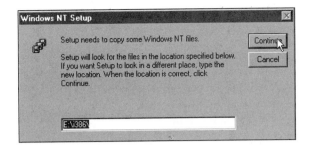

 If a modem has not been installed, the system at this point checks if you want to start the modem wizard to install the modem.

7. The Add RAS Device dialog box shows the remote connection options, such as all installed modems. Select the modem or modems to link with RAS and click **OK** (Figure 9-13).

Figure 9-13

Adding the
modem device
for RAS

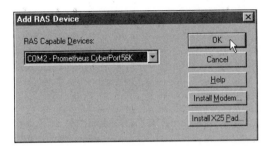

8. Click **Continue**.

9. Dialog boxes appear to confirm whether the RAS and the previously installed protocol access options are for all servers on the network (if there are more than one NT server) or only the server with RAS. A dialog box is used for each active protocol, such as TCP/IP, NetBEUI, and IPX (NWLink). In each dialog box, click **Entire network**. If the server is configured for TCP/IP, a dialog box requests addressing information. Ask your instructor what information to use for the IP addressing. If the computer already is configured for IPX (NWLink), the setup will ask for a network number for the remote connection. In that dialog box, select **Allocate network numbers automatically**. NetBEUI does not require additional connection information. After you have entered the information, click **OK** in each dialog box.

10. Click **OK** in the Setup Message dialog box that announces you have made a successful installation.

11. After the setup is complete, configure the modem for remote access. Back on the Services tab, highlight **Remote Access Service** in the Network Services: scroll box and click the **Properties** button (Figure 9-14).

Figure 9-14

Selecting the
Remote Access
Service
properties

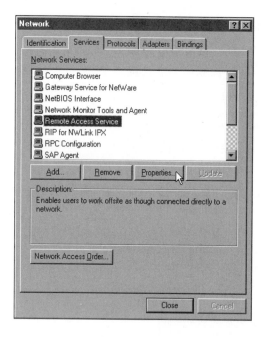

12. In the Remote Access Setup dialog box, highlight the modem device and click **Configure**.

13. In the Configure Port Usage dialog box, click the radio button for **Dial out and Receive calls** (Figure 9-15), to enable the RAS server to receive incoming calls and to call out to a number as a means to authenticate the connection. Click **OK**.

Figure 9-15

Setting the
modem port to
dial out and
receive calls

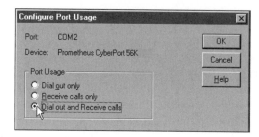

14. After the modem is configured, click the **Continue** button in the Remote Access Setup dialog box.

15. Click **Close** on the Services tab (the system automatically configures bindings for a minute or two).

16. Click **Yes** in the Network Setting Change dialog box to restart the server to enable the new settings to go into action.

17. Once the server is restarted, log in again using an account with Administrator privileges.

18. Click **Start**, **Settings**, and **Control Panel**.

19. Notice that there is a new Dial-Up Monitor icon. Double-click that icon.

20. Click the **Status** tab. Notice that you can view connection statistics for the RAS server.

21. Click the **Summary** tab (Figure 9-16) for information about specific users who have logged on, including currently logged-on users (you won't have any yet).

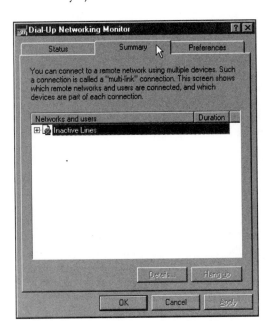

22. Click the **Preferences** tab to see where to set up preferences for monitoring RAS connections on the server.

23. When you are finished, click **OK** in the Dial-Up Networking Monitor dialog box.

INSTALLING REMOTE ACCESS SERVICES AT THE WORKSTATION

You connect Windows 95 and NT workstations to the RAS server by first installing RAS at the workstation. The RAS services support both SLIP and PPP, but PPP should be used as the remote access protocol.

 In this hands-on activity, you practice installing RAS on a computer running Windows NT 4.0 Workstation. Notice how similar this process is to the one used to install the RAS Server software.

To install RAS in Windows NT 4.0 Workstation:

1. Double-click the **Network icon** in the Control Panel and click the **Services** tab.

2. Click **Add** on the Services tab.

3. Highlight **Remote Access Service** in the Select Network Service dialog box and click **OK**.

4. Enter the path to the CD-ROM and the **\i386** directory name. Insert the Windows NT Workstation CD-ROM and click **Continue**. The RAS files are loaded from the CD-ROM.

5. The RAS setup program detects the modem card in the computer or the modem attached to the computer. Check to be certain the modem is correctly detected in the Add RAS Device dialog box (see Figure 9-13). If no modem is detected, click the Install Modem button to run the modem installation wizard. Click **OK**.

6. In the Remote Access Setup dialog box, highlight the modem and click the **Configure** button. Set the port to "Dial out only" or to "Dial out and Receive calls" (see Figure 9-15). For example, the modem needs to be able to receive calls if the RAS server at work is set up to call back users as a security measure to ensure that users requesting access are known to the server.

7. Click **OK** in the Configure Port Usage dialog box, then click **Continue** in the Remote Access Setup dialog box.

8. Windows NT Workstation should automatically configure bindings for the remote access. If there is no message that it is configuring bindings, click the Bindings tab in the Network dialog box to initiate the Bindings configuration.

9. Click **Close** in the Network dialog box.

INSTALLING THE DIAL-UP CONFIGURATION

After you have installed remote services on the remote workstation, it is necessary to create a dial-up configuration to automate the dialing procedures needed to connect to the NT server running RAS. Individual dial-up settings can be created for each type of remote access, such as one for RAS, one for America Online, and one for an Internet service provider.

 In this hands-on activity, you create a dial-up configuration for a RAS connection on a workstation running Windows NT 4.0 Workstation.

To set the dial-up configuration:

1. Double-click **My Computer**, then double-click the **Dial-Up Networking** folder.

2. Click **New** in the Dial-Up Networking dialog box.

3. Enter **RAS** as the name for the automated dial-up connection (Figure 9-17) and click **Next**.

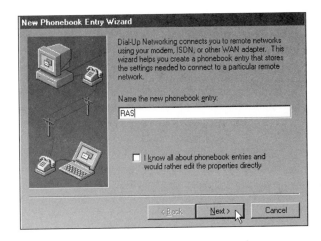

Figure 9-17

Entering
the RAS
connection
name

4. Check **Send my plain text password if that's the only way to connect** (Figure 9-18). Your plain-text password is the password for your account on the NT server. Leave the other boxes blank; you are not connecting through the Internet, and you are not planning to connect to any non-Windows servers at this time. Click **Next**.

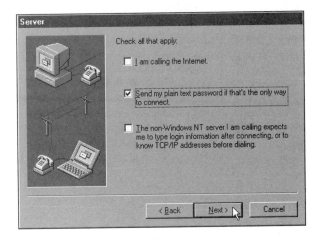

Figure 9-18

Checking the
box to send
the account
password to
the server

5. Enter the telephone number of the line attached to the RAS server's modem in the Phone number: text box in the Phone Number dialog box. Do not click the box for telephony dialing properties; the line is a basic telephone line and does not require specialized information. Click **Next**.

6. Click **Finish** in the last dialog box to complete the installation wizard.

7. Click **Close** in the Dial-Up Networking dialog box.

SECURITY

With today's concern about security, it is wise to set up protection on the remote access server. Microsoft NT Server has that capability through management of user accounts on the server. User accounts can be set up to enforce dial-in security each time a remote user attempts to log on to an NT server, thus discouraging hackers from trying to access the server. With **call-back security**, when a remote workstation calls into the RAS server to access a particular NT server account, the server calls back the remote computer to verify its telephone number. The following call-back options are available in Windows NT 4.0 Server:

- No Call Back. The server allows access on the first call attempt.

- Set By Caller. The number used for the call back is provided by the remote computer.

- Preset To. The number to call back is entered into the text box.

Call-back security instructs the RAS server to call back an accessing workstation to verify that access is requested from an authorized telephone number.

In this hands-on activity, you view where to set up call-back security on an NT server account. You need access to a Windows NT server through an account with Administrator privileges.

To view the call-back setup:

1. Click **Start**, **Programs**, and **Administrative Tools (Common)**.

2. Click the **User Manager for Domains** menu option.

3. Double-click an account, for example, **Guest**.

4. Click the **Dialin** button in the User Properties dialog box (Figure 9-19).

Figure 9-19

Clicking the
Dialin button
in the User
Properties
dialog box

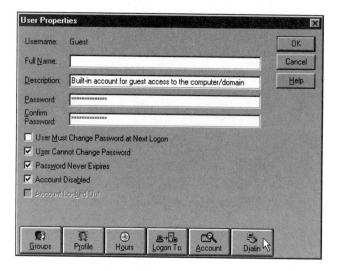

5. Notice the three dial-in security options in the Call Back section of the Dialin Information dialog box (Figure 9-20). Also notice that dial-in access can be denied to an account holder by removing the check from Grant dialin permission to user.

6. Click **Cancel** in the Dialin Information dialog box, then **Cancel** in the User Properties dialog box.

7. Close the User Manager for Domains.

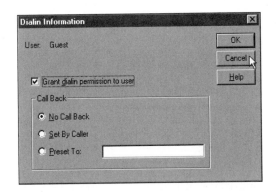

Figure 9-20

Setting up
dial-in security
on an account

CHAPTER SUMMARY

Millions of people work from home or while traveling by using some form of remote communication. Modems have made "telecommuting" a viable work option, particularly as advances have taken modem speeds from 300 bps to 56 Kbps and beyond. The first unofficial modem standards were developed by Microcom, with critical functions such as transmitting in synchronous mode, negotiating modem speed, and data compression. The ITU followed suit by implementing standards, many of which are built on Microcom's original work.

Most modems purchased today are asynchronous for individual communications, but synchronous modes are used as well, for example, where multiple terminals or workstations communicate over a single line using multiplexers. Remote computer access also has forced improvements in telephone communications, particularly in options for leased and ISDN telephone lines.

Other improvements in remote communications are in the options to connect modems and telecommunication lines to a network. Modern access servers provide connectivity for large numbers of modems, T1 lines, X.25 networks, and ISDN communications.

One of the early remote access protocols, SLIP, was developed for UNIX computers. SLIP still is used to enable remote communications involving UNIX-based servers and workstations. PPP is a newer remote access protocol that has more options than SLIP, such as the ability to negotiate point-to-point connection at multiple OSI layers.

Remote access is only as good as the software tools created to provide access to the network. Novell led the way in developing techniques for multiple access through the NAS technology. Microsoft improved on that concept with RAS, which provides remote access directly through a Microsoft NT server. Because remote access is a high priority with network users, modem vendors and the developers of network operating systems will continue pioneering new technologies.

In chapter 10, you discover more about managing a network by studying network monitoring tools. You learn about a protocol that enables network monitoring and about tools that are used to monitor networks and diagnose problems. The Microsoft network monitoring tools are introduced to provide hands-on experience.

REVIEW QUESTIONS

1. Which of the following remote access protocols supports connection authentication?
   a. PPP
   b. SLIP
   c. CSLIP
   d. all of the above
   e. only b and c

2. What type of network device enables you to connect 24 modems and a T1 line to the network for remote access communications?
   a. repeater
   b. ATM switch
   c. access server
   d. Carbon Copy

3. Which of the following would you use to connect an ISDN line to a computer?
   a. synchronous modem
   b. digital modem
   c. asynchronous modem
   d. analog switch

4. Which remote access protocol would you use for communications between a home computer running Windows 95 and an NT server that also is a RAS server at work?
   a. PPP
   b. SLIP
   c. CSLIP
   d. NWLink

5. Which type of modem communication mode transmits a byte at a time, with each new byte prefaced by a start bit?
   a. synchronous
   b. asynchronous
   c. multicast
   d. digital

6. One way to make sure a remote connection request is from a user authorized to access a RAS server is through
   a. call forwarding.
   b. caller ID.
   c. call analysis.
   d. call back.

7. _____ measures modem communications based on the maximum number of signal changes per second.
   a. Bits per second
   b. Bytes per second
   c. Baud rate
   d. Signal rate

8. To have remote communications between a RAS server and an NT workstation,

   a. RAS must be set up at the workstation.

   b. a RAS driver must be installed on the workstation's modem.

   c. the workstation must be set up as a communication server.

   d. all of the above

   e. only a and b

9. Which of the following is an advantage of a leased line compared to a dial-up line?

   a. It is conditioned for data communications.

   b. It does not go through a central switch.

   c. It is a permanent connection.

   d. all of the above

   e. only b and c

10. When operating as a RAS server, an NT server (version 4.0)

    a. can provide up to 256 connections.

    b. cannot provide normal file services on the network.

    c. must be placed on a separate network segment.

    d. all of the above

    e. only a and c

ASPEN CONSULTING PROJECT: REMOTE ACCESS FOR A HIGHWAY DEPARTMENT

The highway department in a neighboring state is centralizing statewide highway construction information on a network located in the highway department headquarters across the street from the state capitol building. Aspen Consulting won the bid for the project, and Mark Arnez has assigned it to you. You are now in the phase of planning for remote access to the four NT servers on their network.

The highway department wants field engineers and technicians to be able to access the four NT servers from anywhere in the state. The remote access is needed so they can check on contracts, update project timelines, access technical information, track budgets, and use other information on the servers.

ASSIGNMENT 9-1

The engineers and project managers have 80486 and Pentium portable computers with different kinds of modems. About 50 portables already are in use by these personnel, all running Windows 95. Some modems operate at 9600 bps, others at 14400 bps, still others at 28800 bps, and a few at 56 Kbps. Ten people currently use cell phone links; the rest use dial-up lines. Review the MNP and ITU-T specifications for modems and make a recommendation on the general specifications for modems to use at the state headquarters, making sure the modems are compatible with those already on the portables in the field.

Use the Internet to find modems with the features you are recommending (some modem manufacturers are AT&T, IBM, Hayes, Microcom, and U.S. Robotics). List the modem models and features in the following space.

ASSIGNMENT 9-2

After talking with the highway department managers, engineers, and technicians, you are recommending that they purchase 20 modems for the main network. Explain how the modems might be connected.

Draw a diagram to illustrate how the modems might be connected, so the highway department management and computer support people can visualize the network.

ASSIGNMENT 9-3

Explain what remote access protocols are available through Windows 95 for remote communications, including the advantages of the different protocols. What protocol would you recommend the highway department use? Why?

ASSIGNMENT 9-4

The highway department wants you to provide training on how to set up a RAS server in Windows NT 4.0 Server. Note that they use only NetBEUI for network communications at the headquarters network. Practice setting up a RAS server and record the steps in the following table as notes for your presentation.

Steps to Install a RAS Server
Step 1:
Step 2:
Step 3:
Step 4:
Step 5:
Step 6:
Step 7:
Step 8:
Step 9:
Step 10:
Step 11:
Step 12:

ASSIGNMENT 9-5

The highway department is concerned about security and wants to make sure only its own employees have remote access to the network. What security measures would you recommend they use?

ASSIGNMENT 9-6

Practice setting security for RAS, so you can explain the procedure to the highway department. Outline the steps in the table that follows.

Steps to Set Up RAS Security
Step 1:
Step 2:
Step 3:
Step 4:
Step 5:
Step 6:
Step 7:
Step 8:

ASSIGNMENT 9-7

The highway department wants to install an ISDN line for Internet access to the main network. Explain how they might accomplish that. Also, add to your network diagram in assignment 9-2 to illustrate how the ISDN line might be connected to the network.

ASSIGNMENT 9-8

The RAS server is installed and you are performing a test run with two of the field engineers dialing in remotely. One engineer encounters no problems. The other reports a message about a problem with the remote access protocol. Explain how she might troubleshoot the problem in Windows 95.

OPTIONAL CASE STUDIES FOR TEAMS

 ## TEAM CASE 1

Mark Arnez asks you to form a team to work with Holly College, which has 10 Microsoft NT servers and two UNIX minicomputers. The college wants to provide remote access for faculty, staff, and students. Develop a list of questions to ask about what type of access is needed, so you have a starting point on which to base your recommendations.

 ## TEAM CASE 2

The highway department with which you have been working reports that the engineers and the technicians are confused about how to set up their portables for remote communications with the headquarters RAS server. Form a team to write step-by-step documentation for field personnel.

 ## TEAM CASE 3

The highway department needs some additional help, so assemble your Case 2 team again. They want you to add a new section in the documentation that discusses how to troubleshoot problems with modem communications and problems with dial-up connectivity for Windows 95.

CHAPTER TEN

MONITORING THE NETWORK

As you learned in chapter 9, remote access to networks is flourishing. Many organizations have found they can use remote access to make life easier for employees while saving money on office expenses. With remote access capabilities, millions of employees work part- or full-time from home. As you have learned throughout this book, people depend on networks to provide all types of services. A network problem can be devastating because it often affects many people. A down network is just as serious as a citywide power outage or a break in telephone service.

This chapter teaches you how to monitor a network to avoid problems before they occur. You learn about establishing baseline network statistics so you can stay alert to developing problem situations. The SNMP protocol is introduced to show you how to take advantage of network monitoring capabilities. In this chapter, you also learn about monitoring equipment and how to use the monitoring tools built into Microsoft Windows NT.

AFTER READING THIS CHAPTER AND COMPLETING THE EXERCISES YOU WILL BE ABLE TO:

- EXPLAIN HOW TO ESTABLISH NETWORK TRAFFIC BASELINE CHARACTERISTICS
- DESCRIBE THE SIMPLE NETWORK MANAGEMENT PROTOCOL (SNMP) AND HOW IT IS USED
- DESCRIBE NETWORK-MONITORING DEVICES SUCH AS MULTI-METERS, CABLE SCANNERS, TIME DOMAIN REFLECTOMETERS, AND PROTOCOL ANALYZERS
- EXPLAIN REMOTE NETWORK MONITORING
- DESCRIBE AND USE MICROSOFT NETWORK-MONITORING TOOLS SUCH AS THE PERFORMANCE MONITOR AND NETWORK MONITOR

AN OVERVIEW OF NETWORK MONITORING

Network monitoring serves at least three purposes. One reason to monitor is to become familiar with your network so that you know the signs of impending problems. It is difficult to see a problem coming unless you know what performance is typical on your network. A second reason to monitor is to prevent problems before they occur and to diagnose existing problems to resolve them. Third, network monitoring enables you to track network growth, so you can plan for expansion and new services before the network is clogged with traffic. Your role is similar to that of a highway planner who tracks the growth in traffic and regional populations and proposes new lanes and bypasses before people are stuck for hours in traffic jams. Network baselines also provide a means of predicting network growth and future expenditures for network devices and new technologies.

Monitoring a network is a complex process. Many factors interact to affect network performance. A new database server that sends the entire database to users who want only a report may suddenly increase the network load. A poorly designed client/server application gradually may tax a network as more users are trained on that application and start using it. An untuned network server may become a bottleneck as users queue up for access to that server. A new print server may broadcast so frequently that it increases network traffic. A portion of the network may need to be segmented to reduce traffic. Bridges may be incorrectly installed, causing packets to loop continuously around a network. Table 10-1 shows some typical sources of network load and the factors that cause them. One key to solving such problems is to have network-monitoring tools and to become skilled at using them.

Table 10-1

Sources of network load

Problem Source	Factors That Can Cause the Problem
Cable plant	Damaged cable, poorly installed cable, shorts, opens, partial grounds
Workstations	NICs, network drivers
Servers	NICs, network drivers, routing information protocols, CPU capacity, memory capacity, hard disk capacity, protocols in use
Software	File sizes, network compatibility
Client/server applications	Design problems, database handling, report-generating techniques, user capacity
Network printing	Number of print servers, protocols in use by print servers, print file sizes, print server setup, multi-protocol print servers, printer setup
Network management system	Data collection and polling (of network nodes) configuration
Network capacity	Adding new workstations, servers, hosts, software
Intelligent network devices	Polling frequency (polling network nodes), configuration problems, broadcast frequency

ESTABLISHING NETWORK TRAFFIC CHARACTERISTICS

The most important way to get to know your network is to use monitoring tools to establish normal traffic characteristics in a process that involves establishing benchmarks. **Benchmarks**, or baselines, provide a basis for comparing data collected during problem situations with data showing normal performance conditions. That creates a way to diagnose problems and identify growth. You establish benchmarks in the following ways:

- By generating statistics on CPU, disk, memory, and I/O with no users on the system, to establish a baseline for comparison to more active periods. Keep a spreadsheet or database and performance charts of the information.

- By using performance monitoring to establish slow, average, and peak periods. Keep records on those periods.

- By gathering performance statistics on slow, average, and peak periods for every new software application installed.

- By tracking growth in the use of servers, such as increases in users, increases in software, and increases in the average amount of time users are on the system.

 A **benchmark**, also called a baseline, is a standard for hardware or software used to measure performance under varying loads or circumstances.

The best way to get a feel for your network is to gather benchmarks and then to monitor network performance frequently after you have the benchmark data. Performance indicators can be confusing at first, so the more time you spend observing them, the better you'll understand them. For example, viewing the CPU utilization on a server the first few times does not tell you much, but viewing it over a period of two or three months, noting slow and peak periods, helps you develop knowledge about how CPU demand varies for that server.

SIMPLE NETWORK MANAGEMENT PROTOCOL (SNMP)

The **Simple Network Management Protocol (SNMP)** is a widely used protocol that enables network managers to monitor network activity continuously. SNMP was developed as an alternative to the OSI standard for network management, **Common Management Interface Protocol (CMIP)**. CMIP has been slow to emerge and has relatively high system overhead. Many vendors have chosen SNMP instead because of its simplicity.

 The **Simple Network Management Protocol (SNMP)** is a protocol that enables computers and network equipment to gather standardized data about network performance and is part of the TCP/IP suite of protocols.

 The **Common Management Interface Protocol (CMIP)** is a protocol that is part of the OSI standards for network management to gather performance data on a network.

SNMP has several important advantages over CMIP. First, it is supported by the following major network management systems and manufacturers:

- NetView (IBM)
- Spectrum (Cabletron)
- Polycenter (DEC)
- Optivity (Bay Networks)
- OpenView (Hewlett-Packard)

Several hundred networking devices also support SNMP, including file servers, NICs, routers, repeaters, bridges, switches, and hubs. In contrast, CMIP is used by IBM in some token ring applications but not on many other networks.

Another advantage of SNMP is that it operates independently on the network, which means it does not depend on a two-way connection at the protocol level with other network entities. That quality enables SNMP to analyze network activity, such as incomplete packets and broadcast activity, without depending on possibly faulty information from a failing node. CMIP, on the other hand, connects to network nodes at the protocol level, which means its analysis of problems depends on the accuracy of a node that may be malfunctioning.

SNMP also has an advantage in that management functions are carried out at a network management station. That is in contrast to CMIP, where management is distributed to the individual network nodes that are also being managed.

Another advantage of SNMP is that it has lower memory overhead than CMIP. CMIP needs up to 1.5 MB at the node for operation, whereas SNMP only needs a maximum of 64 KB.

USING SNMP FOR NETWORK MONITORING

SNMP functions through two entities, the **network management station (NMS)** and **network agents**. The NMS monitors networked devices that are equipped to communicate via SNMP. The managed devices run agent software that is in contact with the NMS. Most devices connected to modern networks can be agents, including routers, repeaters, hubs, switches, bridges, PCs (via the NIC), print servers, access servers, and UPSs.

 A **network management station (NMS)** is a dedicated workstation that gathers and stores network performance data, obtaining that data from network nodes running agent software that enables them to collect the data. The NMS runs network management software that enables it to compile the information and perform network management functions.

 A **network agent** is a network device, such as a workstation or a router, that is equipped to gather network performance information to send to the NMS.

The network administrator can use the console at the NMS to send commands to network devices and obtain statistics on performance. The NMS can build a map of the entire network. If a new device is added, the NMS can discover it immediately. Software on the NMS has the ability to detect if an agent is down or malfunctioning. The agent may be highlighted in red, an alarm may sound, or both. All NMS software is written in GUI format, so it is easy to interpret.

Many NMS software packages have graphical representations of meters to show network utilization, flow of packets, and other network performance information. Application programming interfaces allow customized programming features.

MANAGEMENT INFORMATION BASE (MIB)

Each agent keeps a database of information, such as the number of packets sent, the number of packets received, packet errors, the number of connections, and so on. An agent's database is called the **Management Information Base (MIB).**

 The **Management Information Base (MIB)** is a database of network performance information that is stored on a network agent for access by an NMS.

The NMS uses a range of commands to obtain or alter MIB data. The retrieved data enables the network manager to determine if a device is down or if a network problem exists. The NMS may even allow the network manager to reboot a device remotely.

The messages transmitted between the NMS and the agent are packaged into the User Datagram Protocol (UDP). The packaged unit consists of a message version ID, a **community name**, and a protocol data unit (PDU). The community name is a password shared by the NMS and the agent. The PDU is a command sent from the NMS to the agent (Figure 10-1).

 A **community name** is a password used by network agents and the NMS so their communications cannot be easily intercepted by an unauthorized workstation or device.

Figure 10-1

Network management station monitoring a server and a hub

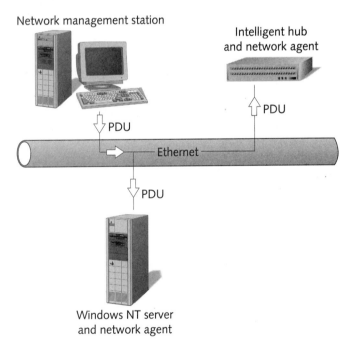

The MIB stores data on network objects such as workstations, servers, bridges, routers, hubs, and repeaters. The core set of variables contained in a MIB is listed in Table 10-2. The MIB table was originally defined according to the Management Information Base-I (MIB-I) standard, and tracks information about a device, incorporating a range of variables. MIB standards are defined by the Internet Engineering Task Force (IETF).

Table 10-2

MIB variables

MIB Variables	Purpose
Address translation group	Converts network addresses to subnet or physical addresses
Electronic gateway protocol group	Provides information about nodes on the same segment as the network agent
Interfaces group	Tracks the number of network NICs and the number of subnets
Internet control message protocol group	Gathers data on the number of messages sent and received through the agent
Internet protocol group	Tracks the number of input datagrams received and the number rejected
SNMP group	Gathers data about the communications with the MIB
System group	Contains information about the network agent
Transmission control protocol group	Provides information about TCP connections on the network, including address and timeout information
User datagram protocol group	Contains information about the listening agent that the NMS is currently contacting

A newer standard, MIB-II, has been developed to improve on MIB-I. The MIB-II standard includes improved security, support for token ring, support for high-speed interfaces, and support for telecommunications interfaces. MIB-II is supported by many network device vendors.

SNMPv2

The original version of SNMP has some shortcomings that are addressed in version 2, which is called SNMPv2. Security is a particularly important issue, since SNMP lacks strict security measures. For example, with SNMP the community name is sent by the NMS without encryption and can be intercepted. Someone might be able to capture the password and gain access to sensitive network management commands, providing the ability to remotely configure a router or a hub, compromising network security.

Compared to SNMP, SNMPv2 provides an encrypted community name, improved error handling, and multiprotocol support. It also adds support for IPX and AppleTalk. Another advantage of SNMPv2 is fast data transmission and the ability to retrieve more MIB-II information at one time.

NETWORK-MONITORING DEVICES

Network-monitoring devices range from simple voltage testers to complex protocol analyzers. Prices go up for devices that have more network-monitoring functions. If you have a small network of 10 or 20 workstations, you probably need only simple equipment, such as a voltmeter or a multimeter. If you manage a large enterprise network with hundreds of nodes, you may need several types of equipment, such as a time domain reflectometer and a protocol analyzer. Some examples of test and monitoring devices are the following:

- Voltmeter, multimeter, and optical power meter
- Cable scanner
- Transceiver monitor

- MAU analyzer
- Time domain reflectometer
- Protocol analyzer

BASIC MONITORING DEVICES: VOLTMETERS, MULTIMETERS, AND OPTICAL POWER METERS

A **voltmeter** tests the voltage on network cable and tests signal strength or voltage levels on any network device. For a few dollars more, you can purchase a **multimeter**, which combines the functions of a voltmeter and an **ohm meter**. The ohm meter enables you to test the cable for opens or shorts.

A **voltmeter** is a device that tests the voltage in an electrical circuit. Some voltmeters use a gauge-type meter to display the test results; digital voltmeters (DVMs) have a more precise digital display.

An **ohm meter** is a device that tests resistance and continuity in an electrical circuit.

A **multimeter** is a device that measures a combination of electrical characteristics such as volts, ohms, and amperes.

To measure the light-signal strength on fiber-optic cable, you need an **optical power meter**. For small- to medium-size networks, the best course is to retain the services of an optical cable expert to measure the signal strength and to troubleshoot other optical cable problems.

An **optical power meter** measures the light signal transmitted through fiber-optic cable.

MONITORING CABLE DISTANCE

Cable scanners test coaxial, twisted-pair, and fiber-optic cable. To test the cable, a connector on a section of cable is attached to the scanner. The scanner measures the cable by transmitting an electrical signal. It times the signal to determine where the signal stops. The information is used to determine the cable length, which is shown on an LCD display, printed out, or both. Scanners are made to test cables at various speeds.

A **cable scanner** measures the length of a cable segment and tests for opens and shorts.

If the signal transmission is interrupted, the scanner determines if an open circuit or a short circuit exists. An open circuit is one in which the connection is severed, such as a cable that is cut. A short circuit is an incomplete or damaged connection, such as when the two conductors in a twisted-pair set come in contact in a poorly built connector. The scanner reports the distance to the problem so it can be located and repaired. Many scanners also can indicate if a cable segment has RFI or EMI.

Some scanners can monitor for cable problems continuously, producing a report of the information they have collected. This feature is useful when you are working to locate an intermittent problem, such as an occasional short or a defective connector.

Optical fault finders are devices that measure power and distance capabilities in fiber-optic cable. These devices are slightly more expensive than power meters, but they have the additional ability to make distance measurements and locate tiny fiber breaks called microbends.

 An **optical fault finder** is a device that measures power and distance characteristics in fiber-optic cable.

 If a 10BASE-T cable scanner is available to you, try this hands-on activity to measure the cable distance on a small network. You need access to a network that is not in use by others, or you need to make your own network. If you make your own, connect two workstations to a 10BASE-T hub using UTP cable and make sure the hub is connected to power. (If the scanner is compatible only with coaxial cable, try building a small 10BASE2 segment with two workstations and two terminators on each end of the segment.)

To measure the end-to-end distance of cable on the network:

1. Review the instructions for using the scanner.

2. Make sure both workstations are turned off and remove the connector to one of the workstations.

3. Attach the cable scanner to that connector (Figure 10-2).

Figure 10-2

Using a cable scanner to check the cable distance

Disconnected workstation

Cable scanner

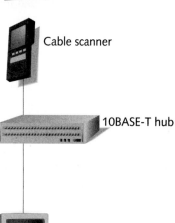

10BASE-T hub

4. Follow the scanner directions to measure the cable distance.

5. Add another workstation to the network and measure the distance again (or remove the second workstation and cable).

It is safest to disconnect the cable from all powered devices to ensure the most accurate measurement and to protect you and the scanner from damaging levels of voltage that may be present on the cable.

TRANSCEIVER MONITOR

Transceivers have low visibility on a network, but they play a critical role. These small devices are part of the attachment unit interface (AUI) for linking backbone cabling into network and computer equipment, such as bridges, routers, hubs, and workstations. A defective transceiver can be hard to identify without the right equipment. The transceiver monitor detects transceiver problems related to power, signal reception, and collision handling.

 A malfunctioning transceiver is one of the most difficult problems to locate and solve, making the transceiver monitor a valuable tool for network administrators.

MAU ANALYZER

A MAU analyzer is used on token ring networks and provides information similar to a cable scanner. It generates a signal for the purpose of locating opens, shorts, and faulty cable connectors. It also determines if the MAU is functioning properly.

TIME DOMAIN REFLECTOMETER (TDR)

A **time domain reflectometer (TDR)** has more options than a cable scanner and is more expensive. It monitors line impedance, opens, shorts, RFI/EMI, cable distances, and connector and terminator problems. A TDR works by transmitting a signal and gathering information on the signal reflection that is returned. TDRs can duplicate the wave pattern of the signal to show impedance, signal strength, signal interference, distance, and other information. Some TDRs have a memory feature to capture several snapshots at different times and to record the information in a printed report. That feature is used to track intermittent cable problems or problems due to occasional electrical interference.

 A **time domain reflectometer (TDR)** is a device that measures network cable characteristics such as distance, impedance, levels of RFI/ EMI, and the presence of opens and shorts.

Optical time domain reflectometers (OTDRs) are available for testing fiber-optic cable. These devices transmit a lightwave instead of an electrical impulse. The reflected signal is measured for distance and strength.

PROTOCOL ANALYZER

The most sophisticated monitoring device for resolving protocol-level problems is the **protocol analyzer.** This device works in promiscuous mode to capture detailed information about the traffic moving across a network, including information about the protocol and the OSI layer. Some protocol analyzers provide information derived from the OSI physical, data link, and network layers. Others can analyze the upper OSI layers also.

A **protocol analyzer** is a device used to monitor one or more protocols transmitted across a network.

At the physical layer, a protocol analyzer detects problems such as opens, shorts, and electrical interference at a very basic level. The analyzer can be attached to the network backbone or to a particular segmented portion of the network. The data link layer analysis produces information on data errors, including packet collisions, incomplete packets, corrupted packets, CRC errors, network bottlenecks, and broadcast storms.

At the network layer, a protocol analyzer monitors routing information contained in data packets. By viewing that information, you can analyze distances traveled by packets. For example, it may show that a packet takes an unusually long route to or from a workstation in one building to a server in another, perhaps indicating the need to adjust a router's setup.

Some protocol analyzers can examine the transport, session, presentation, and application OSI layers. Protocol analyzers contain software that is designed to interpret specific protocols. At the time you purchase the analyzer, you also purchase the individual software modules for designated protocols. For example, if you have a network using TCP/IP and IPX/SPX, you need to purchase a module for TCP/IP and another for IPX/SPX monitoring. As you add new protocols to the network, you can add software to the analyzer to monitor the new protocols.

In this hands-on activity you use the Internet to find out about protocol analyzers on today's market.

To find out about protocol analyzer products:

1. Start **Internet Explorer**.

2. Go to a product site such as Hewlett-Packard at **www.hp.com** (and search for the Internet Advisor product) or Network General at **www.ngc.com** (and search for the Sniffer product).

3. Find out what protocols those products support and if the products are available in portable units.

4. Create a document to record your findings.

REMOTE NETWORK MONITORING

The problem with dedicated network monitoring devices like the protocol analyzer is that they gather data from only one portion of the network. If an analyzer is connected on one side of a bridge, it may not be able to gather data on the other side. If two networks are connected through a remote router, it is necessary to place a protocol analyzer on each network. The same problems exist for monitoring network traffic on different switch ports. Obviously, providing full monitoring coverage can become expensive on a large network.

One alternative to purchasing multiple protocol analyzers is to use software to turn existing network nodes into monitoring devices. **Remote Network Monitoring (RMON)** was developed by the IETF in the early 1990s. RMON is compatible with SNMP and uses a database for remote monitoring called RMON MIB-II. That database is designed to enable remote network nodes to gather protocol analysis data. The remote nodes are agents, or **probes**. Information gathered by the probes can be sent to an **RMON management station**, which compiles it into a database. RMON MIB-II standards have been developed for FDDI, Ethernet, and token ring networks.

 Remote Network Monitoring (RMON) uses remote network nodes, such as workstations or network devices, to perform network monitoring, including gathering information for network protocol analysis. Probes are located on remote sections of the network, for example, across bridges or routers.

 RMON probes are remotely located workstations, servers, and network devices equipped with RMON software used to monitor a network and send information to an **RMON management station**. The management station is a dedicated workstation that gathers and reports on RMON data collected by probes.

Similar to a dedicated protocol analyzer, the probe taps into the network in promiscuous mode, gathering information about network activity. Probes can be placed anywhere there is a need to continuously monitor the network. They even can be placed on the remote side of a dial-up, T1/T3, or ISDN link to gather information from each region of a WAN (Figure 10-3). The probes can be devices dedicated to information gathering or they can be software placed on existing network nodes, such as workstations, servers, hubs, bridges, routers, and switches.

Figure 10-3

Remote network monitoring through RMON

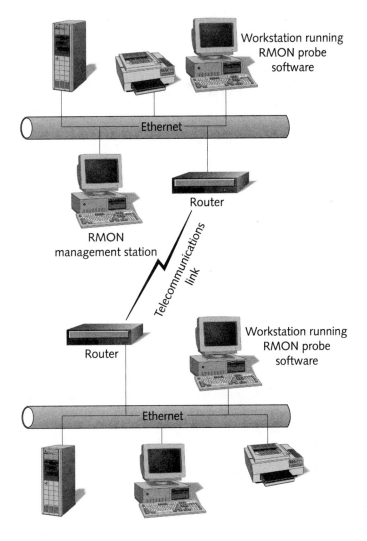

RMON software can create overhead on a workstation, server, or network device. If you implement RMON, find out what overhead is created and the risk of interruption to the normal functions of the host device. Avoid using RMON on a critical network component, such as a server, where the added overhead may cause extra CPU and disk storage load.

MONITORING THE NETWORK WITH MICROSOFT TOOLS

Several software-based monitoring tools are available through Microsoft operating systems or can be obtained from Microsoft. Some of these tools are designed for small Microsoft-based networks where only NetBEUI is used. Others are compatible with SNMP and are used on networks running TCP/IP. Microsoft's monitoring tools include the following:

- Network Monitor Agent
- SNMP Service
- Performance Monitor
- Network Monitor
- Net Watcher
- SNMP Monitor

NETWORK MONITOR AGENT

The **Network Monitor Agent** is a service that can be installed on a network computer running Windows NT Workstation, Windows NT Server, or Windows 95. Once installed, it enables a computer to collect statistics about network performance, such as the number of packets sent from and received at that workstation. The computer running the Network Monitor Agent gathers the information through its NIC. With the Network Monitor Agent loaded, the NIC gathers information about NetBEUI and NWLink (IPX/SPX) traffic that passes through it. A workstation or server running Microsoft analysis software, such as the **Performance Monitor** or the **Network Monitor,** can connect to the computer with the Network Monitor Agent software and use that computer's NIC to capture data for examination. Table 10-3 shows the type of information that the Performance Monitor can capture with the Network Monitor Agent loaded.

The **Network Monitor Agent** enables a Microsoft workstation or server NIC to gather network performance data.

The **Performance Monitor** is a Microsoft monitoring tool that captures and reports performance information about the computer that is running the monitor software and about the network to which that computer is connected.

The **Network Monitor** is a Microsoft monitoring tool that captures and reports information about network performance.

Network Object Being Monitored	Information Collected
NetBEUI	Data on NetBEUI communications, such as communication errors, bytes sent, and data packets sent
NetBEUI Resource	Data on resources used, such as the storage areas (buffers) used by a NIC transmitting NetBEUI data packets
Network Interface	Data that travels through the workstation or server NIC, such as the number of bytes transmitted and received, number of packets sent, and packet transmission and receipt errors
Network Segment	Data on the network segment to which the workstation or server is attached, such as broadcast and network utilization data
NWLink IPX	Data on IPX communications sent from a Novell NetWare server, workstation, or IPX-enabled print server
NWLink NetBIOS	Data on NetBIOS communications, such as bytes sent, packet transmissions, and communications errors
NWLink SPX	Data on SPX communications sent from a Novell NetWare server or workstation

SNMP SERVICE

Loading the SNMP service on a computer running Windows NT Server or Workstation can turn that computer into an SNMP network agent. With the SNMP service loaded, a computer can communicate with an SNMP network management station. Microsoft's SNMP service provides support for MIB information gathering. Although SNMP includes network monitoring for TCP/IP and IPX/SPX traffic, the Microsoft SNMP service monitors only TCP/IP, because Microsoft's Network Monitor Agent is used to gather information on NWLink (IPX/SPX). Table 10-4 shows the SNMP monitoring information available to the Performance Monitor.

At this writing, Microsoft's SNMP service uses SNMP version 1, not SNMPv2, which means the community name is not encrypted over the network. However, it is likely that SNMPv2 soon will be supported.

Network Object Being Monitored	Information Collected
ICMP	Data on network communications using the **Internet Control Message Protocol (ICMP)**, which is used by TCP/IP-based computers to share TCP/IP addressing and error information
IP	Data on Internet Protocol (IP) activity and addressing
NetBT (NBT)	Data for NetBIOS communications that are performed via TCP/IP data communications
Network Interface	TCP/IP performance data on a network interface such as a NIC, including the number of bytes or data packets sent
TCP	Data on TCP, including transmission or connectivity errors
UDP	Data on UDP, which is the protocol used by network management stations and network agents for sending messages between one another

ICMP is a network maintenance protocol used in the Internet Protocol (IP) to assist in building information about routing network packets, including determining the shortest path to use for transmitting data. It also helps determine if a network station is live, to help locate network problems, and to reduce the flow of packets when the network is congested with traffic.

With the SNMP service loaded, the following devices can be remotely controlled by a management station:

- NT servers

- NT workstations

- WINS servers

- DHCP servers

- Internet Information Server (IIS) computers

This hands-on activity gives you an opportunity to load the Network Monitor Agent and the SNMP service on a computer running Windows NT 4.0 Workstation. You need access to the Windows NT Workstation CD-ROM for version 4.0. To start, log on to the NT workstation using the Administrator or equivalent account.

To load the Network Monitor Agent:

1. Click **Start, Settings,** and **Control Panel**.

2. Double-click the **Network** icon.

3. Click the **Services** tab and **Add** (Figure 10-4).

Figure 10-4

Preparing to add a service

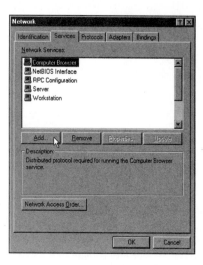

4. In the Network Service: scroll box, double-click **Network Monitor Agent** (Figure 10-5).

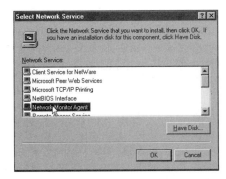

Figure 10-5

Adding the Network Monitor Agent service

5. The Windows NT Setup dialog box requests the path of the disk from which to install the service. Enter the CD-ROM drive letter immediately followed by a colon and the path **\I386**, then click **Continue** (Figure 10-6).

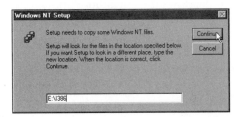

Figure 10-6

Entering the CD-ROM path

6. Back in the Network dialog box, click the **Add** button to view the list of services. This time, find the SNMP Service in the Network Service: box and double-click **SNMP Service**.

7. In the Windows NT Setup dialog box, enter the CD-ROM drive letter, a colon, and the path **\I386**, then click **Continue**.

8. If TCP/IP or Internet services already are loaded, the SNMP agent installation displays the Microsoft SNMP Properties dialog box. Click the **Security** tab. Click **Add** under Accepted Community Names and enter a community name, such as **topsecurity**, as in Figure 10-7. Click **Add** on the Service Configuration dialog box, then **Apply**.

Figure 10-7

Entering a community name

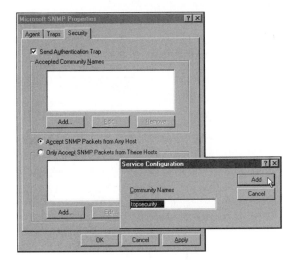

9. Click **Close** at the bottom of the Network dialog box.

10. A warning message notes that the changes will not be implemented until you reboot the workstation. Click **Yes** to reboot.

PERFORMANCE MONITOR

The Windows NT Performance Monitor is available on Windows NT Server and Windows NT Workstation. Many network administrators monitor their networks using a workstation equipped with Windows NT Workstation, because it offers the Performance Monitor and other tools that provide a view into the network. The view available through the Performance Monitor is made possible by loading the Network Monitor Agent and the SNMP service on the administrator's workstation and on other networked workstations and servers. In a Microsoft Windows–based network, the Performance Monitor is useful in two broad respects. One is to monitor how server resources are used, such as CPU, memory, and hard-disk utilization. Those possible sources of load on a server can make network access appear to be slow to that server. The Performance Monitor can be used as a tool to assess insufficient server resources, enabling you to spot a resource that needs to be increased, such as adding more server memory. Increasing a server's resources can decrease that server's response time, which decreases the pileup in workstations trying to access that server. Table 10-5 lists the server resources that can be monitored.

Table 10-5

Resources monitored by the Performance Monitor

Resource or Object Being Monitored	Information Collected
Browser	Activity of the browser service that enables Network Neighborhood to communicate and exchange information with other computers on the network
Cache	Performance information on data caching for the hard disks
LogicalDisk	Information about one or more physical disks that are linked as a single logical disk (one assigned drive letter for multiple disks), such as queue length for disk requests and data transfer speeds
Memory	Information about RAM use, such as percentage of memory in use, input and output activity, and peak usage
Objects	Activities of special objects, such as started processes and started threads
Paging File	Data on paging file performance such as current usage and peak usage
PhysicalDisk	Data on each hard disk drive, such as length of queues to access a disk and data access speeds
Process	Performance data on a specific process that is running
Processor	Demands on the processor, such as percentage in use, number of requests from hardware components, and percentage in use by the operating system
Redirector	Network connection information, such as folder access requests from other computers on the network and information about connected workstations
Server	Information about the Server service, such as number of bytes sent out and received, logon errors, and logged-off sessions
System	File access, system calls, operating system activities, and percentage of the processor used by the system
Thread	Data on a specific thread running within a process, such as processor time used by the thread

With the help of servers and workstations that have the Network Monitor Agent and SNMP services, a second important function of the Performance Monitor is to gather data about network performance. The information it can provide (see Tables 10-3 and 10-4) can be built into monitoring information that shows how much a network is utilized. The network administrator uses that information to examine the load on the network at peak, average, and slow periods. If the average range of utilization is 30% or less, network performance is in an acceptable range. However, an average range of 40–70% utilization, with frequent peaks over 90%, may indicate a serious problem, such as a malfunctioning network component, poor network design, or the need to expand the network capability. Average utilization over 70% is cause for immediate network troubleshooting, for example, to locate a defective network device.

This hands-on activity is an opportunity to see how the Performance Monitor is used to monitor network utilization. You need access to a computer running Windows NT Server or Workstation that also has the Network Monitor Agent loaded (the SNMP agent is optional). You also need to log on to the Administrator or an equivalent account.

To view network utilization:

1. Click **Start**, **Programs**, and **Administrative Tools (Common)**.

2. Click **Performance Monitor** (Figure 10-8).

3. Click the **Add counter** icon on the empty Performance Monitor tracking screen (Figure 10-9).

Figure 10-8

Opening the Performance Monitor

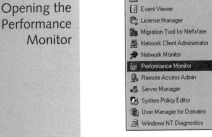

Figure 10-9

Adding an object to monitor

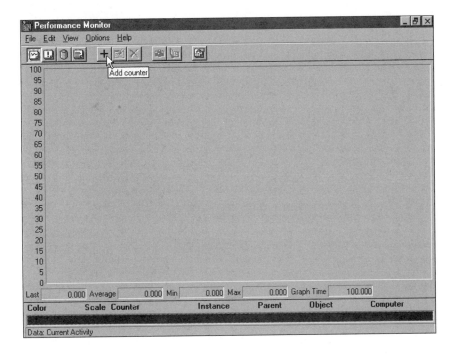

4. Notice that the Add to Chart dialog box shows your computer in the Computer: text box, which means the Performance Monitor is set by default to monitor from your computer's NIC. The Computer: text box is where you can tell it to monitor from another agent, such as a network server or a workstation on another part of the network. Leave your computer as the default for this activity.

5. Click the scroll arrow in the Object: text box and select **Network Segment**.

6. Click **% Broadcast Frames** in the Counter: text box. On a Microsoft-based network, this counter shows how much of the network traffic is due to servers (Windows NT) and workstations (Windows 95 and NT Workstation). Click **Add**.

7. Click **% Network utilization** in the Counter: text box. This counter enables you to view the network utilization statistic (Figure 10-10). Click **Add**.

Figure 10-10

Selecting to monitor network utilization

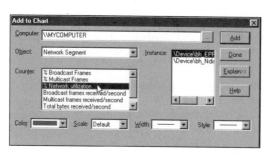

8. Click **Done** in the Add to Chart dialog box.

9. View the network utilization compared to the broadcast frames for information on the utilization and the amount of traffic due to broadcasts from servers and workstations (Figure 10-11). Notice that each counter is graphed in a different color. Spend a few minutes viewing the information to see how it changes.

Figure 10-11

Viewing network utilization compared to broadcast frames (on the actual screen each counter is graphed in a different color)

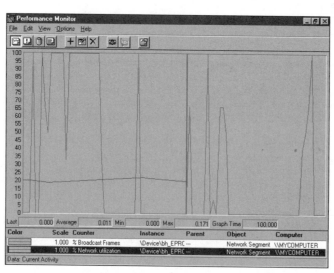

10. Close the Performance Monitor when you have finished viewing the information.

NETWORK MONITOR

The Network Monitor is included with the NT Server operating system. The Network Monitor is installed from the Network icon Services tab. To run, it requires that the Network Monitor Agent is installed. The Network Monitor also gathers SNMP-related data when the SNMP service is installed on the server and on other workstations or network devices. The network monitor tracks information such as the following:

- Percentage of network utilization
- Frames and bytes transported per second
- Network statistics
- Statistics captured during a given time period
- Transmissions per second
- NIC statistics
- Error data
- Addresses of network nodes

The Network Monitor can be customized to present many different pictures of network activity, because it displays four windows of data and because filters can be set to collect only specific types of information. A **filter** is a way to customize the Network Monitor to display or capture only certain information, for example, traffic at particular nodes, only NetBEUI traffic and not TCP/IP, or only network error information. Filters can be built based on addresses, protocols, and properties. You can choose to capture data for a short or long period of time.

A **filter** is a capability in network monitoring software that enables the network administrator to view only designated protocols, network events, network nodes, or other specialized views of the network.

In this hands-on activity, you experience using the Network Monitor. You need access to a Microsoft NT server or workstation with the Network Monitor already installed.

To use the Network Monitor:

1. Click **Start**, **Programs**, and **Administrative Tools (Common)**
2. Click **Network Monitor**. Use the maximize button on one or both Network Monitor screens if the display is not maximized.
3. Click the **Capture** menu and **Start** (Figure 10-12) or click the Start button ▶.
4. View the data capture on the screen, for example, % Network Utilization or Network Statistics (Figure 10-13).

Figure 10-12

Starting the data capture in the Network Monitor

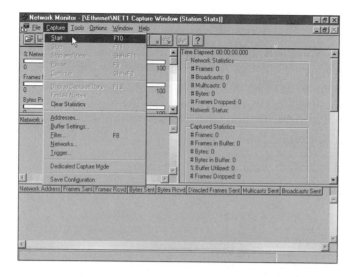

Figure 10-13

The Network Monitor capturing data

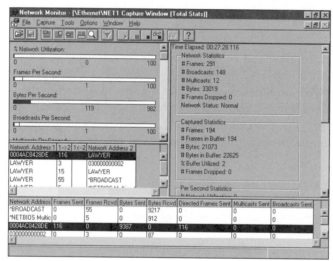

5. Use the scroll bars in each of the four windows to view the information they offer.

6. When you have finished, click the **Capture** menu and **Stop** or click the Stop button .

7. Close the Network Monitor.

> **Caution**
>
> Both the Network Monitor and the Performance Monitor create load on the CPU of the computer where they are running. When, as the network administrator, you implement these tools, plan to run them from your workstation and not from a server; if you are gathering data from a server's NIC, limit the amount of time spent gathering the data so you do not interfere with the users' access to that server.

NET WATCHER

Net Watcher provides a quick view of the shared network resources on a Microsoft-based network, showing which users are connected to those resources. It is a quick way to find out, for example, how many users are connected to a shared network printer or to a shared folder. It also offers a way to make a fast audit of which users are accessing a particular resource. If you notice a user who should not have access, you can disconnect that user through Net Watcher; or you can unshare a folder that is inadvertently shared. Net Watcher is available from Microsoft in the Microsoft NT Server Resource Kit.

 Net Watcher is a Microsoft monitoring tool used to view shared network resources and who is using them.

 In this hands-on exercise, you start Net Watcher to view the information it monitors. You need access to a Windows NT workstation or server with the Microsoft NT Server Resource Kit already installed.

To use Net Watcher:

1. Click **Start**, **Programs**, and **Resource Kit**.

2. Click **Diagnostics** and **Network Watch** (Figure 10-14).

3. Notice the shared printer and folder resources available on the network (Figure 10-15)

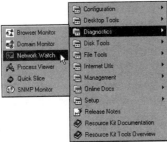
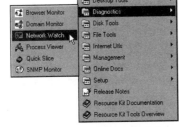

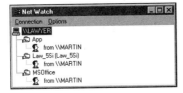

4. Notice the users connected to the shared resources.

5. Close Net Watcher.

SNMP MONITOR

The **SNMP Monitor** can obtain information about network performance that is stored in the MIB of a network agent. Queries are made through commands that are executed in a command line window. It is available as part of the Microsoft NT Server Resource Kit and is intended to be run from a Windows NT server. The SNMP Monitor keeps a log of the collected MIB information that is compatible with ODBC (open database connectivity). That means data can be collected in a log and then periodically updated in a database that supports ODBC, such as SQL Server, Microsoft Access, Oracle, or Sybase. When you start the monitor, a dialog box appears so you can view the number of connections that are monitored (Figure 10-16).

SNMP Monitor is a Microsoft network-monitoring tool that can query MIB information on network agents and store that information to put in ODBC-compatible databases.

Figure 10-16

Running the
SNMP monitor

CHAPTER SUMMARY

There are many ways to monitor a network and many tools available for network monitoring. Before starting to monitor your network, gather and record baseline network statistics so you can establish a way to identify normal network traffic. For example, network utilization statistics on low, average, and peak periods are valuable in helping you recognize out-of-the-ordinary situations, such as sudden problems, the need to make some network design changes, or the need to expand the network.

SNMP has become a staple for network monitoring. Many network devices, servers, and workstations are equipped with SNMP capabilities, so network performance can be tracked through information stored in a database.

Single devices can be attached to a network to monitor specific conditions. For example, a multimeter tests for cable continuity and the presence of signals or voltage. Other devices test cable distances, monitor for electrical interference, find open and short circuits, and monitor protocol traffic. Individual devices have the disadvantage that they monitor from only where they are attached to a network. RMON overcomes that disadvantage by turning designated network nodes into monitoring devices, enabling monitoring of enterprise and WAN networks.

Many vendors offer network-monitoring software. This chapter gave you a hands-on peek at tools used on Microsoft networks. Such tools monitor network traffic, protocols, and other performance characteristics.

In chapter 11, you learn more about network management and management tools. Domains, groups, and management wizards are examples of how Microsoft-based networks can be managed. You also learn about enterprise management tools for large networks available from other vendors.

REVIEW QUESTIONS

1. Which of the following might be an SNMP network agent?

    a. workstation

    b. router

    c. hub

    d. all of the above

    e. only b and c

2. What device would be used to determine that a NIC is sending a high number of partially formed TCP/IP frames?

    a. optical time domain reflectometer

    b. multimeter

    c. protocol analyzer

    d. transceiver monitor

3. An SNMP network agent gathers information to store in

    a. buffers.

    b. a Management Information Base (MIB).

    c. a cache.

    d. an SQL Server database defined by the network manager.

4. You want to determine the number of broadcasts from networked servers and workstations on a Microsoft-based network. Which of the following tools would give you that information?

    a. Microsoft Network Monitor

    b. cable scanner

    c. time domain reflectometer

    d. all of the above

    e. only a and c

5. What software is necessary to enable a Microsoft NT Workstation to gather data about TCP/IP traffic on a network?

    a. Performance Monitor

    b. SNMP Service

    c. IPX Agent

    d. SNMP Monitor

6. You manage three networks in three neighboring cities and want to monitor performance on all three networks from one location. Which of the following would you use?

    a. Intranet monitor

    b. Net Watcher

    c. Common Management Interface Protocol (CMIP)

    d. Remote Network Monitoring (RMON)

7. A community name is a
   a. password.
   b. timeout value.
   c. measure of network performance.
   d. NetBIOS name for a server.

8. The Network Monitor Agent can be installed on
   a. Windows NT Workstation.
   b. Windows NT Server.
   c. Windows 95.
   d. all of the above.
   e. only a and b.

9. The Performance Monitor runs from which of the following?
   a. Windows NT Workstation
   b. Windows NT Server
   c. Windows 95
   d. all of the above
   e. only a and b

10. Once installed, Network Monitor Agent enables network data to be gathered
    a. through a NIC.
    b. through the session layer of the OSI model.
    c. by sending repeated tracer signals throughout the network.
    d. through a customized network cable attachment interface.

ASPEN CONSULTING PROJECT: MORE VARIED ASSIGNMENTS

In these assignments, you are further training Sheila Markovski. You also provide assistance to Winston Research Labs and the highway department. All your assignments today focus on network monitoring issues.

ASSIGNMENT 10-1

One of Aspen Consulting's newest consultants, Sheila Markovski, has some questions for you about SNMP. Use the following space to explain how SNMP works.

List four network devices that might be equipped to use SNMP.

ASSIGNMENT 10-2

Sheila also has questions about the network-monitoring devices that are connected to a network to test various conditions. Complete the following table for Sheila's benefit, listing four devices and what they do.

Device	Purpose

Which of those devices would you recommend for determining that a cable segment is too long?

ASSIGNMENT 10-3

Winston Research Labs took your advice in chapter 5 and linked their Boston, Atlanta, Houston, and Phoenix research centers into a WAN. Because they are a 24-hour-a-day operation, they want to reduce network support costs by having only one network administrator monitoring all four sites for each of the two 8-hour night shifts between 4:00 p.m. and 8:00 a.m. Currently, there are four network administrators at each site per shift. Is network monitoring software available that would make it possible to monitor all four sites from one location? If so, use the following space to describe how it works. Create a network diagram for Winston Research Labs to illustrate how it would be set up.

ASSIGNMENT 10-4

The network administrator for the highway department, with whom you worked in chapter 9, wants to use the Network Monitor on their NT server-based network. He set it up but can collect data only from the server and not from any workstations, even though he owns the full version of the Network Monitor. He calls you for advice about how to monitor the network. Explain in the following space what he is missing and how he should set it up. Also, do you recommend he use the server or his workstation to run the network monitor? Why?

ASSIGNMENT 10-5

The highway department network administrator has called you back. He wants to use the Performance Monitor to graph information about network utilization. Practice setting up the Performance Monitor for that purpose while you explain the process to him. Use the following table to record the steps.

Steps to Set Up the Performance Monitor for Viewing Network Utilization
Step 1:
Step 2:
Step 3:
Step 4:
Step 5:
Step 6:
Step 7:

ASSIGNMENT 10-6

Based on what you know about the Performance Monitor and the Network Monitor, the highway department's network administrator is asking which tool provides the best ability to determine if an NT server NIC is broadcasting at an unusually high rate. Explain the basis of your answer here. Practice with both tools before you provide an answer.

ASSIGNMENT 10-7

Sheila Markovski has stepped into your office with some questions about what monitoring tool to use in particular instances. Complete the following table to answer her questions.

Problem Situation	Monitoring Tool	Reason for Using the Tool
Transmission errors at the server NIC		
Monitoring a network across a bridge or router		
Workstations waiting on the NT server CPU		
Network utilization often over 80%		

ASSIGNMENT 10-8

It is 4:50 p.m. and the highway department administrator has just one more question before you go home. He wants to know about protocol analyzers. Explain in general what they do. What monitoring do they perform at the physical layer, the data link layer, and the network layer?

OPTIONAL CASE STUDIES FOR TEAMS

 ## TEAM CASE 1

Winston Research Labs has never developed a set of network benchmarks. They have contacted you, and you have decided to work with several colleagues to come up with some recommendations for them. Prepare a document describing your recommendations.

 ## TEAM CASE 2

Gary Sharma from the Physicians Group is calling to report network slowdowns. He wants to know whether he should use the Performance Monitor or the Network Monitor to find the problem. You and a couple of other consultants discuss the question. Which do you recommend? What information would you look at to track the source of the problem?

 ## TEAM CASE 3

You are in the coffee room with some of the other consultants when Mark Arnez comes in. He poses an interesting question: What single network-monitoring device offers the most flexibility in troubleshooting network problems for a network engineer who works on all types of networks? Discuss the issue with your colleagues and prepare a written response for Mark.

CHAPTER ELEVEN

MANAGING THE NETWORK

Network monitoring, as you learned in chapter 10, is useful in finding and solving network problems. For example, one morning the network administrator on a college campus received several desperate calls from the administration building, including one from a vice president. The network was down and no one could access two NT servers. The problem was critical because the university trustees were scheduled to start their monthly meeting that afternoon, and several reports were still needed for the administration's meetings with the trustees. That network administrator used the Network Monitor to determine what portions of the network she could access. She traced the problem to a hub in the administration building, which she immediately replaced with a spare hub.

Although network monitoring was helpful in this situation, it would have been better if the network administrator had been warned about the problem before it occurred. In this case, network users had to call the administrator to inform her of the problem. Additional network management software might have avoided the problem altogether.

This chapter covers network management tools that can supplement monitoring and alert a network administrator to problems before they occur. Those tools also reduce hours spent manually setting up and maintaining a network. The information presented in this chapter includes an overview of enterprise management software and of tools that work specifically with Microsoft NT server networks.

AFTER READING THIS CHAPTER AND COMPLETING THE EXERCISES YOU WILL BE ABLE TO:

- EXPLAIN NETWORK EVENT MANAGEMENT
- EXPLAIN HOW TO MANAGE NETWORK DOMAINS
- DESCRIBE TOOLS FOR SERVER AND WORKSTATION MANAGEMENT
- EXPLAIN APPROACHES TO NETWORK PRINTING MANAGEMENT
- DESCRIBE TOOLS FOR MANAGING NETWORK DEVICES
- EXPLAIN FIREWALL SERVICES USED IN NETWORK MANAGEMENT SOFTWARE
- DESCRIBE SYSTEMS MANAGEMENT SERVER (SAM) CAPABILITIES

AN OVERVIEW OF ENTERPRISE NETWORK MANAGEMENT TOOLS

Several network management tools are available that provide a range of services. For example, they can monitor network nodes such as repeaters, routers, bridges, hubs, switches, workstations, servers, and hosts. If a router is down, the software graphically displays this condition and may sound an alarm to the network management station (NMS). Some management packages have the ability to reboot the router from the NMS, monitor network traffic, and provide analysis of traffic based on the data collected by intelligent nodes, such as routers and hubs.

Some management packages are designed to be modular, so specific functions can be added as your network needs grow. Modules can be added that manage domain services, user accounts, groups, virtual networks (VNETs), disk storage capacity, e-mail services, backup and restore services, file server configuration, and printer services. Many network operating systems come with management tools, or additional tools are available from the vendor. On smaller networks, the tools may circumvent the need to purchase additional management systems. Medium-size and large enterprise networks require both the management tools built into the network operating systems and enterprise network management software. In most cases, the network administrator runs the network management tools from a network management station or has different kinds of management stations. For example, some tools run only on UNIX workstations, and some run only on NT workstations. In those cases, the network manager may use one workstation as a small server and log on to it from another workstation. For example, the UNIX workstation may act as a server for some of the network management software, which the administrator accesses from a workstation running Windows NT. Most network management software vendors port systems originally written for UNIX workstations to Windows NT so that all software can be run from one place. Figure 11-1 illustrates network management functions that can be incorporated into one or more software packages running from an administrator's network management station.

Figure 11-1

Components in a network management system

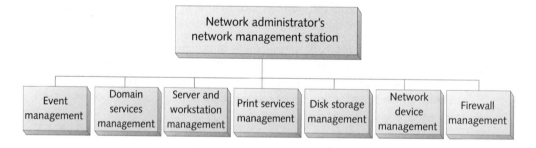

EVENT MANAGEMENT

Event management enables the network administrator to set up filters to capture certain types of events, similar to the filter capabilities of Microsoft's Network Monitor but on a larger scale for enterprise network management. A filter can capture the source of the event, such as a malfunctioning router or a hub module. It also captures descriptive information, including a message about the event, the time and date, and the severity of the problem. Event categories can be established so they are prioritized for the network manager. For example, a switch that is down can be given a higher priority than a partitioned segment containing a single node.

Another capability is data collection of real-time and historical network information. For example, you can compare the present activity of a hub with historical activity. That enables you to judge differences between normal and peak times.

Event management is used in network management software to create filters and track designated network events, such as a device that is down, the network traffic to a server or a segment that is partitioned, or network utilization over a specified percentage.

In this hands-on activity, you build a simple filter to study only the IP traffic into and out of an NT server as a way of tracking present activity. You need Administrator access to a computer running NT 4.0 Server that has the Microsoft Network Monitor already installed. (Your lab may be set up to run the Network Monitor from computers running Windows NT Workstation or remotely through the remote administration setup on a server. Consult your instructor about how to start Network Monitor in those situations and begin at step 3.)

To create a filter:

1. Click **Start**, **Programs**, and **Administrative Tools (Common)**.

2. Click **Network Monitor**.

3. Maximize the Network Monitor and the Capture windows if they are not already maximized.

4. Click the **Capture** menu and **Filter**, as in Figure 11-2.

Figure 11-2

Selecting the Filter option in the Network Monitor

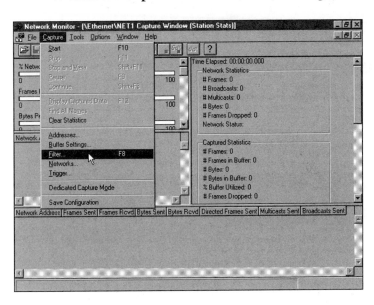

5. If a warning message appears about the capabilities of your version of the Network Monitor, click **Yes** to continue. (Some versions monitor traffic only from a particular server's NIC, and it is necessary to purchase Microsoft's System Management Server for a version with more capabilities.)

6. In the Capture Filter dialog box, double-click the **SAP/ETYPE** line to specify a protocol (Figure 11-3).

Figure 11-3

Selecting a
protocol to
filter

7. In the Capture Filter SAPs and ETYPEs dialog box, click the **Disable All** button.

8. Scroll down in the Disabled Protocols box to find the two IP protocol options (SAP and ETYPE). Hold down [**Ctrl**] and click each **IP** option, as in Figure 11-4. Click **Enable** and then **OK**. Now only IP communications will be monitored.

Figure 11-4

Selecting the IP
protocol

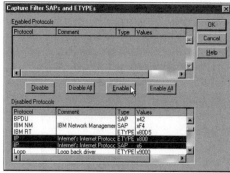
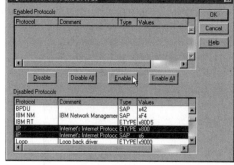

9. Back in the Capture Filter dialog box, highlight any INCLUDE lines and click the Delete **Line** button to remove those lines (Figure 11-5).

Figure 11-5

Deleting
existing
monitoring
filters

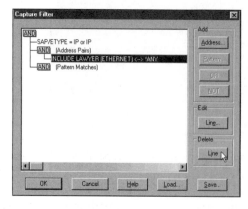

10. Double-click the (**Address Pairs**) line.

11. In the Address Expression dialog box, click the **Include** radio button.

12. In the Station 1 scroll box, select the name of the computer from which you are working (if there are duplicate names, one with a hexadecimal address and one with a dotted decimal address, select the one with the dotted decimal address). This is the server on which you want to collect data.

13. In the Direction box, click the top two-way arrow, because you want to collect data on packets received and sent at that server's NIC.

14. Click **★ANY** in the Station 2 scroll box and click **OK** (Figure 11-6), which means that traffic to and from the server will be monitored from any node on the network.

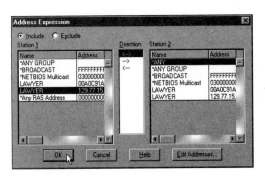

Figure 11-6

Selecting the stations to monitor

15. Click **OK** in the Capture Filter dialog box.

16. Click the **Capture** menu and then **Start** (or click the Start Capture button ▶).

17. View the statistics in the bottom box of the Network Monitor for a few minutes.

18. To exit, click the **Capture** menu and **Stop** (or click the Stop Capture button ■). Close the Network Monitor.

DOMAIN SERVICES MANAGEMENT

One way to manage a network is to divide it into domains, which consist of groupings of resources. The largest domains are the country designations on the Internet. For example, *.us* is the domain name for the United States, and *.se* is the domain name for Sweden. Another Internet domain representation is for organizational types, such as *.edu* for education, *.com* for commercial entities, *.org* for noncommercial groups, and *.gov* for government entities. Yet another type of domain is a network at a business or a university, such as *microsoft.com* for Microsoft and *sewanee.edu* for the University of the South.

Within an enterprise network, a domain may be a collection of network resources, such as servers, workstations, hubs, switches, printers, and other devices on one network. For example, Sun Microsystems' Solstice Domain Manager software is designed to manage an enterprise of multivendor equipment within one network management system that recognizes the network nodes as a domain.

A Microsoft NT Server domain is a collection of resources and users who have access to the resources, which can be servers, printers, CD-ROM arrays, and other equipment. A single domain can have one or more servers as members. Some servers may have generalized functions, such as PDCs and BDCs, which provide log-on services and log-on authentication. Others may be specialized, such as print servers, database servers, or CD-ROM servers. Figure 11-7 shows examples of two domains, A and B.

Figure 11-7

Two domains

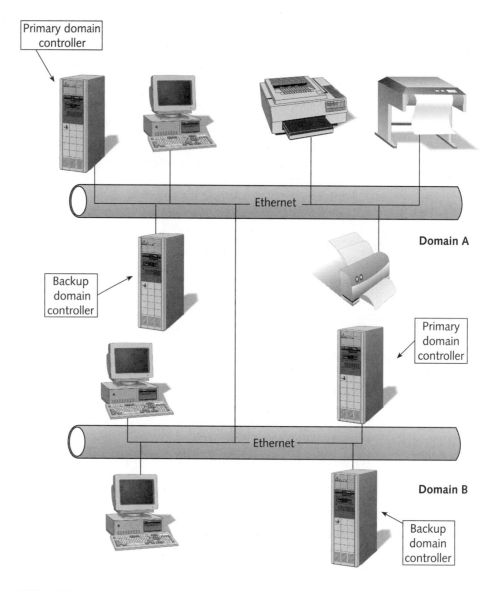

When file servers were first introduced, users logged on to each network server individually. A user might have to log on to three servers: one for word processing and spreadsheet applications, one for CAD applications, and one for accounting data. The user would have an account on each server. Access rights and other services for that user would have to be set on each server, with every server having its own record of the user's privileges. With such networks, having a few servers was manageable but time consuming. As networks have grown, individual server management is not productive for administrators or users.

The domain on an NT server allows the network administrator to manage resources and users as one unit. A user who needs resources logs on to the domain instead of several file servers. The user needs only to log on to the domain once with one password. The domain has a record of the resources the user is allowed to access and makes those available at logon.

Microsoft domains consist of clients and resources used by the clients. User accounts and user groups make up the client side. File servers, print servers, and other network services are the resources. One or more groups can be defined to the domain, with a user having membership in any or all groups. The concept of the domain preserves the idea of work groupings, without the headaches of managing them individually from multiple workstations and file servers. For example, if a business is interested in creating an executive management group with access to the accounting, sales, and inventory software, a group can be created to include each manager on that team. A supervisor who is promoted to a manager's position on the team is added easily by using the NT Server User Manager for Domains tool.

The domain concept saves time because the network administrator sets up users, privileges, and groups. One or more domains can be created to suit the management needs and styles of an organization. For instance, a college with branch campuses in four cities might place the resources of the four branches in four separate domains, each domain controlled by the network administrator at that branch. Another setup might be to have four domains but to centralize domain management under one network administrator through the domain at the main campus. A domain is a powerful management tool because one domain can be home to as many as 26,000 users and 250 groups. Multiple domains can bring many more thousands of users and resources under one roof for centralized management. Multiple domains work well for businesses or colleges with branch sites in different cities or states and for organizations with foreign and domestic locations. With network administration centralized at the domain level, only one SAM database is needed to store information on all users and their security privileges.

In this hands-on activity, you view where to add a new server to a Microsoft domain. You need access to a computer running Microsoft NT Server and an account with Administrator access. (If your lab is set up to run the Server Manager from a workstation running Windows NT or 95 using the remote administration setup on a server, consult your instructor about how to start the Server Manager and begin at step 3.)

To add a computer to a domain:

1. Click **Start**, **Programs**, and **Administrative Tools (Common)**.

2. Click **Server Manager**.

3. Click the **Computer** menu.

4. Click **Add to Domain** (Figure 11-8).

Figure 11-8

Selecting to add a computer to a domain

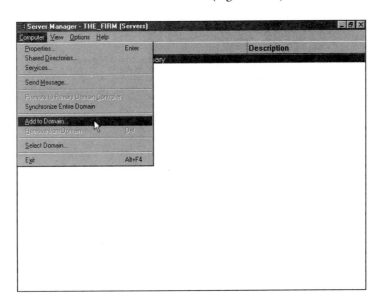

5. Click the **Windows NT Backup Domain Controller** radio button in the Add Computer To Domain dialog box, so that computer can store a backup copy of the SAM.

6. Enter the name of the server (you can make one up for this activity, e.g., **Business**).

7. Click the **Add** button to add the server to the domain (Figure 11-9).

Figure 11-9

Specifying
details to add a
computer to a
domain

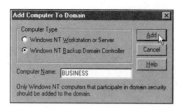

8. Click **Close** to exit the Add Computer To Domain dialog box.

9. Close the Server Manager.

DOMAIN TRUST RELATIONSHIPS

In situations where there are two or more domains, users can access domains other than their own through **trust relationships** set up by the network administrator. Each trust relationship has two parties, the trusted domain and the trusting domain. The trusted domain is the one that is granted access to resources; the trusting domain grants the access. For example, assume a manufacturing business has a main office and branch offices in five states, each with its own NT file server and domain. The main-office domain needs access to all five branch-office domains, which is granted. In this scenario, the main office is the trusted domain, and the branch offices are the trusting domains. There are several combinations of trust relationships, but three are most common: one-way trust, two-way trust, and universal trust relationships.

 Trust relationships establish how resources are accessed in Microsoft domains, providing a way to manage both resources and user accounts. A *trusting domain* is one that allows another domain security access to its resources, such as file servers. A *trusted domain* is one that has been granted security access to resources in another domain.

ONE-WAY TRUST

In a **one-way trust**, the trust relationship is not reciprocated. One domain is the trusted party and the other is trusting. For example, consider a manufacturing company where the business domain is for accounting, human resources, and sales data, and the manufacturing domain is intended for inventory control in the plant. In this case, members of the business domain may need to use resources on the manufacturing side, such as inventory and materials costs information. Access to the business domain from the manufacturing domain must be kept locked due to the sensitive nature of the accounting and human resources information. Members of the business domain can access resources and belong to groups in the manufacturing domain. Users in the manufacturing domain, however, have no access to files, groups, or resources in the business domain. Figure 11-10 illustrates a one-way trust, signified by the arrow going from the trusting to the trusted domain.

 In a **one-way trust** relationship, one domain is trusted and one is trusting.

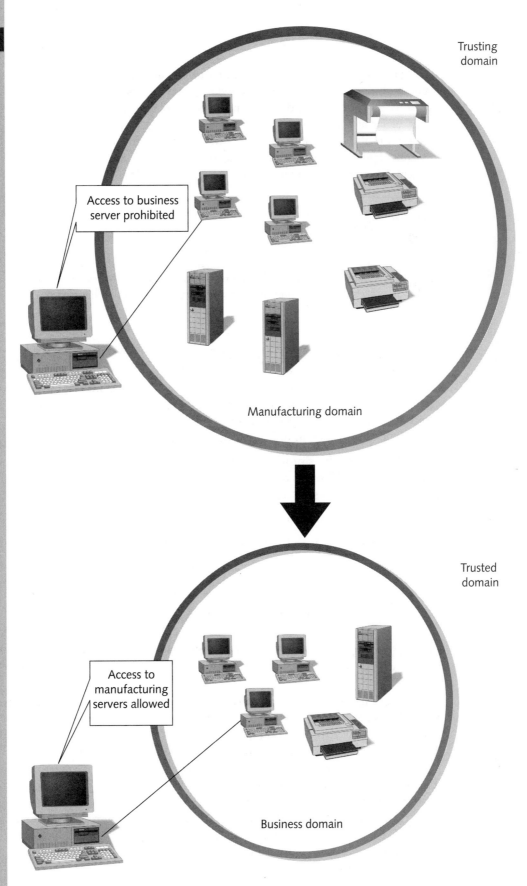

Trusting
domain

Access to business
server prohibited

Manufacturing domain

Trusted
domain

Access to
manufacturing
servers allowed

Business domain

Two-Way Trust

The trust relationship is reciprocated in a **two-way trust**. For example, a chemical company might have its business office downtown and a production plant in an industrial park across town. Two separate domains might be established for the sake of routing e-mail and other electronic communications. However, members of each domain need to access resources in the other domain. A two-way trust enables full sharing of resources between domains (Figure 11-11). Also, members of one domain can belong to groups in the other domain. Two-way trusts set up among more than two domains are called a **universal trust**.

 A **two-way trust** domain relationship is one in which both domains are trusted and trusting.

 A **universal trust** is a domain relationship among three or more domains in which every domain is trusting and trusted with every other domain.

Domain Management

Trust relationships between domains can be set up in many combinations to make the management of resources easier. For example, in a single-master domain model, several domains are controlled from one master domain. The domains may be separate divisions on one large campus or they may be in different cities or states.

The advantage of the **single master domain** is that all users access resources in all the domains. This model works particularly well for small organizations in which several hundred users are spread across several branches or business units. The advantages are the following:

- Accounts and groups are centrally managed.

- Resources are available to all users (as determined by the network administrator).

- One consistent security policy applies across the organization.

- Groups can be tailored across organizational unit boundaries.

- The SAM database is easily maintained and synchronized.

 A **single master domain** model is a relationship in a domain or among domains in which trusts are set up so that management control is centralized in one domain.

Very large organizations that span several states or countries may use the **multiple master domain** model. This model consists of two or more single master domains connected through two-way trust relationships. For example, an international foods company might have single master domains established at company sites in the United States, Brazil, and Norway. Those single master domains are linked in two-way trust relationships, as shown in Figure 11-12. In this instance, the Brazil master domain has a one-way trust with its two local domains and a two-way trust with the United States and Norway master domains. Because users are defined in the master domains in each country, all users have access to the resources of each domain. Administration of this system can be centralized in one domain or decentralized to each master domain. The advantages of this model for a large organization are the following:

- Administration can be centralized or decentralized.

- Thousands of users can share resources across a country or around the world.

- Groups can be formed to span domains.
- Security policies can be standardized for thousands of users and resources.

Figure 11-11

Two-way trust

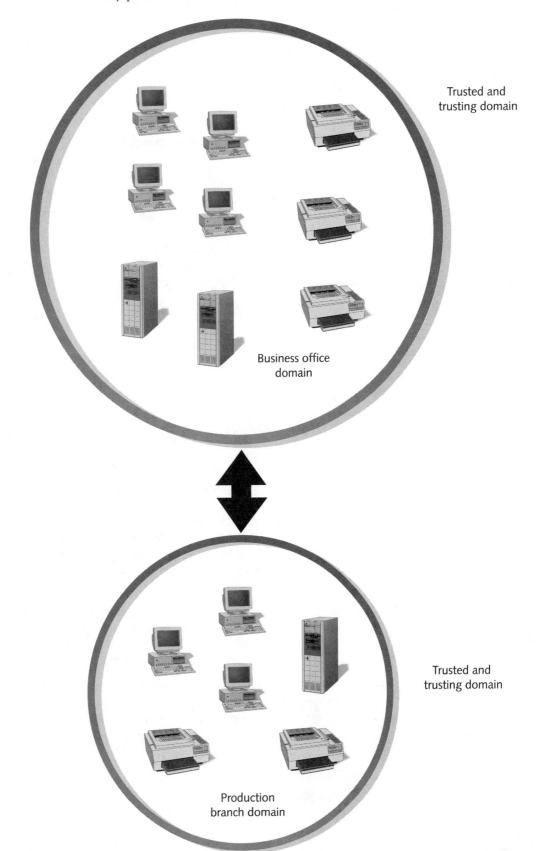

Trusted and
trusting domain

Business office
domain

Trusted and
trusting domain

Production
branch domain

The **multiple master domain** model consists of many domains in which domain management is located in two or more domains.

Figure 11-12

Multiple master domain model

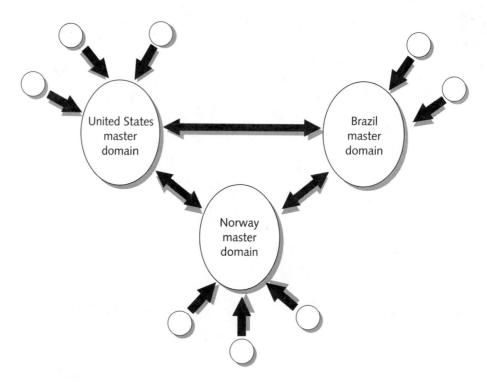

SERVER AND WORKSTATION MANAGEMENT

Enterprise network management software often includes a module to track and manage workstations and servers. For example, Hewlett-Packard's OpenView software can create and delete server accounts through central network management. It also has a problem-warning system to alert the network manager when more people are attempting to access a server than there are licensed server connections. It monitors CPU load, disk usage, disk volume problems, cache problems, and other server activities. On the workstation side, there is software to inventory workstations and determine characteristics about each workstation such as processor type, memory, memory mapping, and disk capacity.

Sun Microsystems' Solstice software is another example of network management software in which administration of multiple servers is performed through a centralized network management station with Solstice software modules. Solstice performs account and work-group management from the network management software.

If you manage a network with only Microsoft or Novell servers (or both), those companies have developed server and workstation administrative tools that can be run remotely from the network administrator's management station. The tools are included with the network operating system. For example, Microsoft provides the following tools for remote network administration:

- User Manager for Domains
- Server Manager

- Performance Monitor

- Event Viewer

- Directory and Printer Controls

Microsoft's tools are set up from Windows NT 4.0 Server by configuring it as a RAS server and then using the Microsoft Network Client Administrator to implement the remote administration tools. The Network Client Administrator places the tools in a shared server directory with strict access controls. The network administrator has the option to run tools from a workstation running Windows 95 or one running Windows NT Workstation.

 In this hands-on activity, you view Microsoft remote network administration tools for Windows NT. You need a workstation running Windows 95 or Windows NT and access to an NT 4.0 Server's shared folder containing the remote administration tools. Before starting, ask your instructor for the name of the shared folder.

To access the remote administration tools:

1. Double-click **Network Neighborhood**.

2. Find the server in the Network Neighborhood display, then find the shared folder containing the remote administration tools (such as **SetupAdm** or **RemoteAdm**). Double-click that folder.

3. Notice two folders. The Win95 folder contains administration tools that can be run from Windows 95; the Winnt folder contains administration tools compatible with a computer running Windows NT (Figure 11-13).

4. Double-click one of those folders (depending on whether you are running Windows 95 or Windows NT), such as **Winnt**.

5. Click the **I386** folder, which contains programs compatible with an 80386, 80486, or Pentium computer (Figure 11-14).

6. Notice the administration tools. As a network administrator, you likely would map a permanent drive to the administration tools and create desktop shortcuts to the tools you use most.

7. Click **usrmgr** to view the User Manager for Domains (Figure 11-15).

Figure 11-15

Remote
Network
Administration
tools

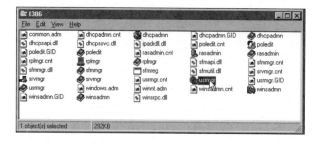

8. Close the User Manager for Domains.

9. Close all the windows you opened from Network Neighborhood.

Besides the remote network administration tools, Microsoft automates server and workstation administration through a series of administrative **wizards** introduced with Windows NT 4.0 Server. For example, there is a wizard to add a new account and one to manage software licenses for applications that are made available from an NT server. The wizards provide a way for the new network administrator to get accustomed to managing a server; they also provide a single place on the server for many management activities. The NT 4.0 server administrative wizards include the following:

- Add User Accounts

- Group Management

- Managing File and Folder Access

- Add Printer

- Add/Remove Programs

- Install New Modem

- Network Client Administrator

- License Compliance

A **wizard** is a set of automated dialog boxes and screens that take you, step-by-step, through a particular setup or administrative function.

This hands-on activity gives you a look at the administrative wizards on an NT 4.0 server. You need access to a computer running Windows NT 4.0 Server and an account with Administrator privileges.

To view the administrative wizards:

1. Click **Start**, **Programs**, and **Administrative Tools (Common)**.

2. Click **Administrative Wizards**.

3. Notice the eight wizards and the descriptions for each (Figure 11-16).

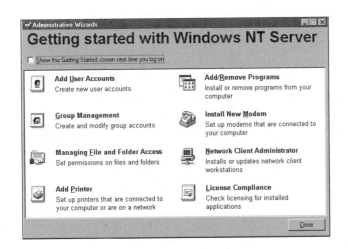

Figure 11-16

Microsoft's
administrative
wizards

4. Close the Administrative Wizards dialog box.

PRINT SERVICES MANAGEMENT

Network printing can be a complex area of network administration. Every network server and host operating system has a somewhat different way of handling print services. UNIX handles them one way, DEC VMS computers handle them another way, IBM MVS computers use still another method. Vendors of print server devices use their own methods; NetWare has its particular method; and Microsoft uses its own method for workstations running Windows. Also, some network printers and print server combinations may use two or more protocols, such as a combination of NetBEUI, IPX/SPX, and TCP/IP.

On an enterprise network with many types of computers, servers, and hosts, network printing can be almost chaotic. The best advice is to keep the printing process as straightforward as possible. One way to do that is to use compatible equipment and to attempt to manage printing through one source. For an enterprise network, you might consider the OpenView module called OpenSpool. The OpenSpool software provides centralized management of network printer services such as printer configurations, print queues, printer forms, font options, and different types of printers, such as color ink jet and laser printers.

If you administer a network that has primarily Microsoft and Novell servers, consider centralizing all print operations through one system or the other. Network printers connected to print server devices, workstations, and servers can be set up to be managed as network printers through one or more servers on the network. For example, from an NT Server, you can manage a printer connected to a user's workstation running Windows 95. That can be done in two ways: (a) by connecting the server to that printer and offering network printing (including the printer driver and security) through the server, or (b) for tightest security, by modifying the Registry at the workstation so printing is forwarded automatically to a setup for that printer on the server.

If you choose to modify the Registry, first learn how to work with the Registry. Then obtain specific Registry-modification information from Microsoft's technical resources or from a Microsoft technician.

DISK STORAGE MANAGEMENT

On enterprise networks that combine different types of systems, there are network management products to manage data storage across different types of computers and storage devices. For example, some systems automatically write data to hard or optical disks, depending on the type of data. Daily accounting data may be written to hard disk, while end-of-year data may be written automatically to optical storage. Some systems automatically migrate old data from expensive storage media to less expensive storage, such as from hard disk to tape. Other systems track disk capacity and give a warning when capacity is low.

Microsoft NT Server has built-in management software that watches disk capacity and issues a warning when capacity is low. The warning is placed in a log file that is accessed by the Event Viewer. The **Event Viewer** displays information about the server system, security accesses, and software applications. Figure 11-17 shows a warning message that disk space is getting low in a particular hard drive.

The **Event Viewer** is a tool with which to view events on an NT server that are recorded in the system, security, and application logs.

Figure 11-17

A message that disk capacity is low

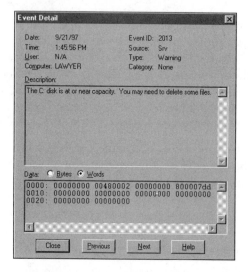

In this hands-on exercise, you look at the contents of the Event Viewer on a Windows NT computer. You need access to a Windows NT Server or Workstation using an account with Administrator privileges.

To use the Event Viewer:

1. Click **Start**, **Programs**, and **Administrative Tools (Common)**.

2. Click **Event Viewer**.

3. Click the **Log** menu and check one of the listed options for System, Security, or Application, such as **System**.

4. Double-click one of the events to view a description of that event (Figure 11-18).

Figure 11-18

Examining the
Event Viewer

Date	Time	Source	Category	Event	User	Computer
ⓘ9/21/97	3:56:27 PM	Rdr	None	3012	N/A	LAWYE
ⓘ9/21/97	3:38:20 PM	Rdr	None	3012	N/A	LAWYE
ⓘ9/21/97	3:28:10 PM	Rdr	None	3012	N/A	LAWYE
ⓘ9/21/97	2:57:17 PM	Rdr	None	3012	N/A	LAWYE
ⓘ9/21/97	2:46:20 PM	Print	None	9	Administrator	LAWYE
ⓘ9/21/97	2:45:02 PM	Print	None	9	Administrator	LAWYE
ⓘ9/21/97	2:45:02 PM	Print	None	2	Administrator	LAWYE
ⓘ9/21/97	1:45:56 PM	Srv	None	2013	N/A	LAWYE
●9/21/97	1:42:42 PM	Service Control Mar	None	7026	N/A	LAWYE
ⓘ9/21/97	1:42:39 PM	BROWSER	None	8015	N/A	LAWYE
ⓘ9/21/97	1:42:39 PM	BROWSER	None	8015	N/A	LAWYE
ⓘ9/21/97	1:42:39 PM	BROWSER	None	8015	N/A	LAWYE
ⓘ9/21/97	1:42:39 PM	BROWSER	None	8015	N/A	LAWYE
●9/21/97	1:42:04 PM	Service Control Mar	None	7024	N/A	LAWYE
●9/21/97	1:42:03 PM	RemoteAccess	None	20008	N/A	LAWYE
●9/21/97	1:42:03 PM	RemoteAccess	None	20105	N/A	LAWYE

5. Click **Close** on the Event Detail dialog box.

6. Close the Event Viewer.

MANAGING NETWORK DEVICES

Some network management software creates a GUI representation of the network to help the network administrator manage specific intelligent devices, such as hubs, routers, and switches. To let the network administrator know there is a problem, a graphical representation of a device that is down or malfunctioning may appear in red, an alarm may sound, or both. Some devices that are down can be booted remotely. Particular segments can be partitioned or reset from the dedicated network management station running that software. Also, event filters can be set in conjunction with the software to provide data on certain events, as well as to provide different levels of warning. Two examples of this type of software are Bay Networks' Optivity and Sun Microsystems' SunNet Manager. Figure 11-19 illustrates a SunNet Manager display of a network.

Figure 11-19

An example
management
screen using
SunNet
Manager

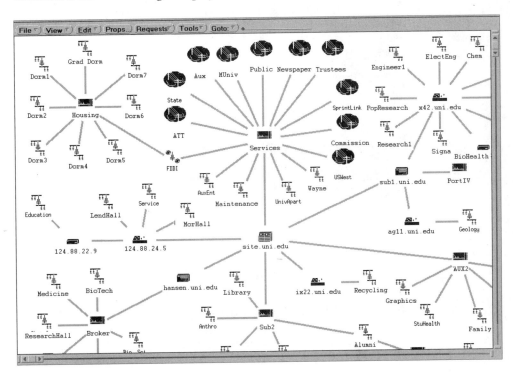

FIREWALLS

Firewall modules are available with some network management software. Software-based firewalls enable you to create virtual private networks for security against intruders. The software also provides data encryption and IP address translation to keep internal network address information from the Internet. Some firewalls use client authentication to control which individuals have access to applications on network clients and servers. Others control access to a server's Web site, for example, by limiting which IP addresses are allowed access from the Internet.

In some cases, network operating systems and Web server software provide firewall-like protection to Web and intranet resources on a network. For example, Microsoft's **Internet Information Server (IIS)** provides security to control access to a Web site or to FTP services on a Web server. This security controls access by IP address, for individual user access restrictions, and by subnet mask, for group access restrictions.

 Internet Information Server (IIS) is a Microsoft application that turns an NT server into a Web server for Internet and intranet communications.

 This hands-on activity gives you a look at the IIS security screen used to control access to an IIS Web site. You need access to an NT server with the IIS software already installed. If an NT server is not available, you can view the same information on a computer running Windows NT 4.0 Workstation with Peer Web Services installed (select Peer Web Services instead of Internet Server in step 1).

To view the IIS access security:

1. Click **Start**, **Programs**, and **Microsoft Internet Server (Common).**

2. Click **Internet Service Manager** (Figure 11-20).

3. Double-click the **WWW** service for your computer (Figure 11-21).

Figure 11-20

Opening the
Internet Service
Manager

Figure 11-21

Opening the
WWW service

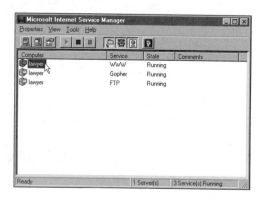

4. Click the **Advanced** tab (Figure 11-22).

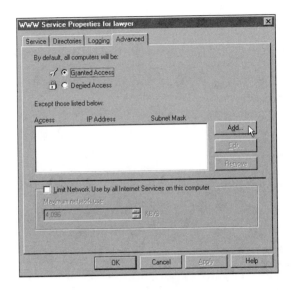

Figure 11-22

The Advanced
tab security
options

5. Notice the options to grant or deny access and to add or remove IP addresses and subnet masks.

6. Click **Help** to find out more about the security options in this dialog box.

7. Close the help dialog box.

8. Click **Cancel** when you have finished viewing the options.

9. Close the Internet Service Manager.

SYSTEMS MANAGEMENT SERVER

Systems Management Server (SMS) is a network management system developed by Microsoft. SMS provides management tools that go beyond those already built into Windows NT Server. SMS runs on a computer with NT Server or NT Workstation, giving network administrators the option to operate SMS from an NT workstation. The SMS tools include the following:

- Expanded capabilities within the Network Monitor

- Diagnostics for network workstations and servers

- Software management capabilities

- Network workstation inventory

- ODBC database compatibility

The SMS network monitor works similarly to the one included with Windows NT Server but with several enhancements. For example, there are more options to filter, decode, and study network packet traffic. Also, Windows 3.11 is added to the list of Microsoft operating systems that can be agents at which the Network Monitor can collect data.

Problems with network workstations can be studied from the SMS management station. The SMS station can remotely monitor workstation performance, run applications, and boot workstations. If a user calls with a problem, the network administrator can remotely control that user's workstation to simulate and observe the problem. Besides remote diagnostics, SMS can inventory the software and hardware at network computers. The inventory data is gathered to be compatible with databases that support ODBC access, enabling the network manager to examine inventory data and to determine where upgrades are needed and what they will cost. Also, an SMS management station can schedule one or more software upgrades to take place from a software distribution server overnight while workstation users are away. For example, if the network administrator finds that 20 out of 280 workstations need an upgrade to Microsoft Excel, those 20 workstations can be scheduled for an automatic upgrade over an evening or a weekend. SMS is compatible with the networks and clients shown in Table 11-1.

Table 11-1

SMS compatibility

Client Compatibility	Network Compatibility
MS-DOS 5.0 or higher	Windows NT Server
Windows 3.1 and 3.11	NetWare 3.1 and higher
Windows 95	Microsoft LAN Manager
Windows NT	IBM LAN Server 3.0 and higher
IBM OS/2	DEC Pathworks (with software from DEC)
Apple Macintosh System 7	OpenVMS (with software from DEC)
	UNIX (with software from DEC)

CHAPTER SUMMARY

No matter how good a network administrator you are, you cannot be everywhere at once. Network management software enables you to be a more effective manager by offering different kinds of tools to extend the range of your capabilities. There are many network management software components you can implement. Some can be united into a single enterprise management package with modular units, such as Hewlett-Packard's OpenView or Sun Microsystems' Solstice software. Other software is built into network operating systems.

One important component is a tool to monitor and capture network events for analysis and the resolution of problems. Filters help target particular events to monitor for specialized information gathering. To consolidate management, the network enterprise can be divided into domains. Microsoft NT Server–based networks, in particular, offer many ways to configure domains to match the management practices of an organization.

Many management software packages offer tools to help manage network servers and workstations. Microsoft's remote administration capability and administration wizards are two examples of tools for server and workstation management.

Packages are available to manage an array of print services on networks with many different types of computer systems. Network printing is one of the most difficult areas to manage because every operating system vendor has a unique way of handling printing. Disk management tools are another important management area to ensure adequate disk capacity and that the right type of storage is used for different kinds of data.

Some network management software can survey existing intelligent network devices and build a GUI representation of the network. Such software also provides the ability to control network devices and to solve problems from the network administrator's management station. Graphical representations show if certain devices are not working or if a network segment is partitioned. Other management tools enable you to build firewalls to protect certain areas of a network.

Microsoft's SMS software is well suited for situations in which you need a way to manage workstations remotely, such as to help a user diagnose a problem or to upgrade software automatically. SMS software provides added network monitoring capabilities and the ability to inventory network software and hardware on workstations and servers.

In chapter 12, you learn troubleshooting tips and techniques. That final chapter shows you how to diagnose connectivity problems with servers and workstations and how to trouble-shoot cable and printing problems. Also, there are tips on how to find and solve network broadcast problems.

REVIEW QUESTIONS

1. A workstation in a _____ domain can access servers and printers in a different domain.

   a. trusted

   b. trusting

   c. reciprocal

   d. reciprocating

2. Which of the following is not an NT Server administrative wizard?

   a. Add Printer

   b. Install New Modem

   c. License Compliance

   d. Network Protocol Configuration

3. Filters are used to help

   a. install software.

   b. set up initialization files.

   c. capture network events.

   d. build GUI representations of networks.

4. Which network tool can inventory how many workstations have word processing software?

   a. Network Monitor

   b. System Management Server

   c. Event Viewer

   d. a protocol analyzer

5. What tool would you use to add a new NT server to an existing Microsoft domain?

   a. OpenView

   b. User Manager for Domains

   c. Server Manager

   d. Domain Wizard

6. Where might you find out if a server is running low on disk space?

    a. Network Monitor

    b. Event Viewer

    c. Server Manager

    d. all of the above

    e. only b and c

7. Internet Information Server can limit access to a Web site by

    a. IP address.

    b. subnet mask.

    c. workstation location.

    d. all of the above

    e. only a and b

8. Microsoft's remote administration can be run from

    a. MS-DOS.

    b. Windows for Workgroups.

    c. Windows NT.

    d. all of the above

    e. only b and c

9. Which tool would you use to remotely run a user's workstation to diagnose a problem?

    a. Network Monitor

    b. System Management Server

    c. Client Administration Wizard

    d. User Manager for Domains

10. Microsoft domain management

    a. always centralizes network management.

    b. enables centralized or decentralized network management.

    c. always decentralizes network management.

    d. does not affect network management techniques.

ASPEN CONSULTING PROJECT: NETWORK MANAGEMENT

Today you are working with two of your old clients, Collectibles and Easton Car Parts. You also are working with a law office and a university. All these clients need assistance with network management issues.

ASSIGNMENT 11-1

Collectibles, the mail order company you have worked with before, has installed an NT server running IIS. The company has a Web site where customers can place orders via the Internet. The Web site has been up for about a month, and a counter records the number of people who have visited the site. Collectibles has contacted you about how it might monitor network traffic into the dedicated Web server. You recommend using the Network Monitor. What capabilities of the Network Monitor make it a good choice?

Use the following table to explain how the Network Monitor might be set up to monitor the Web server traffic.

Steps to Set Up the Network Monitor to Gather Data on Traffic into the Web Server
Step 1:
Step 2:
Step 3:
Step 4:
Step 5:
Step 6:
Step 7:

ASSIGNMENT 11-2

As you know, Easton Car Parts has two NT servers at each of its plants in Wisconsin. The company wants to set up management of the servers from only one site, instead of managing accounts and security at both sites using network administrators at each site. Explain trust relationships to Easton's representatives and how they might use a domain model to set up one-site management of the servers.

ASSIGNMENT 11-3

For Easton Car Parts, explain how you can administer NT servers remotely. What administrative tools can be accessed remotely? How would the network administrator access those tools?

ASSIGNMENT 11-4

Easton Car Parts wants to purchase a tool that would enable its network administrator to find out what software is on workstations at both business sites. What tool do you recommend? What other capabilities come with this tool that might be of benefit to Easton's situation?

ASSIGNMENT 11-5

The new network administrator for a law office is calling you about administering NT servers. The administrator also is new to Microsoft NT Server. Where would you recommend that the administrator start in terms of finding a central means to administer a server? What administrative tools are available from there?

Use the following table to explain how to reach this central way to administer an NT server.

Steps to Access a Central Location for Administering an NT Server
Step 1:
Step 2:
Step 3:
Step 4:
Step 5:

ASSIGNMENT 11-6

The network administrator from the law office is not certain about which NT server administrative tools handle certain functions. Complete the following table to answer the administrator's questions.

Administrative Function	NT Server Tool
Set up IP access controls in the IIS	
Find warning information about disk capacity	
Set up software license compliance	
Add a new server to a domain	
Manage groups	

ASSIGNMENT 11-7

You are working with a client that has NT Server–based networks in Canada and the United States. There are four different network sites in Canada, and each network has 30 to 70 workstations. The three sites in the United States vary between 22 and 50 workstations. Suggest a domain management model that might be appropriate for this client's situation, then create a network diagram to illustrate the model.

OPTIONAL CASE STUDIES FOR TEAMS

 ## TEAM CASE 1

One of the universities in your state has an extensive network with IBM mainframes, UNIX computers, and NT and NetWare servers. Mark Arnez has assigned you to a team to recommend a comprehensive network management system. You are looking at Optivity, from Bay Networks, and OpenView, from Hewlett-Packard. Use the Internet to find out more about these packages. What modules are available with these systems? Prepare a document for the university to briefly describe the modules.

 ## TEAM CASE 2

The supervising network administrator at the university from Team Case 1 has two new questions for you about the management packages. First, with what types of networks are they compatible? Second, what operating system is required at the network administrator's workstation? Create a document to record your findings.

 ## TEAM CASE 3

Mark Arnez has asked you to work with a couple of your Aspen Consulting associates on behalf of a client that has a network of 32 workstations connecting to a Windows NT 4.0 server. Consider the management tools already available to the client through the server. Would you recommend the purchase of any additional network management software? If so, what do you recommend? If not, why not?

TROUBLESHOOTING NETWORK PROBLEMS

As you learned in chapter 11, network management tools can save time by preventing and detecting problems. When problems do arise, good troubleshooting skills enable administrators to address those problems in the most efficient and effective way. This chapter is an introduction to troubleshooting skills and outlines common problems related to servers and workstations. All types of connectivity problems are presented, including NIC, cable, and driver problems. Printer and network device problems also are discussed. You learn to troubleshoot such problems through several hands-on activities. Before you tackle specific problems, however, it is important to develop some troubleshooting strategies.

AFTER READING THIS CHAPTER AND COMPLETING THE EXERCISES YOU WILL BE ABLE TO:

- DEVELOP A PROBLEM-SOLVING STRATEGY AND TROUBLESHOOT NETWORKS STEP BY STEP
- KEEP TRACK OF NETWORK PROBLEMS AND SOLUTIONS TO PROBLEMS
- TUNE NETWORK SERVERS AND WORKSTATIONS
- TROUBLESHOOT SPECIFIC NETWORK PROBLEMS, SUCH AS PROBLEMS WITH SERVER DISKS, CONNECTIVITY, NETWORK COMMUNICATIONS CABLE, NETWORK PRINTING, AND NETWORK DEVICES
- DETECT AND RESOLVE BROADCAST STORMS
- DETECT AND RESOLVE NETWORK PERFORMANCE PROBLEMS

DEVELOPING A PROBLEM-SOLVING STRATEGY

Your best weapon in solving network problems is to develop troubleshooting strategies. Three general strategies are:

- Knowing your network
- Training your users to be troubleshooting allies
- Knowing the business processes of your organization

KNOW YOUR NETWORK

You can take many steps to understand your network better, even if you are the one who installed it originally. One critical step is to create a diagram of the entire network and update the diagram each time an aspect of the network changes. The network diagram should include the following elements:

- Servers
- Host computers
- Workstations and network printers (unless the network is too large to include them)
- Network devices such as repeaters, bridges, routers, hubs, and switches
- Telecommunications links
- Remote links
- Building locations
- Cable link types, such as copper or fiber, and link speeds
- Address locations (TCP/IP)

If you administer a large network, you can develop a general diagram of the network and have more detailed diagrams of each subnet or VNET. Some network managers hang the network diagrams on an office wall for quick reference. Also, develop the baseline statistics, as described in chapter 10, so you can detect any unusual network activity quickly and track growth. Frequent network monitoring or use of network management software is another way to understand the network better.

TRAIN USERS AS TROUBLESHOOTING ALLIES

Another valuable strategy is to train network users to be your partners in reporting problems. If you encourage users to be troubleshooting allies, they are more likely to feel they can take action on a problem rather than to wait impatiently for you to detect and solve the problem. If you train users to gather information and report it to you, they can advance you several steps to the solution. Train users to take the following actions to help you and themselves:

- Save their work at the first sign of a problem.
- Carefully record information about a problem, such as the exact wording of error messages, impact on their workstations, and the impact on other users working nearby.

- Report any protocol information, such as error messages about a protocol or an address.

- Quickly report a problem by telephone or voice mail.

- Avoid sending e-mail about urgent problems.

KNOW THE BUSINESS PROCESSES OF YOUR ORGANIZATION

Your knowledge of how your organization works is another weapon you can use to solve problems. For example, assume you are the network administrator at a college library where the network is reported to be slow just before 1:00 p.m. and 6:00 p.m. Your knowledge of library activities might indicate that the network or a server is slow because large numbers of students are checking out books just before going to afternoon classes or to the dorms for dinner. In another case, say you work at a business where network problems occur each morning when the company president downloads a huge database or runs several giant reports. Your understanding of how people work in your organization can help you take the appropriate steps in finding solutions, such as making network modifications or tuning servers. Another asset in finding solutions is your knowledge of circumstances that affect the network, for example, an adjacent building containing welding equipment or large motors that create high RFI when the equipment is started.

SOLVING PROBLEMS STEP BY STEP

Armed with knowledge of your network, trained users, and an understanding of your organization, you can use the following step-by-step technique to solve network problems.

1. *Get as much information as possible about the problem.* If a network user reports a problem, listen carefully to the description. Even if the user does not use the proper terminology, the information is still valuable. Part of your challenge is to ask the right questions to get as much information as possible.

2. *Record the error message when it appears or when a user reports it to you.* This seemingly obvious step is sometimes overlooked. If you try to recall the message from memory, you may lose some important information. For example, the message "Network not responding" can lead you to a different set of troubleshooting steps than the message "Network timeout error." The first message might signal a damaged NIC, whereas the second message could mean that a database server is overloaded and the application is waiting to obtain data.

3. *Start with simple solutions.* Often the solution to a problem is as simple as connecting a cable or a power cord. For example, a printer may not be printing because the print server to which it is attached is disconnected from the network. A hub may be down because it is it is unplugged at the wall outlet.

4. *Determine if anyone else is experiencing the problem.* For example, several people may report that they cannot load a word processing software package. The problem may be at the server they use to load the software. If only one person is experiencing a problem, it may point to trouble with that user's workstation.

5. *Check if any recent triggered events have been logged.* If you have event monitoring with your network management software, check for triggered or trapped events that indicate problems. Also check to determine if any devices are in a caution or warning status.

6. *Check for power interruptions.* Power problems are a common source of network difficulties. Sometimes a bridge, router, hub, or other device fails to boot properly following a power outage. Some power irregularities, such as brownouts or small surges, go unnoticed but may affect one or more network devices, even though no other equipment seems affected. A simple solution may be to reboot or reset those devices.

In general, it is best to power reset (turn off and on) network devices instead of using a reset button. Also, before you take any action to fix a problem, know the impact your actions will have on users. Provide them ample warning, in case some users are still working and need to save files or data.

In this hands-on activity, you learn about the troubleshooting strategy of a network administrator.

To find out this information:

1. Make an appointment with a network administrator at your school or a local business. Another option is to invite a network administrator to speak to your class or lab session.

2. Ask about the administrator's strategies for solving network problems.

3. Ask about the problem that was the most difficult to solve and why.

4. Ask what problems occur most frequently.

5. Ask what problems are the easiest to solve.

6. Create a document to record the administrator's answers to the questions in steps 2–5.

KEEPING TRACK OF PROBLEMS AND SOLUTIONS

One effective troubleshooting tool is to keep a log of all network problems and their solutions. Some network administrators log problems in a database created for that purpose. Others build problem logging into help desk systems maintained by their organization. A **help desk** system is application software designed to maintain information on computer systems, user questions, problem solutions, and other information that members of the organization can reference.

Help desk software is used to keep data on hardware and software problems, how problems are solved, hardware and software setup information, and general computer documentation.

The advantage of tracking problems is that you soon accumulate a wealth of information on solutions. For example, to jog your memory about a solution, you can look up how you handled a similar problem six months ago. The log of problems also can be used as a teaching tool and reference for other network support staff. Problems that show up repeatedly in the log may indicate that special attention is needed, such as replacing a router that has experienced five problems over two months.

TUNING SERVERS AND WORKSTATIONS

One way a network administrator can prevent slow performance on a network is to tune the servers and workstations that share resources over the network. Servers should be tuned before you try more expensive alternatives, such as upgrading memory or the CPU.

TUNING SERVERS

Network servers experience dynamic variations in demand. One instance of high demand may be when users log on at the beginning of the work day. Then the demand may shift to access of databases or software applications. Later, print services or IIS services may experience heavy loading. Modern network operating systems such as Windows NT Server have several automated tuning features to shift server resources to meet various demands.

In some areas, the network administrator can intervene to troubleshoot performance problems. For example, on an NT Server, **virtual memory** can be tuned, files can be shifted from overloaded hard disks to less busy hard disks, and RAM can be set to optimize connectivity to the server. Applications that are demanding on the system can be scheduled to run at night, and inefficient applications can be replaced with better alternatives. Files on a busy disk can be moved to another disk. Unused server services can be stopped. Full system logs can be cleared and saved to disk. A network administrator should try all these options before purchasing more hardware, such as memory or disk drives.

Virtual memory is disk space allocated to link with memory to hold data temporarily when there is not enough free RAM. On an NT server, that disk space is called a page file and has the name pagefile.sys. The page file size is set from the Performance tab under the Control Panel System icon.

In this hands-on activity, you view where to tune memory for use by an NT server for network connectivity. The use of server RAM can be tuned for small, medium, and large network situations. You need access to a computer running Windows NT 4.0 Server or Workstation and an account with Administrator privileges.

To view where to optimize memory for connectivity:

1. Click **Start**, **Settings**, and **Control Panel**.

2. Double-click the **Network** icon.

3. Click the **Services** tab.

4. In the Network Services: scroll box, click **Server** and then the **Properties** button (Figure 12-1).

5. Notice the optimization selections (Figure 12-2). For example, Balance optimizes memory for a small LAN with 64 or fewer users when NetBEUI is the main protocol. Maximize Throughput for File Sharing is used for a network with over 64 users.

6. Click **Cancel**.

7. Close the Network dialog box.

Figure 12-1

Selecting the
Server service
properties

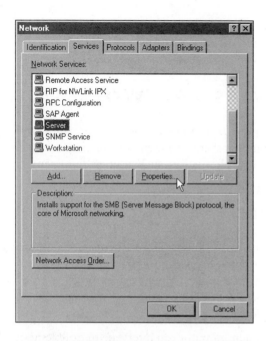

Figure 12-2

Optimizing
memory use
for connections

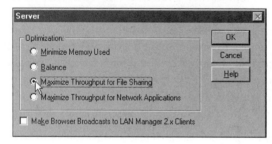

TUNING WORKSTATIONS THAT SHARE FOLDERS

When network users share folders through a workstation running Windows 95 or Windows NT, access to a shared folder can be slow depending on how the workstation is tuned and the number of computers trying to access the folder. You can optimize a workstation to be accessed over the network just as you can optimize servers. To optimize a Windows NT workstation, you follow steps similar to those for an NT Server, as illustrated by the last hands-on activity. A workstation running Windows 95 also can be optimized for folder sharing by setting the system as a network server.

    In this hands-on activity, you set up a computer running Windows 95 to optimize it for sharing folders with other network workstations.

To tune Windows 95 for sharing folders:

1. Click **Start**, **Settings**, and **Control Panel**.

2. Double-click the **System** icon.

3. Click the **Performance** tab, then the **File System** button (Figure 12-3).

4. Click the **Hard Disk** tab.

5. In the Typical Role of this machine: list box, select **Network server** (Figure 12-4).

6. Click **Apply** and **OK** in the File System Properties dialog box.

7. Click **Close** in the System Properties dialog box.

8. If asked to restart the computer, click **Yes** (but first save any work that is currently open).

Figure 12-3

Optimizing workstation connectivity

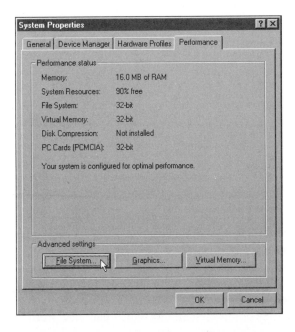

Figure 12-4

Setting the workstation properties

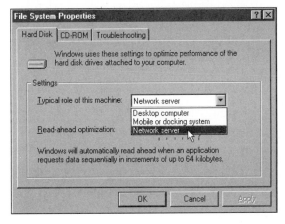

TROUBLESHOOTING SPECIFIC NETWORK PROBLEMS

Now that you have developed a problem-solving strategy and troubleshooting steps, the following sections deal with using the techniques to troubleshoot specific network problems, such as those involving server disks, network connectivity, cable connectivity, network printing, and network devices.

SERVER DISK CAPACITY AND DISK PROBLEMS

A common cause of slow network server or host response is one or more overloaded hard disks. Balancing disk load is important in small server environments and on large mainframes. On a Windows NT server, you can use the Performance Monitor to watch disk activity by selecting Physical Disk as the monitor object. Monitor using two counters, % Disk Time and Current Disk Queue Length. (Monitoring with the Performance Monitor was introduced in chapter 10.) The first counter shows the amount of activity on a disk, and the second shows the number of waiting requests to access the disk. If one disk frequently is busy at the 100% level, information on the number of waiting requests helps to diagnose the problem. If the number of requests normally in the queue is zero or one, the disk load is acceptable. If the queue generally has two or more requests, it is time to move some files from the overloaded disk to one that is not as busy. The best way to determine which files to move is to understand what applications and data are on the server and how they are used. If all the server disks are constantly busy, it may be necessary to purchase disks with more **spindles** or to add data paths.

 A **spindle** is a rod attached to the center of a hard disk platter and to a motor used to rotate the rod and the disk. Individual drives typically have one spindle; RAID drives have multiple spindles within the disk array. A RAID array is a good investment for growing servers because of the combined performance and redundancy features.

When a disk drive, a controller, or a SCSI adapter fails on a server or host, the problem usually is made apparent through messages displayed on that computer's console. The Alerter service sends those messages on an NT server. You also will find information about the problem in a log on the computer. For example, on an IBM mainframe, the information appears in one of several logs, such as the system log and in disk error logging. On an NT server, disk errors are recorded as events in the system log, which you view from the Event Viewer.

Sometimes disk access is slow for networked users because a disk is experiencing errors but is still online. If a particular NT server disk is having trouble accessing certain files or directories, run CHKDSK from the MS-DOS window. The CHKDSK utility works for FAT or NTFS file systems, although it provides better error checking for NTFS. It checks the integrity of volume indexes, security descriptors, total disk space, user files, system files, and other information.

Another way to test for disk problems is from the Windows NT Disk Administrator, which is started from the Administrative Tools (Common) menu. You select the drive having difficulties in the Disk Administrator and click the Tools menu. Next, click Properties and select the Tools tab, which has a Check Now button to perform a lengthy analysis of the disk surface to detect problems.

CLIENT AND SERVER CONNECTIVITY PROBLEMS

A workstation or server may have problems connecting to the network or to other computers on the network for several reasons. When you experience a connection problem, try the following:

- Ascertain if that node is the only one having problems.

- Check that the NIC driver is properly installed and is a current version.

- Use the NIC test software to determine that the NIC is functioning. Reseat or replace the NIC if it fails the test.

- Verify the protocol setup through the Network icon.
- Make sure network bindings are set up for each NIC or dial-up connection.
- Make sure the correct frame type is in use for the NIC setup.
- Check the cable connection into the NIC or reconnect the cable.
- Examine the network cable to the NIC for damage.

For example, if you are using an out-of-date NIC driver, the workstation or server may have difficulty connecting to the network or it periodically may lose connection. Most NIC vendors place driver updates on their Web sites so you can quickly download the latest version. Another problem on Ethernet networks is that the computers may be using different versions of Ethernet. On a Microsoft-based network, check the protocol setup to make sure all computers are using either frame type I or frame type II (802.3 or Ethernet-II), because both types cannot be used on the same segment.

Another problem to check is the cable-medium setting in the software. A NIC set for coaxial cable will not communicate if it is connected to twisted-pair cable. In Windows NT and Windows 95, you can check that setting through the Control Panel Network icon by looking at the properties of the NIC.

In this hands-on activity, you check the cable-medium setting on a computer running Windows NT 4.0 Workstation or Server. You need access to an account with Administrator privileges.

To check the cable type setting:

1. Click **Start**, **Settings**, and **Control Panel**.
2. Double-click the **Network** icon.
3. Click the **Adapters** tab.
4. Click an adapter in the Network Adapters: box and click **Properties** (Figure 12-5).

Figure 12-5

Viewing the NIC properties

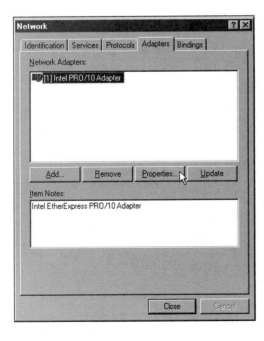

5. Click **Change** in that NIC's setup dialog box (Figure 12-6).

Figure 12-6

Changing
the NIC's
properties

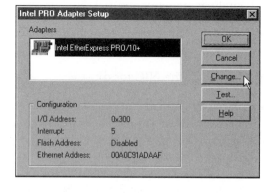

6. Click **Advanced** in the NIC configuration dialog box (Figure 12-7).

Figure 12-7

Changing the
NIC's advanced
properties

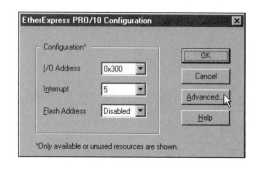

7. In the Property box, click **Connector Type** and check the setting for your connector type in the Value box (Figure 12-8). TPE is twisted-pair Ethernet, and BNC is coaxial. The Auto setting is for combination cards that support both twisted-pair and coaxial and where the driver can automatically determine which type of connection is used. Auto is the best setting for combination cards because it simplifies the setup. However, both cable types cannot be connected to the card simultaneously.

8. Click **Cancel** on the Advanced dialog box (if you wanted to activate a change, you would click OK).

Figure 12-8

Checking the
Connector
Type setting

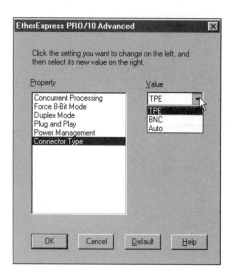

9. Click **Cancel** on the configuration box.

10. Click **Test** in the Setup dialog box to test the NIC connection to the network (see Figure 12-6).

11. Click **Continue**.

12. View the test results to make sure the NIC is working (Figure 12-9).

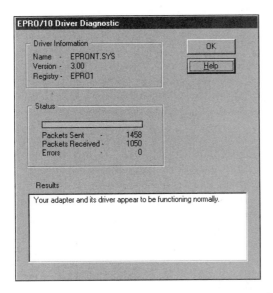

13. Click **OK** in the Diagnostic dialog box and **OK** in the Setup dialog box.

14. Click **Close** in the Network dialog box.

If a single workstation has problems executing software or accessing files, check directory and file permissions on the server. Another place to check is the user's group membership at the server and related permissions. Sometimes a user has permission to execute a program but no permission to write to setup or temporary files required by the program. Also, check that there are enough software licenses to accommodate all users.

When multiple users have trouble accessing a server, make sure the server is on, completely booted, and has a good network connection in terms of the NIC, connector, and cable. Always make sure that servers have the latest NIC drivers. Sometimes users cannot connect to a server because one or more disk drives have failed or a SCSI adapter is malfunctioning. Also, check the network equipment that the user must pass through to reach the server.

NIC Broadcast Problems

Sometimes a NIC malfunctions and broadcasts continuously, creating a **broadcast storm**, which causes the entire network to slow down. One way to locate such a problem is to use network management software or network analyzing equipment, as covered in chapters 10 and 11. On a network with Microsoft servers and workstations that have the network monitoring agent installed, you can use the Network Monitor or the Performance Monitor to trace a malfunctioning NIC. For example, using the Network Monitor, check the network utilization and the number of broadcasts per second in the upper left and right windows. In the bottom window, watch for a workstation or server sending a large number of broadcasts. Once you identify the malfunctioning NIC, reseat it in the computer and check the network traffic again. If that does not work, the next step is to replace the NIC.

A **broadcast storm** is saturation of network bandwidth by excessive broadcasts from devices attached to the network.

TCP/IP Connectivity Problems

One area that network administrators often troubleshoot is TCP/IP connectivity. A common problem is duplicate IP addresses, which can happen in situations where static IP addressing is used, with the network administrator or user typing in the IP address and subnet mask when the computer is set up. Two computers using the same IP address will not be able to connect to the network at the same time, or they are likely to experience unreliable communications such as sudden disconnections.

Some TCP/IP utilities, such as Telnet, have IP troubleshooting tools built in. The same is true for workstations and servers running TCP/IP-compatible operating systems such as Windows NT and Windows 95. You can test the IP address of a Windows 95 computer by opening the MS-DOS window from the Start button Programs option. Type *winipcfg* to view a dialog box showing the adapter address (MAC or Ethernet), IP address, subnet mask, and other information for that workstation (Figure 12-10). You can run a similar test on a Windows NT server or workstation from the MS-DOS window by typing *ipconfig*. If the workstation is using an IP address identical to the address used by another networked computer that is turned on, the subnet mask value is 0.0.0.0 when you run one of those utilities.

Figure 12-10

Testing the TCP/IP configuration in Windows 95

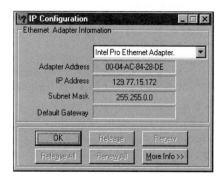

Another tool for testing TCP/IP connections is the PING utility. You can poll the presence of another TCP/IP computer from the Windows 95 or Windows NT MS-DOS window by opening a command-line window and typing *ping* and the address or computer name of the other computer. Many network administrators use PING to quickly test, from their offices, the presence of a server or a mainframe when there are reports of connection problems to that computer. Pinging a server on a network in another state or remote location also enables you to quickly test if your Internet connection is accessible from your office workstation. Figure 12-11 illustrates the PING utility used from Windows NT.

Figure 12-11

Using the PING utility to verify another TCP/IP node

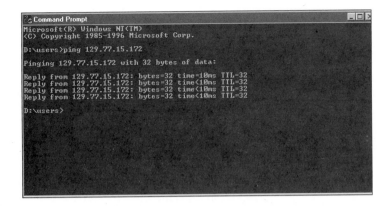

The Windows 95 and Windows NT NETSTAT utility is a quick way to verify that a workstation or server has established a successful TCP/IP connection. The NETSTAT utility provides information about TCP and UDP connectivity.

This hands-on activity gives you an opportunity to try the NETSTAT utility for a computer running Windows NT Server or Workstation that is already set up for TCP/IP communications.

To test TCP/IP connectivity with NETSTAT:

1. Click **Start**, **Programs**, and **Command Prompt**.

2. At the MS-DOS prompt, enter **netstat –a** (to view all connections, including your own).

3. If your computer is successfully connected to the network, the TCP state will be reported as established (Figure 12-12).

4. Enter **Exit** at the prompt to close the Command Prompt window.

Figure 12-12

Testing TCP/IP in Windows NT

```
Command Prompt                                        _ □ X
Microsoft(R) Windows NT(TM)
(C) Copyright 1985-1996 Microsoft Corp.

D:\users>netstat -a

Active Connections

  Proto  Local Address      Foreign Address      State
  TCP    lawyer:1025        localhost:1027       ESTABLISHED
  TCP    lawyer:1027        localhost:1025       ESTABLISHED
  UDP    lawyer:1026        *:*
  UDP    lawyer:135         *:*
  UDP    lawyer:snmp        *:*
  UDP    lawyer:nbname      *:*
  UDP    lawyer:nbdatagram  *:*

D:\users>_
```

Sometimes a TCP/IP session to a server or mainframe computer hangs. You can determine such a condition by entering *netstat -e* from the MS-DOS window at that computer. Two columns of send and receive data are displayed. If the columns contain 0 bytes, it is likely that the session is hung. If it is, reboot the computer and try again. Rebooting resets the NIC and TCP/IP connectivity to ensure a clean connection. The *netstat -e* command also provides a quick indication of the number of transmission errors and discarded packets detected at the computer's NIC. For a more comprehensive listing of communication statistics, type *netstat -s*. Table 12-1 lists some useful diagnostics available from the Command Prompt window in Windows 95 and Windows NT.

Diagnostic Command	Function
winipcfg (Windows 95) *ipconfig* (Windows NT)	Displays information about the TCP/IP setup at that computer
ping	Polls another TCP/IP node to verify you can communicate with it
netstat (-a, -e, -s)	Displays information about the TCP/IP session from that computer
nbtstat (-n)	Shows the server and domain names registered to the network
tracert (server or host name)	Shows the number of hops and other routing information on the path to the specified server or host

 The Windows 95 and Windows NT TCP/IP diagnostics come with switches that enable you to display different kinds of information. To learn more about those switches, type the command and *all*, for example, *netstat all*.

CABLE PROBLEMS

Network cabling is one of the most common sources of network problems. Cabling problems have many symptoms, such as disconnecting workstations, slow network services, high levels of packet errors, and unreliable data transmission. If you have reports of any of those problems, one place to start is by investigating the cable plant. Check cable length, cable type, cable impedance, terminators, connectors, and opens and shorts. Table 10-2 summarizes cable problems you should look for and how to troubleshoot them.

Cable Problem	How to Troubleshoot
Cable segment too long	If a network segment is extended beyond the IEEE specifications, there will be communication problems affecting all nodes on that segment. Use a cable scanner or TDR and test the distance of the cable. Another method is to use a protocol analyzer or RMON probe to analyze the cable length. Those tools will show excessive packet collisions, especially late collisions. A late collision occurs when a node can put a majority of the packet on the cable but experiences a collision toward the end of the transmission of the packet.
Mismatched or improper cabling	Check the labeling on the cable jacket to make sure it is right for your network. For example, coaxial cable should be labeled RG-58A/U. Also measure the cable impedance with a cable scanner that has reflectometry capabilities or a TDR. For instance, coaxial cable must have 50-ohm impedance, UTP 100-ohm impedance, and STP 150-ohm impedance.
Defective or missing terminator on coaxial cable	A segment with a defective or missing terminator responds like one that is too long. Workstations on the segment may disconnect, experience slow network response, or receive network error messages. If your cable scanner or TDR shows that the segment distance is invalid, check the terminators. On an Ethernet network, the impedance of the terminator should be 50 ohms. Test the impedance with a cable scanner that has reflectometry capabilities or a TDR to make sure the terminator is viable. A coax segment with a missing terminator often will not function.
Improper grounding	Proper grounding is critical to packet transmission on the cable. Without it, the network packet transmissions will have many cyclical redundancy check (CRC) errors. Ethernet frames include CRC to ensure the reliability of data transfer from the source node to the recipient node. A protocol analyzer can provide a report of CRC errors. A multimeter also can help determine if there is a grounding problem.

Table 12-2

Troubleshooting cable problems (continued)

Cable Problem	How to Troubleshoot
Opens and shorts	An intermittent open on a cable segment prevents workstations on that segment from connecting to the network. A short may cause intermittent problems, network errors, and disconnection problems. Use a voltmeter, cable scanner, TDR, or protocol analyzer to identify shorts and opens.
RFI and EMI	RFI and EMI result in excessive noise or jabber on the cable. These conditions occur when the cable is run too close to an electrical field, such as over fluorescent lights in the ceiling or through a machine shop with heavy electrical equipment. Use a TDR or a protocol analyzer to trace interference.
Defective connector	A faulty connector can cause a short or an open on the cable. Several workstations on a segment experiencing problems or a segment being partitioned may be caused by a connector on a workstation or a server. Use a cable scanner, TDR, or protocol analyzer to identify shorts and opens due to a faulty connector. The best solution is to replace the connector.
Improper coax connectivity at the wall outlet	A T-connector should not be placed directly on a wall outlet because the topology for a coax segment must be a bus or "in series."
Improper distance between connections	Two adjacent nodes may have network communication problems if the distance between their connectors is too short. The same is true if the distance is too short between a node and a hub. For example, on a thinnet coaxial Ethernet segment, the minimum distance between nodes is 0.5 meter. For STP and UTP, the minimum distance between two nodes, between a node and a hub, or between the wall outlet and a node is 3 meters. Make certain all workstations are separated according to IEEE specifications.

This hands-on activity simulates a defective cable connector. You need a section of UTP cable with a bad connection to the connector at one end and another equivalent section of cable that does not have a damaged connection. You also need a cable scanner and a hub.

To simulate the connector problem:

1. Obtain the cable with the defective connector from your instructor or make it with your instructor's permission. To make a defective connection, remove the outer jacket going into the cable. Use a wire cutter to cut all but one of the wires going into the cable.

2. Attach the end with the defective connector to the hub and the good end to the cable scanner.

3. Test the cable following the directions that come with your cable scanner.

4. Notice the message on the cable scanner display, indicating an open on the cable.

5. Replace the cable with one that is not damaged and check it again with the cable scanner.

FIBER-OPTIC CABLE PROBLEMS

Fiber-optic cable is used for network backbones and for high-speed network segments. Troubleshooting fiber-optic cable presents some special problems, because the signal source is light and the medium is usually glass. Fiber cable is especially susceptible to damage; when problems occur, it should be examined for breaks or opens. Use an OTDR (optical time domain reflectometer) to locate opens or measure power loss on a cable run. Network problems result if attenuation is greater than permitted by the IEEE specifications.

Fiber-optic cable connections and terminations must be installed carefully and precisely. Durable connections and terminations depend on the cable installer having the right tools and being careful in the installation. Improperly connected or terminated cable causes problems. Dirty connectors also cause problems on fiber-optic cable runs. Examine connections and terminations for dirt or for poor installation. If you find that the connectors need to be cleaned, consult a fiber cable installer for the proper procedures.

Another problem area is the angle of the bend around corners, or the **angular circumference**. The maximum angular circumference depends on the cable characteristics and the number of strands. Light does not transmit when the angular circumference is too great.

The **angular circumference** is the measurement of the amount of bend in fiber-optic cable.

Unless you or someone in your organization has the right tools and expertise, leave fiber-optic cable troubleshooting to someone who does it professionally.

NETWORK PRINTING PROBLEMS

Many of the problems that network administrators troubleshoot are related to network print services. For those problems, start with simple steps:

- Make sure the printer has power.
- If the printer is physically connected to a workstation, server, or print server, check that the computer or print server is turned on and working.
- Be certain the printer is online (i.e., the online printer button is active).
- Press the printer reset button, in case the printer did not fully reset after the last print job.
- Make certain all printer trays have paper.
- Check that the printer data cable is connected properly between the computer and the printer.
- Check that the network cable is connected properly when a NIC is being used.

One of the most overlooked solutions is to press the reset button on the printer. When several people share one printer, it may be printing documents with different fonts and formats. A slight miscue at the printer or in a printer connection may cause it to miss the software reset instruction sent at the beginning of each document. Another possibility is that the software may have omitted a form feed instruction on the last page of a document, causing it to stay in the printer's memory without printing. To print the last page, press the form feed (FF) button on the printer, if one is available. If there is no form feed button, it may be necessary to press the reset button.

If the problem is related to the server or the workstation, the most likely areas to check are the following:

- Is the printer driver properly installed and selected for the print job?

- Is the printer share enabled?

- Are the printer share permissions set correctly?

- Is the software used to produce the print job correctly installed at the workstation?

 On Microsoft networks, one way to increase network performance at the server is to install a shared server printer through the Add Printer Wizard in the Printers folder on the client workstation. Do that instead of installing the printer through the Network Neighborhood installation option. When you do so, the printer driver and print services resources are used from the client, saving effort at the server even though the printer is physically connected at the server and access is managed through the share created at the server.

Some printers have a built-in NIC and print server on a card that plugs into a slot inside the printer. Network printers also can be connected to a network through dedicated print server devices that have a NIC and one or more parallel and serial ports for cables to printers. Some of those print servers send frequent broadcasts onto the network. Many dedicated print server devices attached to a network can degrade network performance. Plan to monitor the traffic created by print servers and consider handling part of the network printing through printers attached to servers and workstations as an alternative to dedicated print servers.

PROBLEMS WITH NETWORK DEVICES

Network devices can malfunction or generate problems on the network. The following sections present troubleshooting suggestions for gateways, repeaters, bridges, routers, and hubs.

Gateway Problems

A malfunctioning gateway can have several symptoms. The most apparent symptom is that a node is missing. For example, if an SNA gateway to an IBM mainframe is down, the mainframe is no longer accessible to the network and will appear to be missing. The solution is to reboot the gateway or replace it. Malfunctioning gateways also can generate bad packets and high error rates on the network. Use a protocol analyzer or RMON probe to trace the problem to the gateway.

Repeater Problems

Some repeater problems are relatively simple to troubleshoot. For example, if network traffic is not going through a repeater, check to determine if a repeater segment is partitioned. Check the segment cable, connections, and NICs for problems. Correct any problems you find and reset the partitioned segment on the repeater.

If the entire repeater is down, check the power source and any fuses in the repeater.

Sometimes a malfunctioning repeater sends bad or corrupted packets. To determine if that is the case, place a protocol analyzer on the network and view the traffic into and out of the repeater. The easiest solution is to replace a defective repeater and return it to the vendor for repair.

Excessive collisions, network slowdowns, and network bottlenecks can be caused by an overloaded repeater. You may need to make some design changes, such as installing one or more bridges to segment sections of the network and prevent overloading.

Bridge Problems

Symptoms of an overloaded bridge are similar to those of an overloaded repeater, including a high rate of network collisions, slowdowns, and bad packets. A protocol analyzer can help you determine if the problem is related to a bridge. To solve a problem, you may need to install a router or a hub in that part of the network. Also, be certain that a server or workstation NIC is not creating a broadcast storm and overloading the network.

A defective bridge can generate bad packets, excessive network traffic, and network slowdowns. Another problem is that a bridge may be improperly configured to send **bridge protocol data units (BPDUs)** at a high rate, causing the network to slow down. You can gather information about such situations from a protocol analyzer or from RMON probe data. Check the bridge configuration and power supply. Try resetting the bridge to see if that cures the problem. If none of those steps works, you may need to replace the bridge.

Bridge protocol data units (BPDUs) are specialized packets used by bridges to exchange information with one another.

In this hands-on activity, you practice building a filter to monitor BPDU traffic using the Network Monitor. Try this activity even if there is no bridge in your lab, because you still learn how to monitor for that activity. You need Administrator access to a computer running NT 4.0 Server that has the Microsoft Network Monitor installed.

To create a filter to monitor BPDU activity:

1. Click **Start**, **Programs**, and **Administrative Tools (Common)**.
2. Click **Network Monitor**.
3. Maximize the Network Monitor and the Capture windows.
4. Click the **Capture** menu and **Filter**.
5. If a warning message appears about the capabilities of your version of the Network Monitor, click **Yes** to continue.
6. In the Capture Filter dialog box, double-click the **SAP/ETYPE** line.
7. In the Capture Filter SAPs and ETYPES dialog box, click the **Disable All** button.
8. Scroll down in the Disabled Protocols box and click **BPDU** (Figure 12-13). Click **Enable** and then **OK**.

Figure 12-13

Creating a filter
to capture
BPDU traffic

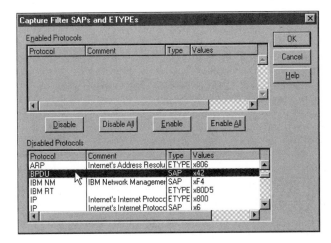

9. Back in the Capture Filter dialog box, highlight any INCLUDE lines and click the Delete **Line** button to remove those lines.

10. Double-click the **(Address Pairs)** line.

11. In the Address Expression box, click the **Include** radio button.

12. In the Station 1 scroll box, click **★ANY GROUP**. In the direction box, click the two-way arrow. Click **★ANY** under Station 2 and click **OK** (Figure 12-14).

Figure 12-14

Setting up to
monitor all
traffic

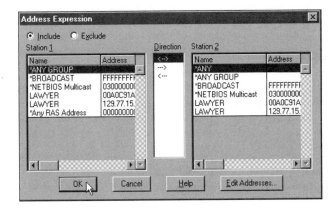

13. Your capture filter should look like the one in Figure 12-15. Click **OK** in the Capture Filter dialog box.

Figure 12-15

Completed
capture filter

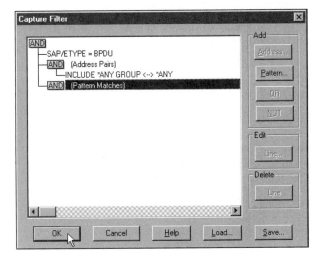

14. Click the **Capture** menu and then **Start** (or click the Start Capture button ![button]).

15. If there is a bridge on your network, take a few minutes to capture data on BPDUs.

16. To exit, click the **Capture** menu and **Stop** (or click the Stop Capture button ![button]). Close the Network Monitor.

Router Problems

As with other network equipment, malfunctioning routers produce bad packets, slow network response, and a high rate of collisions. When a router malfunctions, examine the routing table and related areas. Check the following potential trouble spots:

- Is the routing software up-to-date?

- Is the power supply working properly?

- Is the router memory working and sufficient for the load placed on the router?

A router also may be overloaded. In that case, it may be necessary to redesign the network, upgrade the router, or segment that portion of the network. Another solution may be to replace the router with an intelligent hub or an ATM switch.

 If a router is the cause of bad packets, the problem most likely is caused by a hardware problem, and the router should be replaced immediately.

Hub Problems

On a small network, a nonstackable or stackable hub may be out of service because it does not have power or because it needs to be reset. Check that the hub has power, push the reset button, or power it off and on. If those steps don't work, replace the hub with one you know is working. On a modular hub, all of the hubs may be working except a single board, such as a bridge module. If one module is defective, the hub isolates the problem and shuts it down. The board then can be removed and replaced, often with no interruption of service to other hub modules (depending on the vendor and the hub model).

The symptoms of a defective module are similar to those for repeaters, bridges, and routers, and include bad packets, packet encapsulation errors, network errors, slow network response, and problem reports from users on a particular module. Intelligent hubs can be monitored directly from a network management station or from software provided by the manufacturer.

If there is a generalized failure of a hub, check fuses and the power supply. Also check the hub backplane to be sure it is working. If your network management software or protocol analyzer detects packet timing errors or excessive collisions, check the retiming module in the hub. Often that module is a single board that can be replaced when it malfunctions.

Rebooting Network Equipment

Any time you detect a problem with network equipment, try rebooting it (after you have warned connected users). That technique works in many cases because most network equipment is CPU-based. As can happen on any CPU, some registers may get out of synchronization, register pointers may be lost, or a critical register may be empty. Rebooting the equipment (turning it off and then on) forces the CPU registers to reset to a known state, and the equipment may be fully operational again.

DETECTING AND RESOLVING BROADCAST STORMS

A broadcast storm is a network condition in which so many broadcasts are sent at the same time that the network bandwidth is saturated and the network slows significantly or times out. As you learned earlier in this chapter, a server or workstation NIC can cause a broadcast storm, which you can detect by using the Network Monitor. If the NIC is in a computer running Windows NT, you also can detect broadcast traffic through the Performance Monitor. Once you find the computer responsible for the problem, the fastest solution is to remove it from network access, such as by partitioning its segment through network management software or manually at a hub. Replace the NIC and put the computer back into service.

Poorly configured bridges are another source of broadcast storms, for example, a bridge that broadcasts BPDUs at a high rate or bridges configured so that packets travel in a loop. In the first instance, you learned through the last hands-on activity to set up a Network Monitor filter to detect BPDU traffic. In the second, looping can be prevented by the use of bridges that have the **spanning tree algorithm**. The spanning tree algorithm has two purposes: (a) to prevent looping when there are two or more bridges on a network and (b) to enable packets to be forwarded along the most efficient network route.

The **spanning tree algorithm** is used to ensure that packets are not transmitted in an endless loop. It also enables packets to be sent along the most cost-effective network path as determined by the shortest path from the source to the destination and by the most effective use of cable resources for the type of information sent.

Another source of broadcast problems is non-routable protocols on medium to large networks, including Microsoft's NetBEUI and DEC's **local area transport (LAT)** protocol. For example, on a network of 110 users, NetBEUI performs well without saturating the network. On a bridged network of 425 users, the inability to route NetBEUI can cause unnecessary flooding of traffic to network nodes. For such a medium-sized network and for larger networks, plan to convert NetBEUI use to TCP/IP and implement routing.

Local area transport (LAT) is a protocol developed by DEC for virtual terminal communications.

In this network activity, you practice using the Performance Monitor to assess network traffic related to NetBEUI. You need access to a computer running Windows NT Workstation or Server, which also has the Network Monitor Agent installed.

To view the network utilization:

1. Click **Start, Programs**, and **Administrative Tools (Common)**.

2. Click **Performance Monitor**.

3. Click the **Add counter** button on the empty Performance Monitor screen.

4. Leave your computer as the default in the Computer: scroll box in the Add to Chart dialog box.

5. Click the scroll arrow in the Object: text box and select **NetBEUI**.

6. Click **Frame Bytes Received/sec** in the Counter: text box to chart the total bytes received from the network per second in NetBEUI frames that contain data (Figure 12-16). Click **Add**.

Figure 12-16

Selecting to track received NetBEUI traffic

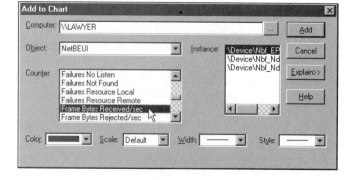

7. Click the scroll arrow in the Object: text box and select **Network Segment**.

8. Click **% Network utilization** in the Counter: text box to track network utilization as you track packet traffic from NetBEUI. Click **Add**. Also, click **Total bytes received/second** so you can compare this with bytes received from NetBEUI frames (Figure 12-17). Click **Add**.

Figure 12-17

Selecting to track overall received network traffic

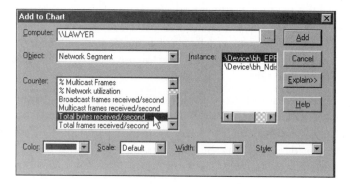

9. Click **Done** in the Add to Chart dialog box.

10. View the network utilization and NetBEUI traffic for several minutes.

11. Close the Performance Monitor when you are finished viewing the information.

DETECTING AND RESOLVING NETWORK PERFORMANCE PROBLEMS

Many of the troubleshooting topics discussed so far are factors that affect network performance, such as malfunctioning NICs and network devices, cable problems, server disk resources, print servers, and the network protocols in use. Some other causes of network performance problems are improperly tuned servers, poorly configured bridges and routers, inefficient software applications, and improper network mail configurations. For example, a mail system that is set up incorrectly can transmit a single message continuously thousands of times. At one college, the finance director and a vice president received over 5,000 duplicate messages in a day from one employee. The repeated messages slowed network response and caused both officials to lose their mail folders and mail. Another source of performance problems can occur when there are several mail servers and mail systems on one enterprise network. Addressing and forwarding problems can develop, causing mail to travel in endless loops from server to server.

One way to tackle network performance problems is to implement an efficient network design and to adjust the design as the network grows. That includes techniques you have learned already, such as the following:

- Follow network standards.

- Choose the right protocol or protocols for your network.

- Segment the network to reduce bottlenecks.

- Implement a centralized design through hubs, routers, and switches.

- Take advantage of VLAN technologies.

- Use fat-pipe communications between high-impact network devices, such as hubs, routers, switches, servers, and hosts.

- Test software and hardware so you know their network impact before they are installed.

Another way to ensure healthy performance is to use network monitoring tools and network management software, as outlined in chapters 10 and 11. For example, on Microsoft networks, the Performance Monitor and the Network Monitor are good sources of performance information, and the NT server domain management tools provide effective management resources.

CHAPTER SUMMARY

Network problems can be complex because often there are many possible causes. Problems are an opportunity to learn more about networking and your network in particular. Solving complex problems can be satisfying and make you a better network administrator. Even the most difficult problems can be solved, if you approach each one with a problem-solving strategy that you perfect with every problem you address. Each time you address a problem, keep a record of the problem and its solution. The next time you or a colleague encounters that problem, you will have documented how to solve it.

Server and host computers can cause network problems when they are not tuned for optimal performance. When they are not properly tuned, multiuser access is slow, which reciprocally slows the network. Workstations also can be tuned for sharing folders and files. Another factor that influences network performance is server disk storage. An overloaded disk or one that has a high level of errors slows server access, which also affects network performance.

Server and workstation connectivity is one of the most common sources of network problems. NIC setup, for example, is crucial to successful communications. Troubleshooting TCP/IP setup and connectivity is another task you likely will undertake as a network administrator. NICs also can malfunction, creating network-wide broadcast storms until you locate the source computer.

Cable problems are another frequent cause of network problems. There are many sources of cable problems, such as segments that are too long, broken connectors, and electrical interference. Printing problems also occur often and have many causes. Sometimes a network printer is brought back into service simply by pressing the reset button or adjusting a cable connection.

Problems with network devices are more difficult to troubleshoot, often requiring use of a protocol analyzer or the Network Monitor. Once the defective device is located, the solution may be as simple as rebooting or resetting the device. Complex network devices such as bridges, routers, and hubs may need to be reconfigured or replaced.

There are many sources of network performance problems and broadcast storms. The Performance Monitor and the Network Monitor are Microsoft tools you can use to detect those kinds of problems and locate their source. The cable scanner is another inexpensive tool that is useful in locating cable problems.

As you solve more network problems in the course of your work, bear in mind that you grow with each solution. Also, you occasionally will encounter problems where the best solution is to contact a colleague or vendor who has experienced that problem and can help you find its source.

REVIEW QUESTIONS

1. If you discover that a router is not working, what would you try first?

    a. Replace its NIC.

    b. Reboot it.

    c. Reinstall the router software.

    d. Repartition it.

2. What tool can you use to determine if you can connect to a computer at another location?

    a. NETROUTE

    b. PING

    c. IPCONFIG

    d. WINIPCFG

3. Which of the following tools enables you to monitor NetBEUI traffic on a network?

    a. Performance Monitor

    b. NETSTAT

    c. NBTSTAT

    d. TRACERT

4. What should be the impedance of STP network cable and how would you measure it?

    a. 100 ohms measured using the Network Monitor

    b. 50 ohms measured using a protocol analyzer

    c. 150 ohms measured using a cable scanner or TDR

    d. 100 ohms measured using a cable scanner or TDR

5. What tool would you use to determine the load on a particular NT server hard disk?

    a. Disk Administrator

    b. Server Manager

    c. TDR

    d. Performance Monitor

6. Which of the following might be the source of a broadcast storm?

    a. server NIC

    b. workstation NIC

    c. nonroutable protocol

    d. all the above

    e. only a and b

7. Which of the following might be a source of problems on fiber-optic cable?

    a. electrical interference

    b. improper bend or angular circumference

    c. dirt on the connectors

    d. all the above

    e. only b and c

8. Which of the following can be a setup problem on a network using TCP/IP?

    a. mismatched frame types

    b. designating the wrong CRC value to use in frames

    c. specifying Auto connect

    d. binding TCP/IP with NetBEUI

9. Which network device might be set up to send BPDUs too frequently?

    a. repeater

    b. MAU

    c. bridge

    d. gateway

10. What is the minimum distance required between two nodes or between a node and a hub on STP cable?

    a. 0.5 meter

    b. 1.0 meter

    c. 2.5 meters

    d. 3.0 meters

ASPEN CONSULTING PROJECT: SOLVING NETWORK PROBLEMS

In these assignments, you work on network troubleshooting issues with regular clients like Winston Research Labs, Easton Car Parts, and network administrators at nearby colleges. You also help Mark Arnez with network troubleshooting tasks for Aspen Consulting while the regular network administrator is away.

ASSIGNMENT 12-1

Winston Research Labs, which has both Windows 95 and NT workstations, is contacting you for a quick way to determine if two nodes are using the same IP address. What tool or tools might you use to determine that?

Experiment with a tool for Windows 95 to solve the problem and explain in the table that follows how to use it.

Steps to Determine if Two Nodes Are Using the Same IP address
Step 1:
Step 2:
Step 3:
Step 4:
Step 5:

ASSIGNMENT 12-2

A network administrator from Winston Research Labs wants to know how to determine if a NIC is causing a broadcast storm.

In the table that follows, explain the steps you would take to diagnose and resolve a broadcast storm created by a NIC.

Steps to Diagnose and Resolve a Broadcast Storm
Step 1:
Step 2:
Step 3:
Step 4:
Step 5:
Step 6:
Step 7:
Step 8:

ASSIGNMENT 12-3

Easton Car Parts is considering the purchase of 25 print server devices to connect printers for network printing. Before making that purchase, they want your advice about setting up network printing. Provide your advice in the space that follows, including how to use a network monitoring tool to test the impact of the devices.

ASSIGNMENT 12-4

Easton Car Parts also wants your advice about what tools to use to troubleshoot certain network problems. Complete the following table for them, showing which tools could be used in the following situations.

Troubleshooting Procedure	Troubleshooting Tool
Determining if there is an open on a cable segment	
Finding out if a bridge is causing extra network traffic	
Determining if a TCP/IP session is hung	
Finding the registered servers on a network	
Determining if there is too little distance between adjacent connectors	

ASSIGNMENT 12-5

The university with which you worked in chapter 11 is considering a mail system for their mainframe computers, a different one for UNIX workstations, and still another one for their NT servers. They want your opinion about implementing different mail systems from the standpoint of network performance. What pitfalls should they be prepared for? What problem areas might they research about mail systems or any software they install to be used over the network?

ASSIGNMENT 12-6

The network administrator for Aspen Consulting is away on vacation for a week, so Mark Arnez asks you to help with a perplexing problem. The network has a modular intelligent hub using a star topology for Ethernet communications. There are 55 consultants with workstations connected to the network through the modular boards in the hub. At least 10 consultants in the same area of the building periodically are disconnected from sessions on an NT server. At other times, access to that server is very slow. The problem is severe enough to interfere significantly with their work. Explain what you would do to solve the problem, including the network monitoring tool(s) you would use.

ASSIGNMENT 12-7

While you are working on the problem in Assignment 12-6, Mark reports a problem connecting his computer to the network in a different part of the building from the problems you are tackling. He just purchased a new computer with Windows NT 4.0 Workstation preinstalled and a NIC that can be connected to twisted-pair or coax. The computer came preconfigured, but when Mark connects it to the 10BASE-T network at Aspen, it does not seem to talk to the network. Mark is set up to use NetBEUI for Aspen's NT server and TCP/IP for Internet access and to use the IIS on the NT server. Mark thinks the problem is related to the problem other users are having on the network. Explain in the following table what you would try to get his computer to work. Experiment with NIC connectivity on a computer running Windows NT 4.0 Workstation as you consider what to try for Mark.

Steps You Would Take to Diagnose Mark's Workstation Connectivity Problem
Step 1:
Step 2:
Step 3:
Step 4:
Step 5:
Step 6:
Step 7:
Step 8:

ASSIGNMENT 12-8

You've solved the network problems at Aspen Consulting and are in your office visiting with the network administrator from a college near your city. Her pager goes off, and she calls in to find out that no one can connect to the IBM mainframe on campus. They can connect to other computers, such as NT servers and DEC scientific workstations. The IBM mainframe and the NT server are in a central computer room on campus, and the mainframe is reported to be running without problems. Users connect to the mainframe through an SNA gateway in a modular hub. The network administrator asks your thoughts on what might be wrong and what to have the college try in solving the problem. What is your advice?

OPTIONAL CASE STUDIES FOR TEAMS

 ## TEAM CASE 1

Mark Arnez has formed a team consisting of you and other consultants at Aspen Consulting. He asks the team to develop two sets of guidelines for network troubleshooting that can be used by consultants and clients. One set is general guidelines to help make troubleshooting go more smoothly. The second is specific steps to help isolate problems quickly. Create a report of your recommendations for Mark.

 ## TEAM CASE 2

Mark is keeping the team together from Team Case 1. Now he wants you to develop recommendations on how to get the best performance from networks. Develop some general guidelines. Include example network diagrams to illustrate your recommendations.

 ## TEAM CASE 3

Steel, Inc., is a large company that manufactures metals in Canada. Its network has thousands of users in Vancouver, Toronto, Montreal, Winnipeg, and Edmonton. The company would like you to develop a set of guidelines for troubleshooting connectivity problems when setting up Windows NT and Windows 95 workstations, particularly for TCP/IP communications. Form a team and document the guidelines for Steel, Inc.

 ## TEAM CASE 4

Steel, Inc., likes your work and has a new assignment. They have many servers and host computers connected to their network. Access sometimes is slow to those computers. They want you to develop some general troubleshooting ideas that their network administrators can use to investigate and solve those problems. Develop your recommendations in a report, including network diagrams that help illustrate your ideas.

GLOSSARY

100BASE-VG or 100VG-AnyLAN
100 Mbps communications that uses demand priority to transmit packets on a star topology network.

100BASE-X The 100 Mbps Fast Ethernet standard that uses the CSMA/CD access method for communications, as specified in the IEEE 802.3u standard.

A

access server A device that connects synchronous and asynchronous communication devices and telecommunication lines to a network, providing routing for those types of communications.

account-level access A security access method that controls security based on the rights and permissions given to an account, either through the account or through a group to which the account belongs.

account lockout A security measure that prohibits logging onto an NT server account after a specified number of unsuccessful attempts.

active hub A network device that connects nodes in a star topology, regenerating, retiming, and amplifying the data signal each time it passes through the hub.

algorithm A block of computer code or logic designed to accomplish a certain task or to solve a problem, such as to control data communications or to calculate a payroll deduction.

American National Standards Institute (ANSI) An organization that works to set standards for all types of products, including network equipment.

American Standard Code for Information Interchange (ASCII) A commonly used character set consisting of 96 uppercase and lowercase characters and numbers, plus 32 non-printing characters.

analog A type of transmission that can vary continuously, such as in a wave pattern with positive and negative voltage levels.

angular circumference Measurement of the amount of bend in a fiber-optic cable run.

AppleTalk A peer-to-peer protocol used on networks for communications between Macintosh computers.

asynchronous communications Communications that occur in discrete units, where the start of a unit is signaled by a start bit at the front, and the end of the unit is signaled by a stop bit at the back.

Asynchronous Transfer Mode (ATM) A transport method that uses multiple channels and switching to send voice, video, and data transmissions on the same network. ATM data transfer stresses efficient, QOS (quality-of-service), high-capacity data transport.

ATM switch A switching device that determines the network channel used to transmit an ATM cell received from a node, taking into account the type of information in the cell (i.e., voice, video, data) and the transmission speed needed.

attachment unit interface (AUI) A network interface that connects coax, twisted-pair, or fiber-optic backbone cable to a network node, such as a repeater, a hub, or a workstation. The interface consists of AUI standards for connectors, cable, interface circuits, and electrical characteristics.

attenuation The amount of signal that is lost as the signal travels through the communications medium from its source (transmitting node) to the receiving node. Attenuation in fiber-optic cable is measured as the drop in decibels.

auditing The ability to track past activities as a means to help identify and solve problems.

B

backbone A high-capacity communications medium that joins networks on the same floor in a building, on different floors, and across long distances.

backbone cabling As defined by the EIA/TIA-568 standard, cable that runs between network equipment rooms, floors, and buildings.

backplane A main circuit board in modular equipment, containing slots as plug-ins for modular cards. The backplane provides connections between the modular boards, a power source, and grounding.

backup domain controller (BDC) An NT server that acts as a backup to the primary domain controller. It has a copy of the security accounts manager database containing user account and access privilege information.

baseband A type of transmission in which the entire channel capacity of the communications medium (cable) is used by one data signal; thus, only one node transmits at a time.

basic rate interface (BRI) An ISDN interface consisting of three channels. Two are 64 Kbps channels for data, voice, video, and graphics transmissions. The third is a 16 Kbps channel used for communications signaling.

baud rate An older measurement of modem speed reflecting that 1 data bit is sent per each signal change (signal oscillation).

bayonet navy connector (BNC) A connector used for coax cable that has a bayonet-like shell. The female BNC connector has two small knobs that attach to circular slots in the male connector. Both connectors are twisted on for a connection. Other interpretations of the abbreviation BNC are bayonet nut connection and British Naval connector.

beaconing An error condition on a token ring network that indicates one or more nodes is not functioning.

benchmark Also called a baseline, a standard for hardware or software used to measure performance under varying loads or circumstances.

bits per second (bps) The number of binary bits (0s or 1s) sent in one second, a measure used to gauge network, modem, and telecommunications speeds.

bridge A network device that connects different LAN segments using the same access method, such as one Ethernet LAN to another Ethernet LAN or a token ring LAN to another token ring LAN, utilizing layer 2 MAC addressing.

bridge protocol data unit (BPDU) A specialized packet used by bridges to exchange information with one another.

broadband A transmission method using several transmission channels on a communications medium, allowing more than one node to transmit at the same time.

broadband ISDN (B-ISDN) An ISDN interface that is being developed to initially provide a data transfer rate of 155 Mbps. The theoretical limit is 622 Mbps.

broadcast storm Saturation of network bandwidth by excessive broadcasts from devices attached to the network.

brouter Also called a multiprotocol router, a device that acts like a bridge or a router, depending on how it is set up to forward a given protocol.

bus topology A network configured so that nodes are connected to a segment of cable in the logical shape of a line, with a terminator at each end.

C

cable plant The total cabling that makes up a network.

cable scanner A test device that measures the length of a network cable segment and tests for electrical opens (breaks) and shorts.

call-back security Used for remote communications verification, a security measure in which the remote server calls back the accessing workstation to verify that access is being requested from an authorized telephone number.

carrier sense The process of checking a communication medium, such as cable, for a specific voltage level, indicating the presence of a data-carrying signal.

Carrier Sense Multiple Access with Collision Detection (CSMA/CD) A network transport control mechanism used in Ethernet networks. It regulates transmission by sensing the presence of packet collisions.

cell A unit of data formatted for high-speed transmission over a network. Typically a cell contains a fixed amount of data and performs less error checking than a packet to achieve faster transmission.

cell relay A communications protocol that uses large fixed-length cells to transmit voice, video, and data.

channel service unit (CSU) A device that is a physical interface between a network device, such as a router, and a telecommunications line.

circuit switching A network communication technique that uses a dedicated channel to transmit information between two nodes.

Class A node An FDDI ring node, also called a dual-attached node, which is a network device, such as a hub that is connected to both rings in the FDDI architecture.

Class B node An FDDI node, also called a single-attached node, which is a workstation, server, or host computer that connects to the primary ring only and through that ring connects to a Class A node (hub).

client A computer that accesses a mainframe, a minicomputer, or a microcomputer that permits access to multiple users. The client may use the accessed computer (host) to process data or may process accessed data using its CPU.

client/server application A software application in which processing tasks are performed on the client or on one or more servers to achieve the best performance and to minimize network load.

cluster remapping A fault tolerance technique used by Windows NT to flag a damaged cluster and find an undamaged cluster on which to write data.

coaxial cable Also called coax, a cable with a copper core surrounded by insulation. The insulation is surrounded by another conducting material, such as braided wire, which is covered by an outer insulating material.

collision A situation in which two or more packets are detected at the same time on an Ethernet network.

Common Management Interface Protocol (CMIP) A protocol that is part of the OSI standards for network management to gather performance data on a network.

communications media The cabling or radio waves used to connect one network computer to another and to transport data between them.

communications server A device that connects asynchronous serial devices to a network, providing only asynchronous routing.

community name A password used by network agents and the network management station so their communications cannot be easily intercepted by an unauthorized workstation or device.

Compressed Serial Line Internet Protocol (CSLIP) An extension of the SLIP remote communications protocol that provides faster throughput than SLIP.

computer virus Software that can spread throughout a computer, damaging files, file allocation tables, and other software components.

concentrator A device that can have multiple inputs and outputs all active at one time.

connectionless services Also known as Type 1 operation, services that occur between the LLC sublayer and the network layer but that provide no checks to make sure data accurately reaches the receiving node.

connection-oriented services Type 2 operation services that occur between the LLC sublayer and the network layer, providing several ways to ensure data is successfully received by the destination node.

Consultative Committee on International Telegraph and Telephone (CCITT) An international standards body that develops telecommunication standards for modems, digital telephone systems, and e-mail. For example, the CCITT X.400 standards are for international exchange of e-mail and the X.500 standards are for creating a worldwide e-mail directory. CCITT is a branch of the International Telecommunications Union (ITU).

cyclical redundancy check (CDC) An error detection method that calculates a value for the total size of the information fields (header, data, and footer) contained in a frame. The value is inserted at the end of a frame by the data link layer on the sending node and checked at the data link layer by the receiving node to determine if a transmission error has occurred.

D

data communications equipment (DCE) A network device that performs packet switching.

Data Encryption Standard (DES) A network encryption standard developed by the National Institute of Standards and Technology (NIST) and IBM.

Data Link Control Protocol (DLC) Available through Microsoft NT 4.0 and Windows 95, this protocol enables communications with an IBM mainframe or minicomputer.

data service unit (DSU) A device used with a channel service unit (CSU) for communications over a telecommunications line. The DSU converts data to be sent over the line and converts data received from the line into a readable digital format.

data terminal equipment (DTE) Terminals, workstations, servers, and host computers that operate on a packet-switching network.

datagram A data transmission method that does not use a particular communication channel, causing data sent from one node to arrive at the destination node at different times, because each datagram may follow a different route to the destination. Datagrams do not use acknowledgment and are transmitted unattended.

defragmentation A software process that rearranges data to fill in the empty spaces that develop on disks, which makes data easier to obtain.

demand priority A data communications technique that transmits a packet directly from the sending node, through a hub, and to the receiving node, without making it available to other network nodes.

digital A transmission method that has distinct levels to represent binary 0s or 1s, such as On or Off or +5 volts and 0 volts.

discovery A process used by routers that involves gathering information about how many nodes are on a network and where they are located.

disk duplexing A fault tolerance method similar to disk mirroring in that it prevents data loss by duplicating data from a main disk to a backup disk; disk duplexing, however, places the backup disk on a controller or adapter different from that used by the main disk.

disk fragmentation A normal and gradual process in which files become spread throughout a disk and empty pockets of space develop between files.

disk mirroring A fault tolerance method that prevents data loss by duplicating data from a main disk to a backup disk. Some operating systems refer to this method as disk shadowing.

domain Network clients and resources used by the clients. User workstations and user groups compose the client side. File servers, print servers, and other network services are the resources.

domain name service (DNS) A TCP/IP application protocol that resolves domain computer names to IP addresses and IP addresses to domain names.

driver Software that enables a computer to communicate with devices like NICs, printers, monitors, and hard disk drives. Each driver has a specific purpose, such as to handle Ethernet network communications.

dynamic addressing An addressing method in which an IP (Internet Protocol) address is assigned to a workstation without the need for the network administrator to hard-code it in the workstation's network setup.

Dynamic Host Configuration Protocol (DHCP) A network protocol, DHCP provides a way for a server to automatically assign an IP address to a workstation on its network.

dynamic routing A routing method in which the router constantly checks the network configuration, automatically updates routing tables, and makes its own decisions (often based on guidelines preset by the network administrator) about how to route frames.

E

electromagnetic interference (EMI) Signal interference caused by magnetic force fields that are generated by electrical devices such as motors.

Electronic Industries Association (EIA) An organization that develops standards for electrical interfaces, such as serial interfaces on computers.

electronic mail (e-mail) Using mail software on a client to compose a message and send it to mail or post office software on one or more servers that forward the message to the intended destination. E-mail is possible due to networks and can span the globe, thanks to the Internet.

encryption Turning data into an unintelligible sequence of characters. A key is used to translate the nonsense into the original information.

encryption key A digital password known to the sending node and the receiving node on a network.

enhanced mode The mode in which the computer processor is set to access computer memory indirectly, enabling it to run several programs at once.

enterprise network A network that reaches throughout a large area, such as a college campus or a city, or across several states, connecting many kinds of local area networks and network resources.

Ethernet A transport system that uses the CSMA/CD access method for data transmission on a network. Ethernet typically is implemented in a bus or star topology.

event management Used in network management software, a module in which you can create filters and track designated network events, such as a device that is down, a partitioned segment, or network utilization over a specified percentage.

Event Viewer A tool with which to view events on an NT server or workstation that are recorded in the system, security, and application logs.

Extended Binary Coded Decimal Interchange Code (EBCDIC) A character coding technique used mainly on IBM mainframe computers and consisting of a specially coded 256-character set.

F

Fast Ethernet An Ethernet communications standard that operates at speeds up to 100 Mbps and that is defined under the IEEE 802.3u standard (100BASE-X).

fat pipe Fiber-optic cable used on a network backbone for high-speed communications, such as between floors of a building.

fault tolerance Techniques that employ hardware and software to provide assurance against equipment failures, computer service interruptions, and data loss.

Fiber Distributed Data Interface (FDDI) A data transport method capable of a 100 Mbps transfer rate using a ring topology.

fiber-optic cable Communications cable consisting of one or more glass or plastic fiber cores inside a protective cladding material and covered by a plastic PVC outer jacket. Signal transmission along the inside fibers is accomplished using infrared or, in some cases, visible light.

file server A network computer that makes software applications, data files, and network utilities available to other network nodes.

file transfer protocol (FTP) An application protocol in TCP/IP used to transfer data files from one computer system to another, such as from a workstation running a Microsoft operating system to a computer with the UNIX or IBM MVS operating system.

filter A capability in network monitoring software that enables the network manager to view only designated protocols, network events, network nodes, or other specialized views of the network.

firewall Hardware and software that protects portions of a network in two ways. One is by securing access to data and resources from outside intruders. The second is by preventing data from leaving the network through an inside source.

flow control A process that makes sure one device does not send information faster than can be received by another device.

frame Sometimes used interchangeably with the term packet, a unit of data formatted for transmission over a network.

frame relay A communications protocol that relies on packet switching and virtual circuit technology to transmit data packets.

frequency division multiple access (FDMA) A form of multiplexing that creates separate channels on one communication medium by establishing different frequencies for each channel.

full backup A backup of an entire system, including all system files, programs, and data files.

G

gateway Hardware and software that enable communications between two different types of networked systems, such as between complex protocols or between different e-mail systems.

global group A type of Microsoft NT Server group used to make one Microsoft domain accessible to another, so that resources can be shared and managed across two or more domains.

group In Windows NT Server, a common entity that contains user accounts and network resources, such as file and print servers.

H

help desk Software that is used to keep data on hardware and software problems, how problems are solved, hardware and software setup information, and general computer documentation.

hertz (Hz) The measurement of the frequency of the alternation of current or a radio wave.

home directory A dedicated location on a file server or a workstation for a designated account holder to store files.

hop The number of times a packet travels point-to-point from one network to the next. Another way to view a hop is the number of times the packet is regenerated, amplified, and placed onto another network by a source-route bridge (token ring) or router.

horizontal cabling As defined by the EIA/TIA-568 standard, cabling that connects to workstations and servers in the work area.

host A computer that has an operating system enabling multiple computers to access it at the same time. Programs and information may be processed at the host, or they may be downloaded to the accessing computer (client) for processing.

hot fix A data recovery method that automatically stores data when a damaged area of disk prevents the data from being written. The computer operating system finds another undamaged area on which to write the stored data.

hub A central network device used in the star topology to join single cable segments or individual LANs into one network.

Hypertext Markup Language (HTML) A formatting process used to enable documents and graphics images to be read on the World Wide Web. HTML also provides for fast links to other documents, to graphics, and to Web sites. The World Wide Web is a series of file servers with software such as Microsoft's Internet Information Server (IIS) that make HTML and other Web documents available for workstations to access.

I

impedance The total amount of opposition to the flow of current. In coaxial cable, a 50-ohm impedance influences how fast a packet can travel in optimal conditions.

incremental backup A backup of new or changed files.

Institute of Electrical and Electronics Engineers (IEEE) An organization of scientists, engineers, technicians, and educators that has played a leading role in developing standards for network cabling and data transmissions.

Integrated Services Digital Network (ISDN) A standard for delivering data services over telephone lines, with a current practical limit of 64 Kbps and a theoretical limit of 622 Mbps.

intelligent hub A hub with network management and performance monitoring capabilities.

International Standards Organization (ISO) An international body that establishes communications and networking standards and that is best known for its contributions to network protocol standards.

Internet A worldwide network that is a collection of thousands of smaller networks linked by a vast array of network equipment and communication methods.

Internet Control Message Protocol (ICMP) A protocol used to build information about the location of network workstations, servers, and other network equipment. ICMP assists in determining the shortest path on which to send packets and helps in locating network problems.

Internet Information Server (IIS) A Microsoft application that turns an NT server into a Web server for Internet and intranet communications.

Internet Packet Exchange (IPX) A protocol developed by Novell for use with its NetWare file server operating system.

intranet A private network within an organization. An intranet uses the same Web-based software as the Internet, but it is highly restricted from public access. Intranets enable managers to run high-level reports, enable staff members to update human resources information, and provide access to other forms of private data.

K

kilohertz (kHz) Equal to 1,000 hertz, a measurement of the frequency of the alternation of an electrical current or radio wave.

L

leased telephone line A line that is conditioned for high-quality transmissions and that is a permanent connection without going through a telephone switch.

line of sight A type of signal transmission in which the signal goes from point to point rather than bounces off the atmosphere to skip across the country or across continents. A limitation of line of sight is that transmissions are interrupted by large land masses, such as hills and mountains.

local area network (LAN) A series of interconnected computers, printers, and other computer equipment that share hardware and software resources. The service area usually is limited to a given floor, office area, or building.

local area transport (LAT) A protocol developed by DEC for virtual terminal communications.

local bridge A bridge that connects networks in close proximity and that is used to segment a portion of a network to reduce heavy traffic.

local group In Windows NT Server, a grouping of any combination of accounts, network resources, and global groups. It is used to manage accounts and resources within a single domain.

local router A router that joins networks in the same building or between buildings in close proximity, for example, on the same business campus.

locking An operating system process that prevents more than one user from updating a file or a record in a file at the same time.

logical link control (LLC) A sublayer housed in the data link layer of the OSI model that initiates the communication link between two nodes as well as maintains the link.

M

Management Information Base (MIB) A database of network performance information stored on a network agent for access by a network management station.

mapped drive A disk volume or folder that is shared on the network by a file server or workstation. A mapped drive gives designated network workstations access to the files and data in its shared volume or folder. The workstation, via software, determines a drive letter for the shared volume, which is the workstation's map to the data.

media access control (MAC) A sublayer of the OSI data link layer that examines addressing information contained in network packets.

megahertz (mHz) Equal to 1 million hertz, a measurement of the frequency of the alternation of an electrical current or radio wave.

message switching A data transmission technique that sends data from point to point, with each intermediate node storing the data, waiting for a free transmission channel, and forwarding the data to the next point until the destination is reached.

metropolitan area network (MAN) A network that links multiple LANs in a large city or metropolitan region.

Microcom Network Protocol (MNP) A set of modem service classes that provides efficient communications, error correction, data compression, and high-throughput capabilities.

mission-critical A computer software application or a hardware service that has the highest priority in an organization.

modem A modulator/demodulator device that converts a transmitted digital signal to an analog signal for a telephone line and converts a received analog signal to a digital signal for use by a computer.

modular hub Also called a chassis hub, a hub that contains a backplane into which different modules, such as retiming, bridge, routing, and ATM modules, can be inserted.

multimeter A device that measures a combination of electrical characteristics such as volts, ohms, and amperes.

multiple master domain A domain model that consists of many domains in which domain management is located in two or more domains.

multiplexer A switch that divides a communication medium into multiple channels so several nodes can communicate at the same time. When a signal is multiplexed, it must be demultiplexed at the other end.

multiplexing A form of circuit switching in which several physical channels are connected to a switch called a multiplexer. Multiple computers also are connected to the switch, transmitting along the channels whose access is controlled by the switch.

multistation access unit (MAU) A central hub that links token ring nodes into a topology that physically resembles a star but in which packets are transferred in a logical ring pattern.

N

Net Watcher A Microsoft monitoring tool used to view shared network resources and who is using them.

NetBIOS Extended User Interface (NetBEUI) A protocol that incorporates NetBIOS for communications across a network.

network A system of computers, communication devices, printers, and software linked by communications cabling.

network agent A network device, such as a workstation or a router, that is equipped to gather network performance information to send to the network management station.

Network Basic Input/Output System (NetBIOS) A combination software interface and network-naming convention. It is available in Microsoft operating systems through the file NetBIOS.dll.

network binding A process that identifies a computer's network interface card or a dial-up connection with one or more network protocols to achieve optimum communications with network services. For Microsoft operating systems, you should always bind a protocol to each NIC that is installed.

Network Device Interface Specification (NDIS) A set of standards developed by Microsoft for network drivers that enables communication between a NIC and a protocol and the use of multiple protocols on the same network.

network file system (NFS) A UNIX-based network file transfer protocol that ships files as streams of records.

network interface card (NIC) An adapter card that enables a workstation, file server, printer, or other device to connect to a network and communicate with other network nodes.

network management station (NMS) A dedicated workstation that gathers and stores network performance data, obtaining that data from network nodes running agent software that enables the nodes to collect the data. The NMS is loaded with network management software.

Network Monitor A Microsoft monitoring tool that captures and reports information about network performance.

Network Monitor Agent Microsoft software that enables a Microsoft workstation or server NIC to gather network performance data.

network traffic The number, size, and frequency of packets transmitted on the network in a given amount of time.

node Any device connected to a network, such as a microcomputer, a mainframe, a minicomputer, network equipment, or a printer.

NWLink A network protocol that simulates the IPX/SPX protocol for Microsoft Windows 95 and Windows NT communications with Novell NetWare file servers and compatible devices.

O

ohm meter A device that tests resistance and continuity in an electrical circuit.

one-way trust A domain trust relationship in which one domain is trusted and one is trusting.

Open Datalink Interface (ODI) A driver used by Novell NetWare networks to transport multiple protocols on the same network.

Open Systems Interconnect (OSI) Developed by ISO and ANSI, a model that provides a framework for networked communications based on seven functional layers. OSI contains guidelines that can be applied to hardware and software network communications.

optical fault finder A device that measures power and distance characteristics in fiber-optic cable.

optical power meter A device that measures the light signal transmitted through fiber-optic cable.

P

packet A unit of data formatted for transmission over a network. A packet normally consists of a header containing information about the packet's source and destination, the data to be transmitted, and a footer containing error-checking information.

packet assembler/disassembler (PAD) A device that converts data from a format used by a DCE to one that can be placed on an X.25 communications network and translates data received in an X.25 communications format to a format that can be read by a DCE.

packet switching A data transmission technique that establishes a logical channel between two transmitting nodes but that uses several different paths of transmission to find the best routes to the destination.

partition The process of shutting down an Ethernet segment because a portion of the segment is malfunctioning.

passive hub A network device that connects nodes in a star topology, performing no signal enhancement as the packet moves from one node to the next through the hub. Each time the signal moves through the hub, it is weakened slightly because the hub absorbs some of the signal.

peer protocols Protocols used to enable an OSI layer on a sending node to communicate with the same layer on the receiving node.

peer-to-peer network A network in which any computer can communicate with other networked computers on an equal or peer-like basis without going through an intermediary, such as a server or a host.

Performance Monitor A Microsoft monitoring tool that captures and reports performance information about the computer running the monitor software and about the network to which the computer is connected.

permanent virtual circuit A data transmission method in which the communication channel stays connected at all times, even after the communication session is over.

permissions In Windows NT Server, privileges to control account or group access capabilities for reading, viewing, and changing files or folders.

Point-to-Point Protocol (PPP) A widely used remote communications protocol that supports IPX/SPX, NetBEUI, and TCP/IP for point-to-point communications (e.g., between a remote PC and an NT server on a network).

Point-to-Point Tunneling Protocol (PPTP) A remote communications protocol that enables connectivity to intranets (private virtual networks).

power budget For communications on fiber-optic cable, the difference, measured in decibels, between the transmitted power and the receiver sensitivity. The power budget is the minimum transmitter power and receiver sensitivity needed for a signal to be sent and received fully intact.

power supply A component in an electrical device that converts power from the wall outlet to the type and level of power required by the electrical device.

primary domain controller (PDC) An NT server that acts as the master server when two or more NT servers are on a network. It holds the master database (called the SAM) of user accounts and access privileges.

primary rate interface (PRI) An ISDN interface that consists of switched communications in multiples of 1,536 Kbps.

primitive A command used to transfer information from one layer in an OSI stack to another layer, such as from the physical layer to the data link layer.

privileged mode A protected area from which the Windows NT operating system runs. Direct access to the computer's memory or hardware is allowed only from the privileged mode. Application programs that need to access memory and hardware issue a request to an operating system service rather than a direct memory or hardware instruction.

promiscuous mode Mode in which network devices read frame destination address information before sending a packet to other connected segments of the network.

protocol An established guideline that specifies how networked data is formatted into a packet, how it is transmitted, and how it is interpreted at the receiving end.

protocol analyzer A device used to monitor one or more protocols transmitted across a network.

protocol data unit (PDU) The information transferred between layers in the same OSI stack.

public dial-up telephone line An ordinary telephone connection that is temporarily switched for the duration of the communication session.

R

radio frequency interference (RFI) Signal interference caused by electrical devices that emit radio waves at the same frequency as used by network signal transmissions.

real mode Mode in which a computer processor is set to run programs so they have direct access to memory locations at or below 1,024 KB and so only one program can be run at a time.

real-time application An application that involves immediate processing results, for example, entering a new employee in a human resources database through an application that immediately updates the database as you are working.

redirector A Microsoft service used via the application layer to recognize and access other computers with operating systems such as Windows 3.11, Windows 95, Windows NT, LAN Manager, and LAN Server.

redundant array of inexpensive disks (RAID) A set of standards to extend the life of hard disk drives and to prevent data loss from a hard disk failure.

Registry A database used to store information about the configuration, program setup, devices, drivers, and other data important to the setup of a computer running Windows NT or 95.

Remote Access Services (RAS) Microsoft software services that enable off-site workstations to access an NT server through modems and analog telephone or ISDN telecommunication lines.

remote bridge A bridge that joins networks across a city, between cities, and between states to create one network.

Remote Network Monitoring (RMON) A standard that uses remote network nodes, such as workstations or network devices, to perform network monitoring, including gathering information for network protocol analysis.

remote router A router that joins networks across large geographic areas, such as between cities, states, and countries.

repeater A network device that amplifies and retimes a packet-carrying signal so it can be sent along all cable segments attached to the repeater.

request for information (RFI) A general planning document sent to vendors to obtain information about what services and products each vendor can offer.

request for proposal (RFP) A detailed planning document, often written from information received in RFIs, that is sent to vendors containing exact specifications for services and products that an organization intends to purchase.

resolution A process used to translate a computer's domain name to an IP address and vice versa.

resource On a workstation, an IRQ, an I/O address, or a memory location allocated to a computer component, such as a disk drive or communications port. On an NT Server network, a resource is a file server, a shared printer, or a shared directory that users can access.

rights In Windows NT Server, high-level access privileges for activities such as logging on to a server, shutting down a server, and creating user accounts.

ring topology A network in the form of a continuous ring or circle, with nodes connected around the ring.

RMON management station A dedicated workstation that gathers and reports on RMON data collected by probes.

RMON probes Remotely located workstations, servers, and network devices equipped with RMON software; used to monitor a network and send information to a RMON management station for analysis.

router A device that connects networks having the same or different access methods, such as Ethernet to token ring. A router forwards packets to networks by using a decision-making process based on routing table data, discovery of the most efficient routes, and preprogrammed information from the network manager.

S

sector sparing Available in Windows NT Server and NT Workstation for SCSI drives, a fault tolerance method that reserves certain hard disk sectors so they can be used when a bad sector is discovered.

security accounts manager (SAM) database Also called the directory services database, stores information about user accounts, groups, and access privileges on a Microsoft Windows NT server.

segment of cable A cable run within IEEE specifications, such as one run of 10BASE2 cable that is 185 meters long and that has 30 or fewer nodes (including terminators and network equipment).

segmenting A technique to isolate and direct network traffic to reduce bottlenecks and to reduce the impact of a network malfunction on other portions of the network.

Sequence Packet Exchange (SPX) A Novell connection-oriented protocol used for network transport where there is a particular need for data reliability.

serial communications Data transmissions that use one channel to send data bits one at time. Terminals and modems use serial communications. The serial communications port on a PC conforms to the EIA/TIA-232 (formerly RS-232) standard for communications up to 64 Kbps.

Serial Line Internet Protocol (SLIP) An older remote communications protocol used by UNIX computers.

service data unit (SDU) The protocol data unit (PDU) with the control and transfer information stripped out.

share-level access A security access method that provides access to a shared resource, such as a folder, by creating a network share and by limiting access based on share permissions.

shielded twisted-pair (STP) Cable that contains pairs of insulated wires twisted together and surrounded by a shielding material for added EMI and RFI protection, all inside a protective jacket.

Simple Mail Transfer Protocol (SMTP) An e-mail protocol used by systems having TCP/IP network communications.

Simple Network Management Protocol (SNMP) A protocol that enables computers and network equipment to gather standardized data about network performance and that is part of the TCP/IP suite of protocols.

single master domain A relationship model in a domain or domains in which trusts are set up so management control is centralized in only one domain.

small computer system interface (SCSI) A 32- or 64-bit computer adapter that transports data between the computer and one or more attached devices, such as hard disks. There are several types of SCSI adapters, including SCSI, SCSI-2, SCSI-3, SCSI wide, SCSI narrow, and UltraSCSI. All are used to provide high-speed data transfer to reduce bottlenecks in the computer.

SNMP Monitor A Microsoft network-monitoring tool that can query MIB information on network agents and store that information to put in ODBC-compatible databases.

spanning tree algorithm Software that ensures packets are not transmitted in an endless loop and enables packets to be sent along the most cost-effective network path as determined by the shortest path from source to the destination and the most effective use of cable resources for the type of information sent.

spindle A rod attached to the center of a hard disk platter and to a motor used to rotate the rod and disk.

spread-spectrum technology (SST) Communications technology used by wireless networks in place of cable for communications between network nodes. Network data is transmitted by means of reliable high-frequency radio signals.

standalone server An NT server used as a special-purpose server, such as to store databases. A standalone server does no account logon verification.

star topology A network configured with a central hub and individual cable segments connected to the hub, resembling the shape of a star.

static addressing An IP addressing method that requires the network administrator to assign and manually set up a unique network address on each workstation connected to a network.

static routing A routing method that involves control of routing decisions by the network manager through preset routing instructions.

statistical multiple access A multiplexing technique that allocates the communication resources according to what is needed for the task, such as providing more bandwidth for a video file and less bandwidth for a small spreadsheet file.

striping A data storage method that breaks up data files across all volumes of a disk set to minimize wear on a single volume.

subnet mask A method to show which part of the IP address is a unique identifier for the network and which part uniquely identifies the workstation. For example, on a simple network, the subnet mask 255.255.0.0 would indicate that the first two sets of digits (denoted by 255) are the network identification for that network and the third and fourth sets of digits (denoted by the zeroes) are used as the workstation identification.

switched megabit data service (SMDS) Also called switched multimegabit data service, a data transport method developed by regional telephone companies to provide cell-based, high-speed communications between metropolitan area networks.

switched virtual circuit A communication channel that is established for only as long as the communication session lasts.

synchronous communications Continuous bursts of data controlled by a clock signal that starts each burst (like a starter at a cross-country foot race who fires a starting pistol at intervals to start different heats of runners on the same course). Each bit that is sent is synchronized at specific intervals.

synchronous optical network (SONET) A fiber-optic technology that allows for high-speed (over 1 Gbps) data transmission. Networks based on SONET can deliver voice, data, and video.

Systems Management Server (SMS) A network management and client troubleshooting system developed by Microsoft.

Systems Network Architecture (SNA) A layered communications protocol used by IBM for communications between IBM mainframe computers and terminals.

T

T-carrier A dedicated telephone line for data communications.

Telecommunications Industry Association (TIA) A group within the Electronic Industries Association that develops telecommunications and cabling standards.

Telnet A TCP/IP application protocol that provides terminal emulation services.

terahertz Equal to 1 trillion hertz, a measurement of the frequency of the alternation of an electrical current or radio wave.

terminal A device that consists of a monitor and a keyboard to communicate with a host computer that runs the programs. The terminal does not have a processor to use for running programs locally.

terminal adapter (TA) Popularly called a digital modem, a device that links a computer or a fax to an ISDN line.

time division multiple access (TDMA) A multiplexing method that enables multiple devices to communicate over the same communications medium by creating time slots in which each device transmits.

time domain reflectometer (TDR) A device that measures network cable characteristics such as distance, impedance, levels of RFI/EMI, and the presence of opens and shorts.

token ring Using a ring topology, a network transport method that passes a token from node to node. The token is used to coordinate transmission of data, because only the node possessing the token can send data.

topology The physical layout of cable and the logical path followed by network packets sent on the cable.

transaction tracking Also called transaction logging or journaling, a fault tolerance method in which a log is kept of all recent transactions until they are written to disk. If a hard disk or system failure occurs, unwritten transactions are recovered from the log.

Transmission Control Protocol/Internet Protocol (TCP/IP) A protocol particularly well suited for medium and large networks. The TCP portion was originally developed to ensure reliable connections on government, military, and educational networks. It performs extensive error checking to ensure data is delivered successfully. The IP portion consists of rules for packaging data and ensuring it reaches the correct destination address.

trust relationships Arrangements that establish how resources are accessed in Microsoft domains, providing a way to manage both resources and user accounts.

trusted domain A domain that has been granted security access to resources in another domain.

trusting domain A domain that allows another domain security access to its resources, such as file servers.

twisted-pair Flexible communications cable that contains pairs of insulated copper wires twisted together for reduction of EMI and RFI and covered with an outer insulating jacket.

two-way trust A domain relationship in which both domains are trusted and trusting.

U

uninterruptible power supply (UPS) A device built into electrical equipment or a separate device that provides immediate battery power to equipment during a power failure or brownout.

Universal Naming Convention (UNC) A naming convention that designates network servers and shared resources. The format for a UNC name is //servername/sharename/folder/file.

universal trust A domain relationship among three or more domains in which every domain is trusting and trusted with every other domain.

unshielded twisted-pair (UTP) Communications cable that has no shielding material between the pairs of insulated wires twisted together and the cable's outside jacket.

user-level access A security access method for a network resource that uses a list of names to determine who can access the resource.

V

virtual circuit A logical communication path established by the OSI network layer for sending and receiving data.

virtual LAN (VLAN) The "network" that results when a network manager uses ATM switches, routers, and internetworking software to configure a network into subnetworks of logical workgroups, independent of the physical network topology.

virtual memory Disk space allocated to link with memory to hold data temporarily when there is not enough free RAM.

voltmeter A device that tests the voltage in an electrical circuit.

W

Web browser A tool that enables the user to view or search for information and display text, graphics, sound, and video from the World Wide Web. Web browsers also can be used to search for information through a private network. Microsoft Internet Explorer and Netscape Communicator are two popular Web browsers.

wide area network (WAN) A far reaching system of networks that can extend across states and continents.

Windows Internet Naming Service (WINS) A Windows NT Server service that enables the server to convert workstation names to IP addresses for Internet communications.

wiring closet A centrally located enclosed room dedicated to house network, telephone, and video cable and associated equipment.

wizard A set of automated dialog boxes and screens that take you, step by step, through a particular setup or administrative function on a computer running Microsoft software.

workgroup As used in Microsoft networks, a number of users who share drive and printer resources in an independent peer-to-peer relationship.

workstation A computer that has its own CPU and that can be used as a standalone computer for word processing, spreadsheet creation, and other software applications. It also can be used to access another computer such as a mainframe computer or a file server, as long as the necessary network hardware and software are installed.

World Wide Web A vast network of servers throughout the world that provide access to voice, text, video, and data files.

X

X.25 A packet-switching protocol for connecting remote networks at speeds up to 64 Kbps.

Xerox Network System (XNS) A protocol developed by Xerox in the early networking days for Ethernet communications.

INDEX

Upgrade to the full version of NetCert 3.0

The full version includes Transcender's new test engine and gives you:

- Four full-length exams, including a Computer Adaptive Testing option
- Detailed Score History - Breaks down your score so you can pinpoint weak areas
- Expanded Printing Options - You can now print by section, string or keyword
- Random Exam Option - Randomize test items from all three tests to create additional exams
- Detailed answer explanations and documented references for every question
- Money Back if You Don't Pass Guarantee*
  - *see our Web Site for guarantee details*

To upgrade to the full version:

1. Install NetCert 3.0 Limited version on the computer system with which you intend to use the full version.
2. When the progam starts, choose "Order Full Version."
3. To upgrade immediately, enable your Internet connection, and go to http://www.transcender.com/upgrade/limited/netcert3.
4. Follow the instructions posted at the above listed URL.
5. If you do not wish to purchase your upgrade on-line, mail us the completed coupon below (no reproductions or photocopies please). Enclose a check or money order, payable to Transcender Corporation, for $129, plus $6 shipping ($25 outside U.S.).

Terms and Conditions:

Maximum one upgrade per person. Pre-payment by check, money order or credit card is required. For your protection, do not send currency through the mail.

Send to: Upgrade Program
Transcender Corporation
242 Louise Avenue
Nashville, TN 37203

Please send me the NetCert 3.0 Upgrade. Enclosed is my check or credit card number, payable to Transcender Corporation for $129 plus $6 ($25 outside U.S.). TN residents add $10.64 for sales tax.

Name _____ School _____

Address _____ Credit Card: VISA   MC   AMEX   DISC

City _____ State _____ CC# _____

Zip _____ Country _____ Expiration Date _____

Phone _____ Name on Card _____

E-Mail _____ Signature _____
_____ CRS042799

Transcender Corporation
SINGLE-USER LICENSE AGREEMENT

IMPORTANT. READ THIS LICENSE AGREEMENT (THE "AGREEMENT") CAREFULLY BEFORE OPENING THE SOFTWARE PACK. YOU AGREE TO BE LEGALLY BOUND BY THE TERMS OF THIS LICENSE AGREEMENT IF YOU EITHER (1) OPEN THE SOFTWARE PACK, OR (2) IF YOU INSTALL, COPY, OR OTHERWISE USE THE ENCLOSED SOFTWARE. IF YOU DO NOT AGREE WITH THESE TERMS, DO NOT OPEN THE SOFWARE PACK AND DO NOT INSTALL, COPY, OR USE THE SOFTWARE. YOU MAY RETURN THE UNOPENED SOFTWARE TO THE PLACE OF PURCHASE WITHIN FIFTEEN (15) DAYS OF PURCHASE AND RECEIVE A FULL REFUND. NO REFUNDS WILL BE GIVEN FOR SOFTWARE THAT HAS AN OPENED SOFTWARE PACK OR THAT HAS BEEN INSTALLED, USED, ALTERED, OR DAMAGED.

Grant of Single-User License. **YOU ARE THE ONLY PERSON ENTITLED TO USE THIS SOFTWARE.** This is a license agreement between you (an individual) and Transcender Corporation whereby Transcender grants you the non-exclusive and non-transferable license and right to use this software product, updates (if any), and accompanying documentation (collectively the "Software"). ONLY YOU (AND NO ONE ELSE) ARE ENTITLED TO INSTALL, USE, OR COPY THE SOFTWARE. Transcender continues to own the Software, and the Software is protected by copyright and other state and federal intellectual property laws. All rights, title, interest, and all copyrights in and to the Software and any copy made by you remain with Transcender. Unauthorized copying of the Software, or failure to comply with this Agreement will result in automatic termination of this license, and will entitle Transcender to pursue other legal remedies. IMPORTANT, under the terms of this Agreement:

YOU MAY: (a) install and use the Software on only one computer or workstation, and (b) make one (1) copy of the Software for backup purposes only.

YOU MAY NOT: (a) use the Software on more than one computer or workstation; (b) modify, translate, reverse engineer, decompile, decode, decrypt, disassemble, adapt, create a derivative work of, or in any way copy the Software (except one backup); (c) sell, rent, lease, sublicense, or otherwise transfer or distribute the Software to any other person or entity without the prior written consent of Transcender (and any attempt to do so shall be void); (d) allow any other person or entity to use the Software or install the Software on a network of any sort (these require a separate license from Transcender); or (e) remove or cover any proprietary notices, labels, or marks on the Software.

Term. The term of the license granted above shall commence upon the earlier of your opening of the Software, your acceptance of this Agreement or your downloading, installation, copying, or use of the Software; and such license will expire three (3) years thereafter or whenever you discontinue use of the Software, whichever occurs first.

Warranty, Limitation of Remedies and Liability. If applicable, Transcender warrants the media on which the Software is recorded to be free from defects in materials and free from faulty workmanship for a period of thirty (30) days after the date you receive the Software. If, during this 30-day period, the Software media is found to be defective or faulty in workmanship, the media may be returned to Transcender for replacement without charge. YOUR SOLE REMEDY UNDER THIS AGREEMENT SHALL BE THE REPLACEMENT OF DEFECTIVE MEDIA AS SET FORTH ABOVE. EXCEPT AS EXPRESSLY PROVIDED FOR MEDIA ABOVE, TRANSCENDER MAKES NO OTHER OR FURTHER WARRANTIES REGARDING THE SOFTWARE, EITHER EXPRESS OR IMPLIED, INCLUDING THE QUALITY OF THE SOFTWARE, ITS PERFORMANCE, MERCHANTABILITY, OR FITNESS FOR A PARTICULAR PURPOSE. THE SOFTWARE IS LICENSED TO YOU ON AN "AS-IS" BASIS. THE ENTIRE RISK AS TO THE SOFTWARE'S QUALITY AND PERFORMANCE REMAINS SOLELY WITH YOU. TRANSCENDER'S EXCLUSIVE AND MAXIMUM LIABILITY FOR ANY CLAIM BY YOU OR ANYONE CLAIMING THROUGH OR ON BEHALF OF YOU ARISING OUT OF YOUR ORDER, USE, OR INSTALLATION OF THE SOFTWARE SHALL NOT UNDER ANY CIRCUMSTANCE EXCEED THE ACTUAL AMOUNT PAID BY YOU TO TRANSCENDER FOR THE SOFTWARE, AND IN NO EVENT SHALL TRANSCENDER BE LIABLE TO YOU OR ANY PERSON OR ENTITY CLAIMING THROUGH YOU FOR ANY INDIRECT, INCIDENTAL, COLLATERAL, EXEMPLARY, CONSEQUENTIAL, OR SPECIAL DAMAGES OR LOSSES ARISING OUT OF YOUR ORDER, USE, OR INSTALLATION OF THE SOFTWARE OR MEDIA DELIVERED TO YOU OR OUT OF THE WARRANTY, INCLUDING WITHOUT LIMITATION, LOSS OF USE, PROFITS, GOODWILL, OR SAVINGS, OR LOSS OF DATA, FILES, OR PROGRAMS STORED BY THE USER. SOME STATES DO NOT ALLOW THE EXCLUSION OR LIMITATION OF INCIDENTAL OR CONSEQUENTIAL DAMAGES, SO THE ABOVE LIMITATIONS MAY NOT APPLY TO YOU.

Restricted Rights. If the Software is acquired by or for the U.S. Government, then it is provided with Restricted Rights. Use, duplication, or disclosure by the U.S. Government is subject to restrictions as set forth in subparagraph (c)(1)(ii) of The Rights in Technical Data and Computer Software clause at DFARS 252.227-7013, or subparagraphs (c)(1) and (2) of the Commercial Computer Software Act—Restricted Rights at 48 CFR 52.227-19, or clause 18-52.227-86(d) of the NASA Supplement to the FAR, as applicable. The contractor/manufacturer is Transcender Corporation, 242 Louise Avenue, Nashville, Tennessee 37203-1812.

PLEASE READ CAREFULLY. THE FOLLOWING LIMITS SOME OF YOUR RIGHTS, INCLUDING THE RIGHT TO BRING A LAWSUIT IN COURT. By accepting this Agreement, you and we agree that all claims or disputes between us will be submitted to binding arbitration if demanded by either party. The arbitration will be handled by the American Arbitration Association and governed by its rules. This Agreement requiring arbitration (if demanded) is still fully binding even if a class action is filed in which you would be a class representative or member. You and we agree that the arbitration of any dispute or claim between us will be conducted apart from all other claims or disputes of other parties and that there will be no class or consolidated arbitration of any claims or disputes covered by this Agreement. You and we also agree that this Agreement does not affect the applicability of any statute of limitations.

General. This Agreement shall be interpreted and governed by the laws of the State of Tennessee without regard to the conflict of laws provisions of such state, and any arbitration or legal action relating to this Agreement shall be brought in the appropriate forum located in Davidson County, Tennessee, which venue and jurisdiction you agree to submit to, and the prevailing party in any such action shall be entitled to recover reasonable attorneys' fees and expenses as part of any judgment or award. The pursuit by Transcender of any remedy to which it is entitled at any time shall not be deemed an election of remedies or waiver of the right to pursue any of the other remedies to which Transcender may be entitled. This Agreement is the entire Agreement between us and supersedes any other communication, advertisement, or understanding with respect to the Software. If any provision of this Agreement is held invalid or unenforceable, the remainder shall continue in full force and effect. All provisions of this Agreement relating to disclaimers of warranties, limitation of liability, remedies, or damages, and Transcender's ownership of the Software and other proprietary rights shall survive any termination of this Agreement.

SingleUserLicense.CT.040699